"Looks Good to Me"

CONSTRUCTIVE CODE REVIEWS

ADRIENNE BRAGANZA
FOREWORD BY SCOTT HANSELMAN

MANNING
SHELTER ISLAND

For online information and ordering of this and other Manning books, please visit
www.manning.com. The publisher offers discounts on this book when ordered in quantity.
For more information, please contact

Special Sales Department
Manning Publications Co.
20 Baldwin Road
PO Box 761
Shelter Island, NY 11964
Email: orders@manning.com

Manning Publications Co.
20 Baldwin Road
PO Box 761
Shelter Island, NY 11964

Development editor: Rebecca Johnson
Technical editor: Miroslav Popovic
Review editor: Dunja Nikitović
Production editor: Keri Hales
Copy editor: Alisa Larson
Proofreader: Jason Everett
Typesetter: Dennis Dalinnik
Cover designer: Marija Tudor

ISBN: 9781633438125
Printed in the United States of America

This is for you . . . you . . . my Number One. Thank you, Mario.

brief contents

PART 1 **CODE REVIEW FOUNDATIONS** 1

    1 ■ The significance of code reviews   3

    2 ■ Dissecting the code review   15

    3 ■ Building your team's first code review process   58

PART 2 **ELEVATED CODE REVIEW ESSENTIALS** 89

    4 ■ The Team Working Agreement   91

    5 ■ The advantages of automation   112

    6 ■ Composing effective code review comments   142

PART 3 **DEALING WITH DILEMMAS** 165

    7 ■ How code reviews can suck   167

    8 ■ Decreasing code review delays   176

    9 ■ Eliminating process loopholes   193

    10 ■ The Emergency Playbook   211

PART 4   PAIRING CODE REVIEWS WITH OTHER PRACTICES 219

        11 ▪ Code reviews and pair programming   221
        12 ▪ Code reviews and mob programming   239
        13 ▪ Code reviews and AI   255

contents

foreword   xii
preface   xiv
acknowledgments   xvi
about this book   xviii
about the author   xxi
about the cover illustration   xxii

PART 1   CODE REVIEW FOUNDATIONS 1

1 *The significance of code reviews   3*

    1.1   Who this book is for   7

    1.2   How this book is structured   9

    1.3   You should want code reviews   10

        Better applications   10 ▪ Elevated team understanding   11

    1.4   Convincing your team   12

    1.5   Making code reviews better   12

2 *Dissecting the code review   15*

    2.1   Code review systems   16

        Human-led   16 ▪ Tool-facilitated   16 ▪ Hybrid   17

2.2   How does a code review work?   19

*The modern code review workflow   19 ▪ Our code review (pull
request workflow)   22*

2.3   Elements of a great PR   22

*Title: The "what"   23 ▪ Description (the "why")   27
Labels   34 ▪ Review states   36*

2.4   Code review participants and expectations   39

*The reviewer   40 ▪ The author   45 ▪ The team   49
Those in charge   51 ▪ The organization   52*

3   **Building your team's first code review process   58**

3.1   Establish your goals   59

*Finding bugs   60 ▪ Codebase stability and maintainability   61
Knowledge transfer and knowledge sharing   62 ▪ Mentoring   65
Recordkeeping/chronicling   65 ▪ Choosing your code review
goals   66*

3.2   Choose your tools   67

Assessing code review functions   68 ▪ Choosing a tool   70

3.3   Set guidelines   73

*What is our workflow?   73 ▪ What is your review focus?   75
What can block a PR from being approved?   77 ▪ What's our
approval policy?   79*

3.4   Refining the process   82

Refinement scenario walkthroughs   85

PART 2   ELEVATED CODE REVIEW ESSENTIALS 89

4   **The Team Working Agreement   91**

4.1   What's a Team Working Agreement?   92

4.2   Setting team expectations with a Team Working
Agreement   92

*Scenario 1: The swift and not-so-swift reviews   92 ▪ Scenario 2:
Mismatched meanings   93 ▪ Scenario 3: To approve or not to
approve?   94*

4.3   Establishing a TWA with your team   95

Do we really need a TWA?   96

4.4 What to consider including in your TWA   98

*More implicit code review expectations   98 ▪ Reasonable response
times   99 ▪ Reasonable PR sizes   102 ▪ Issue identification   102
Self-approving PRs   105 ▪ Nitpicks   107 ▪ Positive review
environment   108 ▪ What happens when a policy is violated?   109*

4.5 This TWA is the team's document now   109

Need to make a change?   110 ▪ Final thoughts   110

5 *The advantages of automation   112*

5.1 Automation as an asset   113

5.2 Automation prerequisites   114

Team style guide   114 ▪ Capable tools   117

5.3 Automations before the review   118

*Formatting   118 ▪ Linting   121 ▪ Static analyzers   123
Automated testing   124*

5.4 Automations during the review   126

*PR templates   126 ▪ PR validators   129 ▪ Reviewer
assignments   131 ▪ PR gate checks   135 ▪ Reminders and
escalations   139*

6 *Composing effective code review comments   142*

6.1 What makes a comment effective?   143

*Objectivity   143 ▪ Specificity   149 ▪ Focused outcome   155
Effective code review comment examples   157*

6.2 Tone of voice   158

6.3 Code compliments   163

PART 3 DEALING WITH DILEMMAS 165

7 *How code reviews can suck   167*

7.1 Code review pain points   168

*The lazy code review   168 ▪ The mean code review   170
The shape-shifting code review   172 ▪ The stringent code
review   173*

7.2 So, what do we do?   174

8 **Decreasing code review delays   176**

8.1 "We only have a single senior developer to review our PRs"   177

8.2 "I don't understand the PR"   181

8.3 "There are too many files to review"   182

8.4 "Feature is too large to review"   183

8.5 "There's too much discussion back and forth"   186

8.6 "Code needs to be refactored (sometimes over and over)"   189

9 **Eliminating process loopholes   193**

9.1 How do loopholes happen?   193

9.2 Loopholes (and how to fix them)   194

An undefined code review process   194 ▪ Lack of time for code reviews   202 ▪ Tool (mis)configurations   204 ▪ Lack of feedback culture   205 ▪ Approval-driven metrics   207 ▪ Taking advantage of emergencies   209

10 **The Emergency Playbook   211**

10.1 What is an Emergency Playbook?   212

10.2 What goes in an Emergency Playbook?   213

Decision trees   213 ▪ Authorization process   215 ▪ Bypassing mechanisms   215 ▪ Next steps   216

10.3 When do we use the Emergency Playbook?   218

PART 4   PAIRING CODE REVIEWS WITH OTHER PRACTICES 219

11 **Code reviews and pair programming   221**

11.1 Do we do code reviews or pair programming?   222

Complementing code reviews with pair programming   223 Pair programming can't replace code reviews   223

11.2 Integrating pair programming   225

Convincing your team to try pair programming   226 ▪ Pairing styles   227 ▪ Considerations for effective pair programming   230

12 Code reviews and mob programming 239

12.1 Do we do code reviews or mob programming? 240

Mob programming strengths 241 ▪ Complementing code reviews with mob programming 243 ▪ Mob programming can't replace code reviews 244

12.2 Integrating mob programming with code reviews 245

Complementary approaches 245 ▪ Mob programming challenges 250

13 Code reviews and AI 255

13.1 Benefits of AI in code reviews 256

Expedited reviews 256 ▪ Code quality improvement 256 Review consistency 257 ▪ Review scalability for large teams and codebases 258

13.2 Limitations of AI in code reviews 258

Difficulty understanding context and domain knowledge 258 Capabilities are highly dependent on training data 259 Over-reliance on AI can hinder human reviewer expertise 260

13.3 What can an AI-powered code review do? 260

13.4 Integrating AI into your code reviews 270

13.5 The future of code reviews: Human-AI collaboration 272

appendix A Team Working Agreement starter template 275
appendix B Emergency Playbook starter template 282
appendix C PR templates 287
appendix D List of resources 290

index 325

foreword

I've been coding for money for over 32 years this year, and coding for free for nearly 40! I've taught coding at two colleges and worked side by side with developers who were far, far better coders than I, at companies all over the world, like Microsoft, Nike, and Intel, among others. Early in my career, I had my code so completely eviscerated in group code reviews that it had me sobbing in my car in the parking lot.

It wasn't until I read Adrienne's book, *Looks Good to Me: Constructive Code Reviews*, that I realized that no one ever formally teaches us how to review code, or how to accept the review. It's somehow just assumed that we'll put a bunch of passionate coders in a room, have them warmly accept "this code sucks" as feedback, and have each happily head back to their desk to make needed changes with an open heart.

You may think programming is about raw competence, you against the machine, putting lightning in a bottle in a caffeine-fueled 2 a.m. coding session. It is—when you're a one-person shop coding for yourself. But engineers nearly always work as part of a team, and even more often, we work on very large systems that can't be held in a single human's mind. Programming is a team sport, and humans are a messy bunch to assemble into teams.

Adrienne knows this and has assembled a practical and human-first guide to constructive code reviews. It's filled with real-world anecdotes from her storied career, and it also looks at the code review process within the larger context of the software development life cycle. What if your team is deep into continuous integration as a culture? What if you work in pairs? What about the "vacation factor?" Should code reviews come in pairs or in mobs? Should you use extensive tooling or just eyeballs and intuition? I appreciate that each of these questions and so many more are delved into in great depth with clear examples.

Reviewing code is as important as writing code, and you'll want to put together a process that works for your team culture. With this book, you'll work to set a Team Working Agreement, set shared expectations, and describe a comfortable environment where everyone can bring their best selves and their best code to the table. You'll then add in automation, PR prechecks, test coverage, and more.

Whether you're just starting out or you've been in the game for years, this book will set you and your team up for an improved code review culture. Thank you, Adrienne, writing a book like this is a massive undertaking. Looks good to me!

—SCOTT HANSELMAN, VP of Developer Community, Microsoft

preface

Ah, code reviews! We need them, but we dread them. We do them, but not well. And despite the tools we have at our disposal, we still manage to mess things up.

How do we deal with gigantic PRs? How do we make code reviews shorter? Why can't we write effective code review comments? Is SSDaaRB (Single Senior Developer as a Reviewer Bottleneck) something we just have to accept? Are we doomed to debate with our colleagues over technical implementations? Will code reviews always be like this?

These questions (and plenty more) are the matters that I gravitated toward in my now 12-year career. I've worked on teams that had no code review process at all. I've worked on teams that had a process, but it was barely enforced. I've worked on teams that had a wonderful process. And I've worked on teams where the process made me want to pull my hair out because it was so tedious. As I gained knowledge in those roles, both in technologies and team processes, I couldn't help but return to those questions. Looking back, I realized a big part of whether I enjoyed working with certain teams was whether our code review process was amicable and effective. Yes, you write code when you become a professional software developer, but you spend way more time reading and making sense of it. You also spend a lot of time reading code you didn't write! This realization made me look at code reviews in a different light.

More recently, I've been earning pretty pennies as a developer advocate, focused on teaching developers how to do "developer things" well. I accidentally fell into this role, but I'm glad I did; my software development background (and apparent skills in public speaking and written communication) really helps in creating technical educational content that shines. A big part of that is because I like to focus on what I believe are essentials—things that we tend to forget or assume that everyone already knows in the software development industry—and teach them in an approachable way. When Manning asked me what topic I would want to write about, given the chance to choose anything, the choice was absolutely clear: code reviews.

Are there other resources on code reviews? Absolutely. Do other developers have insights that may relate better to you? Guaranteed. But one fact remained: there is no "official" or single, comprehensive resource on code reviews, not in the way I imagined. I wanted to answer the questions I previously mentioned. I wanted to focus on the code review process and the team dynamics that surround it rather than list out code smells to watch out for (that would be a *huge* book if I accommodated everyone). I wanted to share all the insights, experience, strategies, and tactics I've learned and collected throughout my career to build a better code review. And I wanted to do it in a friendly, approachable way. I wanted to be THE book on code reviews. So that's what I did.

Now that you're reading this labor of love, I'm excited to guide you through the human side of code reviews. I want you to do better than LGTM 👍. I want your code reviews to be great!

Thanks for caring about code reviews. Enjoy the book!

acknowledgments

Writing a book is no small feat. And it's certainly not just me that does everything. So it's only appropriate that I give my thanks to everyone who has been a part of creating this wonderful book, both directly and indirectly.

I want to thank my first (my last, my everything), my husband, Mario. For the countless conversations we've had about code reviews, the late-night milk teas you've brought me, the patience you've shown while I disappeared into my "writing mode," and the undying support you've given me throughout this entire process, thank you. Mahal na mahal kita ♥ .

To Rebecca Johnson, my editor at Manning: there were many *cough* rearranged deadlines, major changes to the book's content, and questions I had on how to navigate the book-writing process, and you gracefully guided and supported me through all of it. Thank you for pushing me to be a better writer and for being an indispensable editor on this book.

To Miroslav Popovic, software architect and Software Engineering Manager at Qinshift, my technical editor: your feedback was instrumental in keeping this book as approachable for a myriad of developers as possible. Your own insights and perspectives not only enhanced this book but also kept it authentic. Thank you for playing a pivotal role in the creation of this book!

David Alexander, Jonah Andersson, Devlin Duldulao, Denis Kranjčec, Garrett McCullough, Glenn Reyes, and Marilag Svennevig: thank you for the marvelous contributions to the book. Your stories, lessons, and real-life ways of working benefited the book greatly.

Thanks to all my reviewers: Asif Iqbal, Ninoslav Čerkez, Charles Chan, Dave Corun, David Krief, Deborah Mesquita, Edward Lee, Emmanouil Chardalas, Frédéric Flayol, Gowtham Sadasivam, Hazem Farahat, Jakub Jabłoński, Jeff Patterson, Jeremy Bryan, John Kasiewicz, John Pantoja, Jon Moore, Lin Zhang, Louis Aloia, Louis Savart, Marcus Geselle, Marlin Keys, Mehmet Yilmaz, Mustafa Özçetin, Oliver Korten, Regan Russell, Scott Bartram, Sebastian Larsson, Seth MacPherson, Shyam Burkule, Srihari Sridharan, Tim Wooldridge, Xiaoyun Yang, and Ashwani Singh. I'm incredibly grateful for all of your insightful feedback and suggestions. Even though they may have resulted in late nights, tight deadlines, and the use of every spare minute I had to incorporate them, the investment was well worth it. Thank you all for helping me create a truly worthy book.

Alisa Larson, I guess I'm a bit verbose, huh? Thank you so much for going through the muddled version of my book and making it much more succinct. Your excellent edits, refining rewrites, and clarifying cuts make this book even more human-readable than I could have imagined. Thank you.

Manfred Steger, although we've never met, I owe my book's character, charm, and comedic breaks to you. I feel incredibly lucky to have found your set of adorable Pixelchen vectors and even more thankful that you've generously made them free to use. Thanks to you, the readers of the book don't have to endure the limits of my artistic ability.

To Brian Sawyer, my acquisitions editor at Manning: thank you for having that first call, taking a chance on an evergreen topic like code reviews, and eventually agreeing to the title changes of this book!

Erik Pillar also deserves my thanks: without you, I would not have started a conversation with Brian, and this book may not exist at all! Not only that, but your continued efforts in finding podcasts, book clubs, and other opportunities to share my book have been tremendous. Thank you!

Adriana Sabo and Dunja Nikitović: thank you for facilitating the major review rounds, the results of which have been invaluable for the improvement of my book. As well, thanks to the rest of the production team behind the scenes who helped shepherd this book into its final format.

Finally, thank you to my family. I've always wanted to make you proud, so I hope this book does the job. 😁 Thanks for always rooting for me. You know who you are. Ok, in case you don't—Angie Braganza, Joanne Braganza (Hi, Mom 👋), Joel Braganza, JP Braganza, Gerry Braganza, Lucie Lapid, Jill Lapid, Fely Quitevis-Bateman, and Jonathan Abarabar. Maraming salamat! I love you all. 😊

about this book

Looks Good to Me: Constructive Code Reviews was written to be THE code review book. It intends to be the referenceable, immediately applicable, and discussion-starting book on code reviews your team won't stop talking about (in a good way). We start with the "what" and "why" of code reviews and then engage in a step-by-step process of building your team's first code review before teaching you essential skills, like automation, collaboratively creating team agreements, and comment writing, that let you perform code reviews well. We finish with the trickier stuff—dilemmas that can delay your code review or weaken its effectiveness and how to consider code reviews with other practices.

Who should read this book

Do you write and review code? Then YOU should. To be a bit more specific, *Looks Good to Me* would be valuable for developers who want to make their current code review process better, who want to establish a new code review process for their team, or are tired of ineffective reviews and need some inspiration on how to change them. This book is especially relevant for those who have grown resentful of the code review process due to "human bottlenecks" but would like to resolve them to change their feelings on the process! Lastly, technical leads and software development managers who want to support and enable their team to build the best code review process that works for them will also find value in this book.

How this book is organized: A road map

This book has four parts that cover 13 chapters. Part 1 will make sure you have a good foundation for code reviews:

- Chapter 1 introduces you to the code review, its benefits, and why they are significant in the context of software development. It also describes how you may want to go through this book, "choose your own adventure" style.
- Chapter 2 dissects the code review and establishes some core knowledge you should know: what types of review systems there are, what a typical workflow looks like, what the elements of a good pull request are, and who the main characters of a code review are and the responsibilities each one holds.
- Chapter 3 breaks down how to build your team's first code review process step by step. You'll walk through establishing a code review process collaboratively and ask your team to make some important decisions about the code review they are creating.

Part 2 gets into the key skills you'll need to not only perform code reviews but also do them well:

- Chapter 4 explores the important Team Working Agreement. Everything about it, from what it is to why your team needs it and how it helps enforce code review policies to how to maintain it are addressed.
- Chapter 5 focuses on automation tactics, both during development and during the review.
- Chapter 6 teaches us why words matter and how to write considerate yet effective code review comments for almost any scenario.

Part 3 gets into real dilemmas you might face (and how to handle them) once you've been using your code review process for some time:

- Chapter 7 outlines some pain points and real developer stories of code reviews gone wrong.
- Chapter 8 takes a look at the prevailing problem of lengthy code reviews—specifically, why they may get delayed and how to make reviews much shorter.
- Chapter 9 digs into code review process loopholes to watch out for and how to fix them (tech leads and engineering managers, chapter 9 is for you!).
- Chapter 10 introduces the Emergency Playbook, a helpful tool that allows your team to deal with situations that don't fit neatly into your established code review process.

Part 4 analyzes code reviews within the context of other software development practices:

- Chapter 11 explores combining code reviews with pair programming.
- Chapter 12 explores combining code reviews with mob programming.
- Chapter 13 ends the book discussing code reviews and AI: what's possible right now and what I think we should be mindful of as we enter the next age of code reviews.

I highly recommend reading this book cover to cover. As a general rule, I encourage everyone to read chapters 2 through 6 as they are equally valuable to every team, regardless of where you are on your code review journey. The remaining chapters can be read as necessary and when applicable to your team. You can also refer back to chapters as often as you need to, when you change teams, or when you need a refresher on some awesome thing you learned from this book.

About the code

This book contains examples of source code both in numbered listings and in line with normal text. In both cases, source code is formatted in a `fixed-width font like this` to separate it from ordinary text. Sometimes code is also **in bold** to highlight code that has changed from previous steps in the chapter, such as when a new feature adds to an existing line of code.

In many cases, the original source code has been reformatted; we've added line breaks and reworked indentation to accommodate the available page space in the book. In rare cases, even this was not enough, and listings include line-continuation markers (➥). Additionally, comments in the source code have often been removed from the listings when the code is described in the text. Code annotations accompany many of the listings, highlighting important concepts.

You can get executable snippets of code from the liveBook (online) version of this book at https://livebook.manning.com/book/looks-good-to-me. Throughout the book, you'll find templates and examples that will usually be a Markdown file. The complete code for the examples in the book is available for download from the Manning website at https://www.manning.com/books/looks-good-to-me, and from GitHub at https://github.com/adriennetacke/lgtm-extras.

liveBook discussion forum

Purchase of *Looks Good to Me* includes free access to liveBook, Manning's online reading platform. Using liveBook's exclusive discussion features, you can attach comments to the book globally or to specific sections or paragraphs. It's a snap to make notes for yourself, ask and answer technical questions, and receive help from the author and other users. To access the forum, go to https://livebook.manning.com/book/looks-good-to-me/discussion. You can also learn more about Manning's forums and the rules of conduct at https://livebook.manning.com/discussion.

Manning's commitment to our readers is to provide a venue where a meaningful dialogue between individual readers and between readers and the author can take place. It is not a commitment to any specific amount of participation on the part of the author, whose contribution to the forum remains voluntary (and unpaid). We suggest you try asking the author some challenging questions lest her interest stray! The forum and the archives of previous discussions will be accessible from the publisher's website as long as the book is in print.

about the author

ADRIENNE BRAGANZA is a Filipina software engineer, international speaker, LinkedIn Learning instructor, author of *Coding for Kids: Python*, and now, a Manning author, thanks to this book! (Essentially, she's an overachiever.) With over a decade of software development and developer advocacy experience, she's always favored teaching the essential topics, especially how to do them well. But the most important things to know about her? She spends way too much money on coffee and pastries and looks forward to the ungodly amounts of time she can now spend playing *Age of Empires II* and *Manor Lords.*

about the cover illustration

The figure on the cover of *Looks Good to Me*, titled "The Lounge Singer," is taken from a book by Louis Curmer published in 1841. The illustration is finely drawn and colored by hand.

In those days, it was easy to identify where people lived and what their trade or station in life was just by their dress. Manning celebrates the inventiveness and initiative of the computer business with book covers based on the rich diversity of regional culture centuries ago, brought back to life by pictures from collections such as this one.

Part 1

Code review foundations

Hey there! You're here either because (a) you want to learn about this thing called code reviews, (b) you're in desperate need of redoing your existing process, or (c) you know your code reviews are OK but are looking to make them better, or (d) you really like to learn and have good taste in technical books 😊—maybe you're reason (e) and you just appreciate the awesome book title 😎. Regardless of the reason, the first part of the book will make sure you have a good foundation on code reviews, at least the way we'll be talking about them in this book!

Chapter 1 will introduce you to the importance of code reviews, why you should want them, how to convince your team to want them too, and lay out how the rest of this book is structured. Feel free to reference this chapter when you want to skip to certain topics.

Chapter 2 delves deeper into the basic components of the code review; by the end of this jam-packed chapter (that I encourage you to take in strides), you'll understand what types of code review systems there are and what the main parts of a code review are, describe what a pull request is and how to create a fantastic one, and know who participates in the code review and what their specific obligations are.

With the detailed foundation laid, you'll be ready for chapter 3, which guides your team through a step-by-step process in creating your first code review process. Once you complete chapter 3, your team should have their first working code review process in place! To make the best of it, you'll need to learn some key code review skills, which await you in part 2—Elevated code review essentials.

The significance
of code reviews

This chapter covers

- Introducing the code review process
- Who this book is for (and who it's not for)
- How this book is structured
- The benefits of a code review
- How we can make code reviews better

Mike, a developer on a small software development team, just finished a new feature on Friday. He built an entirely new invoice parsing system that would render customers' invoices as PDFs. And he finished it just in time for his vacation in Cancún. Sure, there were some workarounds and hacks in parts of his code, but hey, it *worked*. Excited, he quickly merged his new feature into the demo environment; his colleagues (Adrienne, Erica, and Justin) agreed to demo the new invoice parser to the CEO while Mike was out.

On Monday morning, Adrienne stared at her screen, confused. She began testing the parser and found that it was calculating the invoices incorrectly. Debugging was almost impossible as she couldn't make sense of Mike's code. She asked both Erica and Justin if they could try their hand at understanding the new parser code. After some time, both defeatedly shook their heads no. As they huddled around

Adrienne's screen trying to understand the mystery code, Mike shared photos of his vacation in the team's messaging channel—the beaches he lay on, margaritas he drank, and tasty dishes he ate. The team sighed.

Unfortunately, the team was unable to fix the calculation problem by the time of the demo. Mike's coworkers couldn't "fake" the demo—the code was so difficult, it was impossible to understand enough to know what to manipulate and how to make it do the right thing—and they couldn't reschedule the demo as it had already been rescheduled twice. They had to show the new feature with its major flaw to their CEO. As they performed the demo of the new parsing system, the CEO was not happy. This feature was already supposed to be deployed last quarter. To make matters worse, the fees were wrong—by a lot—and it was glaringly obvious in the demo. Adrienne, Erica, and Justin were under intense pressure to "fix this faster than as soon as possible," a direct quote from the CEO.

As they debugged, they found the relevant code where fees were indeed calculated incorrectly, but they were unsure why. Adrienne and her colleagues spent the rest of that Monday (and Tuesday and Wednesday) working overtime to understand the code and find the problem. After those stressful few days, they finally found it: an incorrect calculation hidden behind "clever" code and single-letter variable names produced the wrong fee. As a (sour) cherry on top, they confirmed that the new invoice PDF parser system irresponsibly pulled the charge amounts from the generated PDF rather than a more durable source of truth. This was a major change from the conventions of the codebase and a wrong one at that. At this point, it was pretty clear that this new parsing system introduced some headache-inducing bugs.

The team worked as quickly as they could to get invoices functioning properly again. It was a bit tricky as there were no tests (tsk tsk, Mike), and the code was cryptic. The team felt that even Mike wouldn't understand his own code once returning from vacation. In the end, Adrienne, Erica, and Justin agreed that they never wanted to go through something like that again.

As you read this story, you may have thought, "Why didn't Mike's colleagues look through his code or give a quick thumbs up before moving forward? Why was there no knowledge sharing between Mike and his team or any explanation of his changes? Were there no automated tools that could have caught some of these bugs?" These are all great questions, and they all lead to what this book is about: code reviews.

So, what's a *code review*? At its core, it's a process software developers use to inspect each other's code, making sure it passes a set of agreed-upon standards. The inspection part can happen over your shoulder, through a more formal meeting with a governing board of approvers, or, as is the focus in this book, through a *pull request* (PR). A PR is a proposal of code changes that can be reviewed, discussed, and commented on before being merged into a larger codebase. Pull requests are common in tools like GitHub, GitLab, Bitbucket, Azure Repos, AWS CodeCommit, Google Cloud Source Repositories, or any number of collaborative code tools backed by private Git repositories.

> **NOTE** To learn more about how to get started with Git, see https://mng.bz/w5Z5.

Code reviews are also the missing piece to our earlier story. Mike's team could have employed a very simplistic review by preparing Mike's new parsing system changes in a PR. Then, at least two of the team—ideally, the whole team—could have taken a look to see whether everything looked good. Since things obviously weren't, Mike's teammates could have given him feedback: the code was too cryptic, was straying from the codebase's conventions, and didn't have accompanying tests for such an important feature. Mike's code would never have progressed to the demo environment in the state it was in.

While this book focuses on code reviews, I need to call out its complementary and co-dependent nature to an overall *continuous integration* (CI) and *continuous delivery* (CD) strategy. CI refers to the automation of building, testing, and integrating code changes within a shared repository. CD refers to the automation of delivering code changes to an environment for approval. Together, they form a *CI/CD pipeline*, which is a set of automated workflows a software development team uses to cut down on manual tasks of the software development process. While a fully automated CI/CD pipeline is an alluring goal we should strive for, it's not foolproof for protecting and maintaining the health of a codebase. Where CI automates and evaluates code quality through static analysis, unit tests, and other "computer-friendly" mechanisms, code reviews allow developers to evaluate code with a nuanced, context-aware, and domain knowledge–aware eye. We need both. Overall, the more safeguards a team can put into place to make sure healthy code is the only code that gets deployed, the better.

A good code review process plays a vital role in an organization's overall approach to supply chain security and build environment security. Securing everyone's participation in and support for code reviews contributes to the overarching goal of building valuable software for your organization.

What about continuous deployment?

When you hear or read about CI/CD pipelines, the acronym "CD" likely refers to *continuous delivery* rather than the equivalently abbreviated *continuous deployment*. In continuous delivery, the automated workflows in a pipeline are briefly paused or stopped since they require human intervention to approve the final push to production. Alternatively, continuous deployment is fully automated: as long as code changes pass all the required tests implemented in the pipeline, they are deployed to customers immediately. I like to remember the difference in this way: continuous delivery *delivers* a sign-off (like a delivery driver asking you to sign for a package), and continuous deployment *deploys* a ready-to-go feature (exactly like the definition of "deploy," which is to move into a position of readiness).

Now, some of you might be thinking, "I know how important code reviews are, and we do have a code review process in place." To that, I say, "Great!" That's a wonderful start. Let's continue to pull on that thread: ask yourself and, more importantly, all the members of your team the following questions:

- Is our current code review process useful?
- Do our code reviews take too long?
- Are we placing the reviewing burden on a single person?
- Do we still like each other after a difficult code review?
- Do we know how to leave a suggestion or constructive criticism?
- Do we know how to deal with feedback effectively?
- Is our review process fulfilling the purpose we believe they are supposed to fulfill?
- Are we aligned on what that purpose is?
- Are we taking advantage of *any* automation?
- Do we know what's expected of each party in our code review process?
- Do we all understand the value code reviews bring to our software development process?
- Can we show why code reviews matter and link them to the business value they deliver?
- Can we confidently say that we *love* our process?

In my conversations with developers around the world and my own experiences on a multitude of teams, I'm willing to bet that you've answered "No" to at least a few of those questions. I can also tell you that there's a consistent theme: software developers *dread* code reviews. Whether that's because it's an inconsistent, unsustainable, inefficient, unfair, uselessly manual, or otherwise nonexistent process, or there is a lack of empathy between teammates during the review itself or some other bottleneck of human origin, code reviews are avoidably the bane of many developers' existence.

Through this book, I want to change this reality. Whether this is the first time you've heard of code reviews or are sick and tired of them, I want you to experience code reviews as they should be—effective, empathetic, and effortless for your team.

One big caveat as you read this book: this won't be a "one-size-fits-all" approach for code reviews. Your team's needs, wants, and limitations will differ (imagine writing a book covering all possible team scenarios)! Rather, this book is a guide to help you set up or improve and then continuously refine and evolve a manageable process. I try to generalize the advice I give to help most teams create a code review process that works within their team and organizational constraints, achieves the goals they wish to accomplish, complements a larger CI/CD pipeline, and is one the team is happy and proud of. Ultimately, this book will make your code reviews better by improving the process, even if that progress is small or incremental.

If you implement just a few tactics today or share a piece of advice learned from this book with a colleague, I'll consider that a success for code reviewers everywhere. Let's get to it.

1.1 Who this book is for

This book will be valuable to anyone who reads, writes, and reviews code. Through actionable advice, automation tactics, collaborative strategies, and team-enforced techniques, this book will guide developers, tech leads, and engineering managers on building a code review process from scratch or upgrading an existing one that's subpar.

- *If you're just starting out in software development*—I want you to understand why code reviews are important and explore how it's critical to create maintainable, understandable, and valuable applications; to acknowledge that organizations need it (even if they don't understand it); and to recognize that we can't just let AI take care of them for us.
- *If you're on a software development team and aware of the importance of code reviews but need help creating a process for your own team*—I want to guide you through creating a code review process from scratch, from convincing your team and establishing a fair and effective process from the start to choosing what your code review process will do for your team and how.
- *If you're a developer who sees your team's code review process could be improved*—I want to share tactics, strategies, and mindsets that you can implement and experiment with, many of which solve common problems that plague many teams' code reviews today. And if "improving" your process means "redoing" your process (☺), I'll advise you on how to define better guidelines and rules you'll enforce as a team.
- *If you're a developer who wants help in navigating difficult reviews*—I want to give you structured processes that help you find middle ground with your colleagues and strategies for handling typical code review disagreements.
- *If you're a developer who has trouble composing code review feedback*—I want to give you reusable comment strategies, from one that helps organize and streamline feedback for both the author and reviewer to one that helps you objectively and effectively ask for a change.

- *If you're a senior or lead developer who's tired of being the only reviewer*—I want to solve this "bottleneck" problem and help you fairly and efficiently redistribute the reviewing responsibility in a way that makes sense and contributes to the overall improvement of the team's skills.

- *If you're a tech lead or lead developer who wants to improve your team's code review demeanor*—I want to help you help your team to be more considerate of each other through code review comment patterns (that your team can use to compose effective, yet considerate code review comments) and introduce you to the Team Working Agreement, a document that can help your team understand each other's expectations around the code review.

- *If you're a tech lead or engineering manager who is frustrated with particularly long code review cycles*—I want to unravel the reasons why code reviews can take so long, train you to spot potential factors that contribute to long code reviews on your own team, and share what can be done to reduce code review times.

- *If you're a tech lead or engineering manager who wants to support and enable a pro-code review culture*—I want this book to serve as a helpful guide on the holistic code review process, even if you don't participate in the review phase itself. I want to help you appreciate the benefits of a code review, anticipate (and deal with) common problems that arise, prevent human bottlenecks, enable your team to build a code review process that addresses their needs, and recognize how you can best support your team's code reviews.

No matter who you are, I'll guide you through the code review process with a human lens to transform a process that's been known to be forgotten, despised, and used to build up one's ego into a much more enjoyable, praised, and supported part of the software development workflow. I mean, for such an integral component of software development—not to mention the countless tools we have at our disposal—there should be a better way. This book will help you get there.

It is worth noting who *this book is not for*: this book may not make sense for you if you primarily work alone, like a one-person army or solo developer at a startup. The tactics and advice shared here focus on solving problems between people, so those sections may not apply. However, learning what's in this book can set a wonderful foundation for you once you start working on a larger team!

Also, while this book presents guidelines on *how* to review code effectively and generalized criteria to judge code on, this book is not for those who want to learn *what* to look for while you review your colleague's code, which will differ greatly between programming languages, application architectures, and your company's internal standards. So, if you are looking for a guide on how to spot code smells, a reference on programming conventions and best practices, or a book that teaches you how to write good code, this is not the book you're looking for 🖐 (waves hand in Jedi-like motion).

If that's what you are looking for, I'd highly recommend Steve McConnell's *Code Complete: A Practical Handbook of Software Construction* [1] or Christian Clausen's *Five*

Lines of Code: How and When to Refactor [2]. Both are excellent references on what to look for in code reviews and how to make the code you're reviewing better.

1.2 How this book is structured

In Part 1 (chapters 1–3), we start with some basics. You're currently reading chapter 1, which introduces you to the code review, its benefits, and why they are significant in the context of software development. It also outlines who this book is for and how it's structured. Chapter 2 dissects the code review and establishes all the basics you should know: what types of review systems there are, what a typical workflow is like, what the elements of a good PR are, and who the main characters of a code review are and the responsibilities each one holds. Chapter 3 breaks down how to build your team's first code review process step by step. You'll walk through establishing a code review process collaboratively and ask your team to make some important decisions about the code review they are creating.

With a foundation laid, Part 2 (chapters 4–6) gets into the good stuff. These chapters delve into specific skills you'll need to perform code reviews and do them well. Chapter 4 explores the important Team Working Agreement. Everything about it, from what it is to why your team needs it and how it helps enforce code review policies to how it's maintained will be addressed. Chapter 5 focuses on automation tactics, both during development and during the review. Chapter 6 teaches us why words matter and how to write considerate yet effective code review comments for almost any scenario.

Part 3 (chapters 7–10) gets into the tricky stuff that can pop up as your team gets used to code reviews. Chapter 7 outlines some pain points and real developer stories of code reviews gone wrong. Chapter 8 takes a look at the prevailing problem of lengthy code reviews—specifically, why they may get delayed and how to make reviews much shorter. Chapter 9 digs into some code review process loopholes—namely, what to watch out for and how to fix them if we spot them in our own code review (tech leads and engineering managers, chapter 9 is for you!). We then end Part 3 with chapter 10, an introduction to the Emergency Playbook. This is a helpful tool that allows your team to deal with situations that don't fit neatly into your established code review process. You'll likely find the actionable pieces of advice that you can use today in part 3 of the book.

By Part 4 (chapters 11–13), you can learn more about code reviews within the context of other software development practices before I leave you with my thoughts on the future of code reviews. Chapter 11 explores combining code reviews and pair programming, while Chapter 12 explores combining code reviews with mob programming. Both chapters answer the questions, "Do we still need code reviews if we do this?" and "How do we do both well?" Finally, chapter 13 discusses code reviews and AI, what's possible right now (at least during the time of writing), and what to be mindful of as we (inevitably) introduce AI into our code reviews.

While I highly recommend reading this from cover to cover, there are other ways to make the most of this book:

- *If you just accepted code reviews into your life but don't know how to start the process with your team*—I'd start with chapter 2, then really dig into chapters 3 and 4. Once you have a good cadence and your team is used to code reviews, you can start making your way through the rest of Part 3 to refine it and tailor the process to your team.
- *If your code reviews are terrible, no good fiascos*—Same as those starting from scratch (you'll be better off redoing your team's code review foundation, trust me); start with chapter 2 and take your time with chapters 3 and 4. Since you've experienced what a *terrible* code review process is like, you'll likely ease into Part 3's chapters a lot sooner than those starting from scratch, as you'll know what to improve or do better this time around.
- *If your team understands the importance of code reviews but can't agree on anything*—Start with chapter 4 and then go through the rest of the book.
- *If your code reviews are alright but you know they can be way better*—You can likely jump straight to chapters 5 and 6 (and beyond) and start experimenting with automation tactics and enhanced code review policies, among other neat things to improve your process. You can also refer back to chapters 2 to 4 as needed.
- *If your team needs some help with constructive feedback (like how to give and receive it)*—Head straight to chapter 6 and then refer back to the rest of the book as necessary.
- *As a general rule*—Chapters 2 to 4 can be equally valuable to most teams, no matter where you are in the code review-building process.

Lastly, this book is meant to keep on giving. Once you have established a process with your team, feel free to refer back to it as needed. Recommend specific sections to new team members or establish it as required reading for all code review participants. Pick and choose different tactics as you need them or when you are refining your process. This book should be your best code review friend.

1.3 *You should want code reviews*

Code reviews should be the norm rather than the exception. They result in better applications, promote clear and readable codebases, and can produce invaluable artifacts that describe how and, more importantly, *why* your codebase has changed over the years. I'm telling you, you should want code reviews.

1.3.1 *Better applications*

Code reviews (paired with a well-rounded CI/CD strategy) keep codebases healthy and secure. When done properly and consistently, code reviews minimize the number of defects that enter production. This has been proven time and time again. IBM's 500,000-line Orbit project used 11 (!) levels of review, resulting in only 1% of expected errors being found without review [1]. AT&T's case study showed a 90% decrease in defects once code reviews were introduced to a 200-person organization within the company [1]. A large-scale study of modern code review and security in open source projects conducted by the University of California at Berkeley shows that code review reduces the number of bugs and security bugs in production [3]. Then there's a case study titled *The Impact of Code Review Coverage and Code Review Participation on Software Quality* that I think sums it up best: "If a large proportion of the code changes that are integrated during development are either: (1) omitted from the code review process (low review coverage), or (2) have lax code review involvement (low review participation), then defect-prone code will permeate through to the released software product" [4].

Code reviews also promote better clarity and readability of code as developers review each other's work. Whether it's because you know someone else is going to look at your code or just generally try to write human-friendly code, the process seems to encourage us to tidy up and present our code changes in the best light. Clear, readable, human-friendly code generally means it's also maintainable code, and a maintainable codebase typically lowers the chances of bugs being introduced in the future. As an important, human-only quality check, code reviews make applications better.

As code quality continuously improves (and stays healthy) and the understanding and maintainability of the code also improve, the number of people and the amount of time and money needed for debugging and fixing the application are reduced later on.

Having a codebase that a team can confidently work on simplifies (and sometimes makes possible) adherence to compliance requirements, regulatory standards, and internal audits of the codebase. This all boils down to a codebase whose overall maintainability improves over time, largely thanks to code reviews. All of these things promote better code, which usually translates to better applications.

1.3.2 Elevated team understanding

Often an overlooked benefit, code reviews can boost a team's overall understanding of their codebase and each other. When prioritized, code reviews can act as both a knowledge-transfer (the deliberate process of moving knowledge from one person or group to another) mechanism and a knowledge-sharing (the exchange of knowledge in a readily accessible environment) mechanism between team members. Thus, code reviews are a useful onboarding mechanism, integrating new team members faster.

With code reviews, the opportunity to share and transfer knowledge between all involved naturally presents itself. Knowledge transfer and knowledge sharing can lead to more people on your team understanding a larger percentage of your codebase. With more knowledge equally spread across the team, you can reduce the overall team's dependency on specific team members. No more feeling guilty for taking time off!

Finally, effective code reviews, combined with automation practices and clear team policies (like proper commit messages, PR descriptions, and a commitment to explaining the "why" of your changes), can be the living record of your codebase's evolution. How powerful would that be to know exactly when, where, and why a particular change caused a problem or produced a positive change?

With some really kick-ass perks, it shouldn't be so difficult to get your team on board. Unfortunately, a few people might not be so excited about code reviews.

1.4   *Convincing your team*

Let's be clear about something: most software development teams are not against a code review process, just the annoyances that surround it. Consequently, it can take some effort to convince your team that they are still worth it, especially if you are starting without a code review process! That's why the key to convincing your team is first to get on the same page (of this book ☺).

As Khalid aptly sings, "Can we just talk?"; convincing your team starts with an open conversation with everyone. Every individual should be invited to this conversation, from the developers who write the code to the tech leads who influence the policies and even the engineering managers who play a part in enforcing the process.

In this conversation, likely more than one, you'll need to find common ground on a lot of topics:

- What are the goals of our code review?
- Who needs to know about this change?
- How do we decide who reviews PRs?
- How long do we give reviewers to approve PRs?
- Do we require a minimum of two approvers? Three?
- What do we do when we need to deploy an emergency hotfix?

When first starting, these conversations can be held every week. Alternatively, this topic is a great thing to discuss during engineering offsites, a typical week-long engagement where teams plan their future vision, goals, and projects. As you start to define and refine the common ground for your team, it should be codified into a living, working document your team can reference. An example is the Team Working Agreement, which will be explained in detail in chapter 4.

By gathering everyone's opinions, actively encouraging every member to participate in these conversations, and building a process around the team's collective goals, you'll have the best chance at convincing your team to give code reviews a try or another shot.

1.5   *Making code reviews better*

Once you have a code review process in place (or if you're reading this book eager to make changes to your existing one), your team will likely want to make updates and improvements to it. To make code reviews better, we need to consider two things.

First, proper engineering discipline has to be a core goal of the team. For code reviews, that means producing an artifact (i.e., the code being written) that is durable and valuable. When the developers on your team can easily understand the code—and can still understand it a few years from now—durability is achieved. Likewise, code becomes valuable when bug fixes are quicker to apply, and extensions to functionality are easier, or even possible, to implement. When a team has durability and value ingrained, the code they write and the code reviews they complete are likely better.

Second, we can't forget the people behind the code. From the practices performed to the conversations held, the foundation of great code reviews is built within an environment that encourages feedback and a cohesive team. What does a cohesive team look like? It's where each team member is able and willing to share their opinion, wants to contribute to key team conversations, feels safe bringing up concerns, can confidently rely on their colleagues to do their best work, and generally trusts that others will treat them with kindness and respect. There's no room for egos on a cohesive team; favoritism, bias, nepotism, selfishness, and a lack of humility also don't have space on a cohesive team.

For a great code review process to be built, a team has to know what it wants, what it doesn't want, what systems work best for the team, what is possible with their organizational and team constraints, what its collective goals and standards are, and have a collective sense of ownership and accountability to the codebases they maintain—this only happens when a team works well together. Only then will a repeatable and worthwhile code review be created.

With all that out of the way, I'm excited to share what I've experienced, learned, developed, experimented with, researched, and corroborated over the years on how to make code reviews the best that they can be. And you know what? This book is the culmination of ideas, automation tactics, templates, patterns, and strategies that you can use to create the code review process of your team's dreams. Ready to get started?

Summary

- A code review is a process software developers use to inspect each other's code, making sure it passes a set of agreed-upon standards. The inspection part can happen over your shoulder, through a formal meeting, or through a pull request (a proposal of code changes that can be reviewed, discussed, and commented on before being merged into a larger codebase).

- Code reviews should be the norm rather than the exception in software development. Why? Code reviews produce better applications (through clear, readable, maintainable code) and elevate a team's understanding of their codebase and each other (through the knowledge-transfer, knowledge-sharing, and record-keeping mechanisms they provide).

- Great code reviews are built on the foundation of a cohesive team, meaning a team where all members feel respected, valued, and treated as an equal part of the team.

References

[1] McConnell, S. (2016). *Code Complete: A Practical Handbook of Software Construction*. Microsoft Press.

[2] Clausen, C. (2021). *Five Lines of Code: How and When to Refactor*. Manning Publications.

[3] Thompson, C., & Wagner, D. (2017). A large-scale study of modern code review and security in open source projects. In Proceedings of the 13th International Conference on Predictive Models and Data Analytics in Software Engineering (pp. 83–92). Association for Computing Machinery.

[4] McIntosh, S., Kamei, Y., Adams, B., & Hassan, A. E. (2014). The impact of code review coverage and code review participation on software quality. In *MSR 2014: Proceedings of the 11th Working Conference on Mining Software Repositories* (pp. 192–201). Association for Computing Machinery.

Dissecting
the code review

This chapter covers

- What code review systems exist
- What's involved in a typical code review workflow
- Who participates or influences the code review process (code review participants)
- What responsibilities belong to each participant (code review expectations)

In the first chapter, we explored why code reviews are essential and why you and your team should want them. Here, we dive deeper into the process itself: types of code review systems, who's involved, what a typical workflow looks like (and which one we'll focus on in this book), and some foundational practices we should know for the workflow we'll be using. Consider this chapter a breakdown of the basics!

> **NOTE** This chapter is packed with lots of good info. Feel free to take it section by section. Take a break if you feel like you need one. Bookmarks are encouraged for this chapter!

2.1   *Code review systems*

There are two code review systems a team can consider: human-led or tool-facilitated. Both have pros and cons, but as a recurring theme of this book, the right decision is what works best for your team. As you delve into what each system offers, note what you like and dislike and see what your team thinks about its characteristics.

Also, consider your team's size, location, industry, organization, budget, and goals. Human-led systems may be perfect for smaller teams in the same city. This quickly changes once your team becomes hybrid, adds more remote workers, or even has one team member move to a different timezone. Similarly, highly regulated industries like finance or healthcare may require additional documentation and historical records, which point to using a tool-facilitated system. Taking everything into consideration, you may find that neither one nor the other will fulfill your team's needs—rather, a hybrid of the two will be what's best!

2.1.1   *Human-led*

The human-led code review encompasses any system that primarily uses synchronous meetings, discussions, or face-to-face review processes to evaluate potential code changes. It can be a formal process, where a team member presents their code to their colleagues at a high-stakes meeting, or it can be as informal as a pair programming session with someone reviewing it over your shoulder.

Choosing a fully human-led code review system can be a great facilitator of both knowledge transfer and sharing and mentoring goals. This can give your team greater awareness of and familiarity with the system they are building—largely because they get to discuss its intricacies with their colleagues more often. Reviews can be much faster, too; requesting an in-person code review is more likely to be done at the time of the request. Uncertainties and questions about the proposed changes can also be answered in a synchronous but shorter timeframe. That's the ideal case, anyway.

Despite these advantages, there are a few things to consider. With its synchronous nature, formal documentation and official records of the code review itself become *highly* dependent on the team to accomplish. As a separate task, these important parts can easily be abandoned. The in-person nature of this system also limits the review to team members who are within reach of each other or go into the same office. While online meetings can still facilitate this kind of system, it becomes harder to coordinate across distributed teams.

2.1.2   *Tool-facilitated*

Probably the most well-known type, tool-facilitated code review systems use software to help teams run their code review process. If you've ever used GitHub, GitLab, Azure Repos, BitBucket, Sourceforge, Google Cloud Repositories, Git Kraken, AWS Code-Commit, Launchpad, or a whole slew of other tools, then you've participated in a tool-facilitated code review system!

Choosing a fully tool-facilitated code review system works especially well for large or distributed teams. When the tool is part of a larger ecosystem your team already works within, conforming to the code review process is easier. Tool-facilitated code reviews also allow parts of workflows to be automated, which is a big reason they are a popular choice. They provide a clear structure for many parts of the review, including the communication between the author and reviewer and the review itself. Tool-facilitated systems also offer integrations with CI/CD tools, like running static analysis checks, unit tests, and deployments to other test environments, making them a very productive choice.

On the other hand, tool-facilitated code review systems do have some downsides. One of them is delayed or lengthy review times. This is due to the asynchronous nature of the tool and having the software facilitate the process. Additionally, if the wrong tool is chosen, your team may introduce unnecessary friction into the code review process, either by working around the tool's shortcomings or adapting to the tool's quirks rather than having the tool adapt to your team's process. If your team has to switch between multiple systems to do a code review and their development work, this is another source of frustration for your team's workflow.

2.1.3 *Hybrid*

As you've likely identified, a hybrid of both human-led and tool-facilitated systems will probably be the right match for your team. You're not alone. According to StackOverflow's 2022 Developer Survey, 85% of respondents say their organizations are at least partially remote [1], about 94% use Git as the version control system [2], and GitHub is the most used version control platform for both professional (~87% of respondents) and personal (~56% of respondents) use [3].

If any part of your team is in more than one location, the use of a tool will be required. Even if your entire team is located in one location, a large codebase, multiple codebases or projects, team sizes of more than five, or multiple teams touching the same codebase will likely still require a tool to help facilitate and keep track of all the changes! Moreover, teams can supplement the tool with human-led tasks where they feel it falls short. For example, additional mentoring and knowledge transfer/sharing can occur through pair programming sessions prior to the submission of a pull request (PR).

Before choosing a system, consider an in-depth discussion with all members of your team who will be engaging in the code review process. Review the items in figure 2.1. In this way, your collective choice will have greater buy-in, resulting in higher chances of acceptance and support from the team.

Choosing a code review system

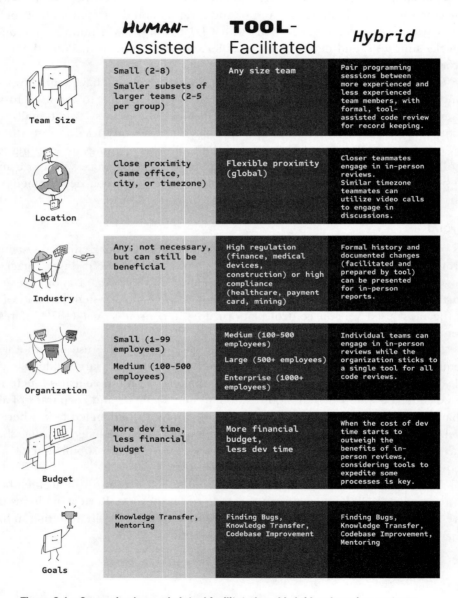

	HUMAN-Assisted	TOOL-Facilitated	*Hybrid*
Team Size	Small (2-8) Smaller subsets of larger teams (2-5 per group)	Any size team	Pair programming sessions between more experienced and less experienced team members, with formal, tool-assisted code review for record keeping.
Location	Close proximity (same office, city, or timezone)	Flexible proximity (global)	Closer teammates engage in in-person reviews. Similar timezone teammates can utilize video calls to engage in discussions.
Industry	Any; not necessary, but can still be beneficial	High regulation (finance, medical devices, construction) or high compliance (healthcare, payment card, mining)	Formal history and documented changes (facilitated and prepared by tool) can be presented for in-person reports.
Organization	Small (1-99 employees) Medium (100-500 employees)	Medium (100-500 employees) Large (500+ employees) Enterprise (1000+ employees)	Individual teams can engage in in-person reviews while the organization sticks to a single tool for all code reviews.
Budget	More dev time, less financial budget	More financial budget, less dev time	When the cost of dev time starts to outweigh the benefits of in-person reviews, considering tools to expedite some processes is key.
Goals	Knowledge Transfer, Mentoring	Finding Bugs, Knowledge Transfer, Codebase Improvement	Finding Bugs, Knowledge Transfer, Codebase Improvement, Mentoring

Figure 2.1   Comparing human-led, tool-facilitated, and hybrid code review systems.

2.2 How does a code review work?

Before we dive into the modern code review (on which this book is based), a brief look at the past is warranted. While there is likely much more history on this topic, many thanks should be given to Michael E. Fagan, an IBM researcher first credited with the invention of the "formal" code inspection process in 1976 [4]. This was the first documented and structured process with the sole goal of examining source code for defects. In contrast to the modern code review (which can be asynchronous, completed remotely, and much quicker overall), Fagan's inspection process was much more formal.

Consisting of several (and sometimes extended) in-person meetings, Fagan's inspection involved three to six participants (each with an assigned role) who discussed and reviewed up to 250 lines of source code. There's a moderator who keeps everyone on task, controls the pace of the review, and acts as an arbiter of disputes [5]. There's a reviewer tasked with critical analysis, a reader who only looks at the source code for comprehension (meaning no critique), and the author, the original creator of the source code [5]. There's also an observer role—someone occasionally called in for domain-specific advice or to learn how to do reviews properly [5].

What's most characteristic of Fagan's inspections is that everyone is handed printed materials—the source code itself and other related note and rubric documents—that are used for the duration of the inspection. Throughout the inspection, meticulous details and metrics are recorded, including those about any defects found and about the inspection process itself. Though variations of this type of code review are still done today, they are not as common as they once were. Still, Fagan solidified the formal inspection system as an effective and very successful way to improve software quality; since introducing it in 1974, IBM reduced the number of defects per thousand lines of code by two-thirds! You can read the interesting and detailed breakdown in Fagan's paper "Design and Code Inspections to Reduce Errors in Program Development" [6].

2.2.1 The modern code review workflow

Today, the intent and goals of the modern code review process are still the same, but the structure is a bit more informal, ad hoc, and tool-based. Numerous workflows can comprise a code review; we'll start with the lowest common denominator between the different permutations today.

> **NOTE** There are plenty of things that can and should be done before even reaching this workflow, like different forms of automation. This book goes into depth about those things; for now, we first need to lay the groundwork before jumping into those topics. Let's crawl before walking before finally running, shall we?

A general code review involves four parts: new or changed code, one or more reviewers (ideally other than the author of the code to be reviewed), a reviewing mechanism, and a signoff condition, as seen in figure 2.2. Let's see what's involved in each part of a code review.

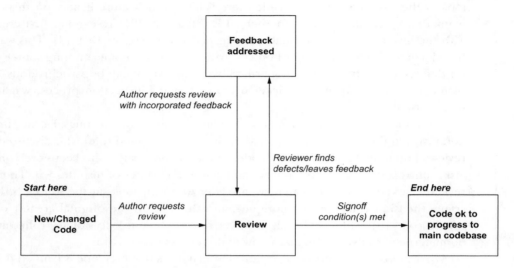

Figure 2.2   A high-level workflow of the typical, modern code review

NEW/CHANGED CODE

Writing new code or changing existing code leads to a code review process being initi-ated. Once the author is finished, the unreviewed segments of code are prepared for someone to review. This can be an email that's sent to a team with the actual code to be reviewed, a scheduled meeting where the code is presented, your own monitor showcasing your code in an integrated development environment (IDE), or, in the case of the workflow we'll be using in this book, a pull request (PR), a reviewing mech-anism that is common on Git-based version control systems.

Pull requests vs. merge requests

PRs are widely understood as the reviewing mechanism of choice. Pulling a request refers to pulling changes from another branch into your own branch/specified target branch. However, GitHub is not the only player in the market! In GitLab, the equivalent feature is called a "merge request" (MR). GitLab chose this name since it is the final action in the process. Both PRs and MRs encapsulate the intent of making changes to your existing code. No matter which one you choose, know that they act as the review mechanism portion in the overall code review.

There's also something called the git email workflow (https://mng.bz/XVnl), where your changes are proposed via "patches." I am not personally familiar with this sys-tem (which is why it won't be discussed in this book), but please feel free to read about it in the link!

REVIEW REQUESTED

When a review is requested, this signals to the team that a pending code inspection needs to be done. The review itself can happen over someone's shoulder, through a conversation, via email, or someplace other than a PR, and it can happen before or in conjunction with a formal PR. Since this book focuses on the PR as the reviewing mechanism, we'll continue describing the remaining parts with that in mind.

Once a PR is opened, the associated repository's team members are notified, either by some configured notification settings in the tool or, more likely, in a manual manner—say, a quick message from the author asking someone to review their PR.

DURING THE REVIEW/ADDRESSING FEEDBACK

While the pull request is open, the bulk of the code review happens. First, it's expected that at least one reviewer (likely obvious but still needs to be said: someone other than the original author) go over the code, look for potential problems, provide feedback, and ultimately ensure that the code being reviewed can safely be integrated into the main codebase without any problems.

This unreviewed code can also be discussed in more detail. If defects are found, clarification is needed, or other feedback needs to be noted, the reviewer can leave comments. As a common feature of version control tools/systems, comments can be added to the PR by highlighting the applicable code and adding the desired note. It is up to the original author to address these comments and resolve them adequately. Sometimes, the reviewer or another colleague pairs up with the author to help fix any problems. While encouraged, the original author can't depend on that assistance; ultimately, the author is still responsible for responding to the reviewer's feedback.

This feedback–resolution cycle can go back and forth for a while. The PR will remain open until the team's signoff conditions are met and the reviewer is confident the code is clear, stable, and won't break the main codebase.

SIGNOFF

Finally, after all feedback is incorporated and signoff conditions are met, the reviewer approves the pull request. This signals the team that the PR is safe and ready to be integrated into the main codebase. At this point, the code review process is complete.

Now, a variety of other tasks may be kicked off after this approval; code can be automatically merged, or other safety checks can be run, usually orchestrated by CI/CD pipelines. These pipelines can consist of automated steps that build, run, test, and deploy code and are just as integral to the software development process as code reviews. We can (and should) engage in many of these tasks before and after the code review—something highly recommended and, again, discussed more throughout this book.

And that's it! Remember, this is the lowest common denominator of what a code review process is. As you go through this book, you'll decide with your team how to change and evolve these steps (if you are starting from scratch) or curate which tactics and strategies to apply (if you are improving or refining your existing code review process).

2.2.2   *Our code review (pull request workflow)*

This book will be based on a *pull request workflow* as the code review process. It's pretty much the modern code review workflow we just discussed with the PR as a core part of the process, as seen in figure 2.3.

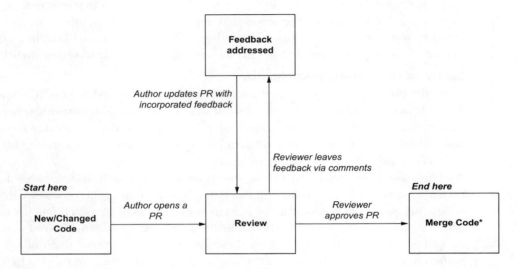

Figure 2.3   A pull request-based code review workflow

We'll initiate the code review process when a PR is opened, use open PRs to signal to our team that reviews are pending, deal with feedback and discussion through comments, and complete the code review process when a reviewer (or two) approves the PR. The rest of this book will consider this workflow when we talk about a code review.

Now that we're familiar with the workflow we'll be working with, we need to make sure we understand the basics and best practices of the pull request. For anyone who's writing code to be reviewed, this next section is essentially "Awesome Pull Requests 101."

2.3   *Elements of a great PR*

First things first (sings to self: 🎵 *I'm the realest*), putting your code up for review is more than just opening a PR and calling it a day. A lot depends on you, the author of the code, to make sure the review goes well. Basically, you need to make sure the PR you submit is properly prepared. In this section, we're going to see what that means.

> **NOTE**   I use the term *pull request* (PR) also to mean *merge request. Pull request* is a GitHub term, while *merge request* is a GitLab term. Both are mechanisms to propose changes to a main repository!

2.3.1   *Title: The "what"*

It all starts with the title. So much can be said with this key element if you let it. And you definitely should. A title needs to be clear, concise, and succinct. It should immediately explain the "what" of the PR—think "elevator pitch" for your code changes. It should make use of categorizations (we'll get to that in a moment), distill the essence of the code changes into a palatable line or two, and ultimately get the reviewer into the correct mindset for their review.

Good titles give you a hint about the PR, with the description filling in the rest of the details. Excellent titles are to the point and self-explanatory without the rest of the PR. These additional details, like the description or tags, ideally add further context; they explain the "why" of the PR. But you want to keep these extra flourishes optional; a reviewer shouldn't need the extra details to understand what the PR is about. In short, the reviewer should be able to understand what they're reviewing based on the title alone. Title-driven review, anyone?

To truly visualize how meaningful titles can be, let's break down some examples. I'm sure that by the end of this discussion, you'll identify which titles would make your life easier as a reviewer (and which ones won't).

Title example 1:
`bug fix for invoice issue`

Let's start with the most frustrating of titles: `bug fix for invoice issue`. On first reading this title, you might think, "OK?" At least we know it's a bug fix. Hopefully 🐛. And it has something to do with an invoice issue. As a reviewer reading this title, you may start going down a rabbit hole. Is this the recurring invoice problem or a *new one*? If it's a new one, what kind of problem is it? Is it urgent (money is being lost) or less so (typo on a label within the invoice)? Better yet, what exactly is the problem? Do we already have a ticket for this, or is this an emergency fix? I think you get the idea.

A vague title (such as this first example) often leads to more questions for the reviewer. More questions mean more cognitive overhead to manage. And more cognitive overhead means not setting up the reviewer for success, but rather, a path toward confusion. To address what may have likely popped into your head: Yes, the author could have placed the rest of the details and answers to those questions in the description of the PR, but that doesn't tackle the inherent problem—that the reviewer cannot easily and quickly understand what this PR is about. They should know after reading the title, not after going through the PR in its entirety.

Title example 2:
`fix issue #1462`

The next title, `fix issue #1462`, may seem slightly better than the first title, but not really. You might be thinking, "Well, it links to the issue it's solving, so the explanation is there." But it's not—at least not in this particular PR. Unless you have personally filed issue #1462, have previously glanced at issue #1462 and remember what it is, or happen to have it open in another tab at that very moment, reading the title alone conveys nothing about what the problem is.

So again, you as a reviewer are unsure about what to expect. You know it's a fix of some sort, but for what, you don't know yet. You're given the additional task of navigating to issue #1462 to see what it is and hope that the title there is a bit more descriptive. Once over there, you're more likely to get distracted by the contents of the issue. After scrolling through a few discussion points, you think to yourself, "What was I doing here? Oh right! I wanted to know what issue #1462 was." Catching yourself, you close that tab and return to the PR. Only now are you (possibly) aware of what this PR is about.

Title example 3:
**fix incorrect invoice
calculation (issue #1462)**

`fix incorrect invoice calculation (issue #1462)` offers another small improvement, but it is still not an excellent title. Here, we finally get a peek at the "what" of the PR: a calculation is not being done correctly. We even have a linked issue adding support. Yet, we still have outstanding questions (as we did with the first title), and we are still required to do our own research (as we did with the second title).

Title example 4:
**fix: invoice
calculates incorrectly
because of decimal
point being in the
wrong place, causing
subtotal to be wrong**

The next title, `fix: invoice calculates incorrectly because of decimal point being in the wrong place, causing subtotal to be wrong`, continues with improvements and finally arrives at a descriptive title. It certainly addresses what the PR will fix; we can clearly understand the problem and mentally prepare for the potential fix—all in one sentence! However, you might notice that this title is way too long. We'll address that in a moment. First, let me slightly divert your attention to something special in this title.

In this fourth example, we are introduced to a PR title tactic: *categorization prefixes*. Categorization prefixes are short phrases or abbreviations used in a PR title to classify them quickly. You may have also seen or used something like Conventional Commits (https://www.conventionalcommits.org/; thanks to Miroslav for the callout), which advocates for the same thing. Categorization prefixes are an incredibly efficient way to describe your PR to the reviewer, allow for changelog generation in an automated fashion, and make searching through your PRs a nicer process. It is totally worth enforcing the use of categorization prefixes in your PR titles as a team.

Categorizing the PR as `fix:` prepares us to shift our reviewer mindset and focus on bugfix-specific goals: Does the PR actually fix the problem? Are there new tests that account for the bug? Are there edge cases that are not considered outside of targeting the bug?

We also expect slightly different details in the description for a fix; items like reproduction steps and before- and after-fix comparisons are likely more important to us than a justification document or use case list, which would be more appropriate for a new feature. Adding this kind of detail to a PR is invaluable for the reviewer without much effort on the author's part, so categorizing PRs in this way is very much recommended. Table 2.1 has a good list of categorizations to consider when using and prepending PR titles.

Table 2.1   PR title categorization prefixes

Categorization prefix	Use for	Examples

`feat:`
 	
Alternatives:
 	
`feat(component or project):`
`feature:`
`feature(component or project):`
	Features, ideally complete, atomic, and encapsulated portions or behaviors
	
	When dealing with large projects or multiple components, it can be helpful to specify the affected component or project as part of the prefix.
		`feat: add common timeouts to registry/digest/head fetches`
		
		`feat: add axis option to slide transition`
		
		`feat(sidenav): customize width using percentages`
		
		`feature: add oci image index support via Accepted headers`

`fix:`	Bug fixes, hot fixes
	
	Code intended to fix unintended or unwanted behavior.
	
	When dealing with large projects or multiple components, it can be helpful to specify the affected component or project as part of the prefix.
		`fix: remove links to nonexistent resources in sitemap`
		
		`fix: omit a11y warning on <video> when aria-hidden="true"`
		
		`fix(svelte:element): race condition with transition #7948`
		
		`fix(flags): detect schedule set from env`
		
		`fix: blinking cursor in <Select> on IE11`
		
		`fix: always add missing slashes to link names`
		
		`fix(registry): image name parsing behavior`

Table 2.1 PR title categorization prefixes *(continued)*

Categorization prefix	Use for	Examples

`docs:`	Anything related to documentation: additions, deprecations, updates to examples, spelling and grammar fixes, improvements to reading flow, etc.	`docs: add "HTTP API Mode" link to nav menu`
		
		`docs(js): update Scrollspy documentation example`
		
		`docs: fix typo in getting started`
		
		`docs: change wording "finished" to "refined" in context api example`

`chore:`	Code changes that deal with developer maintenance tasks or ecosystem changes
	
	Think dependency upgrades, fixing lint rules, reorganizing tests, CI/CD pipeline modifications, and other similar changes
		`chore(deps): bump alpine from 3.17.3 to 3.18.0 in /dockerfiles`
		
		`chore: add missing types to compiler/compile/render_dom functions and variables`
		
		`chore: upgrade to eslint 8`
		
		`chore: a11y tests cleanup`
		
		`chore(ci): run code coverage on main push`
		
		`chore: move textarea tests to the correct place`

`breaking:`	Significant code changes that alter core functionality, drift from previous implementations, remove functionality, or change major dependencies
	
	These are code changes that you want to highlight.
		`breaking: make transitions local by default`
		
		`breaking: set version to 4, remove engines.pnpm and bump engines.node to >=16`
		
		`breaking: remove legacy package.json files`
		
		`breaking: remove the deprecated hooks, methods and options for version 13.0.0`
		
		`breaking: refactor Walkontable Selection rendering module`

Now, as we assumed earlier, while title example 4 is descriptive, it's too long. At 115 characters, the title may be cut off at the 80-character mark, a constraint that has its origins in IBM's punch card [7] and the VT52 [8].

Even though this limitation is mostly obsolete with today's larger screens and higher resolutions, the guideline is still a great one to follow. With PRs, longer titles can be cut off and replaced with some ellipsis, meaning important context could be hidden behind an extra click. This is another unintended hurdle a reviewer has to overcome to understand the intent of the PR. Also, title example 4 is just way more verbose than it needs to be.

By self-imposing a restriction of 80 characters (or less) for a PR title, you flex your communication skills to become more succinct. You can also rest easy knowing your PR title will likely be legible on almost any computer screen or terminal in the world 😎.

Title example 5:
fix: misplaced decimal point miscalculates invoice subtotal

With the fifth title, `fix: misplaced decimal point miscalculates invoice subtotal`, we finally have a pretty good title. We're well below the 80-character limit, use fewer words, and yet know way more about this PR than our previous four titles. Urgency is conveyed through a clear description of the unintended behavior (miscalculates invoice subtotal). A direct answer to what is causing this unintended behavior (misplaced decimal point) primes our brain to the code we expect to see. Without knowing anything else and reading just this title, a reviewer can better prepare for the review they are about to conduct.

To recap, titles are one of the first things reviewers will see on a PR. Make it count!

- Explain the "what" of the PR as clearly, concisely, and succinctly as you can.
- Try to keep titles under 80 characters to reduce the likelihood of them being unintentionally cut short.
- Using categorization prefixes (like `fix:`, `breaking:`, `feature:`, `docs:`, or `chore:`) can be a big help, packing a lot of detail and context into a few characters.
- Finally, remember that titles can get reviewers into the right mindset for your PR. Help them help you and put some effort into creating unambiguous, clearcut titles!

2.3.2 Description (the "why")

If the title explains the "what" of your code changes, the description should detail the "why." Great descriptions add relevant detail about your changes, lay out their context or justification, and supplement the review with items that add value and understanding to the reviewer's process. They answer anticipated questions a reviewer might have and are written in a way that is meant to clarify rather than confuse.

Depending on what type of code changes are being reviewed, which we can easily determine with the categorization prefixes used in the title, descriptions can also differ in how they explain the "why." Table 2.2 gives a quick overview of what a reviewer might expect to find in the PR description based on the PR's classification:

Table 2.2   Description elements based on categorization prefix

If you used this categorization prefix in the title:	These are some expected components to place in the description:

`feat:`
Alternatives:
`feat(component or project):`
`feature:`
`feature(component or project):`
	Context/justification
	Use cases
	How has this been tested?
	Preview (if applicable)
	Documentation
	Tests

`fix:`	Context/justification Linked Issue/ticket # Before-/after-fix comparison How to test it Documentation Tests
`docs:`	Context/justification Linked Issue/ticket # Use cases Preview (if applicable)
`chore:`	Context/justification
`breaking:`	Context/justification How has this been tested? Affected projects Important dates Mitigation/next steps Documentation Tests

Remember, these are just friendly suggestions, a guide you can choose to follow or kickstart your own discussions. You can ignore parts that don't make sense for your team or projects or add missing parts to tailor-fit this tactic to your team. Let's discuss what these individual components are so that you can decide if it's right for your code review.

CONTEXT/JUSTIFICATION

As you may have noticed in table 2.2, context/justification is always included, no matter the type of PR. That's because if nothing else were added to the description, these components would be the most important ones! Context gives us the "why" of the code changes. It's where authors present their stories to reviewers, giving them a glimpse into the section of weeds they've been working on. Context should reveal

- Why items were implemented in a specific way
- Why a different approach was chosen over one that seems more obvious
- What conversations, both public and private, were taken into consideration as this code was written
- What decisions, either your own or those made by others, played a part in the development of these changes
- What steps were taken to get to this point

The more detail, outlined in an organized fashion, that you can provide as an author, the less likely your reviewer will get confused [9].

USE CASES

When you need to give a bit more justification or can better explain the "why" of your code changes through scenarios, you can add use cases to your description. They work equally well for features or fixes as they give the reviewer a workable scenario to base their review on. Use cases can be behavior or functionality deemed missing (either by the team or an open ticket), filed issues that customers are experiencing, or a walk-through of a "happy path" and how the proposed code changes affect that path. You can describe them in detail or paraphrase them and link them to their open ticket/ issue numbers.

Sometimes, your context/justification section may overlap with this one, and that's OK! Other times, your context description is clear and succinct enough that use cases aren't needed at all. As is usually the case, it depends.

HOW TO TEST IT

These are usually a set of steps outlined by the author for a reviewer to follow to confirm that the proposed code changes work as intended. I don't see this too often, but when I do, it makes me very happy as a reviewer. This is especially important if the changes in question have any visual or customer-facing component to them.

Say, a warning modal needs to pop up when certain conditions are met and only on a specific page of your application. It would be incredibly helpful to add some simple steps to guide the reviewer (or QA tester) on how to validate the intended behavior. Something like the following:

- Navigate to the Shopping Cart.
- Enter a test discount code HALFOFFEVERYTHING in the Discount Code input box and then click the Apply button.
- Confirm that the You Have No Items warning appears.
- After acknowledging the warning (by clicking the OK button) or navigating away from the warning (by clicking outside of the warning popup area), confirm that the HALFOFFEVERYTHING test discount code is cleared from the Discount Code input box.

Giving the reviewer a way to test the proposed code changes is always a good idea. It presents the reviewer with an opportunity to make sure the code is doing what the author intends it to do. It also indirectly serves as an additional set of acceptance criteria; if the reviewer can't complete or reproduce the steps outlined, something needs to be fixed.

LINKED TICKETS/ISSUE NUMBERS

Another thing to consider adding is links to related tickets or issue numbers. Usually, you can use the # or @ symbol, followed by the ticket/issue identifier, to link it within a PR. These can be issues that are fixed, initial requests that are fulfilled, or related tasks that may be affected by the proposed changes. While it's common to add these kinds of links to the title, I think it's actually not a good idea to do so. Issue numbers can change, and ticketing systems can be deprecated or migrated over time, leaving an incorrect or unusable link as part of the title. I'd highly suggest adding these links to the description instead.

You may be thinking, "Even if we add them to the description, isn't that still creating a burden for the reviewer by potentially leaving dead links as part of a PR?" To that, I say, yes, you are correct. But here's the caveat: placing that risk within the realm of the description versus somewhere much more important, like the title, is much more forgiving in the long run.

DOCUMENTATION

Documentation is certainly a value-add to a PR description, especially for new features or breaking changes. It can be a link to the docs accompanying the code changes or relevant reference documentation to aid the reviewer with their review. To differentiate between the two, you could opt to have two specific documentation sections—say, *Feature Documentation* and *Reference Documentation.*

Specifically for new feature documentation, many developers won't even consider a feature ready for review unless it has its documentation as part of the code changes. Today, many developers recognize the importance of and advocate for documentation. Figure 2.4 shows some responses to my tweet asking about this topic.

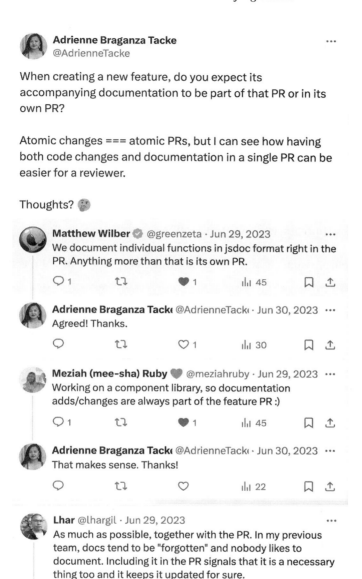

Adrienne Braganza Tacke
@AdrienneTacke

When creating a new feature, do you expect its accompanying documentation to be part of that PR or in its own PR?

Atomic changes === atomic PRs, but I can see how having both code changes and documentation in a single PR can be easier for a reviewer.

Thoughts? 🤔

Matthew Wilber ✓ @greenzeta · Jun 29, 2023
We document individual functions in jsdoc format right in the PR. Anything more than that is its own PR.
💬 1   🔁   ❤️ 1   📊 45   🔖 ⬆️

Adrienne Braganza Tacke @AdrienneTacke · Jun 30, 2023
Agreed! Thanks.
💬   🔁   ♡ 1   📊 30   🔖 ⬆️

Meziah (mee-sha) Ruby 💜 @meziahruby · Jun 29, 2023
Working on a component library, so documentation adds/changes are always part of the feature PR :)
💬 1   🔁   ❤️ 1   📊 45   🔖 ⬆️

Adrienne Braganza Tacke @AdrienneTacke · Jun 30, 2023
That makes sense. Thanks!
💬   🔁   ♡   📊 22   🔖 ⬆️

Lhar @lhargil · Jun 29, 2023
As much as possible, together with the PR. In my previous team, docs tend to be "forgotten" and nobody likes to document. Including it in the PR signals that it is a necessary thing too and it keeps it updated for sure.
💬 1   🔁   ❤️ 1   📊 27   🔖 ⬆️

Adrienne Braganza Tacke @AdrienneTacke · Jun 30, 2023
We also dislike neglected docs so agree with this. Thanks!
💬   🔁   ♡   📊 152   🔖 ⬆️

Figure 2.4   I asked my Twitter followers about documentation in a PR.

BEFORE/AFTER COMPARISON

Sometimes, clearly expressing your intent requires visual aids that are easy to reference—think a layout change, a style guide refactor, or a homepage redesign. Instead of explaining each detail and item changed, a visual before-and-after comparison can be much more effective.

Say a component has been changed to look a certain way on specific devices. There's one layout for tablets, one for mobile devices, and one for TVs. Explaining to the reviewer what results to expect is much simpler via a screenshot, an automatically generated preview deployed to a review environment, or some other visual aid. The highlights and main differences can be summarized in the description, but in this case, a picture truly does the job.

Visuals aren't relegated to just user interface changes, either. If there are any changes that may benefit from a "show, don't tell" approach, consider adding this section to your review description. Things like API endpoint hierarchies and file directory restructures are nonvisual changes in nature but can still benefit from a visual aid to show the change.

AFFECTED PROJECTS (BREAKING CHANGES)

When submitting a PR for breaking changes, the first few things anyone would want to know is whether and, if so, how they may be affected. This is where listing affected projects comes in handy; a quick glance can immediately tell a reviewer what part of the codebase to focus on and to consider any potential causes for concern that the breaking changes might bring.

Again, a reviewer can go through the files and figure out which projects are affected themselves, but why add that extra delay? Instead, and as a diligent author who has all this information fresh in their mind, take the time to fully list the affected projects or components of your breaking changes and what it means going forward. Doing so takes less time for you and saves time for the reviewer by putting them into the correct headspace to review your changes.

MITIGATION/NEXT STEPS (BREAKING CHANGES)

Any breaking changes should be accompanied by a set of steps to migrate, deprecate, or mitigate existing systems, depending on what kind of breaking changes they are. Maybe nothing needs to be done on the consumer's end, but communication still needs to take place internally; both of these things should be noted as well.

- *Migration steps* are non-negotiable if breaking changes means the previous version will no longer work or the changes include important fixes (like a security fix). They also need to consider side effects or possible unintended behavior a consumer may experience and what to do with them.
- *Deprecation steps* should be included if your changes intend to stop providing previous behavior. What does it mean for someone once your changes have completed the deprecation period? Are there items they need to retrieve/download/remove from your platform or application before a specified

deadline? Do they switch to something else (and follow the migration steps you've provided)?

Finally, as an encompassing guideline for any breaking changes, a clear set of next steps (mitigation) or instructions to follow once the code is merged will always be valuable to add to this kind of PR.

To recap, plenty of items can go into a PR description, some more important than others, and some are only necessary depending on what type of PR you are submitting. Check out table 2.3 for a recap of each PR description element and what to consider adding to your PR.

Table 2.3   PR description elements summary

Description element	What this means/what to add
Context/justification	The bulk of the PR description. Anywhere from a few sentences to a few paragraphs that help the reviewer understand why the proposed change is being made and any insider knowledge related to the changes. Context should answer the following questions: ■ Why is something implemented in a specific way? ■ Why was a different approach chosen over one that seems more obvious? ■ What conversations, both public and private, were taken into consideration as this code was written? ■ What decisions, either your own or those made by others, played a part in the development of these changes? ■ What steps were taken to get to this point?
Use cases	Specific, self-contained examples of functionality or behavior the proposed changes fulfill. Example: "Happy paths" (core behavior that should always work in your application).
How to test it	A set of steps, outlined by the author, for a reviewer to follow and confirm the proposed code changes work as intended
Linked tickets/ issue numbers	Relevant links to work tickets, issues, user stories, or other linkable sources of information related to the code changes
Documentation	Links to related documentation (feature or reference) that have also been updated or created as a result of the proposed code changes. Should be required for new features.
Before/after comparison	Visual aids that can be used to compare changes. This can be before-and-after screenshots, before-and-after code diffs, or some other visual aid that makes understanding the proposed changes easier.
Affected projects (breaking changes)	List of projects or components affected by the proposed changes and their effects
Mitigation/next steps (breaking changes)	Set of mitigation, deprecation, or migration steps/instructions to follow before a breaking change

2.3.3   *Labels*

Labels are useful. If your tool or system has them, use them! GitHub is one platform that provides labels that can really help categorize pull requests, as seen in figure 2.5.

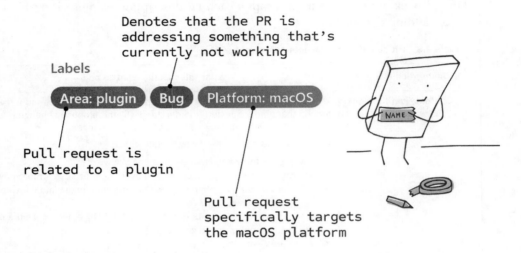

Figure 2.5   Labels and the extra information they carry can add important context to PRs.

While too many labels can negate its benefits, finding a solid handful that works for your team can do wonders. Labels can surgically narrow the scope of the proposed code changes and quickly identify important attributes to a reviewer. You can use labels to denote the affected component or project (especially if you need to save some characters in your title), specify prioritization, indicate status, describe key elements (like browser type, device type, core functionality vs. nice-to-have features, etc.), and so much more. Labels are like the extra spice you add to a review.

I really like Oh My Zsh's (https://github.com/ohmyzsh/ohmyzsh) list of available labels (Oh My Zsh is a community-driven framework for managing your zsh configuration [https://linuxhandbook.com/why-zsh/] and has 300+ optional plugins and 140+ themes). I feel like they cover the majority of scenarios they encounter without going overboard. They also split their labels into logical groupings, such as Area, Platform, and Resolutions. I'm providing them here (table 2.4) in the hopes it will inspire you to find meaningful labels for your projects.

Table 2.4   List of labels used by the Oh My Zsh repository

Oh My Zsh label (api.github.com/repos/ ohmyzsh/ohmyzsh/labels)	Label description
"Area: CI"	"Issue or PR related to the CI pipeline"
"Area: core"	"Issue or PR related to core parts of the project"
"Area: init"	"Issue or PR related to the initializer"
"Area: installer"	"Issue or PR related to the installer"
"Area: meta"	"Issue or PR related to the project itself"
"Area: plugin"	"Issue or PR related to a plugin"
"Area: theme"	"Issue or PR related to a theme"
"Area: uninstaller"	"Issue or PR related to the uninstaller"
"Area: updater"	"Update subsystem"
"Area: website"	"Issues related to the ohmyz.sh website"
"Bug"	"Something isn't working"
"dependencies"	"Pull requests that update a dependency file"
"Discussion"	"Discussion or RFC issue"
"Enhancement"	"Improved user experience"
"Feature"	"New feature or request"
"github_actions"	"Pull requests that update GitHub Actions code"
"Good first issue"	"Good for newcomers"
"Hacktoberfest"	"Issue marked as suitable for Hacktoberfest"
"Invalid"	"Invalid Pull Request (for Hacktoberfest and similar events)"
"New: plugin"	"Request for a plugin or Pull Request that adds one"
"New: theme"	"Pull Request that adds a theme"
"Performance"	"Issue or PR about performance"
"Platform: BSD"	"Issue or PR for a BSD OS (FreeBSD, NetBSD, OpenBSD)"
"Platform: Linux"	"Issue or PR for a Linux system"
"Platform: macOS"	"Issue or PR for macOS"
"Platform: Windows"	"Issue or PR for Windows"
"Resolution: duplicate"	"This issue or pull request already exists"

Table 2.4   List of labels used by the Oh My Zsh repository *(continued)*

Oh My Zsh label (api.github.com/repos/ ohmyzsh/ohmyzsh/labels)	Label description
`"Resolution: not our issue"`	`"Issue or pull request not related to Oh My Zsh"`
`"Resolution: wontfix"`	`"This will not be worked on"`
`"Security"`	`"Security-related issue or PR"`

As for you and your team? If you are just getting started with labels, I'd stick to `"Feature"` and `"Bug"` as the initial labels to work with. Get your team comfortable with consistently using them. Work toward enforcing labels for every PR.

Once your team is used to labeling their PRs, you can slowly start adding new, meaningful labels to your official list. If you find labeling by platform, component, or subtype might make sense to your team, co-create and agree on the new set of labels to be added. Just keep in mind that quality really does matter with labels over quantity. As you discuss new potential labels to use, make sure they can apply to more than a handful of PRs, make sense to the entire team, and will actually help clarify—rather than get in the way of—your PRs.

Again, preparing a solid pull request means putting in some effort as the author. It's on you to ensure the reviewer is set up for success. Thankfully, labels are one of many tools you can use to ensure success.

2.3.4   *Review states*

Finally, we come to review states (or statuses). Do you know how many headaches could be avoided by simply adding a status to our PRs? We add progress bars, spinning wheels, and bouncing balls in our applications to let the customer know, "Hey, we're doing something! So sit tight, relax, and know that things are in motion," but sometimes we forget to apply this notion to our code reviews. It should go without saying that if you have a way to indicate statuses/states on PRs in your code review tool or process, you should absolutely do it. To make review states even more effective, define the list of states your team uses and what each one means and indicate how progressing throughout the states works.

The following statuses should cover most team scenarios and are likely to be helpful.

DRAFT

Ah, the draft PR. Not quite ready for a full review and is usually a work in progress. PRs usually start in this state. Typically, when PR states are not used or inconsistently used, all PRs can look the same. Any open PR can be mistaken for a properly prepared, ready-to-be-reviewed set of code changes (aside from the approved ones, of course). This unintended effect is exacerbated when plenty of PRs are in the queue, as is the case with large teams.

This uncertainty—not knowing whether a PR is truly ready to review—wastes a lot of time for a reviewer. They spend it sifting through incomplete or empty PRs, only to find out the author hasn't intended for them to conduct a review. Meanwhile, other PRs that are ready can get lost in the queue.

To mitigate this, introduce (or start using) the Draft PR state to your team. Many tools and platforms have Draft as an explicit state, like Azure DevOps (https://mng .bz/aVex), Github (https://mng.bz/gA0Z), and GitLab (https://mng.bz/5OR4). You can use this in two ways:

- *An indication of readiness*—Eliminate the frustrations ambiguity brings; clearly indicate to reviewers which PRs are not ready to be reviewed right now. Works in progress, incomplete PRs, or PRs not yet properly prepared and missing context are perfect use cases to mark as drafts. Classifying these drafts helps reviewers filter them out, allowing them to focus their attention on those that are ready to review.

- *A proactive request for feedback*—More popularly, draft PRs can also be used to solicit feedback on an idea/prototype/MVP (minimum viable product) or a more complex change. It's a way to ask if you're on the right track without fully committing to a certain implementation. A colleague of mine used to open draft PRs (that were fully prepared) when asked to experiment with two design frameworks. One draft PR used Materialize (https://materializecss.com/), and another draft PR used MUI CSS (https://mui.com/). The drafts enabled our team to compare how Materialize implemented a card component over MUI CSS. We ultimately chose Materialize, deleted the MUI CSS draft, and promoted the Materialize draft to a Ready to Review PR once my colleague finished their full feature.

What's most important is to align on how your team defines the Draft state. Once you choose your team's meaning, document it somewhere (a good place is a Team Working Agreement, a document we'll discuss in chapter 4).

READY FOR REVIEW

Ready for Review is considered the default state when a PR exists, so you may not need to do much for this state. Generally, PRs in this state mean code changes are properly prepared, self-contained, and ready to be reviewed by others. To progress from a Draft state, you'd explicitly change your PR to Ready for Review (GitHub; https://mng.bz/ 6YRG). In Azure DevOps, you "publish" a draft PR to do the same thing. At this point, the author awaits a review from colleagues.

IN REVIEW

Once a review has started, the waiting game switches between the two parties. Instead of a reviewer waiting for ready-to-review PRs, an author now sits, wondering if and when their code changes will be looked at. Again, erring on the side of overcommunicating is usually better than the opposite. Placing a PR in an In Review state can do all the communicating for you.

My teams always indicated that someone was actively reviewing a PR with this state. As an author, seeing this state meant the review had progressed, and I only had to wait for the reviewer to finish their review. As a reviewer, marking a PR with this state helped cut down on messages from the author asking if I had looked at their PR yet.

In the event you don't have an In Review state as part of your code review tool, an alternative is to use a label. Reserving the In Review label to purely indicate state can help you achieve the same purpose as the built-in states.

Another clever alternative comes from a developer who works on a six-person team at Amazon. When someone on the team has a new PR ready to be reviewed, they add a message to the designated chat channel. Other individuals on the team then use the eyes emoji (👀) in their messaging platform to indicate they are, quite literally, taking a look at that PR at that moment. The emoji reactions don't disturb the team with a notification, and the author can still discern the status of their PR. Seeing that particular emoji lets everyone quickly know how many people have viewed a PR (or have yet to), and hovering over it shows who those reviewers are. It's a great option if you don't have states or labels but still want to take advantage of the tactic.

NEEDS FIXES

An optional but very convenient state is the Needs Fixes state. After a reviewer has conducted their review and assuming only minor fixes need to be made, this state can quickly notify the author of the results of the initial review. Reviewers can also identify which PRs have been sent back for fixes, cutting the time they spend sorting through the PRs when they could be reviewing them.

Extending the Amazon team's emoji technique, this could similarly be achieved using the hammer emoji (🔨). If a reviewer finds the PR needs fixes, they can remove their eyes emoji reaction (since that's only used to indicate an active reviewing state) and replace it with the hammer emoji. Big caveat here: this should only be used for smaller items. For anything else, an offline discussion is usually warranted.

APPROVED

Finally, the state that needs no introduction: Approved. Typically, approved PRs indicate that no further changes need to be made; another human (ideally more than one) has diligently looked through the code changes and found no problems. The code is clear and stable, and the changes are ready to be merged. Once approved, a PR can either be manually merged into the main codebase, typically by the author, or automatically merged if configured to do so.

To refer back to the emoji tactic one last time, when reviewers approve a PR, all other emoji reactions can be removed, and the green check emoji (✅) can be used to indicate approval. This may be a bit much, but it can be done if you don't already have other notifications that communicate a PR approval to the author. Developers truly find impressive ways to make things work!

To RECAP

PR review states can help your team navigate pull requests more efficiently. Much like labels, they carry a lot of additional information about your PR with a word or two. Be sure to list which review states your team will use, what each one means for your specific team, and how a pull request progresses through the states. As a playful summary, Figure 2.6 shows the review states one more time and what they mean.

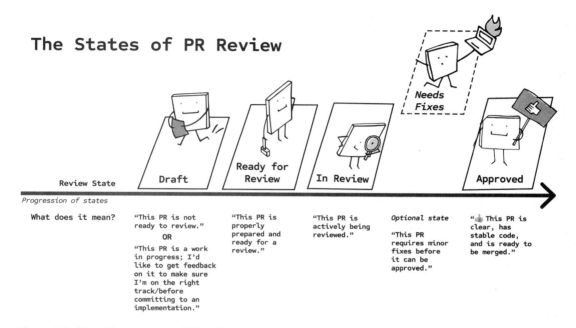

Figure 2.6   The different states of PR review and their meaning

We're almost done dissecting the essential parts of a code review! We know what systems we can choose from, how a typical code review workflow operates, and the pull request-based review we'll be referring to throughout the book. We now know how to prepare a great PR. The final part? The people! Let's see who's involved in making code reviews work (or not 😊).

2.4 *Code review participants and expectations*

We are the primary variables that predict whether or not a code review process will be successful, so it's worth delving into the people who participate in or influence a code review. There's the reviewer, the author, the team, those in charge, and the organization. Each stakeholder is important and has their own obligations in a code review. These obligations—really, implicit expectations—form our understanding of what everyone is supposed to do in a code review. When ignored or lacklusterly performed, our trust is broken, and expectations thwarted, giving the roots of an ineffective code review the opportunity to grow.

Instead, let's spell out what each participant is supposed to do. You'll see a summarized list of responsibilities—what we'll call a contract—after each respective participant's section.

So who's part of this party?

2.4.1   *The reviewer*

As a reviewer, a lot is expected of you in a code review. You need to look for potential defects and make sure you can understand the code. You need to diligently conduct a proper review, leave feedback (when appropriate), and engage the original author in an empathetic but productive way.

Often, a reviewer is also chosen for their unique perspective, skill, subject matter expertise, or historical context to the code being reviewed. Inviting such a person to review is an opportunity to clarify misunderstandings or contextualize missing scenarios found in the proposed code changes. Since code reviews become a permanent record (usually with default repository backup settings), it is immensely helpful to reference these discussions and rediscover this perspective/reasoning when needed.

With all that in mind, two principles are paramount to your role as a reviewer: *you* are given lots of influence, and *you* are responsible for what passes through your review. Neglecting these principles means inadequately fulfilling the reviewer's role.

YOU HAVE THE INFLUENCE

As a reviewer, you set the tone for the review; you decide how long a review lasts (because your approval is the only thing that moves the process forward); you hold the power to create additional work for the author. You have a lot of influence as a reviewer.

What do you do with this leverage?

To start, you must leave your ego out of the review. Forget about job titles, internal squabbles, and personality traits—those shouldn't matter when you review someone's code. Focus on the code and not much else. Let the code, as presented in the PR, dictate your understanding, the judgments you form, and the conclusions you make. Typical questions you should be asking yourself are as follows:

- Is the PR focused on one logical piece of behavior?
- Does the PR give you context on why the proposed change was made (or include a link to that information)?
- Does the code match the context of the PR?
- Does the code fulfill the acceptance criteria (if available)?
- Can you understand the code you are looking at?
- Does it flow logically?
- Are there parts of the code changes you find yourself re-reading because it's confusing?

- Are there scenarios or edge cases the author seems to have forgotten?
- Is there history or nuance you are aware of that affects this code and has not been considered in the proposed implementation?
- Does this change fit into the larger picture? The system as a whole?

Effective reviewers ask these questions and more; they scrutinize the code, never the author.

Next, you may need to leave feedback or request more information from the author. Check yo' self (🎵 *before ya wreck yo' self*)—Are your questions self-explanatory? Can your feedback fit neatly into a few sentences? Are there extremely low chances something gets misinterpreted through the text? If so, it should be OK to start a discussion with the author through the tool itself. This is where leaving comments on the pull request comes into play.

On the other hand, do you see a larger problem? Are there several parts to your inquiry that could each be its own discussion? Is it an urgent or nuanced situation? Do you find yourself writing a novel, trying to fit in all the context and detail necessary to explain your feedback? If so, it'd be better to discuss these items with the author more directly—either in person or over a video call. It's here that your influence needs to be carefully exercised; sure, it could be much easier for you to leave a few comments here and there, trying your best to add context, and then leave it up to the author to understand. But why take the chance of being misunderstood? Especially as a reviewer with more experience or context, why turn a learning opportunity into another occurrence of knowledge being siloed?

As you review the code, it's also important to remember that providing the author with an alternative implementation (simply because you didn't like theirs) is not a goal here. If you can support a better implementation with coding conventions, team standards, missing context, or historical nuance, then, of course, bring it up in the review (or discuss it with the author). If the "better" implementation is something you suggest without any backing or explanation on why it's better, then the author can rightfully choose to ignore it as a preferential, subjective suggestion.

If a 50-line PR can be distilled down to 5 lines with an existing library already being used in the codebase, bring it up! That's a valid use of your influence. However, if those 50 lines are distilled down to 5 due to some magical ternary operations, clever uses of bitwise operators, or shortening of variable names that—while still valid—only you understand, that's a misuse of your influence.

Another thing about influence and setting the tone is you'll likely be responding to the author's work through comments (especially if you are a remote team or use an online tool to facilitate your code reviews).

When you leave comments on a review, you have a choice: to be, well, lazy and vague about your suggestions (like in figure 2.7) or to be focused, effective, empathetic, and clear with your words. Being a better reviewer means choosing comments like the much better figure 2.8.

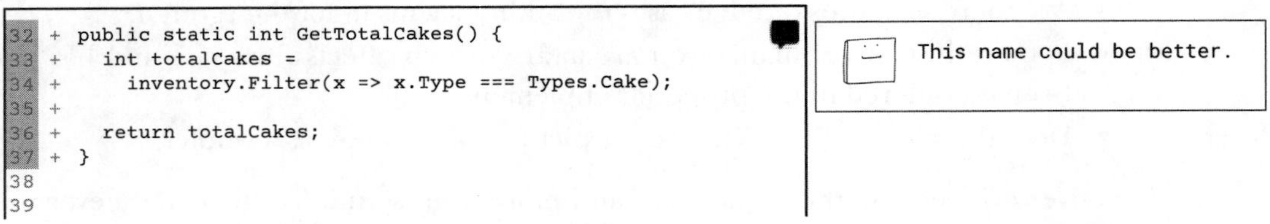

```
32 +  public static int GetTotalCakes() {
33 +     int totalCakes =
34 +        inventory.Filter(x => x.Type === Types.Cake);
35 +
36 +     return totalCakes;
37 +  }
38
39
```

> 🙂 This name could be better.

Figure 2.7   An example of a vague comment left on a code review

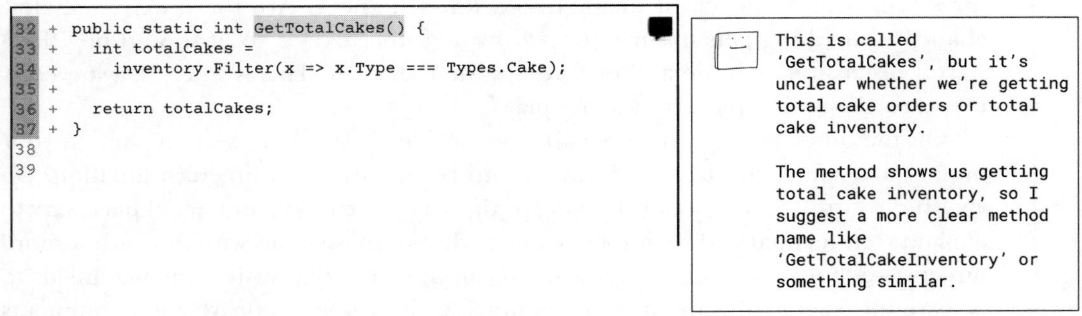

```
32 +  public static int GetTotalCakes() {
33 +     int totalCakes =
34 +        inventory.Filter(x => x.Type === Types.Cake);
35 +
36 +     return totalCakes;
37 +  }
38
39
```

> 🙂 This is called
> 'GetTotalCakes', but it's
> unclear whether we're getting
> total cake orders or total
> cake inventory.
>
> The method shows us getting
> total cake inventory, so I
> suggest a more clear method
> name like
> 'GetTotalCakeInventory' or
> something similar.

Figure 2.8   An example of clear and constructive feedback

Choosing to be clear with your words also means constructive feedback is allowed, contrary to what most developers believe or have experienced. It is so important that I have dedicated all of chapter 6 to crafting effective comments.

So remember, with the influence you have as a reviewer, be kind, focused on the code, and just as effective as you'd like authors to be in a code review.

YOU ARE RESPONSIBLE FOR WHAT PASSES THROUGH YOUR REVIEW

While there are reviewers who seem to nitpick everything and extend the code review process, there are also reviewers on the opposite end of the spectrum: the instant approvers. You've likely encountered this before, either through annoyance at having your PR approved too quickly or giving the ol' LGTM 👍 (looks good to me) yourself, knowing, at best, you barely skimmed the PR. But just like Earth, Wind & Fire sings, there are "reasons, reasons!" why we may do this.

Sometimes, some PRs are prohibitively large: they involve too many files or sections of the codebase, include the fickle legacy stuff, or are a combination of those things. Who wants to go through that? This is ultimately the author's responsibility, though, and we address that in their section.

Other times, you're near the end of the sprint, close to the start of your vacation, or are rushing to adhere to an important deadline. You won't let this one last PR get in the way! You quickly approve it and go about your day.

Sometimes, the reasons are a bit more nuanced. You might be overwhelmed; code reviews gotta happen, you need to be part of every PR, and you just need to get through the week without holding the rest of the team back. So, a quick review here and an LGTM there can seem justified. While I empathize with you (being burned out is not fun or recommended), the problems that crop up with quick reviews will still exist, likely adding even more tasks to your overflowing plate.

Yet another reason? Maybe you're continuously interrupted to get PR approvals. This could be a team thing—a lack of understanding or discussion on implicit team working expectations. I suggest a solution to these kinds of problems in chapter 4. This could also be a management thing—maybe a policy that oversimplifies or ruins the whole purpose of code reviews. One example is dictating that an ask for approval means acknowledging that request as soon as possible. Either way, these environmental factors can make the quick review appealing but detrimental to a reviewer's code review.

Despite all of these reasons, skimming reviews is not something you should do. It's still your obligation as a reviewer to ensure a proper review, no matter the circumstances. Many reviewers conveniently forget that what passes through their review is still their responsibility. If something goes wrong after swiftly approving a PR and production breaks, we're quite quick to blame the developer who wrote the code or the QA team that "didn't test enough." In reality, the reviewer who approved the unhealthy code should be asking themselves, "How did I miss that?"

This situation reminds me of when I worked on a very small team for a year-long project. A "very small team" meant there was one other developer than myself, one quality assurance (QA) engineer responsible for writing automated tests, and one QA tester responsible for manually testing the application. As my colleague and I code-reviewed each other's code and sent it "over the cubicle" to QA, we both implicitly but heavily relied on QA to find our bugs rather than giving it the due diligence we needed to find them ourselves. I remember getting annoyed when a problem would occur in production on something recently released and almost immediately thinking, "Why didn't QA find this?" It was the wrong mindset and, luckily, a lesson I learned early in my career.

Instead of continuing this reliance on our already overburdened QA team, we discussed some changes at our next retrospective. In the end, we decided to carve out some time in our sprints to automate some items in our workflow. Namely, we worked with our QA engineer to build an initial test suite of our key methods and "happy path" methods. With this, we could run our own tests prior to conducting code reviews. Next, we convinced our manager to approve some training on Selenium (an open source project that helps automate functional testing across several web browsers) for our QA tester. We outlined the top five scenarios we always wanted to ensure worked and set that as a goal for them to automate. It took at least four sprints (12 weeks) to get to an ideal state of test coverage and six sprints (18 weeks) to have most of our manual testing scenarios automated. Ultimately, this experience ingrained some of the most important values I've applied to my career: focus heavily on appropriate automation when possible and take accountability for your code.

In these cases, and in a psychologically safe environment, scenarios that can potentially intensify a culture of blame can become a pleasant learning opportunity instead. Like my past encounter, transform these scenarios into a discussion about what went wrong, collectively and individually; take accountability and then make changes to the process to improve it. As a reviewer, you can decide whether such a conversation needs to take place and, if warranted, whether to do so offline, where context and nuance can be better understood. This advice is especially important if the PR you are looking at has too many things to address or needs clarification from the author to understand the broader context of the change.

Giving proper reviews also means keeping in mind how you conduct your review. It's been said that the maximum time a reviewer should spend reviewing code is between 45 and 60 minutes [10]. This amount of time ensures a properly paced, yet thorough review. After 60 minutes (though sometimes well before that), reviewers tend to wear out, get distracted, or lower their ability to focus [11]. To give all of your PRs a proper review, try to limit your review time to shorter bursts of 25 to 45 minutes.

One more thing—ideally, most items in a PR get automated so that you can focus on finding problems that require human judgment. That includes automated syntax and compilation tasks, running unit tests, mocking visual tests, and running prebuild checks, among other tasks. These can be automated during the PR or in the following CI pipeline. However, until you are at that fully automated point in your process, these things still might qualify as items to check as a reviewer.

Sometimes, you may have to pull down the PR's version of the code, run it locally, and ensure things are OK. Sometimes, you may not have automated browser testing that checks user interfaces (UIs) across all supported browsers, so you have to do that yourself. And sometimes, you may need to run some manual integration tests to see that a new change fits into the overall architecture of your system. While none of these scenarios are ideal, the responsibility is still yours. Hopefully, the strategies in this book will help you reach that automated stage sooner rather than later. Whatever the case may be, what's most important is that you understand the full context of the code change in isolation and as it relates to the overall system. As a reviewer, it is up to you to do what is needed to get that context and provide an effective review.

While it can take a bit more effort, an accountable reviewer who owns their part in the code review process is one of the most effective ways to demonstrate its value. By fulfilling these expectations as a reviewer, you contribute reliability and stability to the team and the codebase.

REVIEWER'S CONTRACT

An effective reviewer's responsibilities include the following:

- Leave your ego at the door.
- Focus on the code, not the developer.
- Use comments to leave small or self-explanatory pieces of feedback.

- Communicate directly with the author for larger pieces of or more complex feedback.
- Don't abuse the influence you are given in this role.
- Don't skim through your reviews.
- What passes through your review, thorough or not, is your responsibility.

2.4.2 *The author*

Authors (those who open a PR and submit their code changes to be reviewed) often assume, "I just need to open a PR and wait for the review." That's fine—if you want to be a bare minimum author! To surpass this default expectation and to be a better author, a bit more effort and consideration are needed.

BE YOUR OWN FIRST REVIEWER

The first obligation you have as an author is to be your own first reviewer. Yes, you read that right! Before finishing your final commit and definitely before you open your PR, take a proper break. Get up from your desk, stretch, walk around a bit, maybe (or definitely) grab your favorite beverage, and then return to your desk. It's now time to step into your potential reviewer's shoes.

Pretend you are the reviewer of this code:

- Did you run any automation (things like linters, formatters, static analyzers, or unit tests—things we'll discuss in chapter 5)? Have you fixed any obvious problems that the automations have surfaced?
- Have you fulfilled the acceptance criteria?
- Does your PR contain the relevant files needed for the change and nothing else?
- Could you intelligently explain the code changes based solely on the code and what you've provided in the PR?
- Do any questions come up as you read through your PR? Have they been answered already?
- Can you answer any questions solely based on what's presented (or are you filling in the gaps with your insider/current knowledge)?
- Have you thought about edge cases?
- Does your code fit into the overall architecture of your system?

Answering these questions can help you anticipate what other reviewers might wonder about, allowing you to clarify your code proactively. It can remind you to explain any context that only lives in your head. And if you jot down some of those anticipated questions (and answers) while you do your own review, you'll have them handy once you prepare your final PR. The best part? You can run as many reviews with yourself and revise as necessary before finally setting your PR to the Ready to Review state. The more you do this before the formal PR, the more likely you'll have less back-and-forth with your reviewer.

MAKE YOUR PR MANAGEABLE

The next-most important obligation you have is to make your PR manageable. Far too often, gargantuan PRs are submitted with the expectation that the reviewer will give it a quality review. The truth is, the larger the PR, the lower the incentive for the reviewer to actually look at it, let alone thoroughly review it (figure 2.9)!

Figure 2.9 **The unfortunate truth about code reviews**

On the other end of this spectrum are PRs that aren't ready for the reviewer to go through at all and aren't labeled as such (like using the Draft state). These are unfinished, half-complete, rough versions of proposed changes. Work is likely still underway, and new commits are pushed every so often. The reviewer doesn't know that the PR isn't ready, making it impossible for them to conduct an accurate review. If you've been on the other side of either problem and have received a large, incomplete, or ever-changing PR to review yourself, you can empathize with the frustrations. Instead, be a kind author and break down your PRs into distinct, clear, complete, and feasible portions.

What is a feasible portion? A couple of rough guidelines, as described in figure 2.10, can help you determine that.

One reliable guideline: don't submit more than 500 total lines of code in a PR. In fact, that's more of a hard upper bound; try to stay way below that! A study conducted by Principal Engineer Dragan Stepanovic´ found that PRs with more lines of code have less engagement (fewer comments per 100 lines of code) [12], which can be

A Manageable PR...

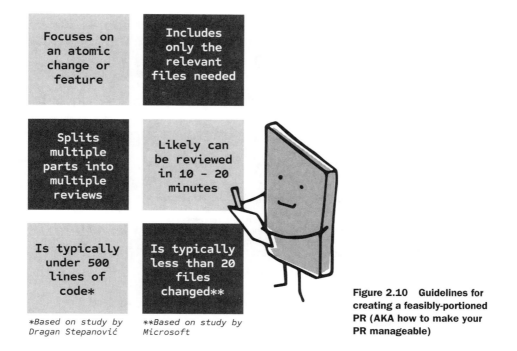

Focuses on an atomic change or feature

Includes only the relevant files needed

Splits multiple parts into multiple reviews

Likely can be reviewed in 10 - 20 minutes

Is typically under 500 lines of code*

Is typically less than 20 files changed**

*Based on study by Dragan Stepanović

**Based on study by Microsoft

Figure 2.10   Guidelines for creating a feasibly-portioned PR (AKA how to make your PR manageable)

indicative of a lower-quality review. This makes sense: large PRs take longer to complete and usually include multiple changes, meaning reviewers are more likely to lose focus once they hit 500 lines of code. On the other hand, PRs with fewer than 500 lines of code had higher engagement (more comments per 100 lines of code).

Another reliable guideline: keep your PRs below 20 total files changed. A study conducted by Microsoft found that code review usefulness is negatively correlated with the size of a code review [13]. The report even states specifically that the more files there are in a single review, the lower the overall rate of useful feedback. Again, this matches our lines of code guideline: the smaller and shorter the reviews you prepare, the more thorough and manageable the review will likely be. If your PR can fit within these limits, you're on the right track.

MAKE YOUR PR UNDERSTANDABLE

The other obligation you own as the author is to make sure your PR can be understood. Similar to the notion of being code-complete, authors need to get their code changes "ready for review" before handing them off to the reviewer. What does being ready for review mean? If you ask yourself the question, "Can the code I'm presenting and the intent I am stating in the PR be clearly understood?" and can confidently answer, "Yes," your PR is ready for review. If you can set your PR to the Ready for

Review state without hesitation or worry that you're missing something, your PR is ready for review. Figure 2.11 shows one such pull request, one that any reviewer would be ecstatic to receive.

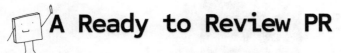

A Ready to Review PR

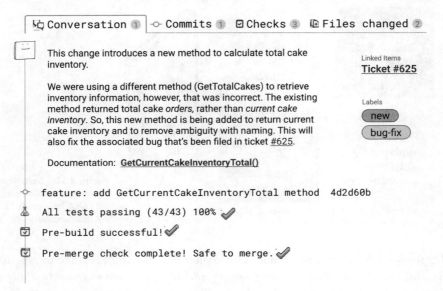

Figure 2.11   A context-filled, properly completed, and ready-to-view PR

More definitively, a PR that is ready to review answers "Yes" to the following questions:

- Do you have a succinct title?
- Is there a clear description of the change?
- Are all the relevant details and context surrounding your changes included?
- Is the accompanying documentation complete and part of the PR?
- Are commit messages meaningful, clear, and atomic?
- Are relevant tests created and/or updated and part of the PR?
- Are ticket numbers/sprint tasks linked?
- Are appropriate labels assigned?
- Are prechecks, test runs, and other automated prerequisites finished running and passing?

Always err on the side of more detail and context in your PR. Make it so clear that if you were to submit this PR and go on vacation, no one would need to contact you to clarify something!

YOU ARE NOT YOUR CODE

Lastly, a key part many authors forget is that they, too, need to leave their ego at the door. It can be difficult; sometimes, the code we write can feel like an extension of ourselves. Sometimes, we also tie our worth or ability as a developer to that same code. When we get any feedback that is not aligned with what we expect, we can respond inadequately. Instead, remember that *you are not your code*. Also, recognize that any feedback left on your PRs is probably worth looking at, discussing, and incorporating into your changes and shouldn't be taken personally. It's usually an opportunity to improve the codebase as a whole.

I know we're all human, and sometimes it's hard to untie those feelings. One thing to try, and as an extra incentive, is to strive for the smaller PRs that benefit everyone. The larger the PR you put together, the likelier it is that you've spent more time on it. The smaller, more manageable the PR, the less time (usually) you've spent on it and the less reason there is to feel "hurt" by reviewers' comments. Right? Focusing on the code rather than you, the author, is part of the reviewer's contract. For you to fulfill your author contract, focus on the feedback rather than the reviewer or even yourself! By doing your part as an author, you can keep the code review on the right track.

AUTHOR'S CONTRACT

An effective author's responsibilities include the following:

- Be your own first reviewer; anticipate what questions your reviewers may ask and proactively answer them.
- Make your PR manageable: keep it short, atomic, and filled with context.
- Make your PR understandable: check off all the items your PR needs to be ready for review.
- Remember, you are not your code. Constructive feedback is not an attack on you or your abilities but an opportunity to improve the codebase as a whole.
- Focus on the feedback, not on yourself or the reviewer.

2.4.3 *The team*

Software engineering teams are hardly ever the same. There are large teams that work well together and smaller sized teams that don't. There are well-functioning, distributed, fully remote teams that work effectively, and there are passive, single-region, in-person teams that disagree about every variable name. The team sets the tempo for much of their processes, and their code review (or lack thereof) is no exception.

Two important principles matter when it comes to team dynamics and a code review process: the team sets the tempo and the code review process is only as good as the entire team makes it.

THE TEAM SETS THE TEMPO

Code review processes can and will be influenced by the way a team works together. When a team has been working together for years, is fully apprised of the system it is working on, and has established communication patterns and channels with each other, a less strict, quick version of a code review might be employed. On the other hand, a team that has frequent changes (like new employees every year or frequent reorganizations), a mix of skill levels or domain knowledge, or work in a highly regulated industry might warrant a more thorough and extensive code review process. Both are valid; the team decides how their code review processes go.

These decisions are made by the team, ideally directly, but also indirectly. As the collective team builds trust with one another, understands each other as colleagues, builds out their CI pipelines, and witnesses how the application progresses with their current tempo, they can decide to become looser with their established process. They can voice their comfort level with the team, validate that they are on the same page, and decide together that their code review process does not need to be as strict. Alternatively, when team members don't trust their colleagues' work, find several mistakes during code reviews, have a higher recurrence of production fires, and other hesitation-inducing scenarios, the team might indirectly enforce a stricter process. It makes sense; the more "issues" a team encounters, the more likely it will decide to introduce more rigorous steps to the overall process.

THE CODE REVIEW PROCESS IS ONLY AS GOOD AS THE ENTIRE TEAM MAKES IT

It's one thing to have a code review process in place that team members are aware of. It's a completely different thing to instill in everyone how important the process is and motivate them to participate. As mentioned in the first chapter, what's the point of having code reviews if not everyone participates?

With this in mind, your team's most difficult obligation is to keep each other accountable. How do you do this? Don't bypass the process because you can or because it's a colleague you get along with. If your team anticipates emergency bypass scenarios, like a hotfix or other infrequent but urgent event that warrants the team to ignore the established process, plan and build them together. These are sometimes called "break-glass" procedures and are sanctioned steps a team completes during an emergency. Or even better, co-create an Emergency Playbook, something we discuss in chapter 10. Most importantly, instill within your team that these emergency bypass processes should rarely be used.

Finally, ensure that any actions that do circumvent the established code review process clearly document what is being done and why and that it is communicated to everyone. In the end, the easier it is for everyone to understand the process they've built and the benefits it awards them, the easier it is for everyone to keep the process intact and want to participate in it.

THE TEAM'S CONTRACT

An effective team's code review responsibilities include the following:

- Enforce the process for everyone.
- If tools allow, let them do the enforcing automatically.
- Develop emergency processes together. Use them as rarely as possible.
- Iterate on all processes frequently, not just during or after emergencies. When something doesn't feel right, chances are, it isn't.
- Communicate any circumvention of the process to everyone.
- Keep each other accountable.
- Share the responsibility and collectively own the codebase you maintain.

2.4.4 Those in charge

As a tech lead, engineering manager, or an individual whose colleagues naturally look up to, enablement and encouragement are your top priorities when it comes to code reviews. With your influence, reputation, and possibly your budget, your team can flourish or just get by. Why not do the former?

ENABLEMENT CAN BE MANY THINGS

You can explicitly carve out time for the team members to discuss their code review goals and refine their Team Working Agreement. You can build in the time to do code reviews for each sprint. You can request more resources for better tooling or more training. You can advocate for your team's code review efforts to your superiors. You can instill their necessity in the development process, not special, one-off tasks or "additional" work. And you can require strict guidelines around code reviews in the same way you require automated tests or travel budget approvals. If you can normalize code reviews, you've laid a wonderful foundation for your developers to flourish.

Enablement can also mean keeping an eye out for bottlenecks, seeds of a negative review environment, potential code review delays (which we discuss in chapter 8), or process loopholes (chapter 9) and proactively stopping or eliminating them before they become a bigger problem for the team.

ENCOURAGEMENT IS FACILITATING A PRO-CODE REVIEW CULTURE

Discourage taking shortcuts and cutting corners. Work with product stakeholders to make code reviews nonnegotiable for your team. Applaud attention to detail and doing things the right way. Actively participate in team discussions of the code review process, reinforcing support for their existence and a willingness to improve them. Ultimately, the more you can boost your team and its efforts to build a great code review process, the more everyone benefits.

CONTRACT FOR THOSE IN CHARGE

To effectively be in charge and promote code reviews, responsibilities include the following:

- Do what you can to enable code reviews for your team.
- Promote a pro code review culture.

- Proactively track and stop or eliminate problems that could affect the code review process and the team.
- Normalize code reviews as a necessary part of the software development process, not as "additional" work or a "nice to have."
- Enforce the process for everyone.

2.4.5   *The organization*

The final, and sometimes forgotten, role in code reviews is the organization a team works for. Companies can have strongly defined cultures, which can heavily influence engineering organizations. If code reviews are important at an organizational level, resources and support are easier to obtain. If they aren't, the opposite is clearly felt and seen.

HOW ORGANIZATIONS VIEW CODE REVIEWS

You may ask yourself, "Why would an organization be against such a beneficial and proven practice?" Some feel that it wastes too much of an engineering team's time—time that's better spent on producing organizational value (in the form of new features). Others have grown used to an environment where fixing production fires after the fact is the norm. Some organizations may have tried to implement code reviews before, but due to a myriad of reasons—they were poorly enforced, caused interpersonal team problems, or did not catch every bug that led to a production outage—code reviews were deemed ineffective.

If you think about it, organizations treat code reviews like turn signals on a car. A car drives perfectly fine without turn signals, just like some organizations can operate without code reviews. However, with turn signals, you drastically lower the chance of getting into an accident by announcing where you're going, just like organizations that implement code reviews decrease the chance of deploying problematic software. Sometimes, value is subjective. Overall, when organizations view code reviews as a hindrance rather than a help or fail to see their value, they probably won't support them.

PERSUADING A CODE REVIEW-RESISTANT (OR CODE REVIEW-NAIVE) ORGANIZATION

If you find yourself in this kind of organization, it can seem like an uphill battle to advocate for code reviews; it's a lonely and thankless battle. However, if there's even the slightest prospect of making it work within your team, it is worth trying! The focus is on helping your organization understand that code reviews are, in fact, a worthy process:

- *Start locally*—Get your team on the same page and agree to a standard of quality they will hold themselves to. Usually, the hardest part is getting your team just as excited and adamant about code reviews as you are. If you do, you'll have a greater chance of that enthusiasm spreading past your team. Some things to try:
  - Introduce the concept of code reviews at your next engineering offsite, sprint retrospective, or another team meeting where everyone is involved.

Engage in discussions about the process, what would be useful to you as a team, or what previous incidents may have been prevented by having a code review in place.

– Go through this chapter and then chapter 3 with your team and document your process. Record how you chose tools and configured settings and identify which policies worked (and which ones didn't), among other things.

– As items solidify and workflows become ingrained into your team, make them official. Chapter 4 helps with this. Even if it's just saying, "Let's code review each other's code before merging into production," it sets the tone for the team and slowly introduces process changes. This produces an artifact for your team's historical records and is something you can share with others.

■ *Share the guidelines you develop with other engineering teams*—As you start to incorporate code reviews into your team, the reviews become less experimental and more routine. That's a good thing! When it comes to processes like a code review, routine *evolves* into expectations and standards. Sharing these standards, how they help your team, how they improve your applications, and how to get started can be an eye-opening experience for other teams! Some things to try:

– Take advantage of lunch-and-learns, monthly all-hands meetings, engineering offsites, and other opportunities to share how code reviews *can* work at your organization.

– Encourage other teams by leading by example. Keep track of team highlights, like on-time or early delivery of big features, reduction in post-deployment defects or rollbacks, or increases in customer satisfaction that can be directly attributed to the code reviews taking place.

■ *Talk to your tech leads and managers*—Whether those in charge hear it from each individual during their one-on-one meetings or collectively as a united team, discussing why code reviews are wanted and needed can be an effective strategy. Whether you like it or not, having technical leaders involved and on your side can be a big factor in convincing the overall organization. Pairing these discussions with hard facts and metrics can make it even easier to convince your tech leads and managers (or help them convince those above them!).

■ *Advocate for code reviews if you are the tech lead or manager*—Just as your team can advocate the benefits of code reviews to other teams, *you* can also play a pivotal role in influencing your peers to be open to them. Share how your team's dynamic has improved since implementing them. Tout how your production fires have decreased. Cite as many tangible (and intangible) advantages your team has experienced as a direct result of a code review process!

Of course, the best way to show the advantages of code reviews is through verified metrics. But with so many random numbers floating around and potential insights to capture, which ones will actually matter when making the case for code reviews?

The DevOps Research and Assessment (DORA) team at Google has some interesting prospects.

DORA conducted a six-year program to measure and understand DevOps practices and capabilities. It wanted to validate that (1) software engineering team performance can be measured in a meaningful way and (2) high-performing software engineering teams (based on the measures they found) do, in fact, bring high value to organizations [14]. After surveying thousands of teams across multiple industries, the team identified four key metrics that indicate the performance of a software engineering team [14], described in depth in table 2.5.

Table 2.5   DORA engineering metrics on software engineering team performance

DORA metric	How it's measured and how to interpret the metric	Why it's important	Why an organization should care
Deployment frequency How often a software engineering team deploys code to production	Deployments per day 👍 Good: On-demand, high frequency, multiple deploys a day 👎 Bad: Low frequency, between once a month and once every 6 months	Indicative of how efficient a team's working and releasing processes are	Indicative of how often a team provides value to customers
Mean change lead time Time it takes from code being committed to code successfully running Change lead time is also known as *cycle time.*	Average time for committed changes to run successfully in production 👍 Good: >1 day 👎 Bad: 1–6 months	Tracks the pace of a team; faster teams have optimized processes; slower teams can be a sign of waste or inefficiency in the process.	Faster delivery encourages an increase in revenue and improved customer renewal rates
Mean time to restore How quickly a software engineering team recovers from failure	The average time between a production bug/failure being reported and that problem being fixed 👍 Good: Less than 1 hour 👎 Bad: Between 1 week and 1 month	Indicative of how quickly a team can understand and resolve problems that occur in production; low mean times to recovery give teams confidence that they can restore to a functional state if production is affected	Any downtime has negative effects on an organization. The quicker your system gets back to a functional state, the less severe the effect on the organization.
Change failure rate How often a software engineering team releases a change to production that causes a failure	Ratio; number of failures to number of deployments (*calculated as a percentage)* 👍 Good: Rate 0–15% 👎 Bad: Rate 46–60%	Indicative of the quality of software the team builds; high change failure rates suggest lower-quality software that frustrates customers.	Fixing bugs and rolling back code is costly; doing so takes time away from building new features that bring value to customers.

With these metrics, the DORA team was also able to categorize teams into four differ-ent performance categories: elite, high, medium, and low [14]. Table 2.6 shows a breakdown of team performance as it relates to the DORA metrics.

Table 2.6 Comparison of elite-, high-, medium-, and low-performing teams based on DORA metrics

DORA metric	Elite	High	Medium	Low
Deployment frequency How often do we deploy to production? *Calculated as deployments per day*	On-demand, high frequency, multiple deploys a day	Between once a day and once a week	Between once a week and once a month	Between once a month and once every 6 months, low frequency
Mean change lead time How long does it take for committed code to run suc-cessfully in production? Change lead time is also known as cycle time	>1 day	Between 1 day and 1 week	Between 1 week and 1 month	1–6 months
Mean time to restore How quickly can we recover to a functional state from a production issue? *Calculated as the average time between a production bug/failure being reported and that issue being fixed*	>1 hour	>1 day	>1 day	Between 1 week and 1 month
Change failure rate How often do we release changes that cause produc-tion failures? *Calculated as a percentage: ratio of the number of failures to the number of deployments*	0–15%	0–15%	16–45%	46–60%

I'm sure your peers will at least be curious to see whether they can achieve the same with their team.

If you do all this and still find yourself in a discouraging scenario, it can be useful to start documenting some key facts. Consider recurring problems, time spent on production fires, new features delayed due to frequent debugging sessions, and reve-nue lost to a recurring bug—really any tangible measurement that quantifies an anti-code review environment. Sometimes, seeing the value of a code review in terms the organization will respond to is what's needed.

In the most unfortunate—and, hopefully, rare—case, these clear signs of lost pro-ductivity and resources will still mean nothing to an organization. It can happen, and when it does, it's up to you to decide if it's worth it to fight that battle at that particular organization or to find a new one that better aligns with your opinions on code reviews! You'll find that organizations that support and have ideal code reviews don't require convincing. Instead, they invest their efforts in enabling their engineering teams to optimize their code reviews.

Summary

- Code review systems can be human-led, where code changes are evaluated through the use of synchronous meetings, discussions, and/or face-to-face review processes; tool-facilitated, where software or online platforms facilitate the review process; or a hybrid of both.
- The typical code review workflow involves four parts: new or changed code, one or more reviewers (ideally other than the author of the code being reviewed), a reviewing mechanism, and a signoff condition.
- This book will focus on code reviews that use pull requests as the reviewing mechanism.
- A great PR includes a clear and concise title and a detailed and context-filled description, takes advantage of labels to add additional info to the PR, and uses PR review states as it goes through the stages of review.
- Reviewers are given lots of influence and are responsible for what passes through their review. To be an effective reviewer, don't abuse the influence you are given, give a thorough review every single time, leave your ego at the door, and focus on the code rather than the author when doing your review.
- Authors are responsible for making their pull requests as manageable and clear as possible. This means breaking PRs into easy-to-review chunks of no more than 500 lines of code, which can be reviewed in detail within 30 minutes and includes as much context and information as necessary to understand the PR. Authors also need to leave their egos at the door, avoid taking feedback personally, and embrace the cycle of incorporating feedback into their original code.
- Teams decide the tempo of the code review process; with greater trust, cohesion, experience together, and communication patterns, code review processes can be more lenient. Without these traits, a stricter code review process may be warranted. To keep up with the designated tempo, the team must hold each other accountable and work together on process changes and enforcement.
- Those in charge, like a tech lead or engineering manager, are responsible for enabling and encouraging optimal processes for the team. Through resources, influence, enforcement, and enthusiasm, they must do what they can to establish, maintain, and promote a pro-code review environment.
- Organizations usually don't support code reviews if they can't clearly see their value, and sometimes value is subjective. In this situation, convincing your team, your manager, and even other teams within your department may be a worthy strategy to try within an anti-code review organization. Documenting

real, negative metrics due to a lack of code reviews can be an effective alternative. If all else fails, it's worth understanding that the organization may not change and deciding what to do with that realization.

- The four DORA metrics (deployment frequency, mean change lead time, mean time to restore, and change failure rate) are excellent base metrics to begin collecting and analyzing for your team. Use these metrics to categorize your team's current state (elite-, high-, medium-, or low-performing team) and then work your way up, if necessary.

References

[1] Work environment. (2022, June 22). *StackOverflow Developer Survey 2022.* https://mng.bz/aVam

[2] Version control systems. (2022, June 22). *StackOverflow Developer Survey 2022.* https://mng.bz/eVOV

[3] Version control platforms. (2022, June 22). *StackOverflow Developer Survey 2022.* https://mng.bz/pxNK

[4] Fagan, M. E. (2001). Advances in software inspections. In *Pioneers and Their Contributions to Software Engineering: SD&M Conference on Software Pioneers* (pp. 335-360). Springer Berlin Heidelberg.

[5] Cohen, J. (2006). Five types of review. In *Best Kept Secrets of Peer Code Review: Modern Approach: Practical Advice* (pp. 21–22). Smart Bear.

[6] Fagan, M. (1976). Design and code inspections to reduce errors in program development. *IBM Systems Journal, 15*(3), 182–211.

[7] The IBM 029 Card Punch. (2018, June 23). https://mng.bz/Om8w

[8] Why did 80x25 become the text monitor standard? (n.d.). *StackExchange: Retro Computing.* https://mng.bz/YVoz

[9] Ebert, F., Castor, F., Novielli, N., & Serebrenik, A. (2019, February). Confusion in code reviews: Reasons, impacts, and coping strategies. In *2019 IEEE 26th International Conference on Software Analysis, Evolution and Reengineering (SANER)* (pp. 49–60). IEEE.

[10] Makszy, M. (2020, June 10). Code review—from a PM's perspective. https://mng.bz/GNYD

[11] Smartbear. (n.d.). Best practices for code review. https://mng.bz/znvl

[12] Stepanović, D. (2022, November 8). From async code reviews to co-creation patterns. https://mng.bz/0MqJ

[13] Czerwonka, J., Greiler, M., & Tilford, J. (2015, May). Code reviews do not find bugs: How the current code review best practice slows us down. In *2015 IEEE/ACM 37th IEEE International Conference on Software Engineering* (Vol. 2, pp. 27–28). IEEE.

[14] Peters, C., Farley, D., Villalba, D., et al. (2022). *2022 Accelerate State of DevOps Report.* Google Cloud, DevOps Research & Assessment (DORA). https://mng.bz/KDKX

Building your team's first code review process

If you're brand new to code reviews and don't currently have a process in place, this chapter is for you! Using three phases, you'll build your first code review process together with your team. First, you'll establish your team's code review goals. Next, you'll decide on the tools or platform you'll use and the basic workflow your team will follow. Then (in my opinion, one of the most important phases), you'll set some guidelines around your review. After spending some time trying out your process, you can use the fourth phase to learn how to make changes to and refine your code review. Get ready for a lot of conversations and open discussions with your colleagues!

For those who already have a code review process in place

Feel free to skim or completely skip sections 3.1 and 3.2. These sections focus on the typical goals teams can set to achieve with their code reviews and discuss code review tools and workflows you may already be familiar with. Though these sections may not apply to you now, you can always refer back to them if you join a new team or want to redo your process.

I'm sure you're still interested in improving your existing code review process, which is great! If that's the case, I'd highly recommend skipping ahead to section 3.3, which focuses on setting guidelines around your code review and may be more relevant to you. Or you can go through the whole chapter anyway if you feel like your team needs a refresher in all of these areas!

3.1 Establish your goals

You've passed the hardest part—you've either convinced your team that it needs a code review process or that your current process needs to be overhauled. The next phase will be filled with a lot of conversations, the first of which is deciding what your team's ideal code review goals and expectations are. Some teams try to achieve as many goals as possible, while others focus on a few. Most teams pick at least one. All teams eventually achieve all their intended goals over time, but never overnight. In the end, what works for your team will be found through some introspection, collaboration, and a transparent look at how your team and engineering department operate (or want to operate).

Regardless of whether you are starting from scratch (you may be working on a team that does not currently engage in code reviews) or need to completely revamp the current process (because your existing one is not working), the basis is the same: your team needs to decide what it wants out of their code review process. Establishing this foundation is the starting point for any team—a lot of things are decided based on these fundamental questions:

- What do we want our code review process to do?
- What goals do we want to achieve with our process?

By answering these questions together, you can start building your code review process together. These answers (as well as the answers to other questions you'll decide in this chapter) will serve as a great draft for your Team Working Agreement (chapter 4), which we'll discuss in depth in the following chapter.

The most common code review goals—finding bugs, codebase maintainability, knowledge sharing and knowledge transfer, mentoring, and recordkeeping/chronicling—are all worthy candidates for your team's code review process. Take a look at each to see what makes sense for your team.

3.1.1 *Finding bugs*

Finding bugs is one of the most obvious goals cited, but it is actually quite debated [1–4]! I think it's rare to find a developer that doesn't want to find a defect in the code before deployment. However, questioning whether the code review is the right place to find these defects is debated among developers.

On one side of the debate, many argue that obvious bugs should never make it to the code review stage because responsible developers are expected to check the proposed changes before even submitting a review [1]. Another argument is that, despite the intent, bugs aren't actually found at this phase, which contradicts its value. This has been validated across many studies and teams; most code review comments do not point out functionality defects [2] or only cover small, low-level concerns [3]. Some bugs sneak past the review by being too subtle or hidden. Unfortunately, it's also too common for reviewers to improperly or lacklusterly review the code. Lastly, if a team chooses to do mob or pair programming in addition to a separate code review process, finding bugs would be a redundant goal already previously covered. With these arguments, proponents believe finding bugs is a misleading goal.

In contrast, many maintain that finding bugs is a feasible goal that should happen within the code review process. Some studies [3,4] and many developers [5–8] cite finding bugs as a big benefit of code reviews. Code reviewed by multiple sets of eyes (and really smart brains) can reveal errors or defects the original author missed [5].

Above all, code reviews are intended to catch different bugs than those caught in unit tests. Let's walk through an example I've encountered. A new feature has been added—a small amount of data needs to be retrieved from a cache—and I'm currently reviewing the pull request (PR). The PR is lovely; it has a detailed explanation of the change, links to the ticket that warranted its creation, and is implemented in a totally valid way. It even has a suite of passing unit tests to accompany it. However, I noticed something subtle: while the code does retrieve data from a cache, it retrieves it from the *wrong* cache! This is a common but important example of the fact that reliance on passing tests is not a safe measure of quality; it's certainly not indicative of bug-free code! These kinds of glaring bugs are usually not caught by unit tests, but they are easily spotted in a code review. And it's only through such a process that reviewers are enabled to find these kinds of bugs. Finding bugs also extends the value of the code review process by covering any gaps where static analysis or automated tests may fall short.

FINDING BUGS AS A CODE REVIEW GOAL?

Should our team choose to find bugs as a code review goal? So, how about your team? How do you determine if finding bugs is a goal you should be focused on? First, determine what your team's current development workflow is like. Introduce some metrics to help you capture how your team operates today. As mentioned in the previous chapter, the DevOps Research and Assessment (DORA) metrics are a good start. Once you have enough data to compare, say, a baseline and metrics a few months in, analyze where you fall on DORA's team categorization. If you are somewhere in the Low to Medium ratings, finding bugs should likely be a goal you incorporate into your process.

Other questions to ask yourself as you start to evaluate your metrics include

- Do you naturally collaborate with your team to find problems?
- Do colleagues ask one another for a second look before merging code?
- Even if you have any sort of testing in place, do you still find problems that make it into production?

If your team leans "yes" to any of those questions, that's another good indicator to make finding bugs a formal goal in your code review process.

Alternatively, do you find that your metrics land you in the High to Elite team categorizations? Does your codebase lend itself well to catching a majority of bugs through static analysis and automated tests? Are your processes already more rigorous and have built-in review phases? If that's the case, then finding bugs may not be a necessary goal for your team—as in your process already has that goal built in, and you likely don't need to incorporate it into your overhaul. Also, if you engage in extreme pair programming (where every written line of code is reviewed by at least one other person in real-time) in addition to a code review process, then finding bugs may be a redundant goal.

3.1.2 *Codebase stability and maintainability*

One goal most team members can agree on is that code reviews can be used to maintain the stability of the codebase. Code reviews excel at achieving this goal because human judgment, being context-aware, and the ability to understand nuance make a big difference in reviewing code for clarity and readability. As we discussed in chapter 1, clear and readable code means it's maintainable code. Maintainable code lessens the likelihood of bugs and makes extensibility easier.

Choosing codebase stability and maintainability as goals mean focusing on things like complexity, consistency, scalability, and tests, as well as adhering to coding conventions and team standards, pointing out and eliminating code smells, always adding accompanying unit tests, considering edge cases, and thinking about how the isolated code changes fit into the bigger picture are common for these goals. Anything and everything that helps contribute to stable, maintainable code is what these goals are all about. (I mean, are you even doing code reviews if you don't keep an eye out for maintainability? ☺)

As always, what constitutes codebase stability and maintainability will differ by team. And yes, it will require discussions and agreement from the whole team.

CODEBASE STABILITY AND MAINTAINABILITY AS CODE REVIEW GOALS?

Should your team include codebase stability and maintainability as code review goals? I mean, if you don't want to, that's your team's prerogative. But I think this is *the* goal to start with, especially for your first code review process. Using the DORA metrics from earlier, if your team falls within the Low to Medium categorizations, codebase stability and maintainability should be high on your list of code review goals. Additionally, if you're fighting more production fires than you'd like to admit, this can be a sign to make codebase stability and maintainability a top priority for your code review.

On the other hand, if you're rating within the High or Elite team categorizations, there's a great likelihood that your code is pretty stable and maintainable (cheers to you)! While you may not have to choose it as an explicit goal to begin working toward, it may be one you wish to continue fulfilling.

3.1.3   *Knowledge transfer and knowledge sharing*

Two complementary goals, *knowledge transfer* (the deliberate process of moving knowledge from one person or group to another) and *knowledge sharing* (the exchange of knowledge in a readily accessible environment) among team members, are worth consideration. Code reviews are a normal place for a team to exchange knowledge with one another. They also facilitate the literal movement of code changes into the codebase (if approved) with accompanying knowledge about the changes officially recorded (in the PR).

Even before submitting your PR, knowledge transfer and sharing already happen naturally: conversing with your colleagues during development, gaining insights through team meetings and discussions, or holding small, informal pair programming sessions with a teammate all involve gathering or sharing some information about the code. One of the nicest things about using code reviews to distribute this knowledge is that you reduce your team's dependency on a single person. Established and long-standing members of the team tend to know all the quirks, nuances, and history behind why the codebase is the way it is today. But it's exactly that information that should be shared rather than sheltered in any one person's mind. By choosing knowledge transfer and knowledge sharing as goals for your team, you can improve your "Vacation Factor."

THE VACATION FACTOR (AKA THE BUS FACTOR)

There's a concept (which turned into a measurement of risk) dedicated to this problem of isolated knowledge called the "Bus Factor." Quite macabre, it describes the minimum number of team members that have to suddenly disappear (like being hit by a bus) before a project stalls due to the lack of knowledgeable team members. We often use the phrase in the software development industry to point out key developers on the team and to evaluate how dependent the team is on those specific developers. Side note: I like the alternative "Vacation Factor" much better because it exchanges the violently hurt people in the Bus Factor for happy, full-of-life, and out-of-the-office people who just happen to be away for a significant period of time.

Ultimately, minimizing the effect of the Vacation Factor on your team is something I'd highly encourage you to pursue. Removing your reliance on a single person or a few individuals (and likely the pressure they feel since they probably know they know the most about your codebase) will yield a more resilient, competent, and cohesive team. Knowledge transfer or knowledge sharing of any sort, regardless of whether you include it in your code review process, will always be a good thing.

Those new to the codebase (or new to coding in general) benefit greatly from knowledge sharing, too. Seeing the norms and conventions the team sticks to, witnessing how changes are made and where, understanding how different parts of the codebase affect each other, and having referenceable examples of accepted code all contribute to leveling up the team.

If you decide to use your code review process as a mechanism for knowledge transfer and sharing, remember these pivotal practices:

- *Document the why rather than the how*—Ideally, the code itself is self-explanatory, and adjacent code comments explain why the code looks the way it does; if not, that's a starting point for effective knowledge sharing and should be addressed in your code. Next, to effectively share knowledge, explain why things were done a certain way, add relevant history or past decisions that affect the current state, and get as much as possible of that "insider knowledge" out and documented. This would be shared through the PR detail itself or on an active documentation portal/wiki that is easily accessible to all. This is the stuff everyone on the team should know—the bits of info that, when shared, reduce any dependency on a single person to understand the entire system. It's the information that lets anyone pick up where someone left off or handle a production issue, no matter who is working that day.

- *Pick the right reviewers*—For any kind of knowledge transfer or sharing to happen, knowledge needs to be shared by those who have it. The most potential for learning occurs when someone more experienced reviews a PR from someone less experienced. This doesn't just mean overall years of experience either! This could be someone who's quite familiar with a particular part of the codebase reviewing a new team member's change in that area, someone well-versed in one language reviewing someone else who is just transitioning to that language, and other similar structures.

- *Include new or less experienced team members as Informational Reviewers on PRs*—All too often, we leave team members out of critical PRs, namely because we think they can't give a proper review. Instead of leaving them off the PR entirely (and in the dark with that particular morsel of knowledge), add them as Informational Reviewers! An Informational Reviewer is someone who is added to a PR solely for knowledge-sharing purposes. They are also known as *Optional Reviewers*. Their approval is optional, but they are asked to acknowledge that they have taken a look at a PR they have been assigned to. This is a great way to encourage team members to be aware of complex changes or get exposure to the intimidating parts of the codebase, which, over time, will get them more comfortable with it. Consider a probationary period where these types of reviewers must observe and learn for, as an example, two to four months before they are added as required reviewers with approval privileges. Paired with some mentoring, it is also a great way to begin transferring that knowledge, which increases everyone's ability to meaningfully contribute to the code review responsibilities of the team.

KNOWLEDGE TRANSFER AND SHARING AS CODE REVIEW GOALS?

Should our team choose knowledge transfer and sharing as code review goals? My suggestion is a resounding yes; what I think will differ is how you implement it in your process, how detailed and formal the mechanism will be, and if the code review will be the *only* process where knowledge transfer and sharing will occur.

If you have separate processes that already account for critical knowledge transfer and sharing opportunities, then it may be less important to ensure it happens within the code review itself. These opportunities include team deep dive meetings, reporting mechanisms that are shared with the entire team, active and ongoing lunch and learn sessions, pair or mob programming sessions, or other collaborative practices that effectively transfer knowledge among team members.

Alternatively, if you don't engage in such mechanisms before the code review, a larger responsibility is placed on the author to share and transfer their knowledge during the review, making it a higher priority goal to seek.

Whether you choose them as explicit goals or not, knowledge transfer and sharing will likely occur on your team, and there's nothing wrong with that!

3.1.4   Mentoring

Paired with knowledge transfer, mentoring is an admirable goal of a code review process. Its focused nature lends itself well to constructive feedback, direct evaluation of the code changes proposed, and valuable guidance from colleagues on the codebase as a whole. In-person reviews make this goal much more feasible, though mentoring is still possible regardless of proximity. Even if you don't explicitly choose this goal, you may find yourself engaging in mentoring anyway, especially as your team grows and the levels of experience among team members vary.

It goes without saying that if there are less experienced team members, juniors, or interns on your team, including a form of mentoring through code reviews would be ideal. This is where (with a good process) they will learn *a lot* of things. They can learn how to iterate on code, build confidence in their programming skills, train their eyes to look at code holistically and within the context of a larger codebase, and develop their communication skills, especially when it comes to giving and receiving constructive feedback.

MENTORING AS A CODE REVIEW GOAL?

The biggest indicator is likely the capacity of your team. If you have enough developers willing and able to step into the mentoring role without putting their workload at risk, mentoring might be a great goal. If you can equally distribute a dedicated Senior or Principal developer per mentee, that's also a good sign that mentoring may be a feasible goal for your team.

However, if you have a single senior developer as the only available mentor to the rest of your team, mentoring might be a challenging goal. It's hard enough to mentor one developer effectively—adding a second mentee will increase the senior developer's responsibilities and decrease the quality of mentorship. Similarly, if the senior or principal developer's current workload doesn't allow for any other tasks, mentoring may become more of a burden than a goal to strive for.

3.1.5   Recordkeeping/chronicling

In my opinion, code reviews are an excellent way of chronicling the changes that your codebase goes through. This makes it a great goal to seek as a team. It is also one of the goals I think your team should start with alongside codebase stability and maintainability.

With collective accountability to clearly describe changes in a PR, your team can benefit from a chronological timeline of what has happened to your codebase. This makes debugging, knowledge transfer, knowledge sharing and refactoring a bit easier, as any context you need can be referred to right in your code review tool.

Even if you decide to engage in more human-led review processes (like pair or mob programming) now or later on, you'll still need to keep track of the insights and outcomes that result from those interactions. As a result, recordkeeping/chronicling is a goal that helps achieve that.

RECORDKEEPING/CHRONICLING AS A CODE REVIEW GOAL?

Should our team choose recordkeeping/chronicling as a code review goal? This will be another resounding yes from me. Also, if you choose to use a PR-based workflow, you'll be doing this anyway. What matters is how much effort you individually put into preparing PRs fully and how well you can hold each other accountable for doing so. There are ways to make this easier, either through some tool features (see chapter 5) or even through AI (see chapter 13)!

A consideration: some teams use a separate system to put all this detail into, like a bug-tracking system, kanban board, or other project-tracking platform. If this is the case, just be sure to link to those external platforms' tickets, stories, etc. in the PR! Still, it can be a good idea to at least include the important bits of context directly in the PR in addition to the link; over time, external systems can change or be deprecated, making an even greater case for using the PRs as the records themselves.

3.1.6 *Choosing your code review goals*

We've covered the goals you'd want to consider for your code review. Figure 3.1 sums them up nicely, along with reasons to choose a particular goal.

When just starting out, it can seem daunting to try to achieve all of these goals! Launch your code review process with codebase stability and maintainability as your first goal and work from there. Make that goal the priority of the team. Tweak how you achieve that single goal. See what processes and behaviors move your team closer to that goal and reinforce them. Go through part 2 of this book and refine your process with automation, policies, and tactics that help you continuously achieve codebase stability and maintainability.

Finally, and just as important, see what doesn't work or what moves you away from achieving codebase stability and maintainability. Try iterating on things to make them work. Find bottlenecks and eliminate them. Target actions that push you away from your goal and remove them completely. Over time, your team will naturally incorporate actions that contribute positively to this goal.

When your team feels confident that it has successfully implemented one goal, consider introducing another. As an ideal second (or for the ambitious, parallel goal), I'd suggest recordkeeping/chronicling. Get your team familiar with properly preparing PRs. Coach them to use categorization prefixes in their titles. Experiment with labels and linking. Encourage a habit of adding context and meaningful details to all PRs.

Choosing code review goals

Knowledge transfer & sharing

Understand norms and conventions of the codebase.

Would like to reduce dependency on a single team member.

Structured format to introduce codebase to new team members.

Distribute "insider knowledge" more freely.

Decrease debugging and root cause analysis times.

Finding bugs

No other review system in place (like pair or mob programming sessions).

Team naturally requests feedback on their code prior to merging.

Nuances in codebase require a human eye to properly review.

Have experienced issues that were not caught by static analysis or automated unit tests.

Mentoring

Encourage new/less experienced developers to be part of the process.

Receive direct feedback and opportunities for growth.

Reduce ramp up and onboarding time with internal processes.

Receive valuable reviewer feedback from a fresh set of eyes.

Pass on "insider knowledge" sooner, reducing time it takes for new/less experienced developers to be contributing members of the team.

Codebase stability & maintainability

Increase clarity and maintainability of codebase.

Increase testing and documentation coverage of codebase.

Encourage best practices through referential and historical samples of correct code.

Decrease mental overhead caused by unconventional or non-standard code.

Recordkeeping/ chronicling

Produce a chronological timeline of how and why your codebase has changed.

Support debugging, knowledge-transfer & sharing, and refactoring efforts.

Capture insights and outcomes from human-led reviews (like pair or mob programming).

Enable traceable features; all changes can be linked to a PR.

Figure 3.1   Choosing code review goals for your team

Repeat the practices from the first goal: tweak, iterate, reinforce, and/or remove actions and behaviors as necessary. It will take time for each goal to transform into something the team just naturally achieves or gravitates toward. Be patient, especially during the introductory phases of new goals. In the end, the investment you make to integrate these goals into your code review system will pay off.

3.2   Choose your tools

With a guiding star to point you in the right direction, your team now needs to decide how to get there. The next question you'll be answering is: How will we facilitate our code review process?

Outcome of step 1

Establish your goals:

- Identify what your team wants out of its code review.
- Choose your code review goal(s).

To answer this question, it will be helpful first to explore your team's needs and then compare the tools available. Some functions will be absolutely necessary for your team and its goals, while others are not required or irrelevant. Let's go over what these different functions are; by knowing what you want, choosing between tools becomes a bit easier.

3.2.1   Assessing code review functions

Different code review tools offer all kinds of functions to help with your code review. There may even be some functionality you didn't know you needed until you learned about it! Table 3.1 outlines the functions I think are bare necessities to have in a tool.

Table 3.1   Code review functions

Function	What is it?	Things to consider
Version control/source code management system integration	The ability to integrate with or support the source code management system your team is using	Make sure the tool you choose supports your source code management system. Popular systems include Git, SVN, Mercurial, Perforce, CVS, and TFS.
Project management platform integration	The ability to integrate with or support the project management system your team is using	Make sure the tool you choose supports your project management platform. Using the same tools within an ecosystem can make integrating easier and less cumbersome than piecing together different systems and platforms. Popular platforms include Jira and Azure Boards.
Continuous integration/continuous deployment tool integration	The ability to integrate with or support CI/CD pipeline tools	Ensure your tool supports integrating with your CI/CD tools (or at least the most common and popular ones if you have not created a CI/CD pipeline yet). Without this integration, the ability to automate and include extra safeguards in your overall process is diminished.
Self-hosting	The ability to host your own instance of the software or tool in a location you control and administer	If you are required to self-host due to compliance, regulatory, or security policies, your tools must give you the option to self-host.

Table 3.1   Code review functions *(continued)*

Function	What is it?	Things to consider
Web hosting	The ability to have an external party host an instance of the software or tool in a location you do not control or administer	Backup and redundancy are great things to consider for web-hosted tools/systems. Highly distributed teams may benefit from a web-hosted version of their review tools.
Change history	The ability to search through your changes and/or view a timeline-style overview of your code changes.	A robust search, like being able to search by date, commit, comment, or reference, can be an indispensable function your team may need. Visual representations of changes can be helpful, especially if you use Git as your version control system.
Code-diff	A side-by-side comparison of changed code with original code; see added, deleted, and edited code.	A visual representation of code diffs can help reviewers see exactly what changed. Bonus: If you can compare code across custom parameters, say your current commit versus a change made two months ago, that can also be a helpful tool to have during troubleshooting or debugging.
Pull requests	The mechanism to propose the integration of a set of code changes into a branch	Ideally (and since we've been talking about these the whole book), your tool has some form of proposing changes and a way to handle their integration to or rejection from the main codebase. It may be called something other than a PR, but if you are able to facilitate a reviewing mechanism through this function (as discussed in this book), it's worthwhile to consider.
Inline comments	The ability to highlight specific lines of code and leave a note	The ability to highlight code as specifically as you need to is a bonus. Highlighting by line should be a bare minimum capability.
Conflict resolution	The ability to assist in resolving simple code conflicts between proposed changes and your main codebase	Some tools can do some simple conflict resolutions automatically. This includes visually viewing changes that conflict and manually sorting through them using a graphical interface. It is worth considering as an additional safeguard if your team uses Git or if you expect code clashes with your team.

This is the next vital discussion to have with your team. Once you align on which functions are nonnegotiable and which ones are nice-to-have, it'll be easier to compare the tools available before ultimately deciding on one.

3.2.2   *Choosing a tool*

With a list of your required code functions handy, the next step is to research and compare different tools. It might save time if you can split your team into researching a tool per developer and then regrouping to compare your results. However, if you'd like to research different tools together, that works too! Choose what works for your team.

The following list of tools is not at all comprehensive, sponsored, or the "best" tools you should choose from. However, they are ones I have personally used, other developers have used and suggested to me, or I've heard good things about. I'll go through a quick summary of each and then give you a more comprehensive table at the end of this section for easier comparison.

GITHUB

Of course, I have to start with GitHub (https://github.com/). I have personally used this platform, and many peers I have spoken to use it as well. GitHub not only offers all of the code functions we've discussed, but it also provides a unified platform for developers to manage their code. GitHub pull requests are built-in.

GITLAB

While very similar to GitHub, GitLab (https://about.gitlab.com/) sets itself apart by offering teams a single tool to facilitate an entire DevOps lifecycle. This means, along with all of the code functions mentioned, you can also build your CI/CD pipelines through GitLab and use their integrated CI/CD tools and security features with their merge requests (their version of PRs). I use GitLab for my personal projects and have also used it on some teams I've worked on.

GERRIT

A free and open source choice, Gerrit (https://www.gerritcodereview.com/) is a web-based code review tool for Git repositories written in Java. This means you'll need to download the source code for Gerrit and run it in Java to use it. Aside from reviews, Gerrit is also commonly used as a bug tracker. And somewhat unique to Gerrit is the voting system. As a reviewer, you can vote on labels, one of which is Code-Review, and indicate a negative, neutral, or positive review using a –1, 0, or +1 vote.

CRUCIBLE

Crucible (https://www.atlassian.com/software/crucible) is a collaborative code review tool by Atlassian. I have not used this tool, but I know plenty of teams who do. Since quite a few teams use Atlassian's suite of tools, Crucible was a reasonable choice to also select for code review purposes. Crucible covers all of the code review functions we've discussed and more, including discussing plan changes and identifying bugs across several version control systems.

RHODECODE

Another tool I haven't personally used but have heard praises for is called Rhodecode (https://rhodecode.com/). Despite only supporting Mercurial, Git, and Subversion, it has been quite popular among teams that work at enterprises. It promises "unified collaboration across Git, Subversion, and Mercurial," meaning it can allow teams to conduct code reviews across repositories that may exist in all three.

COLLABORATOR

One common tool I've seen is SmartBear's peer code and document review tool called Collaborator (https://smartbear.com/product/collaborator/). I have not used it myself, but I have heard a few good things about it from several development teams. While it is a paid tool, it has some functions that could make it worth it, like reporting and analysis tools to track metrics about your code review process, audit management, and bug tracking.

REVIEW BOARD

Though the first version of Review Board (https://www.reviewboard.org/) came out over a decade ago, it's still in active development! I have not personally used it, but I hear it as a great alternative to GitHub's PRs. Review Board is a web-based, open source tool that you can self-host or choose to use as a service (Review Board hosts RBCommons; https://rbcommons.com/). It offers pretty much all of the code functions we've discussed, but some unique things, too! Check out pre-commit reviews, post-commit reviews, and image review capabilities (using side-by-side image diffs).

With some tools to kickstart your search, your team hopefully has a small idea of what's available. What follows is my attempt at a comparison chart of the mentioned tools. Please be aware that some tools might become deprecated by the time this is published, some info might change (like pricing tiers or version control support), some pros and cons become better or worse, or heck, all of these things can happen! What I'm trying to say is that the info in table 3.2 is subject to change ☺.

Table 3.2   Comparison of code review tools

Tool / Platform	VCS support	Pricing tiers	Scalability	Pros	Cons
GitHub	Git	Free and paid plan	Good for all team sizes	Free basic plan, widely used, easy to learn, good integration with GitHub ecosystem	Limited review features in the free plan
GitLab	Git	Free and paid plan	Good for all team sizes	Feature-rich, good value for open source projects	Can be overwhelming for some teams; limited self-hosting features in the free tier

Table 3.2   Comparison of code review tools *(continued)*

Tool / Platform	VCS support	Pricing tiers	Scalability	Pros	Cons
Gerrit	Git	Free and paid plan	Good for large code-bases	Open source, highly scalable, advanced features for code reviews	Requires self-hosting, steeper learning curve, and Java to run
Crucible	Git, SVN, and Mercurial, CVS, Perforce	Paid only	Good for large teams	Security and quality focus, powerful integrations with other Atlassian tools, and advanced code quality checks	Paid only; might be too much for smaller teams
Rhodecode	Git, SVN, Mercurial	Paid only	Good for large organizations	Open source, self-hosted, highly customizable workflows; supports multiple VCS	Paid only; may require more technical expertise to set up and manage; less active development community
Collaborator	Git, SVN, Mercurial, CVS, TFS, Perforce	Paid only	Good for small/medium teams	Strong SVN support, advanced features like code search and integrations; self-hosting option	Paid plans only; aging interface
Review Board	Git, SVN, Mercurial, CVS, Perforce, Azure DevOps/TFS, Bazaar, HCL VersionVault	Free and paid plan	Good for all team sizes	Mature tool with flexible deployment options (self-hosted/web-hosted), strong access control features, open source, customizable, and good community support	Paid plans can be expensive; some features require paid plugins

When you've narrowed your potential list to your top three or so, it's time to get testing! Usually, tools will have free plans or a trial; use these with your team to help you assess whether the tool fits your team's needs. Ideally, one will shine and stand out, making it the choice for your team.

Outcome of step 2

Choose your tools:

- Decide which code review functions are most important for your team's process.
- Choose a tool/platform your team will use to facilitate code reviews.

3.3 Set guidelines

With the collective goals set and the tool or platform chosen, a really important step is next: setting guidelines. These guidelines help your team perform the code review you unanimously set out to do. They answer questions that might come up during the code review. They lay out the ideal path your team should follow. They can also act as arbiters of disagreements or unclear situations. For now, place these guidelines in an open document that everyone can access and edit. In chapter 4, we'll discuss something called the Team Working Agreement, a beefier, more formal, and more thorough document; you'll eventually upgrade this set of guidelines to a Team Working Agreement.

There are PLENTY of guidelines you can discuss when it comes to code reviews. I encourage you to start with the ones we talk about in this section, then adapt and refine them over time. You'll find some might be missing as you work through different kinds of projects or teams, and that's OK. You can change your guidelines as your team sees fit. We talk about how to do that later in this chapter. For now, consider discussing and agreeing to the following guidelines with your team.

3.3.1 What is our workflow?

It's time to lay out the actual workflow your team will engage in to perform their code reviews. Having a referenceable workflow to share with your team serves multiple purposes:

- It helps new team members understand how your code review process works.
- It helps all team members have a clear reference to the steps of your workflow.
- It helps anyone going through the workflow understand what can be expected at each stage and what happens before and after each step.
- It helps your team be on the same page as your workflow.

For these reasons, this is an ideal item to have as your first guideline.

Using your selected tool/platform, discuss what happens during a full cycle of your team's code review. Specifically, you'll need to decide

- The starting point
- The review-requesting action
- The review mechanism
- The feedback-cycle mechanism
- The signoff conditions
- The ending point

Then, elaborate on and discuss the following questions with your team:

- *What's your starting point?* Describe what or how you enter into a code review. What kickstarts the process? For most teams, the catalyst for review will be new or changed code.
- *What's your review-requesting action?* Next, outline how you request a review from your team. For those using Git-based code review tools, that is likely opening a PR. Be sure to add all details about what opening a PR means on your team, too! This could include anything from properly filling out the PR or assigning

two or more reviewers to dropping a quick message in a specified chat room to your team.

- *What's your review mechanism?* Describe the tool you're using and what a reviewer is expected to do during the review. In our continued example, we might link to our GitHub repositories, the topics we expect reviewers to focus on, and even a link to these very guidelines you're creating right now.

- *What's your feedback-cycle mechanism?* Explain how feedback is left on code and how authors can address it. Also, describe how an author is expected to address feedback. In our flow, that's through the use of comments on a code review platform. Additional details that your team considers part of the feedback cycle, like making sure all comments are addressed or limiting how many updates can be made to the same PR, are also helpful to describe here.

- *What's your signoff condition?* Identify what needs to be done or fulfilled before the endpoint of your review. Typically, this is the approval of a few reviewers, a passing set of automated checks, or other conditions that a team wants to ensure before completing the review and progressing to the ending point.

- *What's your ending point?* Finally, what is the outcome of the review? After the entire workflow has been traversed, what happens here? Is it the merging of code? Is it kickstarting some automated checks? Is it deploying that code to a QA environment? The ending point of your workflow will be the last step of the review that, once fulfilled, considers it "complete."

If we use our workflow from Chapter 2 and expand on it, we can add the detailed steps of our workflow, as shown in figure 3.2.

3.3.2 What is your review focus?

Another key guideline to establish early with your team is what to focus on during a code review. This will be different for each team. Some teams might be starting in a wonderful state, where things like consistency and documentation are already in place. Their code reviews might focus more on complexity or security concerns. Other teams might not be so lucky and *need* to focus on consistency, tests, and adding more documentation. Whatever your team decides, be sure to give everyone a chance to give their input on what would make their code reviews effective. At a minimum, some things to discuss and decide on (all of which contribute to maintainable code) include

- *Complexity*—Can you understand the code? Is it easy to follow? Will it still be clear to a different developer (or even the original author) when they revisit it in the future? Are there any opportunities to make the code more "human-friendly" and straightforward? Will you be able to make changes to this code in the future? Are there "workaround" or "temporary" bits of code that need to be addressed in a more permanent way?

Our Code Review Workflow

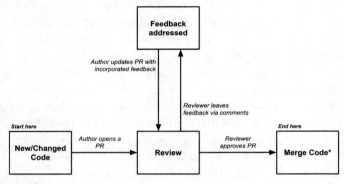

1 Start here

Whenever code is changed or new code is written, a code review needs to be completed.

Author opens a PR
To start the review process, open a PR into our development branch of our main repository.

Be sure to:
- Include a concise title and explain the "why" of the changes in the description.
- Link to relevant resources.
- Link to work ticket.
- Use an appropriate label to categorize the PR.
- Fix any pre-check issues that fail.

2 Review

If you are assigned to review a PR:
- Review the code changes according to our review focus guidelines.
- 🔄 If the code changes do not meet the team's passing criteria or there is further feedback required, enter the feedback cycle (outlined next).

3 Feedback cycle

*If you need to **leave feedback on a PR**:*
- Remember to be kind and focus on the code!
- Leave constructive feedback or necessary changes through comments in GitHub. Remember the Triple-R pattern for crafting objective comments!
- Have an offline discussion with the author to clarify larger issues or to discuss more complex (but possibly warranted) changes.

*If you **receive feedback on a PR**:*
- Remember that the other person is not attacking you! They are communicating opportunities to improve your code.
- Address (or further clarify) all comments with blocking issues. This can either be an update to the original PR or a sufficient discussion and recorded outcome with the reviewer.
- Optional: leave a response on non-blocking issues before closing them.

Reviewer approves PR
👍 If the code changes meet the team's passing criteria (clear, consistent, checks passed) and your review requires no further feedback, you can approve the PR.

Two approvals are required before completing the review.

4 End here

Code can be merged, either by the reviewer or the author.

Figure 3.2 Composing your detailed workflow steps

- *Consistency*—Do the proposed changes follow any working, reliable, and established design patterns and practices already within the project? Is there an opportunity to reuse existing code or libraries?
- *Conventions*—Are industry-wide conventions being followed? Does the code follow any library, framework, language, or other established conventions?
- *Cross-platform compatibility*—Does your codebase need to consider cross-platform compatibility? Are there dependencies included that are not platform agnostic? Will other developers have a hard time running this code "out of the box"?
- *Documentation*—Will missing documentation be a blocker for approval (I think it should!)? Will updates to relevant documentation be a PR checklist item? Do explanatory comments in the code count as documentation? Do you differentiate between technical, user, architectural, and other forms of documentation? If so, which types are valid to address during the code review?
- *Error handling*—Are there clear guidelines on how to handle errors and exceptions? Are they implemented consistently across the codebase? Are there edge cases not handled?
- *Naming*—If your team has naming conventions, are they followed? Are variables, methods, functions, classes, and other key parts clear and understandable? How about a multilingual team? How strict will you be on naming, and what rules regarding its enforcement will be important enough to add to your team working agreement?
- *Resource management*—Are the management of resources (like memory, network connections, I/Operations, etc.) properly considered?
- *Scalability*—Does the code lend itself to refactoring or rewriting without much regression? Can it handle future scenarios that are slightly different?
- *Security*—Are there glaring security vulnerabilities that are not caught by automated means? Are there security standards imposed by the industry you are in that are not followed?
- *Tests*—Are missing tests a blocker for approval? Will tests that purely increase code coverage be accepted? Are there acceptable scenarios where no accompanying tests will be allowed?

You can use this list (and the questions reviewers should be asking themselves) as a starting point and adapt it to your team. Remove items that are irrelevant to you. Add items I haven't listed. Consider other questions that may be important for your team to consider as reviewers. With the review focus established, you set the stage for every reviewer to know exactly what to look for and how to prioritize their review time.

3.3.3 What can block a PR from being approved?

Once everyone agrees on the intent and focus of the review, the next thing to figure out is what prevents a PR from being approved (and what doesn't)! This is one of the most important things you can discuss as a team, and if you figure this out beforehand, you could save yourselves from many disagreements and delays during the code review.

Spell out exactly which issues are allowed or not allowed to block a PR. Figure 3.3 outlines some suggestions on what to block versus what not to block. As you encounter new scenarios that aren't listed in your initial guidelines, take some time to discuss them at your next retrospective or team meeting and determine where that issue falls. While most issues will clearly fall into the nonblocking or blocking category, some might need your best judgment to determine whether the issue is severe enough to block approval.

NONBLOCKING ISSUES

First, decide which issues are nonblocking for your team. These refer to issues that won't impede, stop, or prevent a PR from being approved, as agreed to by the whole team. Remember, this list will be different for each team! Some will be more strict, while others will be a bit more lax. For the most part, the issues I list here generally fall within the nonblocking territory:

- *Style preferences*—Code style preferences that differ from your own
- *Small formatting discrepancies*—Minor things like inconsistent spacing or indentation
- *Documentation nitpicks*—Minor inconsistencies, typos, or discrepancies in documentation
- *Missing but optional features*—If a PR fulfills core functionality but doesn't have an optional feature that was mentioned in passing
- *Minor refactor opportunities*—Code improvements that don't affect functionality but can be addressed in a separate PR
- *Unrelated improvements*—Suggestions that are unrelated to the original PR but can be addressed in a separate PR

BLOCKING ISSUES

Where there are non-blocking issues, there are certainly blocking issues. These refer to issues that definitely need to be addressed and are allowed to stop a PR from being approved. Again, the severity to which certain issues block a PR will vary greatly between teams; the ones I list here are generally a good idea to block a PR on:

- *Core functionality*—The code doesn't meet the intended functionality, as outlined in the PR description or acceptance criteria.
- *Security issues*—The code introduces vulnerabilities that can expose personal or sensitive data or compromise the system.
- *Code standards violations*—The code deviates from established team, project, or style conventions and guides in a major way.
- *Code smells*—The code has poor structure, readability, or anti-patterns.
- *Regression*—The code introduces unintended side effects or breaks existing functionality.
- *Performance issues*—The code negatively affects performance or resource usage.
- *Failed tests*—The code changes cause existing tests to fail.

Blocking Issues

Issues that need to be addressed and are allowed to stop a PR from being approved.

- Core functionality
- Security issues
- Code standards violation
- Code smells
- Regression
- Performance issues
- Failing tests

versus

Non-blocking Issues

Issues that shouldn't stop a PR from being approved; can be addressed in a separate PR or through constructive feedback.

- Style preferences
- Small formatting issues
- Documentation nitpicks
- Missing, but optional features
- Minor refactoring opportunities
- Unrelated improvements

Figure 3.3 Blocking vs. nonblocking issues

The most important thing to remember is that your team's goal is to strike a balance between keeping your codebase maintainable, secure, and human-friendly and keeping your development workflow running smoothly. If problems can be addressed through separate PRs, minor updates, or constructive feedback, they may not require a full block. Reserve the option to block PRs for truly critical problems that affect functionality or security.

3.3.4 What's our approval policy?

Clearly communicate the PR approver policy for your process. There are numerous ways to go about this, but start with the basics: Who gets to approve PRs, and how many approvals are needed before the PR can be merged? Clear-cut answers to these two questions may be all your team needs. You can choose to expand on these two decisions if your team needs a more complex answer.

WHO GETS TO APPROVE PRs?

Usually, any team member who writes or reads code holds approval privileges. Depending on the tooling you choose, you'll either have a binary decision (this person can/cannot approve a PR) or you'll be able to configure more granular permissions (this group can view but not approve; only these PRs can be approved by this group; etc.). Depending on your team, a single person may be responsible for these permissions, or perhaps everyone is given equal access.

As you think about who gets PR approval permissions and develop your reviewer pool (the individuals that make up the group of potential reviewers/PR approvers), consider the following:

- Ideally, everyone on the development team should be able to approve PRs. Are there unique scenarios where this may not be the case for your team? Will titles matter when it comes to PR approval permissions? Do all senior developers get them by default, while approval permission for junior developers is decided on a case-by-case basis? Does your current tooling allow for this scenario?
- Do managers, tech leads, program managers, quality assurance engineers, and other roles that may not code daily get PR approval permissions?
- Will you implement Informational Reviewers with full approval capabilities? We discussed Informational Reviewers earlier in this chapter as a mechanism for knowledge sharing. They did not have approval capabilities. However, when I spoke to some developers at a German tech conference, one of them had implemented Informational Reviewers with approval capabilities! Their guidelines state: "You can approve a PR as an Informational Reviewer, but if something goes wrong, you're on the hook to fix it. Of course, you can ask the original author questions and work with them to get it fixed, but ultimately, you will be responsible for submitting the bug fix." This deeply encouraged accountability and skyrocketed the time-to-contribution for their new team members, resulting in greater cohesion for the team and quicker output for the team as a whole.
- Do external teams (meaning those not core to your team, not those outside your organization, typical in larger organizations) get to approve our PRs? Within those teams, are there specific people who may have historical knowledge or context that would be valuable in a reviewer role? In contrast, including reviewers from other teams—purely to increase the total number of reviewers available—means some reviewers will lack the context and background for each code change. They may not have the sense of buy-in or ownership to be motivated to prioritize the review.
- Another note on artificially increasing the number of available reviewers is that with so many other people who could pick up the review, developers may choose to pawn off the review to someone else rather than do it themselves.
- Will you have a limited selection of people with approval powers for emergency situations?

After thoroughly discussing these questions with your team (and possibly other scenarios that come up in conversation or are not listed here), this pool of approvers should be solidified. This can mean adding them to the tool's list of reviewers, granting them PR review and approval permissions, or making specific people explicit owners of particular portions of the codebase (which we discuss how to do in chapter 5).

HOW MANY APPROVALS?

As another rare, opinionated stance in this book, I strongly suggest having *at least two reviewers approve a PR*. This is a neutral, bare-minimum policy that can positively affect your code reviews. I'm not the only one who implements this! Devlin Duldulao, a chief consultant at Inmeta and Microsoft MVP, also follows this guideline:

> *We have a rule that the more eyes on the code, the better it is, so we ensure that at least two other people review each pull request.*

Who those two approvers end up being is up to your team. They could be any two developers on the team other than the original author: one senior developer and one junior developer, an external team member with background knowledge and one core team developer, or one frontend developer and one backend developer—the options are boundless.

Start with this policy, see how your team handles it in different scenarios, and change it if necessary. Maybe you need more approvals? Maybe a specific developer's approval is more important than just the number of approvals? Decide what happens in each scenario that applies to your team.

If the PR contains changes that affect the whole team—say, an update to your Team Working Agreement or migration to a new API version—I strongly suggest that all core team members need to approve. If your team will be maintaining it, they should know about it!

The scenarios your team encounters will help you shape this policy. And hey, you may find that you don't need to change this bare minimum policy at all! The most important factor is that having more than one person review code changes is always a good thing.

Outcome of step 3
Set your essential four guidelines:

- *Workflow*—Map it out and outline the detailed steps of your code review.
- *Review focus*—Outline what reviewers will concentrate on during their review.
- *Nonblocking vs. blocking issues*—Spell out exactly which problems are allowed to block a PR and which ones aren't.
- *Approver policy*—Determine who gets to approve PRs and how many approvals are needed before the PR can be merged.

After this step, you are ready to pilot your code review! Take it easy and start with smaller issues or code changes. Be patient with each other as you get accustomed to the new process you've established. If you find rough patches or confusing steps, jot those down! At your next team meeting, you can engage in the last part of this chapter, which is refining your code review process.

3.4   *Refining the process*

The greatest part about building your code review process as a team is that you can refine it as a team. As your project, team, or engineering style evolves, so can your code review! If you've found some areas for improvement in your process, your team should be aware of and embrace the ability to refine it. In this final phase, which helps you improve your process, think about the following questions:

- Do we notice any limitations that affect the code review process?
- Do we have clear problems that we need to address in our workflow?
- Are there parts of our process that we can make better, modify, or completely remove?

A "yes" to any of these questions can certainly be a candidate for refinement. You can refine your code review process using three steps: Discussion, Decision, and Dissemination. What's most important to remember is that any changes are *discussed* by all, *decided* by all, and *disseminated* to all. Let's look closer at each of these important steps in figure 3.4.

DISCUSSION

When a part of your code review no longer works and an adjustment needs to be made or something entirely new needs to be added, a team member should bring it up with the larger team and start a discussion. This is the first step to making a change. Having a definitive way to propose these potential changes makes this step much easier. This could be a dedicated portion of a monthly team meeting, a line item discussed during a retrospective, or a purposeful messaging space for such changes; the options are endless! Find the most natural way your team can engage in this kind of discussion and make it the official way to kickstart the refinement process.

Code review process change?

It's as simple as 1, 2, 3!

1. Discuss

Start a discussion and propose the change to the team.

Any team member can propose an improvement or suggestion.

2. Decide

After listening to each team member's thoughts and concerns about the issue, **make a decision together.**

Consider alternative approaches or combining different ideas to come to a decision everyone can agree to.

3. Disseminate

Communicate the collectively agreed upon change publicly and to all those affected by the change.

Don't forget to update or reconfigure any tools to reflect the change.

Figure 3.4   Making a change to your code review process is as easy as discussing, deciding, and disseminating.

One useful tactic I like to use to elicit these discussions is through something I call *refinement checkpoints*. These are scheduled, dedicated times for a team to think about, discuss, and propose refinements to the current code review process. Table 3.3 offers some practical checkpoint times.

Table 3.3   Refinement checkpoints

Checkpoint time	Always required?	Questions to consider
End of sprint	No, but can still be applicable depending on sprint	*Consider:* Was there a task or process that indicated a potential bottleneck in the future?
End of major feature	Maybe; larger features	Was this feature too much to review in one sitting? Is there a way to break apart logical portions of larger features that make the code review process less cumbersome?
End of quarter	No, but good to consider	*Consider:* Were there any quarter-specific projects, initiatives, or company-wide events that affected the code review process?
End of year	Yes	How did our code review process work for us? Were there any recurring pain points/hindrances in our process?
End of project	Maybe	Can we use the same code review process for each project we start? Were there any project-specific "quirks" that affected our code review process? Which pieces of our code review should always exist, regardless of the project?
After production outage	No, but good to consider	*Consider:* Should this incident be added to our Emergency Playbook? *Consider:* Did anything different happen with this outage that challenged the established process? *Consider:* Were there any parts of the root cause that should have been caught in the code review process? If so, what was missing or what needs to change to make sure it doesn't happen again?

Once a proposal has been made to the team, the discussions that follow can be quite quick or heavily involved, depending on the significance of the change and how much the team is in agreement.

DECISION

Once discussions have played out, you'll know that further conversations are no longer needed when a decision can be made. At this point, each team member's concerns, experiences, and thoughts about the proposal have been heard. More importantly, the decision is one the team arrives at together. All are comfortable adopting the change. No one should feel surprised by the change, when or why it was made, when it will go into effect, and how it affects the process going forward. This heavily depends on the final step of dissemination.

DISSEMINATION

Refinements can only work if they are made known to the applicable people. That's why the dissemination of your team-approved changes is one of the most meaningful factors in successfully updating your code review process. To properly disseminate the change that has been made

1 Update your team working agreement to reflect the change you've just decided on.
2 If applicable, reconfigure your tools to put the change into effect.
3 If applicable, update any automated scripts, alerts, or jobs affected by the change.
4 Officially announce the refinement in a team meeting or public team messaging space.
5 Any time someone forgets about the change, kindly remind team members of the refinement you all decided on and be patient while everyone adapts to it.

3.4.1 Refinement scenario walkthroughs

It's always easier to understand these concepts with examples. Let's walk through the steps of discussion, decision, and dissemination to see how some scenarios might play out.

SCENARIO 1: REMOVING A REQUIRED LINE ITEM FROM A PR TEMPLATE

A PR template was created to ensure everyone's PRs are consistent. In it, a few required line items were added to make sure all authors could ensure their PRs were properly prepared. This includes required links to documentation, appropriate tags to categorize the PR, and a self-reported acknowledgment that a manual script (that runs some checks) was executed without errors.

After a few quarters, your team slowly improves its code review process by automating a few things. One of those improvements includes the manual script—instead of relying on the author to run it and acknowledge it in the PR, your build pipeline automatically runs it for you and displays the results.

- *Discussion*—Someone brings up this outdated line item during a quarterly engineering offsite. Questions are asked, and conversations occur. Does the team pretty much agree that they should remove the line item, as no one really uses it? Have most team members individually concluded that they also ignore that line item since it has been replaced with the automated check? Does the automated check have full parity with the manual script?
- *Decision*—Remove the manual script acknowledgment line item from the PR template.

- *Dissemination*—A PR is submitted to your Team Working Agreement to remove the line item. Key takeaways and justifications from the discussions are added to ensure that context and understanding are clear when reviewing why the change was made. At the next team meeting, your tech lead or manager announces the change and a quick synopsis of how the team came to that decision.

However, things are hardly that easy. Even more rare is when the entire team is in agreement! Let's see what happens when there's some disagreement with a proposed refinement.

SCENARIO 2: REQUIRING A MINIMUM OF TWO APPROVERS FOR ALL PRS

Say your team has established a policy to require at least two approvers for all PRs. The tool you are using can be configured in this way and is currently set up to do so.

A few production issues occurred in the past few sprints while a few key teammates were out. This made it harder to get PRs approved, as the two-person minimum could not always be fulfilled. How do we deal with that?

- *Discussion*—A retrospective item to discuss the two-PR approver minimum is added. On the one hand, everyone still agrees that all PRs should have at least two people reviewing and approving any change. This aligns with your team goals of knowledge transfer and codebase maintainability. On the other hand, the fixes to the last few production fires were artificially delayed due to the policy and the surrounding circumstances. It's suggested that the policy be changed to require a single approver; that way, similar scenarios in the future won't introduce unnecessary delays. This suggestion splits the team into opposing sides.

  Both sides have valid arguments. Fundamentally changing the entire process (by only requiring a single approver) seems too drastic. Yet, having delays due to process bottlenecks is also unacceptable to the team. Another thing to consider is that the current tool being used cannot distinguish between these "regular" and "emergency" scenarios; in other words, the minimum approver policy cannot be configured per individual PR. This means one policy has to be chosen.

  Your team discusses a lot of things: Are we working around the limitations of the tool rather than finding a tool that can accommodate our workflows? Have we proven to be reliable and communicative team members who can be trusted with elevated rights in the existing tool being used? If changes were to happen, what assurances can be put into place so they don't weaken the existing process?

- *Decision*—Since the current tool has limitations on how to apply policies, it has been decided that the author of the PR can approve their own PR—with some caveats! First, the author can only be considered a valid second approver during emergency scenarios. This is designated with a new tag, `emergency`, and must be included in PRs that meet that description. Second, the team has been trusted with this change, meaning it's every developer's responsibility to always go through the regular process and not abuse the mechanism intended for emergencies. Lastly, as an additional check (and to dissuade misuse of the self-approving power), developers will be asked to input a justification reason after a PR is detected to have been self-approved. In an emergency scenario, the team has decided that it is enough to link to a bug report. In all other scenarios, the developer will have a logged record of when and why they were self-approving a PR, making it harder to justify and much less appealing to do.

Alternatively, another solution could include opening up the pool of approvers to the next-level managers, again, only during an emergency. In this way, the policy of authors not approving their own PRs can still be enforced.

- *Dissemination*—A PR is submitted to your team working agreement to update the approver policy. Key takeaways and justifications from the discussions are added to ensure context and understanding are clear when reviewing why the change was made. Your tool is configured to adapt to the new changes: an `emergency` tag is added and made available to PRs, any options to prohibit self-approving PRs are removed, and a new post-approval check is added that prompts authors to enter a justification reason when a PR has been self-approved. This new process is added to your emergency playbook, detailing the exact steps and actions to take in case this incident happens again.

Summary

- Building your first code review process involves four stages: establishing your goals; choosing your tools and workflow; setting guidelines; and, when needed, refining the process.
- First, decide what your team's code review goals are. There are several goals to choose from when establishing a code review. These include finding bugs, codebase stability and maintainability, knowledge transfer and sharing, mentoring, and recordkeeping/chronicling. Not all of them are required, nor will they all be relevant to every team. The key is to decide which ones work for your team.
- Next, choose the tool/platform you'll use to facilitate your code review. Understanding what code review functions you need and want for your process can help you compare tools.
- Finally, set guidelines around your code review. Initially, you'll want to solidify your workflow, determine your review focus, outline your nonblocking versus blocking issues, and describe your approver policy. These are a good start, but your team can and should expand them as you get more comfortable with your code review process.
- Refinements are encouraged and part of a successful code review process. They can happen when team members discuss a proposed change, decide on an outcome, and disseminate the new change to the entire team.
- Make changes as needed and as often as your team warrants it.

References

[1] Górka, B. (2021, September 8). Code review is not for catching bugs. https://mng.bz/x6zW

[2] Czerwonka, J., Greiler, M., and Tilford, J. (2015). Code reviews do not find bugs: how the current code review best practice slows us down. In *2015 IEEE/ACM 37th IEEE International Conference on Software Engineering* (pp. 27–28). IEEE.

[3] Mäntylä, M. V., & Lassenius, C. (2008). What types of defects are really discovered in code reviews? *IEEE Transactions on Software Engineering, 35*(3), pp. 430–448.

[4] Bacchelli, A., & Bird, C. (2013). Expectations, outcomes, and challenges of modern code review. In 2013 35th International Conference on Software Engineering (ICSE) (pp. 712–721). ICSE.

[5] Hodgson, P. (2019, May 10). 6 Practices for effective pull requests. https://mng.bz/Aarz

[6] Barrett, W. (2022, January 31). How to catch injection security vulnerabilities in code review. https://mng.bz/ZVjP

[7] Orosz, G. (2019, September 30). How to make good code reviews better. https://mng.bz/RNpK

[8] Malik, K. (2022, April 27). Code review: Manual vs automated. https://mng.bz/2gY0

## Part 2

Elevated code review essentials

I f you're thinking, "I'm ready for the good stuff, Adrienne," this part is where it's at. The skills you'll learn in part 2 are all the things you'll need to know how to do properly; otherwise, your code reviews won't be as effective as they should be (let alone supported or loved).

Chapter 4 is dedicated to the ever-important Team Working Agreement. Without one, your team will likely run into (unnecessary) troubles with your code review process.

"Why is my PR being blocked on such an insignificant issue?"

"I'm spending all my time in the review pointing out indentation mistakes. Ugh."

"What do you mean? One week is a perfectly reasonable amount of time to respond to a PR!"

If you've ever argued or disagreed over the "obvious" things about your code review process with your team, start reading chapter 4 right now!

Chapter 5 focuses on all the wonderful things we can automate to make our lives easier and our code reviews objective, repeatable, and manageable. This includes actions we should definitely take care of before the review and things we can automate during the review.

Then we come to one of my favorite chapters, chapter 6. Communication is a vital component of code reviews. If we don't know how to talk to our colleagues, give or receive feedback, and write practical code review comments, code reviews won't work. So, chapter 6 is dedicated to teaching you how to do all of that.

As you continue iterating and refining your process, there will come a time when more complex challenges start to pop up. That's where part 3, Dealing with dilemmas, will be waiting for you.

The Team
Working Agreement

This chapter covers

- What a Team Working Agreement is
- Why your team should want their own Team Working Agreement
- What to consider in your Team Working Agreement
- Understanding the meaning of a "living" document

As guidelines are established and things are set in motion, it can get difficult to enforce and remember everything your team may have discussed, debated, and ultimately decided on for your code review. Having an official, public, documented, and referenceable record that your team acknowledges can ease the burden—it could even be the key to many interpersonal issues that crop up between team members.

Can *only* a document of policies and agreed-upon standards by the team really be meaningful? This chapter aims to show that, if implemented successfully, taken seriously by the whole team, and effortless to change, it may be the greatest thing your team incorporates into your culture.

4.1   What's a Team Working Agreement?

While its origins come from the Scrum framework (a set of values, principles, and practices that help cross-functional teams deliver products and services in short cycles [1]) and facilitated by product owners or product managers, the Team Working Agreement (TWA) has found a fitting home within engineering teams as well.

A TWA transforms implicit social expectations into *explicit* enforceable ones. And with the code review process, plenty of expectations—which can turn into annoyances—can and should be handled properly through a TWA.

A TWA can start as a literal document shared with all members of the team. Whether it's a Google doc, Word doc, or even a Markdown file in a shared folder, the most important part is that all team members can access and edit it. What's the best way to start this document? In its own repository! Make the TWA the first item that goes through the code review process your team develops. 🏠

One key thing to keep in mind as you read through this chapter is that anything that can be done automatically, *should.* Whether that's through tooling, scripts, or software, your team can ensure a repeatable, objective, and scalable process if you make automation its backbone. In the following chapter, we discuss everything possible to automate, and those are items you should certainly strive to automate. For all other things that can't be automatically implemented or enforced, the TWA comes into play.

4.2   Setting team expectations with a Team Working Agreement

Every individual on your team has different professional expectations and needs—things that, when unknown to the larger team, become incorrect assumptions and a recipe for disappointment. The TWA provides a practical way to have a team's needs collectively known, making them more easily met. This is all very ethereal at the moment, so let's talk through some examples!

4.2.1   Scenario 1: The swift and not-so-swift reviews

Evan submitted a PR around 9:00 in the morning and is awaiting two approvals, per team policy. In this case, the reviewers are Anthony, a mid-level developer who has worked on the codebase for about a year, and Emily, a senior developer who has in-depth experience and context of the project Evan is making a change to. Everyone is in the same office in Palo Alto, California.

Anthony was able to give a thorough review after lunch and has already approved the PR. The remaining reviewer, Emily, has yet to approve or comment on the PR. As the end of the workday approaches, Evan begins to get impatient. From his perspective, the team has some spurts of downtime available. He doesn't understand why he hasn't received his second PR approval yet. He chooses to message Emily, asking if she can take a look at his PR sometime soon.

Emily gets annoyed. She has been reviewing a few other PRs, and one in particular has been taking up a lot of her time. She's spent most of her day having clarifying conversations with the developer of the time-consuming PR, which is why she has not been able to get to Evan's PR yet. Upon receiving Evan's message, she replies, "Hi Evan. Thanks for your patience. I've been reviewing other PRs assigned to me, so I've yet to start on yours. I'll get to it as soon as I can."

In this situation, having explicit response times codified in the TWA does two things. First, it sets expectations for Evan and, if necessary, justifies his need to follow up with Emily if she is unable to adhere to the expected response time. Second, this gives Emily more flexibility in planning her tasks to ensure she can meet the expected response time. While she may not respond as quickly as Anthony, she can feel less anxious about Evan's PR: she can review it the following morning, but well within the reasonable response time expected.

> **Ideal TWA guideline 1**
> Reasonable PR response times

4.2.2 *Scenario 2: Mismatched meanings*

Priya has received feedback that she disagrees with regarding her PR. One of the variables she uses, `postEvaluationCleanedData`, was a bit confusing to reviewer Jonah. Jonah added this feedback and suggested using `postFilterPreCalculationEstimate` as the variable name instead.

While Priya's variable name is explicit, it is still ambiguous in the context of the method it is used in. Jonah pointed out that two evaluation steps occur in this particular method—a filtering step and then a calculation step. Priya considers both steps as an evaluation of sorts, so she chose the variable name she did. Using Jonah's suggested variable name will remove the ambiguity on whether it's the first or second evaluation step. Nevertheless, Priya continues to defend her original variable name, resulting in a back-and-forth that is going nowhere.

In this situation, the first thing to try is an offline conversation. If the PR has been stagnant for a few days or over 10 comments continue to discuss a single problem, let that be a signal to your team to escalate the conversation away from the tool. Ideally, move it to an in-person coffee chat or set up a face-to-face video call, if remote.

When that still doesn't resolve the conflict, having a ranking of attributes, from most important to least important, on naming standards could be what it takes to resolve this scenario. Something like Figure 4.1 would be invaluable.

Using the sample naming standards in the TWA, we can see that both variable names in question fulfill the coding conventions. Eventually, it's the ranking that breaks this stalemate. Clarity is ranked as the most important attribute of naming, and since `postFilterPreCalculationEstimate` is more descriptive, better clarifies which evaluation step it relates to, and is understood by the larger team, it is chosen as the more appropriate variable name.

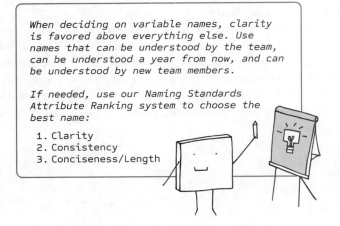

Naming Standards
Attribute Ranking

When deciding on variable names, clarity is favored above everything else. Use names that can be understood by the team, can be understood a year from now, and can be understood by new team members.

If needed, use our Naming Standards Attribute Ranking system to choose the best name:

1. Clarity
2. Consistency
3. Conciseness/Length

Adding a small section like this into your Team Working Agreement can help your team understand what's most important to the team's codebase standards.

Figure 4.1   An example of a naming standards attribute ranking. Added to your team's working agreement, it can help resolve debates over variable names.

Ideal TWA guideline 2
Team naming conventions and standards

4.2.3   *Scenario 3: To approve or not to approve?*

Jimmy is reviewing Jana's PR. In it, he finds a few things he doesn't like: a missing line break in this function and some indentation. The typical details Jimmy always finds. By the time he finishes with Jana's PR, there are about 35 comments left for Jana to review.

As anyone with 35 comments on their PR, Jana is first a bit nervous but then irked. She quickly accepts most of Jimmy's subjective suggestions but ignores the others—specifically, the comments about the line breaks. She returns the PR for Jimmy to re-evaluate. Jimmy quickly scans his comments and is happy to see that Jana has accepted them—that is, until he sees that his line break suggestions were ignored. He restores those comments and returns the PR to Jana. I'm sure you can see where this is going.

Jana reviews the "new" comments. Visibly frustrated, she starts a conversation with Jimmy and explains that his preferences make no difference to the codebase. Further, he shouldn't be withholding her PR's approval because of these things. Jimmy disagrees. He says that the cleanliness of the codebase is important and that his coding style has been the cleanest of the team members. He won't approve the PR until the code is to his liking.

This is another classic scenario where a TWA would be helpful. As we can see, Jimmy cares about the cleanliness of the codebase, and that isn't a bad thing. The way he goes about it, however, isn't the best way to do it. By favoring his personal coding style and using his reviewer privileges to enforce them on the team, he rightfully builds resentment and mistrust with the rest of his colleagues. Instead, team coding standards should be developed, discussed, and agreed upon before adding to the TWA. In this way, everyone's input can be combined into a cohesive set of standards the whole team can follow.

Jana, on the other hand, rightfully gets upset when Jimmy doesn't approve her PR. Small, subjective items like the ones Jimmy pointed out should never hold back a PR. In lieu of this disagreeable exchange, two things can be done. First, a style guide and formatter should be used to enforce the team's coding style during development. This step alone would likely eliminate PR comments like Jimmy's. Second, a policy clearly stating what constitutes withholding a PR approval is perfect for a TWA. In this case, trivial items, like the ones Jimmy pointed out, would not warrant the withholding of approval. Exceptions, like waiting for a planned maintenance window to finish before integrating code, could constitute withholding approval. It would also be wise to distinguish what withholding an approval means versus rejecting a PR outright. Clearer policies and spelled-out examples in the Team Working Agreement will make it more effective for everyone.

> **Ideal TWA guidelines 3 and 4**
> Blocking versus nonblocking issues
>
> Team style guide

4.3 Establishing a TWA with your team

There are many components a TWA can include. Some are more important than others and should always be part of your own. Remember those guidelines you established in chapter 3? That's a perfect starting point for your Team Working Agreement. So, really, you've already established a TWA with your team; they just don't know it yet 😊. As we'll see in the rest of this chapter, there are other components you can consider adding, like your codebase standards, team policies, and any relevant items that might affect your code review process. As you consider the options, remember the decisive questions you must answer as a team: How do we want to interact with each other, and what kind of team atmosphere do we endeavor to create? These guiding questions will enable your team to come together, co-create, and collectively own how your team operates.

To truthfully answer these questions, it will take input from all individuals on your team, so make sure to accommodate everyone. At first, it might seem silly to ask your colleagues to discuss their thoughts on professional behavioral expectations. If done in an empathetic and structured way, though, these conversations may yield the most valuable insight into your team—insights that will shape the policies and guidelines you add to your unique team working agreement.

4.3.1   *Do we really need a TWA?*

If you're still having trouble getting your team to talk, ask them to consider this question: Would you rather have clarity around our code review expectations or assume we all know and agree to our process? Yes, it's a bit of a loaded question, but it should kickstart some thoughts your team may not have considered. Let's look at a common scenario.

Say Magnus leaves detailed feedback on his code reviews as a reviewer. He leaves many comments but ensures they are all context-filled and have a focused outcome. On the other hand, Matthew barely leaves feedback on the PRs he reviews. Maybe there's a comment or two, but they are vague and don't really help the author. This kind of disparity happens often when teams don't discuss what level of detail is expected in reviewer feedback.

As another example, say Hannes places his code up for review in a PR. He receives a few pieces of feedback, addresses some of the comments, marks the other comments as resolved without addressing them, and continues to ask the reviewer for approval.

Reviewer: Have you had a
chance to look at my feedback?

Author: Yep.

What should be done in this scenario? Do all reviewer comments need to be addressed? Can a code review be considered complete simply by closing all comments on it? Can reviewers reopen comments that were not addressed but marked as resolved? Without clear and documented expectations, these kinds of scenarios can break trust and confidence in the system over time, regardless of whether they're intentional or not.

I'll state the following many times in this book: expectations that are not clearly defined usually lead to undesirable outcomes. In our first example with varying feedback levels, the undesired results are twofold. First, the review is inconsistent for everyone involved. Reviewers don't know or aren't expected to leave an acceptable amount of feedback. Second, there is unnecessary uncertainty for the authors. Sometimes authors get an "easy" reviewer who gives the good ol' thumbs up right away. Other times, they get the person that nitpicks everything. Without some assurance that each review will be done thoroughly and with the same diligence each time, developers can start to mistrust or dread reviews altogether.

In our second example regarding addressing comments, real resentment and frustration can grow between colleagues. Reviewers may feel their reviews are futile if authors don't address their feedback. Authors may feel frustrated if they must address feedback they think is irrelevant. While common sense and assumptions dictate that you address all meaningful feedback, what counts as meaningful to some may not be meaningful to others. If a reviewer leaves feedback that says a unit test for a really unlikely edge case is missing, should the author address it? You can hope to have a diligent author who agrees, adds the unit test, and goes on their merry way. You can expect some authors won't want to do the extra work, ignore the feedback, and wonder why their PR isn't approved yet. You can also be sure that every developer knows what's fair to address by outlining that information in your Team Working Agreement.

There are different questions to answer and things to consider depending on the role. As an author, you should consider the following questions:

- What level of detail is required before opening a PR?
- Do I have to address every comment a reviewer leaves?
- How long should a review take? If I hear no response or see no activity, when is it appropriate to follow up with the reviewer?
- What's a reasonable response time to addressing feedback on my PR?
- How is feedback handled? Do I make an update to the original PR with new commits or open a new PR with the changes?
- What options are possible when I don't agree with a reviewer's feedback or requested changes?

As a reviewer, you should consider the following:

- What should I be looking for during my review?
- What scope of feedback is reasonable to include in my review?
- When should I take a conversation offline?
- How should I request major changes to a PR?
- How many feedback/address feedback cycles should be considered normal?
- How do I handle pushback or disagreements with my feedback?
- What are the approval guidelines?
- Do my responsibilities end once I've approved the PR? If not, what are the next steps?

These items cover many foundational topics your team should consider and have explicit answers for in your TWA. If your team has trouble deciding how to answer these questions or needs some inspiration from how other engineering teams have outlined their process, I highly encourage you to check out the following resources:

- *Google's Engineering Practices—Code Review* (https://mng.bz/1aOj)—Google's engineering team has a dedicated documentation devoted to all the things their teams could possibly want to know about code reviews at Google. From "How to Do a Code Review" (https://mng.bz/PNgn) to "Writing Good CL Descriptions" (https://mng.bz/JN4V) to Handling Pushback in Code Reviews (https://mng .bz/w5GP), their documentation is a great start to writing your own.

- *GitLab Code Review Guidelines* (https://mng.bz/q0ar)—A lengthy guide that combines best practices and advice for performing code reviews and having your code review, GitLab provides another great resource to draw from and adapt in your own team. From defining what a Domain expert is (https://mng.bz/759v) and why they should be considered as a reviewer to listing out the responsibilities of the merge author (https://mng.bz/mRQa), GitLab has done an excellent job spelling out the implicit expectations that surround their code review processes.

- *U.S. GSA Technology Transformation Services Guide—Code Review* (https://engineering .18f.gov/code-review/)—Part of a broader best practices guide, the U.S. General Services Administration's Technology Transformation Services department (that's a large name, phew) crafted this document to be the standard way their development teams operate. One of those best practices is their code review guide, which focuses on "a friendly guide for reviewing code—and not each other—at TTS." How awesome is that?

- *Yelp Engineering Code Review Guidelines* (https://mng.bz/5O0O)—Although written a few years back, the content remains relevant and is another good example of how to clearly define code review expectations. Yelp's engineering team chooses to separate the guidelines sequentially by the phases of their review. So, if you want to know what to expect when preparing your code for review (https:// mng.bz/6YKe) or what to do when reviewing code (https://mng.bz/o0yZ), their guidelines walk you through the entire process.

These should give your team a great start and act as meaningful conversation starters. Feel free to reference these while you go through this chapter and as you put together your own team's TWA.

4.4   *What to consider including in your TWA*

The most important and, arguably, the most difficult component to include in your TWA is the team's social expectations. These are items often categorized as "obvious," "known to everyone," or "simply understood." Yet, the opposite is more likely the case. This component makes the TWA invaluable as it resolves—and can even prevent— many of the grievances we have with bad code reviews. We've covered the essentials in chapter 3; let's take a look at some more topics that will likely be beneficial to add to your TWA.

4.4.1   *More implicit code review expectations*

Everyone knows what a complete and properly prepared PR looks like, right? Everyone agrees that nitpicks are fair to point out in a code review, right? Oh, and everyone should know that 6 hours is more than enough time for a reviewer to respond to a PR, duh!

Not exactly.

These kinds of implicit expectations are radically different among individuals on a team. They vary based on every developer's experience and preference. They can change over time and throughout their career. As previously mentioned, these are the crucial but potentially divisive items to discuss and agree on with your colleagues. However, once everyone's expectations are made explicit and clear to the entire team, you'll find that processes and team dynamics will flourish.

In the last chapter, we discussed some essential guidelines for your team to set. Codify them and upgrade that document into your first TWA! Now it's official. With those as a starting point, let's see some other code review expectations to discuss with your team and consider including in your TWA.

4.4.2 *Reasonable response times*

Response times to both the initially submitted PR and PR comments are an excellent thing to codify in your TWA. Everyone has different expectations. Faster-paced developers may expect their teammates to review their PR right away, even expecting a 2- to 4-hour turnaround time. Others may take their time to give a thorough review, doing it during random spurts of free time. This review method could lead to turnaround times of one or two days. Then, there are the outliers that either never respond, never review others' PRs, or just take too long, rendering the code review process inefficient. Add to that the complexity of globally distributed teams. What makes sense then?

To counter these effects and to transform implied expectations into openly stated ones, decide reasonable response times for your team. Then, codify them into your team working agreement.

DETERMINING RESPONSE TIMES FOR YOUR TEAM

What's "reasonable" will highly depend on the size and composition of your team. Are you a small group located in a single office? A 12-hour response time could be quite reasonable. A team of 14 spread across Pacific and Eastern time zones may need a bit more flexibility of, say, a 24- to 36-hour response time. How about a fully distributed team all around the world? A two-day response time keeps things manageable but reasonable. An ideal way to find a starting point is to first see how you compare to three of the four DORA metrics.

- *How fast do you deploy?* If your team falls within the Low to Medium categorizations (either deploying once a week to once a month or once a month to once every six months, respectively) for the deployment frequency metric, a look at your current review phases is valid. If not, great; you can likely look to other parts of your deployment pipeline to see whether there are other bottlenecks.
- *How quick is your lead time for changes?* Another metric to consider is how long it takes for committed code to successfully reach and run in production. A low-performing team takes between one month and six months, while a medium-performing team takes between one week and one month. If you fall into one of these categories, taking a look at your review process is warranted.

- *What is your change failure rate?* Lastly, what percentage of changes to production (or released to users) result in production issues (either an outage or impairment to service)? Low-performing teams have a high change failure rate, between 46% and 60%. Medium-performing teams are also quite high, with a change failure rate between 16% and 45%. As before, this warrants a look at your code reviews to see whether they contribute to a higher change failure rate.

WHAT TO DO IF YOUR CODE REVIEWS ARE A BOTTLENECK

If you find that code reviews take too long or contribute to longer deployment times, slower lead time for changes, or higher change failure rates, try to determine why:

- *Consideration 1—Is there a single person whose approval is generally required, causing the bottleneck?* Try spreading that person's knowledge over time to lessen the dependency and burden of being "the most important PR approver." We talk more about this subject in chapter 8.
- *Consideration 2—What if you work with a team halfway around the world?* This situation is quite common and can cause all kinds of delays, the most significant one likely being the time offset between the teams. One great suggestion for this problem is to "bookend your day" [2] with these other teams. This method advocates for at least two meetings (or periods of active availability) between the teams, once during one team's morning and another during their afternoon (figure 4.2). This process allows both teams to communicate more than once, answer any questions raised since the first meeting, and provide feedback within the same day. It also lessens the effect of the time offset and sets up the "currently awake" team for success, picking up where the "about to go offline" team left off. However, this option may be limited to teams who have less than a 7-hour offset between them.

  Make no mistake—this arrangement can be physically taxing as one team will either have to be awake really late or really early to make that second "bookend" meeting happen. A more realistic and less involved approach may be to proactively check your messaging platform or email to see whether you can answer any quick questions that may unblock your distributed teammates. Otherwise, the other bookend might be committing to answering questions and responding to the distributed team's feedback within the first few hours of your team's workday. There's also the possibility of asking for AI's help, which is discussed in chapter 13 🐾.

- *Consideration 3—Are many discussions and clarifications happening during the code review, inevitably causing a delay (and maybe even some rework)?* Encourage your team to have earlier and more frequent discussions to rule out misunderstandings. See if requirements, work tickets, or assigned tasks can be made clearer, filled with more context, and are not missing vital information the developer needs to do their job successfully. As a tech lead or engineering manager, continuously find opportunities for your team to gain understanding and context

Bookending Days

"Bookend" your days with distributed teams.

Have at least one meeting where you can all be together and answer questions or pass on updates to the next team.

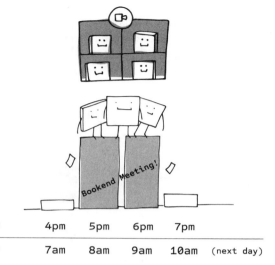

Las Vegas (Pacific Standard Time)	4pm	5pm	6pm	7pm	
Baguio City (Philippine Standard Time)	7am	8am	9am	10am	(next day)

Figure 4.2   Distributed teams can use bookend meetings to decrease code review delays.

faster and earlier and support them in their knowledge-sharing and gathering tasks. The more you can do before the code review, the less likely it is for the code review to become the bottleneck.

Lastly, have a simple chat with your team. Ask each individual to recount a positive PR workflow. Plot out some key data points from each person's experience: How long did the process take from submission to approval? How many people were involved? What time zones were the involved parties in? How easy/difficult was it to get in contact with either the reviewer or author when needed?

After aggregating all this information, determine whether there are clear ranges of response times that people are happy with that coincide with improving your metrics. Say the ideal response time is 10 hours, but the expected response time is two workdays. Ranges like this can keep your team happy while slowly contributing to faster deployments, faster lead times for changes, and lower change failure rates. As your team gets comfortable with the pace of code reviews and keeps steady metrics, you can choose to be more aggressive with your response times. Incremental improvements like this can take you from those initial Low or Medium categorizations to High or Elite!

> **TIP**   If you have some trickier situations, check out chapter 8, which focuses on even more reasons why a code review can be delayed (and how to deal with it, of course)!

4.4.3   *Reasonable PR sizes*

Another excellent guideline to establish in your TWA is the definition of a reasonable PR size. It's a great way to officially say, "No, Josh, 544 files in a single PR is *not* reasonable." This determination will also serve as a helpful guideline for anyone who expects to change your codebase. Feel free to reuse the standards on PR sizes in figure 4.3 (just as I reused my own figure 😊).

A Manageable PR...

Focuses on an atomic change or feature

Includes only the relevant files needed

Splits multiple parts into multiple reviews

Likely can be reviewed in 10 - 20 minutes

Is typically under 500 lines of code*

Is typically less than 20 files changed**

*Based on study by Dragan Stepanović

**Based on study by Microsoft

Figure 4.3   Reasonable PR size guidelines (yes, you've seen this image before)

Even better, find examples of PRs that your team considers manageable or showcase the ideal PR. If you don't have those yet, keep an eye out for them as your team starts to adjust to their code review process.

4.4.4   *Issue identification*

Code reviews can do a lot for the team, but without some clear boundaries, they can also be overloaded with too many responsibilities. This is clearly seen with the variety of topics that tend to come up during this phase. Instead, spell out which problems should be caught way before the review and which ones can still be dealt with if found during the review. Doing so can help the team avoid PRs with tough problems—problems that, if found during the code review, are almost impossible to rectify in time.

Usually, the issues that surface during a code review fall into one of three categories: obvious, expected, and tough. Let's dive into each of these categories.

OBVIOUS ISSUES

Obvious issues are usually matters that can—and should—be caught much earlier than the code review. With the plethora of tooling available, fixes for these problems can be applied right away. Alternatively, these are also great candidates to run through an automated precheck on PR submission. If this precheck fails, it should not be considered a properly prepared PR. These things include

- *Abandoned* TODOs—You've seen these (`//TODO: Maybe, but probably never`). If these are still lying around, the code could be unfinished. If it's a forgotten remnant, it should be flagged and fixed.
- *Spelling and grammar*—Spelling and grammar tools are quite prevalent and usually built-in, even in IDEs (integrated development environments). They should be run as part of a precheck before submitting a PR!
- *Forgotten code*—Unused variables, code that has been commented out but not removed, debugging code (looking at you, `console.log()`!), and other snippets that shouldn't sneak their way into a PR.
- *Comment concerns*—Add missing comments, if required by team standards or if they would better clarify certain lines of code; remove incorrect, incomplete, or unnecessary comments that don't add value; and check for copypasted blocks of code where comments have not been updated.
- *Lint*—Simple or common mistakes; items that don't meet best practices or recommended style guides for your used languages/ frameworks. (We'll discuss linters in more detail in chapter 5.)
- *Style consistency*—Code doesn't look like the code around it (excluding refactors or architectural cleanups); fails to meet team style standards.
- *Language conventions*—Code is inappropriate for the current language or framework.
- *In-house coding standards*—Code doesn't follow team/company guidelines or rules for coding standards.

I strongly suggest keeping obvious issues out of the code review! You may find some things still escape your linter or prechecks and make it into your PRs. When this happens, make sure to take note of and monitor it. If the problem reoccurs more than three times, a new linting rule may be warranted, or a tweak to your pre-checks may solve the problem. We'll get into the whole slew of automations that help you in chapter 5.

EXPECTED ISSUES

Next up, expected issues. These are typical problems developers expect to look for and point out in a code review. They include

- *Readability and maintainability*—Code may not be understood in the next six months (or right now, for that matter); if the original author leaves the company (i.e., the "Vacation Factor"; see chapter 3, section 3.1.3), no one will be able to maintain it.

- *Complexity*—The code is too hard to follow; maybe two giant classes cram everything within them, maybe there are too many layers to jump to for a simple method, or maybe things are a bit too abstracted and the original intent is lost. Depending on how complex things get, complexity could easily turn into a tough issue.
- *Security*—Code introduces vulnerabilities that could compromise the system or personal, sensitive, or proprietary data. Depending on the severity, security could also qualify as a tough issue.
- *Smells and patterns*—Code is poorly structured or features a familiar code smell. It might be misapplying a pattern or could benefit from using a pattern.
- *Naming*—Things are not well named; functions/methods/classes/variables are unclear or ambiguous; methods can only be understood by reading the comments.
- *Approach consistency*—The same area of code uses two (or more!) different approaches to do the same thing.
- *Performance*—Code will start having problems once it hits production or any sort of scale. Depending on the severity, performance could also qualify as a tough issue.
- *Edge cases*—Code hasn't considered or does not handle rare but possible use cases; code could act in an undefined manner in some circumstances.
- *Insufficient logging*—Not enough logging in place (especially for risky code) to tell that it has gone wrong or why.
- *Hacks*—Something just doesn't feel right. It looks like a hack or workaround. It could be fine, but clarification to understand the thinking behind the code is warranted.
- *The old way of doing things*—Best practices change. Engineering team standards can also change. Sometimes, you don't realize you're using an outdated approach until the code review.
- *Reinventing the wheel*—This task could have been completed using some preexisting code; a shared library could have been used; utility code has been reimplemented.
- *Coverage*—New functionality is not covered in unit tests. Significant use cases are not covered.
- *Common pitfalls*—Lessons you've learned the hard way; quirks in a framework, library, or shared component you've experienced; specific customers with unique setups that require additional care.

Your list of expected issues may vary or even fall into the other categories. Whatever they may be, clarify to your reviewers exactly what they should be spending time looking for. By focusing on the things that matter, less time is wasted on the fluff.

TOUGH ISSUES

Finally, we have the tough issues. These are sometimes difficult to spot during a code review. Ideally, they are also issues that are better caught earlier in the development process. What makes these issues tough is that finding them during the code review complicates the choices: Is the current code unacceptable enough that rework is warranted, resulting in a delayed timeline, or do you accept the work already done and willingly introduce technical debt into your system? Tough issues include the following:

- *The PR is too large*—The PR has too many unrelated changes combined into a single PR, has too many files or lines of code to review in a single sitting, or is otherwise too difficult to effectively leave feedback on as it will be tricky to implement. This is especially true if the author can't unravel the PR and organize them into smaller, logical changes.
- *Architectural problems*—Overall, the high-level approach taken is incorrect.
- *Introducing new things*—PR introduces new patterns, libraries, or tools to the team or project *without* prior discussion or agreement.
- *Doesn't meet the requirements*—Code doesn't address what the business requested, partially implements requested components, or fails to meet acceptance criteria.
- *Misunderstood requirements*—Code solves the wrong problem.
- *Bugs*—Subtle, hidden, or unnoticed problems; bugs not caught in static analysis or automated tests or require a deep history of the application or its nuances.

As much as possible, try to prevent tough issues from ever making it into a code review. Some methods you can implement are thoroughly discussing new features and developing clear acceptance criteria for each feature. Facilitate an environment where anyone can ask anyone else a question or for clarification, especially if it's during the development phase. Make clear that asking for help—within reason—is not a negative thing. You'll notice that these all depend on one key component: affording your team the psychological safety to engage in these behaviors.

As a team lead, principal engineer, manager, or someone in a mentoring position, it is especially important to keep an eye on these things. Encourage junior developers, new team members, and less talkative members to contribute to discussions. Allow everyone to contribute in different ways—some people are more comfortable speaking up during an in-person meeting or unmuting their mic and giving their opinions. Some fare better by typing their thoughts in the chat; some prefer to write their ideas down before, during, and after a meeting before submitting them to the larger group. Some are most at ease when in a one-on-one discussion. Find what works for your team so that none of your developers' voices are ignored.

4.4.5 Self-approving PRs

While self-approving PRs is something that can be automatically enforced, I still want to discuss it here because (a) you may not have configured your tool to enforce something like this yet (and are working on the honor system) or (b) even with a tool configured to prohibit self-approvals, there may be crafty workarounds or explicit permissions given to your team that still allow for a self-approved PR. So, still worth a discussion 😊.

Another implicit expectation most teams have is "Don't approve your own PR!" Many developers understand this principle as something obvious. Many developers also understand that self-approving a PR intentionally skips the review process. Others think it's no big deal to approve their own PR. And yet, depending on the current environment of your team, their expectations on this matter could fall on either end of this spectrum.

Does your team naturally encourage conversations with each other? Do they feel like they can discuss implementation strategies without it becoming a heated debate? Does soliciting an opinion or having someone double-check a line or two of code seem "normal"? If so, your team likely also understands that approving their own PRs is not something the team does. It should also be an easy policy to add to your team's working agreement.

On the other hand, do the individual members of your team usually keep to themselves? Do conversations about features or bugs only happen once, either during a planning or design phase? Is there a competitive undertone to the way your team works? Is producing something and deploying it as quickly as possible praised and indirectly rewarded? Then your team might not realize approving one's own PR has many consequences. Similarly, they may take issue with a policy prohibiting doing so in the TWA.

If your team struggles to agree on this topic, consider reminding everyone of the TWA's purpose: to define how the team wants to interact with each other and what kind of team atmosphere they endeavor to create. This discussion is particularly important if you are a team lead or manager and doubly so if you're also trying to improve the dynamics of your team. Encouraging an objective and sustainable path forward for your code review should be reassuring to the team.

Another evidence-based strategy? Bring up any recent production problems or a negative change in DORA or other team metrics that can be traced back to a self-approved PR. Doing this in a nonconfrontational way with the self-approver can show the direct impact of their unreviewed, self-approved PR. Discussing this during a one-on-one meeting can give the developer a chance to grow from the feedback; if your team is already comfortable with more direct and open feedback during group settings, then colleagues may already have brought this up as well.

There is exactly one exception to this rule: if previously discussed and documented by the team, a developer can approve their own PR through an exception with a valid purpose. This statement means a few things. First, the code review tools you use need to have this capability. If so, these settings need to be configured to allow a PR to be approved by its author. Second, exceptions with a valid purpose usually describe one-off or emergency scenarios. So, engaging in self-approving a PR is truly an exception and should never evolve into a norm. Third, since self-approving PRs should only occur during emergencies, the process should be paired with an Emergency Playbook entry (something we discuss in chapter 10). The acceptable reasons to self-approve a PR should be listed clearly, and again, it should be emphasized that this is a one-off scenario. Lastly, but most significantly, the team's understanding of this process needs to be clear: approving your own PR is only allowed under very specific, documented, and clear circumstances.

4.4.6   Nitpicks

Indentation, inconsequential naming preferences, line spacing, and more—these are the nitpicks we hate getting blocked for! (*Pats self on the back for unexpected rhyme.*) Nitpicks, which are small, trivial, and insignificant items flagged by a reviewer that don't affect the quality of the code, should never reach the PR. More importantly, they shouldn't block a PR from being approved. I explain how to enforce this point through the use of a team style guide, automated tools, or both in chapter 5. We also discussed them as a nonblocking issue in chapter 3.

A formal definition of nitpick reads "to criticize by focusing on inconsequential details" [3], which is pretty apt! In the context of a code review, nitpicks are things like a missing space, a seemingly unnecessary line break somewhere in the code, or some other purely subjective preference. It neither improves nor deteriorates the codebase as a whole. It is truly a *nitpick*, as seen in figure 4.4.

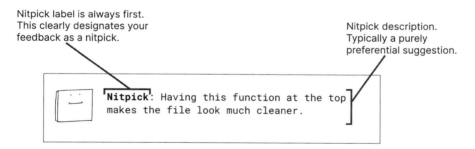

Nitpick label is always first.
This clearly designates your
feedback as a nitpick.

Nitpick description.
Typically a purely
preferential suggestion.

Nitpick: Having this function at the top
makes the file look much cleaner.

Figure 4.4   Nitpick in a code review. Eww.

Nitpicks aren't always a problem; they only become a problem when a reviewer withholds approving a PR because of one. While many things in this book will rely on what works for your team, on this one aspect, I have a much more opinionated stance: label nitpicks as nitpicks and do not withhold PRs because of a nitpick.

This behavioral expectation is very common and should be stated and clarified in your TWA. Even self-proclaimed code perfectionists can attest to the value of leaving nitpicks behind. If you have some team members like this, try conducting a one-month experiment: stop nitpicking altogether—no comments pointing out nitpicks, no blocking PRs because of nitpicks, and no conversing with the PR author about nitpicks. At the end of the month, discuss how the team handled the experiment.

What are your predictions? Will your team love this or hate this? Will the *signal-to-noise* ratio, the number of actual critical problems spotted compared to the number of insignificant ones—in this case, nitpicks—be better or worse? Will the code review process be seen in a more positive or negative light? You'll likely conclude with the same results as Dan Lew, a programmer who did the same experiment with his team [4]: signal-to-noise ratio improves, and everyone's relationships with code reviews and those who conduct them improve.

It isn't hard to see why Dan, and likely your team, will arrive at the same conclusion: think of a PR with four nitpicks and one critical problem to address. When receiving the list of comments with this feedback, the author will want to finish addressing them all as quickly as possible. As the author fusses to fix those nitpicks, the single critical problem can fall to the wayside or seem less important. In the worst-case scenario, it gets overlooked or forgotten. Eliminating nitpicks altogether, there would be a single, valid comment on the PR. With this arrangement, the author can instead focus all their attention on the critical problem—they can look into the signal and ignore the noise (the nitpicks).

Make no mistake—nitpicks can still pop up unintentionally in a PR. That's where your CI pipeline comes into play, acting as a safeguard to your codebase and working hand-in-hand with your linters. Again, more on that in chapter 5, which focuses on automation.

4.4.7 *Positive review environment*

One of the silliest but necessary guidelines to set is that of being civil with each other. You might think, "Do we really need to codify 'Don't be a jerk!' in official documentation"? And I'll answer with an enthusiastic yes! It's no secret that code reviews can sometimes bring out the negativity in people.

While we hope that's not the norm on your team, it never hurts to have explicit guidelines on conduct during your process. Think of it like a conference's Code of Conduct (aka "the Code"). Attendees are expected to behave a certain way, with expectations that may seem obvious to everyone. Still, these social and behavioral expectations of what is allowed and what isn't are clearly defined, along with the consequences if someone goes against the Code. The Code is also clearly displayed on the event's website, reaffirmed on social media, and, most of the time, is even a requirement to acknowledge when buying a ticket. Finally, a Code gives the organizers recourse and justification to kick someone out of the event should an attendee fail to adhere to the Code. Further consequences may follow that person, like being banned from the event indefinitely.

Your team's code of conduct can be set through the TWA. A dedicated section is likely all you'll need. Be as explicit or straight to the point as it fits your team. You can get by with a "Respect each other and make the review about the code, not your colleague" to something closer to a full code of conduct. By establishing this in a public and official location like your TWA, "obvious" professional behavioral expectations are made explicit to everyone (as are the consequences if these expectations are not met), and tech leads or managers can justify any further consequences if needed.

4.4.8   *What happens when a policy is violated?*

For the policies you set forth in the TWA to be useful, consequences must also be stated when a serious violation occurs. Generally, the best place to state these consequences is right next to the policy it belongs to. Additionally, all team members are encouraged to call out any violations and bring them up in the appropriate forums—like your team retrospectives or one-on-one meetings.

"Higher stakes" violations should always be reprimanded. Self-approving a PR without an emergency (when the team has agreed to prohibit it) could be met with revoking PR privileges. Harsh or nasty comments could be met with required empathy training and a documented record of the occurrence. Depending on the severity, not adhering to the team's reasonable response times could result in more frequent reminders (like sending a notification email every hour until the reviewer responds) or even escalation to a manager (when reminder emails make no difference and it is well past a reasonable response time). These are just a few examples; the consequences for your own team's policy violations can be lighter or harsher. It's up to your team. If possible and willing, bringing in your company's HR department can be an option to help enforce the most drastic of violations.

On the other hand, "lower stakes" consequences (like buying coffee for everyone at the next meeting if you're late to today's meeting; coffee gift cards for your remote teammates) can be an alternative way to enforce policies if it makes sense for your team. The most important thing to remember with these kinds of consequences is that they should still be enforced! Otherwise, team members won't take them seriously, making it easier to carelessly or willingly violate the policies your team has set forth.

4.5   *This TWA is the team's document now*

The TWA is a "living" document, meaning changes are possible, encouraged, and expected. The first edition you co-create is not set in stone; rather, it's written on an Etch-A-Sketch (the one with a stylus because who wants to deal with knobs?). Just as you can easily shake this mechanical board to erase what you've previously drawn to create something new, you can continuously revise, revamp, and rewrite your TWA.

The TWA is also the responsibility of the entire team. Therefore, all members should be co-creators, enforcers, and maintainers of the TWA. The TWA needs to be visible to all and easily accessible to all. And when team members leave and new ones join, ease of user management is critical. All things considered, this makes the TWA an excellent item to keep version controlled! Moreover, the TWA should be the first item that passes through your team's newly established code review process.

Maintaining your TWA through a system you'll already be using makes it possible to refine. This is essential: if the process of changing or updating your TWA is too cumbersome, it will be easier for your team to ignore. The longer your team ignores and does not use the TWA, the easier it will be to neglect it.

4.5.1 *Need to make a change?*

As your team, application, and certainly your processes evolve, refining your TWA to match is critical to keeping it a useful document. The key is to make the change process a manageable one. So how do you do that?

Assuming you have taken the suggestion to keep your TWA in a repo, anyone can propose a change (via a PR, of course), and it can be done at any time! If your team notices that something is not working out, a process needs a slight tweak, or a policy is missing, it should be as simple as filing an issue ticket and then, eventually, a PR. Everyone on the team should be notified of the proposed change. A discussion can be held on the PR itself, and after gathering and ruminating on everyone's thoughts, the change is approved by all or not. Notice that this requires everyone's approval. This means the PR rules for this repository need to be slightly different, especially if your normal code review process requires fewer approvals. This usually leads to further discussion and an eventual decision or compromise. Most of the time, however, changes that clearly benefit the entire team will have no problem being accepted by the entire team.

4.5.2 *Final thoughts*

The team working agreement is just like any other work your team is responsible for—even this code review process you've set out to build. You need to keep it up-to-date, make changes to it when something's not working, ensure changes are possible and easy to do, and evolve it over time as the team requires it. Just as a collective sense of ownership and accountability of your codebase can create a great application, collectively owning the TWA and keeping each other accountable to the guidelines and policies can create a great team.

Summary

- The TWA transforms implicit social expectations into explicit, enforceable ones. It includes policies and standards developed and enforced by the team.
- TWAs should be used for policies and guidelines that can't be automatically enforced. Whether through tooling, scripts, or software, your team can ensure a repeatable, objective, and scalable process if you make automation its backbone. For all other things that can't be automatically set, the team working agreement comes into play.
- A lack of clear expectations around your process can build mistrust and animosity among your team. In addition to documenting the process, document the implicit expectations your team, both authors and reviewers, has for a code review in your TWA.
- TWAs should clearly state how you want to interact with each other and what kind of team atmosphere you endeavor to create. Include implicit expectations,

like reasonable response times and dealing with nitpicks and reviewer focus areas, among other things.

- A TWA's usefulness is determined by the team; keeping the TWA visible and accessible to all is paramount. Continuously refining it to meet the needs of the team is key to keeping it relevant.

- The TWA is the entire team's responsibility. Therefore, all members should be co-creators, enforcers, and maintainers of the TWA. As team members leave and others join, access to the TWA should follow accordingly.

- The TWA is a living document, meaning it is not set in stone once the first version is completed, which is a good thing. Refinements, updates, and changes to the TWA are encouraged.

- Making the TWA easy to change is essential; the more cumbersome the process, the likelier your team will ignore or neglect it. The best way to maintain it is to keep it version controlled and use your code review process with it!

- Treat your TWA just like any other bit of work; collectively owning the document and keeping each other accountable to the policies you've codified makes it effective and invaluable.

References

[1] Scrum Alliance. (n.d.). What is scrum? https://www.scrumalliance.org/about-scrum

[2] Rasch, N. (2020, November 17). Things I've learned working effectively with offshore teams. https://mng.bz/n0X5

[3] Nitpick. (n.d.). Dictionary.com. https://www.dictionary.com/browse/nitpick

[4] Lew, D. (2021, February 23). Stop nitpicking in code reviews. https://mng.bz/vJYp

The advantages
of automation

5

This chapter covers

- The importance of automation
- Automation tactics and strategies
- Optimization opportunities that produce a more effective code review
- Building objectivity into the process through automation

As developers, we get paid a pretty penny to solve complex problems. Our skills and experience play a part in this, but our judgment and reasoning allow us to command generous compensation. It's the understanding of nuance, the clarifying of the unclear, and the creative application of code that help us solve intricate problems. Unfortunately, many of us hardly get the uninterrupted time and space we need to use these strengths. Especially in the context of code reviews, there's busy work, manual errands, and tedious tasks that get in the way.

This is where automation steps in to save the day. By letting the robots take care of the tedious, we can create the space we need to truly focus—and do what we do best.

NOTE The first part of this chapter discusses the importance of a team style guide and introduces formatting, linting, static analysis, and automated testing. If you already know what those things are or are currently employing these automations during your development process, feel free to skip those sections and head straight to section 5.4!

5.1 *Automation as an asset*

Imagine reviewing a PR in 20 minutes. Sounds impossible, right? With the right things automated, it is actually quite possible. Code reviews can take a while because of several factors. The majority, however, is noise. Okoye is new and unsure who to add as a reviewer. Stan is focusing on low-stakes problems, leaving an overwhelming amount of comments. Emilio is searching for context and clarity that should have been provided with the PR. Xiu is following up with Rosa (again) to fix her PR title and description to match their team standards. And Tim hasn't looked at his assigned PRs for more than a week. Our energy (except for Tim's, apparently) is wasted on minor tasks like these. However, by automating them away, you'll find that code reviews can be performed much faster—not to mention, with better quality.

On one of my former teams, there was a constant battle with colleagues forgetting to remove debugging code from their PRs. Countless hours were wasted as we all sifted through files carefully, making sure we didn't have a spare `console.log("here!")` or two hiding in our code. One particularly busy week, I had enough of the long, tedious PR reviews due to this manual scanning of leftover code. After a few hours of research, I proposed using ESLint (https://eslint.org/) to my team, even if we only started with a single rule. With an extension (https://mng.bz/XV4v) for VSCode available, I was able to convince my team to install ESLint on their development environments and simply set `no-console: "error"` in the configuration file. I wish I had done this sooner.

Immediately after implementing this, my team no longer left a comment about a spare `console.log()` in a PR again. Once we saw the power of this single rule, we started seeking out other time wasters and low-stakes issues that bogged down our code review process: enforcing camel casing, preferring `const` declarations for variables that are never reassigned, and spacing and indentation preferences our team followed. As we automated more of these collective team style decisions and code conventions, we went from releasing once or twice every two weeks to once or twice a day! Of course, other factors played a role, but the most significant change came after adding the automations we could no longer live without.

Automation excels at the boring and annoying—the mundane and uninteresting tasks like linking associated work items or emailing review reminders, status checks on progress, and looking for missing line breaks in code. Often, these tasks are still necessary and important; they've just become the annoying part of code reviews. By the time we've completed these tasks, we've exhausted our mental focus and capacity. We'd rather quickly skim, or worse, carelessly approve a PR and hope for the best. Instead, we should be reserving the time we code review, along with our precious focus, to do a thorough and effective job. With automation, we can make sure that happens.

What cannot be automated is the human perspective and judgment—nuance, context, history, putting pieces together, and seeing the larger picture. These are all things that we, as developers, bring to code reviews and software development in general.

Automation can remind us that we are using an outdated library, recommend that we update it soon, and even do the upgrade for us. Human judgment tells us we can't proceed with the upgrade just yet because a few services rely on a particular feature—a feature that has unfortunately been removed in the latest version. Automation can enforce a const declaration for a variable; it can even change any var declarations it finds. However, it's our human understanding that recognizes a properly declared constant should have been a block-scoped variable rather than a global one and is the cause of a problem you are currently trying to debug.

As you begin analyzing your own team's process, look for the bottlenecks and time-wasters. Look for tasks that bog down your code reviews with low-stakes comments and nitpicks. Even if you start with a single automation, as I did with flagging leftover debug code to my colleagues, you'll start down a path that will likely optimize and refine your team's workflow. In the end, you'll find that through automation, the intent of the code review can be protected and preserved, permitting your team's human judgment, perspective, and understanding to decide whether the code they're looking at makes sense and adds value to the codebase and team.

5.2   *Automation prerequisites*

The possibilities automation promises are vast, but they do require some preparation. For tools and robots to do their job, some parameters need to be set; otherwise, how would they know what to do? And if we'd like to expand on the things we automate, we also need to ensure the capabilities exist in the tools we choose. Let's discuss some important prerequisites you should have for you to take advantage of automation.

5.2.1   *Team style guide*

While there are immutable conventions and best practices that shouldn't be changed when it comes to how we write, structure, and organize our code, there are still plenty of preferences around code style that usually lead to debates. Do we separate logical lines of code with a line break or two? Pascal, camel, snake, or kebab case? And let's not get started on spacing and indentation. Ultimately, we all (hopefully) want the same thing—to write good code. How we approach that and what defines good code stylistically are harder theories to qualify. Your team can try to do both through a style guide.

A style guide outlines a cohesive set of code style expectations a development team will adhere to. Through the use of rules, the core building block of formatting tools, good programming style can be automated and built-in rather than a debated afterthought.

As you might imagine, a good programming style is highly subjective: we know it when we see it. "Good" style also differs across languages and frameworks. However, if we rely on humans to make this judgment each time, it makes the action impossible to automate. Instead, a style guide captures the team's code style decisions into a ruleset that can be consistently enforced (or, better yet, applied) by a machine.

As a quick example, say your team would like to enforce a consistent brace style. As a team that primarily develops in JavaScript, you've opted to use a tool called ESLint to enforce this rule, among others. Deciding to use the Stroustrup brace style, a variant of one true brace style in JavaScript, the ESLint rule would be written like in the following listing.

Listing 5.1 ESLint Rule enforcing Stroustrup brace style

```
// eslint rule that enforces Stroustrup brace style.

brace-style: ["error", "stroustrup"]
```

Stroustrup brace style enforces the `else` statements (in an `if-else` construct), `catch` statements, and `finally` statements to be on their own line after the preceding closing brace. So, all of the JavaScript code in the following listing would not trigger the brace-style rule as they all correctly adhere to this rule.

Listing 5.2 Code adhering to Stroustrup brace style

```
/* examples of code correctly adhering to ESLint brace-style rule,
   currently set to Stroustrup style.
*/

function goodFunction() {
  return true;
}

if (goodStroustrup) {
  dontError();
}

if (goodStroustrup) {
  dontError();
}
```

```
else {
  error();
}

try {
  somethingRisky();
}
catch(e) {
  handleError();
}

class Customer {
   static {
       getCustomer();
   }
}

// when there are no braces, there are no problems
if (isValid) proceed();
else if (isNotValid) cancel();
```

To compare, the following shows examples of JavaScript code that *would* trigger this rule and flag it for the developer to see.

Listing 5.3   Code that triggers errors with Stroustrup brace style rule

```
/* examples of code incorrectly adhering to ESLint brace-style rule,
   currently set to Stroustrup style.
*/

function goodFunction()
{
  return true;
}

if (goodStroustrup)
{
  dontError();
}

if (goodStroustrup)
{
  dontError();
} else {
  error();
}

try
{
  somethingRisky();
} catch(e)
{
  handleError();
}
```

```
class Customer
{
    static
    {
        getCustomer();
    }
}
```

Can you see where this is going? This is just one of many rules that can be set up in your development environment. While these examples show some common JavaScript style options, the intent is the same for your team and language: having as many of your team's code style preferences enforced by rules like these (rather than through debates during a code review) saves so much time in the long run. No more arguing over brace styles indefinitely. Your team can fix low-stakes issues like these as they happen, keeping them out of the review phase for good.

5.2.2 *Capable tools*

Before diving into the opportunities automation presents, it's important to dedicate some time to choosing the appropriate tools. Specifically, a tool that helps your team put its intended automations into practice.

While not all of the following features must be present, they are needed to take advantage of the automation scenarios presented in this chapter. Here is a list of "must-haves" any code review tool you consider using should possess (and why):

- *PR prechecks*—The number of tedious tasks you can offload to an automated precheck is not trivial. The more complex the capabilities, the better! Look for tools that allow you to set up automated tasks when a PR is opened, integrate with bots that can perform more complex tasks, or even allow you to create your own tasks or scripts to run. Bonus points should be awarded if this tool can integrate with any development tools you already use. Having this feature in your proposed code review tool is also key to automating your author's responsibility of preparing their PR.

- *PR templates*—One specific invaluable feature is the PR Template (which we'll learn about shortly in section 5.4.1). If your tool can support the use of these, it is a tool worthy of consideration.

- *Linking*—Tools that allow linking mechanisms to files, ticket numbers, documentation, and any other supplemental information make PRs so much more valuable. Having all that context and info where you need it is another time-saving feature that is worth having. Extra bonus points if they can be configured as required items in a PR.

- *Threaded discussions/conversations*—As PRs are reviewed, feedback is discussed, and decisions are made, having a way to capture that in the context of a PR is quite helpful. Not only does this feature provide a historical account and record of what was discussed and decided, but it also provides remote workers—really any colleagues—a way to communicate in an asynchronous but tracked way.

- *Group and individual reviewer assignment*—Another "smart" feature to look for? The ability to assign reviewers to a PR in a variety of ways. At a minimum, assigning PRs to individual people or groups of people you create should be available. Fancier options, like auto-assigning specific people to specific PRs or the ability to "rotate" reviewers (randomly choose an assigned reviewer from a specified list), are interesting options to look for if you plan to take advantage of those automation opportunities.
- *Time-based notifications*—Finally, a small but mighty feature is the ability to automate the act of following up with others. Over time, all those nudges to look at a PR, "just checking on the status of . . ." messages or emails, or even walking over to your colleague's desk to follow up on a PR really add up. Finding a tool that lets you configure these kinds of follow-up notifications in a way that works with your team is another key feature your chosen tool should have.

As you've read through this list, you may have a tool in mind or could even be using it already. As we move onto the next few sections in this chapter, we will look into automation tactics that can be applied through open-source or free tools. At the end of this book will be an appendix that lists further suggestions based on language/framework or style of development, which can serve as a starting point for your team.

5.3   Automations before the review

The starting point for code review automation? The low-hanging fruit. The petty stuff. The stuff that shouldn't even reach the PR in the first place. If there's one area where your team can immediately apply and begin to see the benefits of automation, it's before the actual code review and during development.

Through formatting, linting, static analysis, and automated testing, you'll be able to reduce or even eliminate many unnecessary debates, fix lower-stakes issues proactively, and leave room for reviewers to focus on the more important issues in a code review. These mechanisms often overlap—both in the general understanding of developers and in some tools, which makes it a bit confusing to discuss these topics in a general way. For this section, I'll explain what each action generally entails before distinguishing how the actions might differ between programming languages and ecosystems. Regardless of *how*, let's see what we all should be doing long before the code review even begins.

5.3.1   Formatting

Starting at what I consider should always be automated, formatting is what makes sure code looks good (or at least consistent). I know, you might be thinking "good" looking code is subjective, and you're right.

Consider just three possible scenarios that could arise when it comes to line spacing. Developer A likes to leave spaces between variable declarations and the next line of logic, as the following listing demonstrates.

> **Listing 5.4 Line break spacing between variable declarations and logic (JavaScript)**

```javascript
function GetTotalDonutCalories() {

  const donutLog = [
    { day: 'Monday', totalEaten: 2 },
    { day: 'Tuesday', totalEaten: 1 },
    { day: 'Wednesday', totalEaten: 3 },
    { day: 'Thursday', totalEaten: 2 },
    { day: 'Friday', totalEaten: 4 },
  ];

  const caloriesConsumed = donutLog.reduce((lastCount, currentEntry));

  return caloriesConsumed;
}
```

Developer B doesn't, as the following listing shows.

> **Listing 5.5 No spacing between variable declarations and logic (JavaScript)**

```javascript
function GetTotalDonutCalories() {
  const donutLog = [
    { day: 'Monday', totalEaten: 2 },
    { day: 'Tuesday', totalEaten: 1 },
    { day: 'Wednesday', totalEaten: 3 },
    { day: 'Thursday', totalEaten: 2 },
    { day: 'Friday', totalEaten: 4 },
  ];
  const caloriesConsumed = donutLog.reduce((lastCount, currentEntry));
  return caloriesConsumed;
}
```

And yet, we have another option: Developer C, who is inconsistent. Sometimes they have line breaks, and sometimes they don't. The following listing gives us an example.

> **Listing 5.6 Inconsistent spacing between variable declarations and logic (JavaScript)**

```javascript
function GetTotalDonutCalories() {
  const donutLog = [
    { day: 'Monday', totalEaten: 2 },
    { day: 'Tuesday', totalEaten: 1 },
    { day: 'Wednesday', totalEaten: 3 },
    { day: 'Thursday', totalEaten: 2 },
    { day: 'Friday', totalEaten: 4 },
  ];
  const caloriesConsumed = donutLog.reduce((lastCount, currentEntry));

  return caloriesConsumed;
}
```

Some people get very passionate about how code should be styled. Developer A could be reprimanding their team and saying line breaks are the way to go. Others are so used to their personal preferences that any other way looks wrong. Developer B could stand firm on their no-line breaks stance and keep their code that way, despite Developer A saying otherwise. Then there are others who may not have a preference at all, don't have enough experience to know what options exist, or are quite inconsistent in their code style. This results in code like Developer C's.

To manage all of these scenarios (and many more that have not happened yet), automate the formatting of your team's codebase. This is where your team style guide comes into play. With the rules codified, a formatting tool can be used to determine and enforce the chosen style.

Say the team style guide states that the official stance is to leave space between variable declarations and business logic. A formatter can (i) provide real-time feedback to developers B and C and surface any offending code for them to fix, (ii) run in a developer's local environment prior to committing their work, just as you would run a spelling and grammar check before submitting a paper, and (iii) be used as a PR gate check (we talk more about these awesome things in section 5.4.4). PRs failing style guide checks (indicated by PR gate checks) can be confidently ignored by the team as they haven't passed basic formatting standards. Alternatively, you can point out these PRs with labels if you have that feature in your code review system.

Using a formatter is especially convenient for this mundane task. You don't have to remember all the particular rules and conventions your team has agreed to. Your codebase will be much more consistent (and stay that way). Newer developers (in general and to your team) can begin to learn your team's style through the formatter. Much of this unimportant stuff is eliminated from the PR, allowing the reviewer to be less distracted. In the words of Mario Tacke, software engineer and architect at Amazon:

> ♀ *Developers are much more susceptible to change when a robot yells at them rather than another human. It takes out any subjectivity and frees up human cycles, which allows us to focus on what matters.*

I agree wholeheartedly with this statement. I don't know about you, but I'd rather have my IDE or a development tool tell me to fix some spacing issues in my code, *not* my colleague 😊.

You're missing a semicolon, silly!

With the most superficial items automated away, we can step into more intermediate and advanced mechanisms.

5.3.2 *Linting*

If formatting accounts for how our code looks, linting considers how our code syntactically behaves. Linting is the act of inspecting code for any potential and realized faults. Things that we consider "code smells," like calls to deprecated methods or uses of undeclared variables, are the faults we try to catch through linting. We get this clever term from Stephen C. Johnson, a computer scientist at Bell Labs. Johnson came up with a "lint" tool while trying to port Unix to a 32-bit machine [1]. The tool came about as he had a bit of difficulty debugging some Yacc (Yet Another Compiler Compiler) grammar he wrote for C. Just as a drying machine's lint trap catches little bits of fluff and fiber shed by our clothes, the lint tool would catch and flag small errors in his ported code.

That was back in 1978, specifically for the C language; today, we have a linting or lint-like tool for almost every programming language. Some tools may even include formatting capabilities in addition to linting (though you typically want to avoid using a linting tool to enforce formatting since it's slower and less consistent than dedicated formatters). With this, the second automation opportunity presents itself.

Linting your code during development can uncover all kinds of concerns as you write code, meaning you can proactively fix them before the code review. Through the use of rules (the same building blocks used to define a style guide), linters scan your code and flag any parts that break said rules. Typically, a rule is a specific check for a single item, like a rule against unused variables or a rule against methods that have too many parameters. How granular you get with your rules and how severe you want each violation to be flagged is, of course, up to your team.

Going back to my earlier story of proposing ESLint to my team, you already know about `no-console: "error"` and how that rule alone made a significant difference. I wanted to share a few other rules we ended up using as a team that was transitioning into the ES6 era of JavaScript. The following listing outlines them.

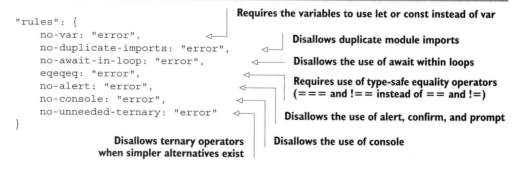

Listing 5.7   ESLint Rules used by Adrienne's team

```
"rules": {
    no-var: "error",
    no-duplicate-imports: "error",
    no-await-in-loop: "error",
    eqeqeq: "error",
    no-alert: "error",
    no-console: "error",
    no-unneeded-ternary: "error"
}
```

Requires the variables to use let or const instead of var

Disallows duplicate module imports

Disallows the use of await within loops

Requires use of type-safe equality operators (=== and !== instead of == and !=)

Disallows the use of alert, confirm, and prompt

Disallows the use of console

Disallows ternary operators when simpler alternatives exist

As we migrated parts of our application to use ES6, we initially set these rules to `"warn"` to help us get used to the linting system and to make sure we truly needed the rule. As we acclimated to our rules, we slowly changed some rules to a full `"error"` to be more rigorous with our frontend codebase.

The `no-var` (https://eslint.org/docs/latest/rules/no-var) rule forced us to re-evaluate whether something needed block scope and to explicitly and properly declare them if it did. Sometimes, our components import quite a few modules, and a duplicate one could easily be missed. Adding the `no-duplicate-imports` (https://mng .bz/yoPB) rule helped with that. Then, silly bugs popped up due to not taking advantage of parallelization or the proper use of equality operators. That's where the `no-await-in-loop` (https:// mng.bz/M1zW) and `eqeqeq` (https://mng.bz/aVX7) rules, respectively, came in handy. As part of cleaning up our code, we added the `no-alert` (https://mng.bz/ gApV) and `no-console` (https://mng.bz/5Oxa) rules. This reminded us to clean up some of those "in the moment" debug code remnants. Finally, to simplify some of our conditional checks, we added the `no-unneeded-ternary` (https://mng.bz/6YJA) rule to help us understand them more quickly and without much extra cognitive load. For example, listing 5.8 shows a common check found in our code (premigration).

Listing 5.8   Unnecessarily complicated check using a ternary operator

```
let thingToCheck = input === 3 ? true : false;
```

When you're down the debugging rabbit hole or trying to follow the execution path of something, conditional expressions like those in listing 5.8 sometimes throw you off track. Instead, a much simpler way to conduct that check could be written, as shown in the following listing.

Listing 5.9   Straightforward conditional check

```
let thingToCheck = input === 3;
```

As with formatting problems, we are much better at receiving warnings about deviations from coding standards from our IDEs than a colleague. And as Mario cleverly reminded us, we're also more likely to fix it and be on our merry way rather than starting a debate. By finding it during development, we give ourselves a chance to fix it in a more lenient and forgiving environment.

While linting is suggested for all, it is especially useful for dynamically typed languages like JavaScript, Lua, Python, and Clojure. Unlike statically typed languages that know the types of their variables before execution, dynamically typed languages don't and instead infer their types during execution. With less information available prior to execution, dynamically typed languages can only run a limited set of diagnostic checks. Linting can fill in those gaps and check for more of these issues prior to execution.

Linter, formatter, or both?

Prior to reading this chapter, you may have thought linting and formatting were the same thing. I don't blame you! Many tools today do both (or more) to a certain degree. Some, like ESLint, for example, imply a focus on linting with its name, even though you can set both code style and linting rules. And when we do talk about linting and formatting, they are usually discussed together. For these reasons and more, the two actions sometimes get mistaken for each other.

Whether or not you choose a specific tool for each or one that does it all, be sure there's a way for you to export your rulesets in case you ever move to a different tool.

5.3.3 Static analyzers

Next, we get to static analyzers. Here, we go a bit deeper than syntax checks and coding standards. With static analyzers, we can perform static analysis—a process that goes through our code line by line and checks for deeper-rooted issues without having to execute the code.

For most of my career, I wrote software with C# and worked within the .NET ecosystem. I was first introduced to the concept of static analysis through Roslyn (https://github.com/dotnet/roslyn), which is .NET's compiler platform. Different kinds of code analysis could be performed, including code style and code quality checks. As I wrote code in Visual Studio (the most popular IDE for working in the .NET ecosystem), the compiler would let me know when there were errors; it added them to a little window toward the bottom of my IDE. I remember first being annoyed at all the little warnings and errors that would appear in my Error List window. I would soon grow to appreciate and depend on that window and understand how invaluable static analysis was. That window became my safety net to catch errors before the review.

Static analysis finds more complex issues that we might miss: more intricate code smells like really long methods or classes, nested conditionals, and things like cyclomatic complexity (a measure of possible execution paths through the code; high complexity means code might be hard to understand or maintain) and primitive obsession (overdependence on primitive types, like strings or integers, which can reveal code that is not designed with object-oriented principles). Security vulnerabilities, like SQL injection, buffer overloads, cross-site scripting, and authentication and authorization gaps also fall within static analysis's reach, as do performance issues like memory leaks, dead code, and computationally expensive functions or loops.

While we are also responsible for looking out for these issues during the code review, we can rely on static analysis to do the heavy lifting. It can scan the entire codebase for these problems and critically examine each line every time it does. That's A LOT to ask of a human! Instead, we can spend our time fixing the actual issues that surface and let static analysis tools be our 24/7/365 watchdog running behind the scenes. Right now, tools like SonarQube (https://mng.bz/o0jp), Veracode (https://www.veracode .com/), and Codacy (https://github.com/marketplace/codacy) have been popular to use.

As an important reminder, static analysis is something that can assist us in catching plenty of issues beforehand, but it can never replace what we do in a code review. This is because static analyzers can't determine developer intent (does the code actually do what it's supposed to do) or enforce rules that aren't possible to enforce statically (for example, a rule to "make sure comments indicate the why, not the what of the code"). It takes a human eye to comprehend these use cases and make a decision based on their understanding.

5.3.4 *Automated testing*

Last but not least, we come to automated testing. If you've ever written a unit test, you already have experience with it! This method of testing software is an effective way of cutting down on manual testing and repetitive tasks and giving you extra assurance that your code is of decent quality.

There are a few types of automated testing that you may choose to employ:

- *Unit testing*—The testing of the smallest possible parts of an application for proper functionality. The unit test—when written correctly—should test that your code does what you intended it to do rather than the implementation of it. A bunch of related unit tests are typically put together in a suite. Running suites of tests after adding or changing code is a good way to self-check that you aren't regressing the code.
- *UI testing*—The functional testing of UI controls. Does the button work, and does it change states according to respective use cases? Are "happy paths" accessible and working in the entire application? Does your application adapt to different devices, browsers, or operating systems? If you've used a tool like Selenium (https://www.selenium.dev/), Puppeteer (https://pptr.dev/), or Protractor (https://www.protractortest.org/), you've done automated UI testing. By automating this kind of testing, a lot of time can be saved by replacing the manual effort these kinds of checks would require.
- *API testing*—The testing of application programming interfaces (APIs). Here, you'd likely test the API endpoints directly or as part of integration testing to make sure they are working properly and returning the expected responses. Sometimes, APIs can have many endpoints or multiple supported versions, which can make testing quite tedious. With automated API testing, you can cut down

on the manual effort needed to test your APIs thoroughly. Postman (https://www.postman.com/automated-testing/) and Newman (https://mng.bz/n092) are popularly used together to achieve automated API testing.

If you have the ability to run any automated testing for your projects, you should take advantage of it! Support the effort and add onto any existing test suites that may already exist. And if you don't have any automated testing in place, you can certainly be the pioneer for your team. Start with some unit tests or work with your QA testers to plan out how to automate some of their typical tests. All of this effort results in a particularly powerful verification of stable code you can rely on during development. The more you can do to ensure your code works before the code review, the higher the likelihood that it will pass the review in an uneventful manner.

By combining the benefits of each of these automations—formatting, linting, static analysis, and automated testing—I can guarantee that you'll cut down on silly bottlenecks in the code review. Let's take a lesson from Captain Planet (does anyone remember that show?) and put their collective powers to great use!

5.4   *Automations during the review*

With the fluff out of the way, let's focus on what we can automate (or make easier for ourselves) during the review. There are several tactics that can be implemented here. While most of them help the author create properly prepared pull requests, others help the whole team with communication bottlenecks.

5.4.1   *PR templates*

Ah, the good ol' template. No matter what industry a template is used in, its purpose is the same: to establish or serve as a pattern. It can be a document with a preset format, a starting point that does not have to be re-created each time it is used, or a file that is prepopulated with default values. In a code review, we can use PR templates to make a portion of your process more consistent.

PR templates are preset outlines of questions or checklist items that are automatically generated when a PR is created. This is an effective tactic to consistently produce properly prepared PRs.

As an author, you can go through the template, self-acknowledge that nothing is forgotten or missing, and be confident you've primed the PR as much as possible for the reviewer. Much better than trying to remember everything you need every time you open a PR!

As a reviewer, you can enjoy consistent, context-filled PRs, enabling you to perform a better and quicker review. The less back and forth you have to do with the author to obtain more information, the better!

So, yeah, the elephant in the room: the use of PR templates isn't necessarily "automated"—authors still need to check and acknowledge the items themselves on the list—though the creation of one is. A widely used example is the PR template on GitHub (which also works in Azure DevOps, specifically Azure Repos). To use it, you create a Markdown file named `pull_request_template.md`, outline the reminders, questions, or checklist items you'd like authors to answer/acknowledge in it, and store the file at the root of a repository. With this in place, all who open a PR against the repository will be presented with this template automatically! For example, a simplistic checklist for a new feature PR template could look like the following listing.

> **Listing 5.10   New feature PR template (simple example)**

```
- [ ] Description - Why is this change being made? (Please add any relevant
➥ context, history, or decisions related to this feature):
- [ ] Linked Work Ticket/Issue #
- [ ] Linked Documentation:
- [ ] New Feature label assigned
- [ ] Accompanying unit tests included
- [ ] Minimum of 2 reviewers assigned
```

As part of your pull request template, this checklist will be presented to an author each time they open a new feature PR. It would be ready for them to fill out/acknowledge, as explained in figure 5.1.

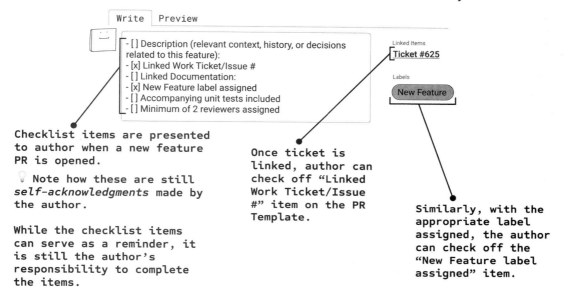

Figure 5.1 A new feature PR template

This checklist becomes even more useful as different templates can be used for different kinds of PRs. Authors likely want to describe the acceptance criteria, add documentation links, and confirm accompanying unit tests for new features. Bug fixes, on the other hand, might ask for different pieces of information in addition to a checklist to make sure the bug is actually fixed. Things like reproduction steps, root cause, and a testing strategy make more sense to add here than to a new feature PR template.

Since these templates use Markdown, it's simple enough to create a slightly more complex PR template. I've created a starting point for a bugfix template that you can use and adapt in the following listing.

Listing 5.11 Bug fix PR template

```
# Bug Fix PR Template
---


## What's happening?
Provide a sentence or two to describe the bug.

## Reproduction Steps
Outline the steps you took to reproduce the bug. Be sure not to forget any
    steps and that they are in the right order!
```

```
1.
2.
3.

## Root Cause
What was the root cause of the bug? How did you identify it?

## Fix
Explain the fix in a sentence or two. Then, go into detail about **why** this
    fix solves the problem.

## Testing Strategy
How was the fix tested to make sure the bug is truly resolved?

## Impact
Are there any implications this fix may have on other parts of the
    application?

## Regression Risk
Are you confident this fix does not introduce new issues? If you think this
    fix may have some regression risk, what steps have been taken to
    mitigate it?


## Bug Fix Checklist

- [ ] Issue # is linked
- [ ] Fix has been tested locally and works
- [ ] New unit tests have been added to prevent future regressions
- [ ] (If applicable) Relevant documentation has been updated


## Notes
Is there any other context or information to share in order to understand the
    fix or its impact?

## Thanks for (hopefully) squashing this bug!
```

And if you're purely updating documentation, that will also have its own set of check-list items. Here's another template for you to use and adapt to your liking.

Listing 5.12 Documentation Update PR template

```
# Documentation Update PR Template
---

## What are we changing in the docs?
Provide a sentence or two about the documentation update.

## Why are we changing this?
Explain **why** these documentation changes are necessary. Feel free to
provide more details about the changes here.

## Items Impacted
Briefly list the components, pages, versions, etc. affected by this change.
```

```
## Screenshots (if applicable)
If there are significant visual changes, please attach some  before and
after screenshots.


## Review Checklist

- [ ] Spelling and grammar check has been performed and is correct
- [ ] All links are working and correct
- [ ] Documentation accurately reflects the current state of the project
- [ ] Changes are clearly highlighted and easy to understand


## Notes
Any other context or information to share that may be helpful for reviewers?

## Thanks for keeping our documentation current and correct!
```

I'll also have these templates as appendix items in the back of the book and in a GitHub repo for easier, uh, borrowing. ☺

5.4.2 *PR validators*

Want to make sure your PRs are as consistent and as organized as possible? It's worth considering some automated checks on the PR itself, things I call PR validators (I also talk about PR gate checks later on in this chapter, but those focus solely on automated quality checks on the code changes, which are also important). Here, I go over some of my favorite automations that help reinforce the guidelines we've set for our PRs.

PR TITLE FORMAT

We spoke about the importance of PR titles in chapter 2. We've also encouraged using a format similar to Conventional Commits, as doing so can form succinct yet information-packed titles. With automation, you can automatically enforce this format! One great tool you can use is a GitHub Action called `semantic-pull-request` (https://mng.bz/vJB4), which validates that your pull request titles match the Conventional Commit spec (https://mng.bz/4pxj). So, as long as your title has a categorization prefix (what it calls a "type") and a succinct title (what it calls a "description"), it will pass the validation. You can configure some other options, but overall, it should be ready to go after installing as a GitHub action (https://mng.bz/QVjv).

LABEL MANAGER

We also spoke about the utility of labels in chapter 2. If your team wants to use labels to describe PRs, this GitHub Action is one to consider for lots of automation capabilities (https://mng.bz/XVBa)! From the age of the PR to the state of the PR body (description), you can set multiple labels based on the rules you configure. Labels are great to use for flagging PRs that have been open too long, checking that the PR description is not empty, and many other validations your team may need.

PR SIZE LABELER

This minimal GitHub Action adds size labels to your PRs based on the number of code lines and files changed (https://mng.bz/yoPd). You can configure what different PR sizes mean for your team or use the defaults. For example, a PR with 20 lines of code changed or five files changed will be considered "small" (the default) and will get corresponding labels. This means two labels will be added: a `"lines/S"` and a `"files/S"` label. You can configure this action to use one or the other (just files or just lines of code) if you prefer. The default will use both.

I like this action as it's quite straightforward; other than configuring how many lines of code or what number of files equate to which size, colors for labels, and an option to omit certain files/directories based on a regex pattern, there's not much else to configure, and that's a good thing! Using this with your team can help you enforce smaller PR sizes and quickly point out which PRs may need some whittling down.

PULL REQUEST STATS

To capture how the review workload is actually being spread across the team, the GitHub Action `pull request stats` is one to consider (https://mng.bz/M1zB). At its most minimal configuration, this action can calculate reviewer statistics for the current repo in the last 30 days, add links to historical data, and sort results by "total reviews" by default. It would print out something like figure 5.2.

	User	Total reviews	Median time to review	Total comments
	jartmez	37	22m	13
	manuelmhtr	35	48m	96
	ernestognw	25	1h 27m	63
	javierbyte	12	30m	0
	Phaze1D	4	34m	1

Figure 5.2   Pull Request Stats GitHub Action: Minimum configuration output

Alternatively, there is a Visual Configuration that calculates reviewer statistics for the last 7 days, displays visual charts for some metrics, removes links to the detailed charts, and sorts results by the Total Comments column, as shown in figure 5.3.

Whatever configuration you decide, this can be a great way to track how your team is doing on code reviews, spot potential bottlenecks, or understand if the workload is equally shared overall. Remember, don't use these metrics in isolation—it's easy to misuse metrics and say that one individual is doing more work than another. You might even build a story around that single metric to say that the less busy developer is

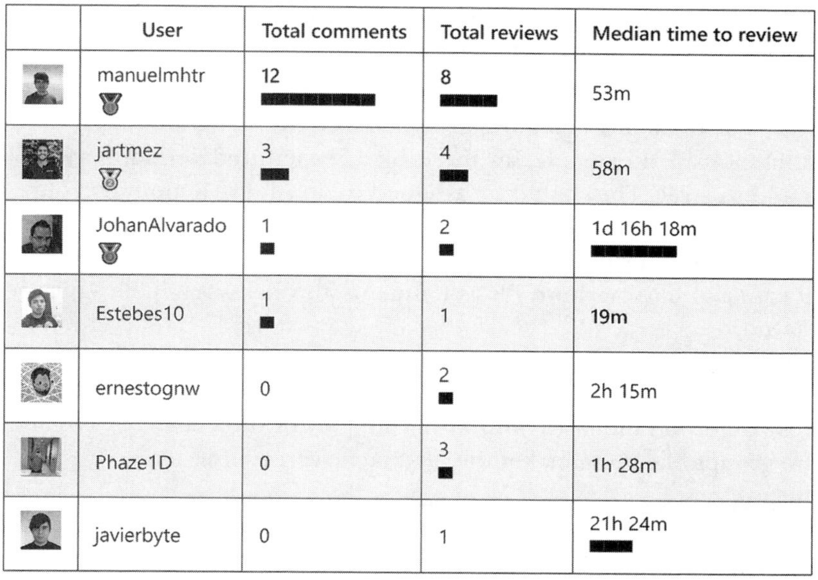

	User	Total comments	Total reviews	Median time to review
	manuelmhtr	12	8	53m
	jartmez	3	4	58m
	JohanAlvarado	1	2	1d 16h 18m
	Estebes10	1	1	19m
	ernestognw	0	2	2h 15m
	Phaze1D	0	3	1h 28m
	javierbyte	0	1	21h 24m

Figure 5.3   Pull Request Stats GitHub Action: Visual configuration output

lazy or not pulling their weight in reviews. Instead, use metrics to track trends over time and in conjunction with team discussions and overall workloads. Did someone have "worse" statistics because they were out sick for a few days? Did someone have "better" statistics because the PRs that week were much smaller than a typical PR? Take everything into consideration and use these metrics as a signal to either improve or change something about your process if the metrics seem to trend negatively or continue with what you're doing if they are trending positively.

5.4.3   Reviewer assignments

Who needs to review this PR? Who should be assigned? Why is this person always reviewing that person's PRs? These questions can go away, along with the extra mental effort it takes to answer them, by automating some or all of the PR assignment process.

There are several ways to go about this; it really depends on your team (yes, this book will say this a lot). I outline several options that you can discuss with your colleagues. They range from the bare minimum tactics to the ultra-fancy ones.

AUTO-ASSIGNING THE WHOLE TEAM TO EACH PR (BARE MINIMUM)

When opening a PR, adding your colleagues one by one every single time gets old. Instead, have the PR immediately add your team to each open PR, which removes bias (automatic assignments take care of that) and lends itself well to those who use code reviews for knowledge transfer. Now, if your team is fairly large (like eight or more people), this might seem spammy. Here, group assignments may come in handy to "break" apart your team into more manageable, "auto-assignable" numbers.

GROUP ASSIGNMENTS (KIND OF FANCY)

If your tool has the ability, creating groups of reviewers can lend itself to more complex automations! For example, say there are a few tenured developers who are always good to add to a PR. They could be assigned to an Always Required group. And let's say there are a few individuals who should be kept apprised of changes but don't need to approve. These individuals could be an Informational group. On larger teams, this makes it easier to narrow down PR assignments and helps new colleagues get a sense of who's who.

Another option is to group similar functions or teams together. Create frontend and backend groups, groups based on individuals' expertise in specific technologies, or groups based on familiarity with a specific part of the codebase. Organizing your team into groups like these makes the next tactic very useful, too!

AUTO-ASSIGN BASED ON CHANGED FILES AND TEAM EXPERTISE (ULTRA FANCY)

Ideally, your team will reach this level of automation or pretty close to it. Here, you'll have the relevant people automatically assigned when a particular part of your codebase changes.

Say a PR focuses on a minor change to a React component. When the PR is opened and recognizes that the code changes affect `.jsx` files, Vittoria, the team's React engineer, is immediately added to the PR reviewer list. Or, imagine all PRs that touch your codebase's legacy systems automatically add Renato and Wendy, the two senior engineers on your team. Sounds neat, right? Glenn Reyes, a software engineer at Kadena, and his team think so:

> 💬 *We have "code owners" which basically describes the authors of different parts in the SDK. We typically request code reviews to at least one code owner. Depending on the size and security vulnerabilities included in the code updates, we sometimes include and require more than one reviewer to look through and have the changes approved.*

In some tools, there is support for this capability: PR assignees can be added based on the files changed. Using a designated file or set of configurations, you can specify conditions to be met, along with the appropriate individuals or groups that will be assigned based on that condition. For those using GitHub, these conditions are stored in a special file called the CODEOWNERS file. Using file patterns, a complex set of conditions can be set up, providing thorough coverage and ownership for all parts of your codebase. The following listing shows a sample CODEOWNERS file.

Listing 5.13   An example of a CODEOWNERS file

```
# This is a comment.
# Each line is a file pattern followed by one or more owners.

# These owners will be the default owners for everything in
# the repo. Unless a later match takes precedence,
```

```
# @global-owner1 and @global-owner2 will be requested for
# review when someone opens a pull request.
*          @global-owner1 @global-owner2

# Order is important; the last matching pattern takes the most
# precedence. When someone opens a pull request that only
# modifies JSX files, only @vittoriak and not the global
# owner(s) will be requested for a review.
*.jsx    @vittoriak #This is an inline comment.

# You can also use email addresses if you prefer. They'll be
# used to look up users just like we do for commit author
# emails.
*.py nico@example.com

# Teams can be specified as code owners as well. Teams should
# be identified in the format @org/team-name. Teams must have
# explicit write access to the repository. In this example,
# the docwriters team in the dev-org organization owns all .md files.
*.md @dev-org/docwriters

# In this example, @nozomiw owns any files in the build/logs
# directory at the root of the repository and any of its
# subdirectories.
/build/logs/ @nozomiw

# The `docs/*` pattern will match files like
# `docs/getting-started.md` but not further nested files like
# `docs/build-app/troubleshooting.md`.
docs/*  docs@example.com

# In this example, @pedrob owns any file in an apps directory
# anywhere in your repository.
apps/ @pedrob

# In this example, @trangv owns any file in the `/docs`
# directory in the root of your repository and any of its
# subdirectories.
/docs/ @trangv

# In this example, any change inside the `/scripts` directory
# will require approval from @ndidio or @waltera.
/scripts/ @ndidio @waltera

# In this example, @lucjar owns any file in a `/logs` directory such as
# `/build/logs`, `/scripts/logs`, and `/deeply/nested/logs`. Any changes
# in a `/logs` directory will require approval from @lucjar.
**/logs @lucjar

# In this example, @mirav owns any file in the `/apps`
# directory in the root of your repository except for the `/apps/github`
# subdirectory, as its owners are left empty.
/apps/ @mirav
/apps/github
```

When you create a CODEOWNERS file, create it in the root, docs/, or the .github/ directory of the repository in the branch where you'd like to add the code owners [2]. Figure 5.4 illustrates the three options.

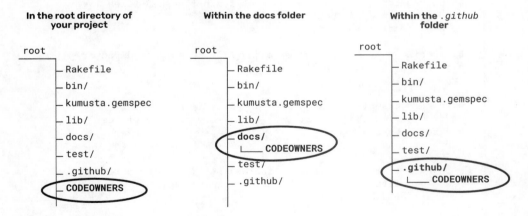

Where does the CODEOWNERS file go?

Elliot should be a reviewer when any Ruby files are changed (see simplified CODEOWNERS below).

CODEOWNERS

```
# E. Alderson is a code owner
# for any Ruby files
*.rb @ealderson
```

In order for Elliot to receive these review requests, the CODEOWNERS file needs to be in **one** of three places:

In the root directory of your project

```
root
    ├─ Rakefile
    ├─ bin/
    ├─ kumusta.gemspec
    ├─ lib/
    ├─ docs/
    ├─ test/
    ├─ .github/
    └─ CODEOWNERS
```

Within the docs folder

```
root
    ├─ Rakefile
    ├─ bin/
    ├─ kumusta.gemspec
    ├─ lib/
    ├─ docs/
    │    └── CODEOWNERS
    ├─ test/
    └─ .github/
```

Within the .github folder

```
root
    ├─ Rakefile
    ├─ bin/
    ├─ kumusta.gemspec
    ├─ lib/
    ├─ docs/
    ├─ test/
    └─ .github/
         └── CODEOWNERS
```

Figure 5.4   Where does the CODEOWNERS file go?

If you want code owners to receive these automatic review requests, make sure that the CODEOWNERS file is on the base branch of the PR. For example, if your main branch is where all PRs integrate into (meaning PRs typically ask to merge into the main branch), the CODEOWNERS file should be on the main branch. That way, any time a PR is opened between a feature/fix/some other branch and the main branch, the respective owners will be notified.

In other tools, such as Azure Repos or Bitbucket, these conditions can be specified through configuration in the tool rather than a file. For example, when I worked for a financial company, my team made use of Azure Repos branch policies to set these conditions. Based on the rules we specified, we automatically assigned the required reviewers to our PRs. We configured a rule to auto-add the Backend/Infrastructure team group when C# files were changed and another rule to auto-add the React/Frontend team group whenever .JSX, JS, or CSS files were changed. In the end, the result is the same: specific reviewers can be assigned to specific PRs automatically.

> ## CODEOWNERS file and repo settings
> Excited to use the CODEOWNERS file in your codebase? Great! Here are some things to remember when using them:
>
> - Each CODEOWNERS file applies to a single branch in the repository. You can have different code owners for different branches! Just create another CODEOWNERS file for each intended branch to which you wish to assign code owners.
> - Only developers with owner or admin permissions on the intended repository can set up a CODEOWNERS file.
> - Individuals or teams you assign as code owners within the file need to write permissions on the intended repository.
> - If you assign a team, the team cannot be "secret"; only visible teams can work with CODEOWNERS files.
>
> Additionally, make sure these branch settings are activated:
>
> - A branch ruleset is created targeting the branch you'd like to protect.
> - The Require a Pull Request Before Merging option is checked within your branch ruleset.
> - The Require Review from Code Owners option is checked within your branch ruleset.
>
> For additional help or to read more about GitHub's CODEOWNERS file, visit https://mng.bz/aVXm.

Don't feel like you have to start out with something like a CODEOWNERS file for reviewer assignments! If your team finds group or whole team assignments work just fine, you may not need to complicate your process with something like the CODEOWNERS file. Knowing that it is an option may be appropriate for right now. If your team evolves, either by growing in size, including external/noncore teams, or some other factor that requires more precise reviewer assignments, you'll be ready!

5.4.4 PR gate checks

In a code review where quality checks are left to the reviewer, too many low-stakes issues can become the focus, resulting in a less thorough review overall. Asking a reviewer to make sure the code is properly linted and formatted, confirm that no sensitive information is present, and confidently acknowledge that there are no security flaws in the code, among so many other things, is a lot to ask of them! With all of that extra work, and a lot of noise to sift through, it can be harder to see any critical, high-stakes issues in the code—those that need a human to be recognized.

PR gate checks help you eliminate a lot of that "noise." Sometimes called *quality gates*, PR gate checks are verifications specific to pull requests that prevent code from being merged if it doesn't meet the specified quality criteria. They can be placed before, during, or after a PR is opened or submitted. If you've used GitHub before, you may have seen some automated checks already, like the prebuild merge check that ensures the proposed code changes are safe to merge, as shown in figure 5.5.

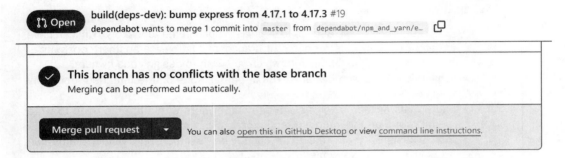

Figure 5.5   Built-in GitHub precheck validates that proposed changes do not result in a conflict with the base branch and are safe to merge.

These checks aren't specific to PRs, though; quality gates can be placed throughout the entire software development workflow. Many of them exist within a CI/CD pipeline. However, it is quite common to place these checks near the code review phase. As a result, PR gate checks serve as a protective shield for your codebase, adding additional safeguards to ensure quality code.

The more gate checks you add, the better off your code reviews will be. Through bots, third-party tools, tasks, and AI, a dizzying array of items can be inspected, tested, simulated, analyzed, measured—you get the idea—when a PR is opened. We go into a selection of these items in the following sections. Note that none of these are endorsements or paid recommendations—they simply had capabilities that I consider important to check in an automated fashion. The more quality checks you can offload to the machines, the less your team has to worry about them, the more time they have to look for critical, human-recognizable problems during the review, and the more confident your team can be about the code once it's integrated into the main codebase. Let's talk about the most important checks you should consider adding and automating.

LINTING

Even though we've encouraged linting prior to opening the PR, it's still a worthwhile gate check to have. Developers could easily miss a lint warning or intentionally ignore one during development, making this check even more important.

FORMATTING

Same thing as linting: this check captures any lingering formatting problems that were missed or ignored. Providing another check at this stage makes it easier for authors to fix these low-stakes issues before the reviewer ever starts the review.

STATIC ANALYSIS

And, of course, we can't forget static analysis. As with all the items we ideally fix during development, it is still a good idea to add an automated check for them once we open the PR. SonarQube (https://mng.bz/gApv) is a popular choice as it supports the most popular programming languages. It is also available as a GitHub Action (https://mng .bz/eVgV).

INCLUSIVE LANGUAGE

Offensive or exclusive language is something that may not come to mind as a gate check, but it should be! Being humans first and developers next, we may use terms and stereotypes within our code despite no malice intended. To help rewire our brains and rewrite our code to be as inclusive of all, a gate check like this can be a great addition. Microsoft's Inclusiveness Analyzer (https://mng.bz/pxWK) is one way to implement this quality check.

SECURITY

From known security vulnerabilities in dependencies to potential flaws analyzed in the code, security is a major gate check teams should be performing.

There are gate checks, such as Zaproxy's ZAP Baseline Scan (https://mng.bz/ OmKw), that test if your code is susceptible to injection, broken authentication, cross-site scripting, or other common security faults in a web application.

Jfrog's Frogbot (https://mng.bz/YVdz) scans new pull requests for vulnerabilities in binaries and dependencies, misuse or misconfiguration of open source libraries and services, or malicious or unexpected packages in your code, among other security composition analysis functions. It then leaves any found issues as a comment on the pull request.

Zimperium's Zimperium zScan (https://mng.bz/GNgD) inspects mobile app binaries (iOS or Android) and identifies security, privacy, and compliance-related vulnerabilities along with recommendations and remediation options.

SecureStack's SecureStack Web Vulnerability Analysis (https://mng.bz/znP1) searches for out-of-date application components, identifies whether basic security controls like firewalls and security headers are being used, finds web application firewall (WAF) bypass attacks for popular content delivery networks (CDNs), and addresses other web application security and availability problems.

It'd be impossible for reviewers to scan for these items to the extent, consistency, and accuracy that a bot would. So, let's leave it to the bots!

DEVELOPMENT SECRETS

Ever scan through someone's PR and see their personal API key? How about a database connection string? Plain text usernames and passwords? These secrets about your team's development environment (or worse, production!) should never make it out into the world. With several prebuilt bots and actions that check for this, having a gate check scan for secrets can be one of the most important things you add to your list of automations. Actions like Nightfall AI's Nightfall DLP Action (https://mng.bz/0MxJ) and SecureStack's All-In-One GitHub Action (https://mng.bz/KDYX) are solely focused on scanning for these items, as well as sensitive consumer information (which we talk about next).

This gate check is certainly one that warrants a "broken" PR status—meaning, if these inspections fail and sensitive secrets are found, the PR should not be allowed to move further in the overall pipeline, let alone be assumed ready to review. This should also be considered a blocking problem—a really major one!

SENSITIVE INFORMATION

Along similar lines as development secrets, when applications work with external, private data, we'd rather not see that as part of the codebase. Think credit card numbers, bank account information, home addresses, or medical histories: information that should be kept private and confidential should be scanned for and checked.

Using the same policy as development secrets found, a PR containing sensitive information should not be allowed to move further in the pipeline or be reviewed until the sensitive information is removed. The PR should be labeled "broken" or have some other clear status that denotes that the PR needs to be fixed. The problem is severe enough to be considered blocking. It's also likely that a rebase (or some kind of altering) of your branch needs to be done to remove the sensitive information from your source control version history.

> **TIP**   Consider anything that has been previously exposed as "out"; it may very well exist somewhere else, even if you've cleaned up your own history. For this reason, be sure to change any keys, passwords, or other info that you can regenerate. Also, I think most forms of "removing the information" and truly cleaning your own history will involve some form of rewriting your git history. This is unfortunate because your other devs may need to reclone the rebased version of their repo to get the removed history.

I think we can all agree: let's not commit sensitive info in the first place! Prevention is better than cure.

TEST COVERAGE

Any time code is changed, optimal codebases usually maintain relevant and thorough test coverage. This is another automation that can be added and calculated when a PR is opened. If test coverage falls below previous numbers or does not meet your team's thresholds, then a PR can be changed to a "broken" status. This can alert the author to fix their PR. Actions like Codacy (https://github.com/marketplace/codacy) and Code Climate (https://github.com/marketplace/code-climate) can help provide text coverage reports automatically.

Ideally, these gate checks run at the time a PR is opened. When a gate check does not pass, the PR should be given a "broken" or "needs fixing" status. This tells the author that there's still work to be done on their PR. It also saves the reviewer time; they can safely ignore any PRs that don't pass a standard set of checks.

When all gate checks pass, a reviewer can confidently start their review, knowing a lot of fluff is taken care of, thus giving them the ability to focus on the code. I strongly recommend you have these gate checks in place. As with most tactics in this book, start with those suggested in the chapter and slowly adapt them to your team's needs over time. Add them in one by one and see whether they hinder or help your team's review phases. Even if you only add the linting and formatting gate checks to start, you'll likely find your code reviews improving in quality by focusing on more pressing problems than a misplaced comma or extra space.

There are far more gate checks than the ones mentioned here. In fact, if you take a look at GitHub's Action Marketplace, there are over a thousand actions under the Code Review category (https://mng.bz/9o2j) alone! If you find that your team needs more gate checks, add them to your process. And if one doesn't exist today, you can always consider creating your own.

5.4.5 Reminders and escalations

Two annoying things that take up too much of our time are PR reminders and escalations. This applies to those nudges you give to your colleagues to progress the state of your PR, like "Hey, I'm still waiting on you to address the comments I left," and "It's been a week, and no one has reviewed my PR." These are, unfortunately, common conversations we have with our team. However, this task is another great candidate to automate!

If you've developed some reasonable PR response times with your team, put them to use and consistently enforce them with some bots or automated email notifications. Here's a suggested list of reminders to consider:

- A new PR is opened.
- A new PR has not been reviewed after 24 hours (and every subsequent day thereafter with no interaction).
- Reviewer comments have been left.
- Reviewer comments have not been addressed after 24 hours (and every subsequent day thereafter with no interaction).

And here are some escalation scenarios to consider:

- A PR has not been reviewed after a week.
- Reviewer comments have not been addressed after a week.

- An outstanding question/blocker needs to be clarified.
- Emergency scenario requesting emergency PR approval.

As with the PR gate checks, these reminders can be done through automated actions (like in GitHub) or configured in your tool (if available). For example, in Azure DevOps, you can set up some of these notifications in your project settings. We also mentioned a PR validator from earlier (the Label Manager; https://mng.bz/XVBa) that can automatically add the PR age as a label.

Doing this manual work once means automating away the hundreds of notifications you manually performed in the past. Now, newly created or updated PRs will always be made known to your team. And aging PRs can be brought to your teammates' attention. Remove yet another mental burden from your team; let the robots enforce reasonable response times and free up your developers' minds!

Summary

- Automation excels at the boring and annoying, the mundane and uninteresting. Code review tasks that fall under this category should be automated as much as possible.
- With automation, we reserve our time and focus to do a thorough and effective job during a code review.
- Easy candidates for automation? Linting, formatting, static analysis, and testing! All of these tools can and should be used during development, eliminating the most tedious yet least important issues from the code review itself.
- PR templates help authors properly prepare their PRs. Automate its creation and use different templates for different PR types, like bug fixes, documentation fixes, new features, and a standard template.
- PR validators help enforce the quality and consistency of your pull requests. Automatically enforce title formats, label management, PR sizes, and the tracking of how your team performs code reviews as a whole.
- Automate reviewer assignments to eliminate bias and assign the right people to review your code! GitHub has a CODEOWNERS file that can be used per repository to assign specific people or teams to PRs based on the files changed.
- PR gate checks eliminate a whole host of noisy tasks and mental clutter for the reviewer. Adding these to your process can help the reviewer focus on what really matters in the code review. It also gives your team more confidence in the code they are merging, as multiple quality checks have been offloaded to more accurate, fast, and thorough bots!
- Reminders and escalations should be left to the robots. Set automated email or messaging reminders for key PR events, like new ones being opened, PRs that have not been reviewed, or PR comments that the author has not addressed in 24 hours.

References

[1] Johnson, S. C. (1978, October 25). Lint, a C program checker. *Computing Science Technical Report (Bell Labs)*, 65, 78–1273.

[2] About code owners: CODEOWNERS file location. (n.d.). GitHub Docs. https://mng.bz/j0Ga

Composing effective code review comments

This chapter covers

- Why code review comments are so important
- What makes a comment effective
- How to write effective comments
- The 5P process for determining whether suggestions are valid to add
- The MMG Exchange for finding a solution that is clear to devs with opposing "objective" viewpoints
- Comment signals, MoSCoW categories, Conventional Comments
- The Triple-R pattern for requesting changes or additional work

Have you ever been in a social setting where multiple people are conversing? Genuinely interested and engaged individuals are sharing their thoughts on a subject—some even ask questions to better understand the person they are talking to. Some people interject, try to impress, rarely listen, and try to place the spotlight back on themselves (sometimes, we might even get into a debate with these folks!). One or two don't employ emotional or social intelligence, usually replying with a snarky, harsh, or inappropriate tone. And there are those who don't say much, if at all.

These individuals are just like the types of comments we may receive (or give!) on a code review. Comments can be thoughtful and relevant or propose unsolicited, "better" implementations with no reasoning to support why. They can be rude, condescending, or mean and add little to no value to the review (life is just a bunch of patterns, huh?). Much of the dread we feel comes from anticipating comments that could start a conflict.

Code reviews shouldn't be battlefields, though! They provide chances to improve the codebase as a team. That means the comments we write can and should have some meaning or positive purpose. They should progress the conversation, provide clarity, or level up the whole team in some way. Otherwise, why bother adding a comment at all?

Writing constructive comments hinges on effective communication and the team's commitment to codebase maintainability. Consequently, I've dedicated an entire chapter to how to write code review comments that are clear, helpful, and move the conversation forward. Let's obliterate that code review comment dread together, shall we?

6.1 *What makes a comment effective?*

After writing countless comments over the course of my career, I've found that the most effective ones are *objective, as specific as possible*, and *clearly define an outcome*. In reflection, it kind of makes sense: These comments directly negate the characteristics of the comments we despise receiving—comments that are subjective, vague, and aimless. Let's consider which characteristics to aim for instead.

6.1.1 *Objectivity*

When I gave my first talk on code reviews, I pointed out how developers absolutely detested subjective code review comments. What's subjective? Anything from missing indentation or preferential styling to unsupported and seemingly random suggestions qualify here. Subjective comments don't trace back to anything objective, like a work ticket or a coding convention. They certainly don't enrich developer happiness; rather, they splinter it because they focus on someone's personal preferences. Discussing this specific type of comment always brought the most agreeable head nods and "I can relate" type of sighs when I surveyed the audience.

WHAT DO SUBJECTIVE COMMENTS LOOK LIKE?

Subjective comments are not hard to find in the real world. Sifting through public projects on GitHub, I was able to find common examples. Figure 6.1 shows a subjective comment.

The changes shown could be better, but as an author receiving this feedback, I have to spend time figuring out why. Why is it better? What about my valid implementation makes it subpar to this suggestion? If I can't figure it out, I'll have to add another comment asking the reviewer to explain their reasoning (which should have

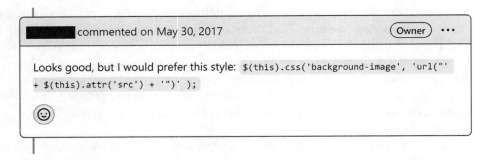

Figure 6.1   From a pull request for the materialize repo

been done in the first place). This is an all too common reason why code reviews can be delayed. This kind of interaction can also breed resentment among team members, especially if both the author and reviewer think their solution is the better one (we'll discuss what to do in this situation later in this chapter).

One other thing to remember is that subjective comments are just that: *subjective.* As reviewers, we need to remind ourselves not to let personal preferences influence our review. Take, for example, figure 6.2.

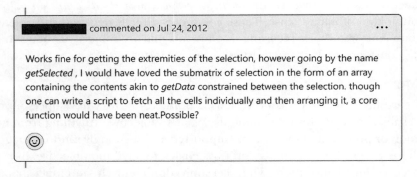

Figure 6.2   From a pull request for the handsontable repo

In this pull request (PR), someone opened a PR for a new method `getSelected()`. This method was implemented according to previous discussions about the requested functionality. Nonetheless, the reviewer (whose comment we are viewing) points out several "nice-to-haves" and additional behaviors they "would have loved." These preferences were not part of the discussion that led to this new feature. They do not point out an obvious flaw or edge case the current implementation may have missed. Instead, they share an idealized version of this method and suggest additional, but at the moment, unnecessary functionality to the original PR author. Can it get any more subjective than this?

A better option for the reviewer is to take these thoughts and place them within a new feature request. That way, their ideas are captured and documented, but they are not stalling the original PR. When the time is right, the team can discuss the additional behaviors and decide whether they are truly worth extending the `getSelected()` method to include.

AS REVIEWERS, WE NEED TO BE OBJECTIVE

Being objective reviewers doesn't mean that alternative ideas or suggestions are taboo; that's not the case at all. If you'd like to suggest a better implementation, please do. Just do it with facts. Why is your implementation better? Is it faster? Show some comparison metrics to prove it. Does it adhere to a language's coding conventions or your own team standards more closely? Say so, and link to that resource or section in your Team Working Agreement that supports your claim. If you just implemented the same behavior in a different way without being able to explain or demonstrate why it's better, it's probably best to leave it out of the review. Figure 6.3 shows a great example of an objective comment that uses a use case that is not considered to argue their position.

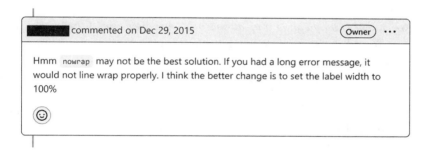

Figure 6.3   From a pull request for the handsontable repo

This discussion brings us to a pretty simple tactic: before you suggest a code review change, ask yourself *why* you want to make that suggestion. In a study on code review comments, researchers found that doing this forces developers to "expose the reasoning to themselves first before they post a comment" [1]. It can save so many code reviews from "review creep" (extra changes or work introduced during the code review that's outside the scope of the original work) and never-ending discussions about suggestions to consider.

To give a bit more structure to the advice "Ask yourself *why*," I've come up with the 5P process: Pause and Ponder and then either Pass, Propose, or Postpone (yes, I like alliterations very much).

Anytime you find yourself ready to suggest a change, always Pause and Ponder first:

- *Pause*—Literally take a moment to pause. Take a breath. Don't start writing that suggestion into a comment just yet.

- *Ponder*—Walk through your thought process. What prompted the suggestion in your head? Why is it necessary? Is it necessary to change right now? Can you justify the change with objective facts? Writing or drawing your thoughts out is encouraged and can help you through your pondering.

After you're done pondering, you'll end up choosing one of three options:

- *Pass*—Thinking it through, you may find it isn't a valid suggestion at all. In fact, you couldn't put words together or clearly understand it yourself. Until you can, pass on this suggestion, and don't add it to your review.

    OR

- *Propose*—If you find that after pondering, you do have a valid suggestion, go ahead and propose it! Understanding the rationale behind your thinking and validating your suggestion beforehand lets you better communicate it and articulate it in the comment you'll be leaving.

    OR

- *Postpone*—Alternatively, let's say that through your introspection, the suggestion is not appropriate for the review but is still worth remembering or discussing. You could

    - *Keep a note of it and bring it up at your next team discussion.* Ideally, you'd discuss this around the same time you are planning and organizing your upcoming work.
    - *Have an offline conversation about it with the author.* This would either lead to an agreement and a potential update to the PR, a new ticket to address the suggestion in a separate PR, or a mutual understanding that the suggestion is not needed (aka a double pass ☺). Remember to update the PR with the outcome of your conversation!

As an objective reviewer, when you can decide what's important for the review and what's not, you help streamline the review for everyone. You focus on leaving comments that are vetted and can be justified. You leave out the "would be nice" and "this would be cool" comments, letting the author breathe a sigh of relief, but still have a way to make sure those ideas are considered. While reviewing others' code, a little self-reflection on your part can make a big difference. Feel free to share the summarized 5P process, as shown in figure 6.4.

FINDING MIDDLE GROUND

As I was reviewing my own reviewer feedback on this book, one person asked a great question: "What do you say when someone suggests a personal preference change because they say your way is 'too confusing' or 'too clever,' and their way is 'clearer,' but you think their way is more confusing than yours?" (thank you, Reviewer 17 ☺). That is quite the subjective conundrum!

I think the final outcome of this situation should be finding a solution that's maintainable and clear. That's the ultimate goal. How do we get there? Take part in

The 5 Ps of Suggesting a Change

*Anytime you find yourself ready to suggest a change on a code review, go through the **5 Ps**. Always **Pause** and **Ponder**, then choose what to do with the suggestion: **Pass, Propose**, or **Postpone**.*

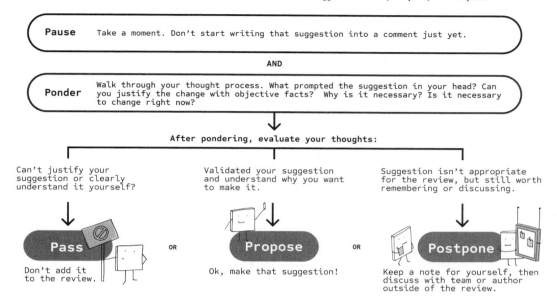

Pause   Take a moment. Don't start writing that suggestion into a comment just yet.

AND

Ponder   Walk through your thought process. What prompted the suggestion in your head? Can you justify the change with objective facts? Why is it necessary? Is it necessary to change right now?

After pondering, evaluate your thoughts:

Can't justify your suggestion or clearly understand it yourself?

Validated your suggestion and understand why you want to make it.

Suggestion isn't appropriate for the review, but still worth remembering or discussing.

Pass   OR   **Propose**   OR   **Postpone**

Don't add it to the review.

Ok, make that suggestion!

Keep a note for yourself, then discuss with team or author outside of the review.

Figure 6.4   The 5P process for suggesting a change during a code review

something I like to call an MMG Exchange, or Maintainable Middle Ground Exchange. Yes, it's literally just a discussion, but with some very key guidelines. The short version is as follows:

1   Remember that tone is key! Keep it professional and respectful, even if you disagree.
2   Acknowledge the reviewer's concern and then open a discussion with them.
3   Aim to understand each other. Explain the reasoning for each of your approaches.
4   If small modifications aren't enough to come to an agreement, find middle ground.
5   If middle ground still can't be found, consider bringing the team into the discussion.
6   In the end, the solution that makes sense to the majority of your team's developers, including future developers, should be the one decided on.

That's the quick version! For more detail, let's dive deeper into each step.

First and foremost, remember that tone is key: a whole section is dedicated to the tone of voice later in this chapter, but it's also listed here first because it's that important. As an author who receives and a reviewer who gives this kind of debated suggestion, remember to keep the conversation you are about to have professional and respectful, even if you disagree. Actively listen to each other's point of view and be open to modifying your own solution based on valid arguments. Remember, you're not the code that's about to be discussed! And you're both humans at the end of the day!

Next, acknowledge the reviewer's concern and open a discussion: As an author who is open to constructive feedback, let the reviewer know you heard them and want to discuss this potential issue of code clarity further. Invite them to an offline discussion, either in person or over a video call, to continue the conversation.

Start the discussion with the goal of understanding each other: Ask the reviewer what they found confusing. Don't take offense to what they may say, even if you think your solution is as "clear as can be." The point is to understand where your reviewer's confusion is coming from. In the best-case scenario, there might just be some small aspect of your solution that needs to be modified. This could be

- Adding an explanatory comment in your code where the reviewer initially felt confused.
- Comparing against existing guidelines. If there are team conventions, established best practices or patterns, or project style guides, see if either approach aligns better with those established guidelines.
- Adding documentation to guide the developer through the code.

In more involved cases, further discussion may be required. Here, both of you should explain the reasoning behind your solutions. Go through

- The thought process behind your approach (I chose this over this because . . . ; I initially tried this, but found . . .)
- The goals you aimed to achieve (This approach focuses on efficiency . . . ; With this particular section, readability was most important . . .)

Just as pausing and pondering can make things make sense to you, explaining your thought processes to each other can surface potential misunderstandings. It can also help you understand the strengths and weaknesses of each other's solution.

Ideally, you now have some background on each other's solutions. The next step is to find middle ground between the two. There are a few ways to find that middle ground:

- Ask the reviewer if they have a specific suggestion that would improve clarity for them without sacrificing the intended goal of your solution.
- See whether there are elements from both implementations that can be combined. Maybe their approach has a clearer variable naming convention, while your approach structures the logic more effectively.
- Conduct a mini pair-programming session with each other and come up with an entirely new solution together.
- Consider the readability of this solution for future developers unfamiliar with this code.

Remember that finding middle ground isn't about debating whose code is "better" and choosing that approach; it's about finding a solution that is clear and maintainable to both—and, really, all future, developers.

In the event that middle ground still can't be found, it may be time to add some fresh pairs of eyes to the discussion. Consider bringing the team into this exchange for their perspective. There might be an insight, idea, or opinion that moves the conversation in a completely different direction, but one that can address both the author's and reviewer's clarity concerns.

At the end of the day, the goal is to find a balance between a clear and maintainable solution that achieves the initial objective, even if it's not exactly either developer's original preference.

6.1.2 Specificity

Much like incomplete or unclear PRs, obscure and fuzzy comments introduce confusion into the code review. As we'll see over and over again, confusion equals delays and frustration. Let's avoid that. Let's be *helpful* and *practical* reviewers. Instead, aim to be as specific as you can in your comments.

BE CLEAR IF SOMETHING NEEDS TO BE DONE

When I go back to a PR I've opened and see some comments, I tend to assume some sort of additional work or change is tied to each of those comments. This is not always the case. To make it clear whether a change is needed, explicitly call out what needs to be done (or not) in the *comment*. This immediately signals to the PR author, "Hey! I'm important and need you to do something" or "This is good to know, but nothing needs to be done about it." By doing this, authors no longer have to guess. Instead, they can use that time effectively and direct their attention to the comments that do require consideration and confidently close the others that don't.

You can choose how explicit and formal you want to be with this callout. There are different systems to consider!

COMMENT SIGNALS

Our team labeled comments with what we called "signals." These are quick categorizations of comments used for specific purposes. In the same way we labeled `nitpicks`, we labeled comments with necessary changes, as shown in the following listing.

> **Listing 6.1 Needs change comment signal used by Adrienne's team**

```
needs change: This is importing the wrong module 'ts/widgets'.
It should be importing 'ts/components'.
```

Code review comment using a 'needs change' label; quickly signals that something needs to be done

As long as the author can quickly tell the difference between a comment that requires changes and one that doesn't, you're doing it right. Table 6.1 shows the signals I used often with my teams.

Table 6.1   Comment signals used by Adrienne's team

Comment signal	Use for
`needs change:`	<ul><li>Smaller changes and fixes that can be resolved in a single commit Small updates to current PR</li><li>Suggestions that result in a Propose outcome when going through the 5 Ps</li><li>These changes can't be ignored and block the PR by default.</li></ul>
`needs rework:`	<ul><li>Larger changes that require major rework or refactoring</li><li>Typically, these initiate an offline discussion as there's a lot to discuss.</li><li>These changes need to be addressed and block the PR by default.</li></ul>
`align:`	<ul><li>Changes that work and are technically valid but don't follow team conventions/project style guide</li><li>These changes can't be ignored and block the PR by default.</li></ul>
`levelup:`	<ul><li>Suggestions, improvements, or other feedback that can improve the code but don't need to be considered or revised at the moment</li><li>These changes are strongly encouraged for consideration in a future PR but are nonblocking by default.</li></ul>
`nitpick:`	<ul><li>Purely subjective commentary that does not affect the code</li><li>If you must add a nitpick, clearly identify it as such. But try not to include nitpicks at all!</li><li>These changes can be ignored and are nonblocking by default. In fact, they should never block a PR!</li></ul>

MoSCoW COMMENTS

Another way to categorize your feedback is through something called MoSCoW comments. (https://mng.bz/WVlg). Adapted from the world of project management and how requirements are prioritized, MoSCoW stands for Musts, Shoulds, Coulds, and Woulds. These map pretty closely to how code review comments might be categorized, as shown in Table 6.2.

Table 6.2   MoSCoW categories and their uses

MoSCoW Category	Use for
`Must:`	<ul><li>Changes that have to be addressed to be approved. These can't be ignored.</li></ul>
`Should:`	<ul><li>Suggestions that are an obvious and clear improvement. As an author receiving a `Should` comment, you have to give a reason to ignore it, and the reviewer has to agree. Third parties can be brought in when there's no consensus on what to do.</li></ul>
`Could:`	<ul><li>Improvements or niceties that the reviewer thinks will improve the overall codebase in some way but are likely going above and beyond what the original task requires</li><li>Ignorable by the author; no reason needed by the author to ignore</li></ul>
`Would:`	<ul><li>Those "I wouldn't have done it this way" comments that are 100% personal preference</li><li>Guiding suggestions for junior developers with the intent to educate</li></ul>

To use MoSCoW comments, each comment would begin with M:, S:, C:, or W: followed by the comment.

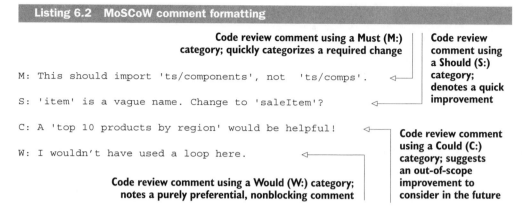

Listing 6.2 MoSCoW comment formatting

Code review comment using a Must (M:) category; quickly categorizes a required change

Code review comment using a Should (S:) category; denotes a quick improvement

```
M: This should import 'ts/components', not 'ts/comps'.

S: 'item' is a vague name. Change to 'saleItem'?

C: A 'top 10 products by region' would be helpful!

W: I wouldn't have used a loop here.
```

Code review comment using a Could (C:) category; suggests an out-of-scope improvement to consider in the future

Code review comment using a Would (W:) category; notes a purely preferential, nonblocking comment

MoSCoW comments are a decent way to organize your code review comments, especially if you don't currently use a system. Try introducing this system to your team and experiment with it.

My team tried MoSCoW comments (prior to using comment signals), and it worked out initially. We found that the lines between Must and Should and between Should and Could were too blurry for us. I received far too many Musts; each time a specific reviewer looked at my PRs, I came back to 10 or 12 Must comments when, really, over half of them were Shoulds and Coulds. We tried to set clear boundaries on what these categories meant within the context of our team, but it didn't really clear the confusion. More critically, it caused more arguments about the appropriate categorization to userather than debates on the suggestions themselves!

We did agree on the recurring types of comments our team would give each other. This is what led us to use comment signals instead. We could customize the labels used and define what they meant for our team. We started with needs change and nitpick while transitioning away from MoSCoW. Over time, we added the ones I discussed earlier (needs rework, align, levelup) to further refine our signals, and it worked out really well for us.

While my team didn't have success with MoSCoW comments, it doesn't mean your team won't! I share my story in the hopes that you'll consider what my team didn't:

- Get on the same page for the categories. Understand what Must, Should, Could, and Would categories mean for your team. Make it official in your team working agreement.
- See whether the categories fit the majority of your comment types. Do they neatly fall within the MoSCoW categories, or do you constantly run into suggestions that blur the lines?
- Consider whether your team uses each category equivalently. Can your colleagues agree on what constitutes a Must from a Should or a Could from a Would?

Keeping these things in mind, MoSCoW comments could be a great addition to your team's code review!

CONVENTIONAL COMMENTS

For those that want to get real science-y about comments, you can consider Conventional Comments (https://conventionalcomments.org/). If you're familiar with Conventional Commits, you'll likely feel accustomed to Conventional Comments in no time.

Working off the same premise that I encourage, Conventional Comments aim to be a standard for formatting comments of any review/feedback process so that they are actionable and useful. Conventional Comments follow the format in the following listing.

Listing 6.3   Conventional Comment format

```
// Source: https://conventionalcomments.org/

<label> [decorations]: <subject>
[discussion]
```

Conventional comment format. <label> denotes what kind of comment it is, [decorations] are optional decorator labels that further describe the comment, and <subject> contains the main message of the comment.

[discussion] is an optional part of the conventional comment format that contains supporting statements, context, reasoning, or anything else to help communicate the "why" and "next steps" for resolving the comment.

From the official Conventional Comments site, each component is used for the following:

- *Label*—This is a single label that signifies what kind of comment is being left.
- *Subject*—This is the main message of the comment.
- *Decorations (optional)*—These are extra decorating labels for the comment. They are surrounded by parentheses and comma-separated.
- *Discussion (optional)*—This contains supporting statements, context, reasoning, and anything else to help communicate the "why" and "next steps" for resolving the comment.

Pretty organized, right? Well, Conventional Comments go one step further and denote which labels to actually use. According to their official site, the labels in table 6.3 are strongly suggested for use.

Table 6.3   Conventional Comment labels

Conventional Comment Label	How to use them
suggestion:	Suggestions propose improvements to the current subject. It's important to be explicit and clear on what is being suggested and why it is an improvement. Consider using patches and the *blocking* or *non-blocking* decorations to further communicate your intent.

Table 6.3   Conventional Comment labels *(continued)*

Conventional Comment Label	How to use them
`issue:`	Issues highlight specific problems with the subject under review. These problems can be user-facing or behind the scenes. It is strongly recommended to pair this comment with a `suggestion`. If you are not sure if a problem exists or not, consider leaving a `question`.
`praise:`	Praises highlight something positive. Try to leave at least one of these comments per review. Do not leave false praise (which can actually be damaging). Do look for something to sincerely praise.
`todo:`	TODO's are small, trivial, but necessary changes. Distinguishing todo comments from issues: or suggestions: helps direct the reader's attention to comments requiring more involvement.
`question:`	Questions are appropriate if you have a potential concern but are not quite sure if it's relevant or not. Asking the author for clarification or investigation can lead to a quick resolution.
`thought:`	Thoughts represent an idea that popped up from reviewing. These comments are non-blocking by nature, but they are extremely valuable and can lead to more focused initiatives and mentoring opportunities.
`chore:`	Chores are simple tasks that must be done before the subject can be "officially" accepted. Usually, these comments reference some common process. Try to leave a link to the process description so that the reader knows how to resolve the chore.
`note:`	Notes are always nonblocking and simply highlight something the reader should take note of.
`nitpick:`	Nitpicks are trivial preference-based requests. These should be non-blocking by nature.

Source: https://conventionalcomments.org/

To go one more step further, the notion of decorations is also used with Conventional Comments. These are decorators that give additional context to a comment. They also further classify comments that have the same label. In figure 6.5, we see a security suggestion versus a test suggestion.

@cheshirec
suggestion (security): I'm a bit concerned that we are implementing our own DOM purifying function here...

Could we consider using the framework instead?

@cheshirec
suggestion (test,if-minor): It looks like we're missing some unit test coverage that the cat disappears completely.

Figure 6.5   Conventional Comment decorators distinguish a security suggestion from a test suggestion. Source: https:// conventionalcomments.org/

Conventional Comments suggest establishing a minimal set of decorations to use that are clear in their intent. These may be specific to an organization or team and can be customized to their needs. Of the ones they suggest using, the `non-blocking` and `blocking` decorations are quite practical and can apply to almost every team, as shown in table 6.4.

Table 6.4   Conventional Comment labels

Conventional Comment Decoration	How to use them
`(non-blocking)`	A comment with this decoration should not prevent the code changes under review from being accepted. This decoration is helpful for organizations that consider any comment blocking by default.
`(blocking)`	A comment with this decoration should prevent the code changes under review from being accepted until they are resolved. This decoration is helpful for organizations that consider comments non-blocking by default.
`(if-minor)`	This decoration gives some freedom to the author in that they should resolve the comment only if the changes are minor or trivial.
Area of focus e.g., `(ux)`, `(ui)`, `(security)`, `(frontend)`, `(backend)`, `(infrastructure)`	This decoration can further classify a comment with a focus area. The wider the stack your team is responsible for, the more useful these classifications may be.

Source: https://conventionalcomments.org/

What's the most important thing to remember about decorations? Adding one to a comment should improve its understandability and maintain readability, not worsen it. Decorations that don't add much to the comment or too many decorations on a single comment conflict directly with their purpose.

Personally, I haven't worked on projects that required the breadth of labels that Conventional Comments offers and suggests. As mentioned earlier, my team was able to work with just a few curated ones. However, I do think following the standard they present helps create more actionable comments. I also really like the notion of decorations to help give more context to the comment. If your team finds any of these attributes of Conventional Comments useful, it's worth checking out!

QUOTE OR HIGHLIGHT THE SPECIFICS OF THE CODE YOU ARE DISCUSSING

In most code review tools and platforms, you can highlight the specific parts of code you are referring to when adding a comment. Sometimes, the entire line gets highlighted, while other tools allow more granular highlighting. Regardless of how much you highlight, here are a few things to keep in mind to make sure you are as specific and clear as possible:

- When possible, only highlight the applicable lines of code. If you're having trouble with some logic in a specific part of a method, only highlight the portions that are confusing rather than the entire method. If you see three lines of repeated code in five places that could be replaced with an extracted method, highlight and leave a comment on each instance of the repeated code rather than adding a top-level comment. Yes, it's a bit more work, but it makes it much easier to pinpoint these changes and shows some due diligence on your part.

- When highlights can't clearly convey what you mean to communicate, add extra context by quoting method names or variables in the comments. Some tools even have Markdown capabilities; take advantage of that and use code formatting for these items to distinguish them further in your comment.
- If necessary or likely to add helpful context, call out the line numbers of the code you are referring to. Again, this should already be available by default through your code review's highlighting function, but if not, it won't hurt to specify exactly what part of the file you are referring to in your comment.

The more specific you can be for the author, the less potential delay you introduce into the review. Pinpointing exactly what needs to be changed, reworked, moved, or fixed makes those actions easier for everyone and is one of several ways to cultivate developer happiness.

6.1.3 Focused outcome

In a study on useful comments, transformation verbs—words that denote some kind of state change—made up a larger part of what was considered useful comments, while comments classified as nonuseful had more verbs that did not denote any change in state [1]. This interesting finding can be applied to how we write comments, especially those that ask the author to fix something or make a change. Here's how.

ASKING THE AUTHOR TO MAKE A CHANGE

As a reviewer, first, ask yourself what needs to be done. Think of all the concise, actionable verbs that you may use to describe your request: rename, remove, consolidate, expand, fix, rewrite, move, reorganize, etc. By focusing on these kinds of transformation verbs, your requests can be concise for the author.

Next, what does the end state look like? How will the author know when they are complete or have properly fulfilled the change or fix you are about to ask them to do? Distill that into an actionable task you can add to your comment.

Finally, where there's an ask, there's a need to explain why. Similar to leaving meaningful comments in code (i.e., explaining why something was implemented in a particular way rather than regurgitating what the code does), giving the author your rationale behind a proposed change brings clarity and justification. Going through the 5P process is a good place to start; if the process leads you to propose your suggestion, you likely have some thoughts that can help you form your suggestion.

THE TRIPLE-R PATTERN

If you find yourself struggling to compose a comment that asks for a change, try what I call the Triple-R pattern (alternatively, R-Cubed or, affectionately, the RRR! pattern):

- *Request*—A sentence explaining what you'd like the author to do.
- *Rationale*—A sentence or two explaining why the request is warranted. Include references or links to justify and support your request.
- *Result*—A measurable end state the author can compare their change to. It could be a metric to reach, a screenshot of an intended state, or, quite literally, what the code should look like after the change.

By explicitly spelling out what you'd like the author to do, there's less chance for misinterpretation and, ideally, a shorter response time for feedback to be addressed. Let's walk through some examples.

- *Moving a method*
  - *Request*—Can we move the `AuthenticateUser()` method into our `AuthenticationUtilities` library?
  - *Rationale*—Similar methods are in the `AuthenticationUtilities` library (like `ReauthenticateUser()` and `AuthenticateThirdPartyUser()`). `AuthenticateUser()` is also called more than a few times, which warrants its place in the library. Lastly, our Team Working Agreement advises us [link] to place any authentication behavior within the `AuthenticationUtilities` library.
  - *Result*—After this change, calls to `AuthenticateUser()` should be through the library rather than a standalone declaration.
- *Use a* `for` *loop instead of* `map`
  - *Request*—Can we replace the map on line 32 with a `for` loop?
  - *Rationale*—The `map` seems to be used solely for iteration and does nothing with the new array that it generates. If there's no need for additional manipulation and we aren't expecting to create a new array, a `for` loop would be a better way to iterate through these items.
  - *Result*—The `map` is replaced with a `for` loop on line 32.
- *Request a more meaningful variable name*
  - *Request*—Can the variable `"item"` be renamed to something less ambiguous?
  - *Rationale*—The variable name `"item"` is vague and provides little context within its scope. Specifically, the notion of discounts being applied to this object is lost, making the function a bit unclear.
  - *Result*—The variable name `"item"` is changed to something more meaningful; suggestions include `"discountEligibleItem"` and `"discountEligibleProduct"`.

In each of these examples, I composed the request using the respective R of the Triple-R pattern. While a bit more work, these comments can make requests for changes easier to read and, ideally, more concise to write. If this is something you choose to employ with your team, try it out until your team gets the hang of it. You may find that after some time, your team will naturally start writing comments in this way and choose to get rid of the labels altogether. Paired with comment signals, your comments could eventually look like this:

```
needs change: Can we update this endpoint to use version 3 (v3)? The call
to our getCoordinates() method currently references version 2 (v2), a soon-
to-be-deprecated (link) version, which will cause functionality to break.
Also, our other endpoints are already using v3; updating this will keep our
code consistent.
```

If you decide to keep the labels or at least write comments this way, the captured rationale and decisions behind every change will persist. While some of this information may be found in design documents or the initial work tickets, the choices agreed upon and revisions made during the code review can sometimes get lost. By having the same clarity and context in your comments, their value extends beyond the current PR and even the current project [1]. You'll be left with incredibly detailed artifacts that could be invaluable to future teammates or even yourself a couple of months later.

6.1.4   *Effective code review comment examples*

Now that you know what makes a comment effective, we can go through some more examples. As you read through them, take note of the characteristics we discussed: How quickly are you able to recognize what it's about and what it's asking for? What contributes to the comment's objectivity? What needs to happen as a result of this comment? You'll start to seek out these cues in the comments you read and ideally, integrate them into the comments you write.

Listing 6.4   Effective comment example 1

```
needs change: The SanitizeCustomerInput() method could go into our utils
library. Since it's reused more than three times, it should probably go into
our utils library with our other reusable methods. This also follows our
coding convention for repeating methods.
```

Here, we see a comment that suggests moving a method into a utility library. This suggestion is made because the reviewer has seen the same method used more than three times and that similar methods are housed in the utility library. As a second point of support, the team's coding convention sets this precedent for repeating methods. Using an objective set of arguments to motivate the change makes it easier to acknowledge this comment as one that intends to make the codebase better—and nothing else. Assuming the referenced coding convention is in this team's Team Working Agreement (of course, it is; why wouldn't it be?), we also see how effective it can be as an objective resource in a code review.

Listing 6.5   Effective comment example 2

```
needs rework: Can we fix the notification to pop up on the bottom-right of a
user's screen? I've run this on several browsers and this notification
actually pops up on the top-right, but our ticket (#1249) specifies bottom-
right. As of today, the actual behavior doesn't match our requirements. Let's
discuss rework commitment offline.
```

This example of an objective comment shows some due diligence on the reviewer's part. A fix is requested because the code changes don't match the requirements of the related ticket. This disparity alone qualifies as an objective reason to make a change and suggest a fix. By running the code changes on their own machine and confirming they don't actually output the intended outcome, the reviewer can likely post some supporting screenshots to show the notification in the wrong place. Finally, by referencing the ticket that states the intended outcome—in this case, a notification that pops up on the bottom right—the reviewer brings another objective resource to support their comment. As discussed previously, rework typically initiates an offline discussion, and that's included as well.

Listing 6.6   Effective comment example 3

```
needs change: Can we replace this method with the authenticateUser method
from our authentication library? The current change uses a method that will
be deprecated in two weeks. #134 and #147 were similar PRs and were also
advised to use the authenticateUser method.
```

In this example, the reviewer voices a valid concern: a method being used is going to be deprecated. The review suggests replacing it with an equivalent method recommended by an existing library. This suggestion is supported by two other linked PRs (#134 and #147) that were asked to do the same thing.

As you start to review others' code and come across items that need to be fixed or changed, don't be hesitant to bring up valid concerns. If you focus on writing objective, specific, and outcome-focused comments, your comments should be received without ill intent and with fewer misinterpretations of your words.

6.2   *Tone of voice*

When we talk to each other, it's typically understood that we should treat each other with respect. When those conversations happen through a written format, respect partly manifests in the tone of voice you choose to use (knowingly or unknowingly) with your words. In code reviews, keeping your tone of voice in mind is especially important, as it could make or break your team dynamic. Take the story of Jonah Andersson, a Microsoft MVP and senior Azure consultant for Solidify, as an enlightening example:

> ✑ *I had an experience where a fellow developer who was senior to me who was not really nice in writing his code review comments to me. As a junior developer back then, I thought it was not so nice or humane to criticize my code on a personal level. It affected me so emotionally that I had to bring it up and talk to that teammate and tell him that I did not like his tone in his PR comments.*

While we hope our own code reviews never employ personal attacks or a focus on items other than the code, it's a relevant reminder I bring up today. If there's anything that you take away from this section, it's to focus on the code, not the developer.

THE POWER OF "YOU"

In an interesting study on detecting interpersonal conflict in issues and code review, researchers explored whether patterns exist in the code review discussions labeled as "toxic" versus "nontoxic." After conducting an exploratory analysis, the authors found that the second-person pronoun "you" was more frequent in comments classified as toxic text [2]. Even more interesting, when they further investigated both toxic and nontoxic comments that included "you" to determine any differences, they found that the toxic text was more likely to begin with "you," rather than appearing elsewhere in the sentence [2]. Their examples showed that toxic comments were typically direct attacks on the person: "You don't care to be a part of the project," "You are expected to comply," "You decided to insult . . ." [2]. Figure 6.6 shows a breakdown of the words that rated statistically more likely to appear in toxic and nontoxic comments.

	unigram	z-score	bigram	z-score	ngram	z-score
Toxic	you	12.172	it is	5.555	if you want	3.397
	people	7.292	you want	4.81	it is not	2.712
	even	7.097	that is	4.272	do you think	2.576
	do	6.71	going to	4.256	you need to	2.397
	what	6.644	you are	4.187		
	is	6.373	trying to	4.053		
	want	6.078	if you	3.682		
	your	5.796	to do	3.668		
	because	5.657	do not	3.556		
	why	5.547	you think	3.539		
Non-toxic	tests	-4.773	could you	-2.815		
	unit	-4.858	the pull	-2.889		
	vs	-4.982	as the	-3.137		
	file	-5.15	and the	-3.143		
	files	-5.165	of files	-3.296		
	for	-5.574	we can	-3.48		
	test	-5.76	pull request	-3.668		
	from	-5.872	code to	-3.856		
	at	-6.732	to the	-4.031		
	line	-6.782	instead of	-5.004	the pull request	-2.276

Detecting interpersonal conflict in issues and code review: cross pollinating open-and closed-source approaches.

Qiu, H. S., Vasilescu, B., Kästner, C., Egelman, C., Jaspan, C., & Murphy-Hill, E. (2022. May)

Figure 6.6   Toxic comment unigram breakdown. "You" is statistically more likely to be found in comments labeled toxic.

Conversely, a focus on technical discussion was clearly representative of nontoxic discussions. Terms like "test," "files," and "pull request," among other technical terms, were almost nonexistent in toxic comments but quite prevalent in nontoxic ones [2]. We see this in figure 6.7.

unigram	z-score	bigram	z-score	ngram	z-score
Toxic					
you	12.172	it is	5.555	if you want	3.397
people	7.292	you want	4.81	it is not	2.712
even	7.097	that is	4.272	do you think	2.576
do	6.71	going to	4.256	you need to	2.397
what	6.644	you are	4.187		
is	6.373	trying to	4.053		
want	6.078	if you	3.682		
your	5.796	to do	3.668		
because	5.657	do not	3.556		
why	5.547	you think	3.539		
Non-toxic					
tests	-4.773	could you	-2.815		
unit	-4.858	the pull	-2.889		
vs	-4.982	as the	-3.137		
file	-5.15	and the	-3.143		
files	-5.165	of files	-3.296		
for	-5.574	we can	-3.48		
test	-5.76	pull request	-3.668		
from	-5.872	code to	-3.856		
at	-6.732	to the	-4.031		
line	-6.782	instead of	-5.004	the pull request	-2.276

Detecting interpersonal conflict in issues and code review: cross pollinating open-and closed-source approaches.

Qiu, H. S., Vasilescu, B., Kästner, C., Egelman, C., Jaspan, C., & Murphy-Hill, E. [2022, May]

Figure 6.7   Nontoxic comment unigram breakdown. Technical terms, like "tests," "files," or "pull request" are statistically more likely to be found in comments labeled nontoxic.

Hopefully, it goes without saying that personally attacking or calling out the author in a code review is never acceptable. We need to be kind and empathetic in our code reviews, and a big part of that is understanding how to communicate via text.

YET, IT'S NOT ALL ABOUT "YOU"

If you received the following comment, how would you respond?

```
You should move the Vehicle class to a separate file.
```

You could interpret that as, "Hey there! Just a thought: it's probably a good idea to move that into a separate file." More likely, though, you may interpret that as, "Hey, YOU. Move that into a separate file, pronto!".

It can sound extreme, but that's what text can do. Void of facial expressions (which we can try to mitigate; more later) and the actual way your voice would speak a comment out loud, text can be misinterpreted very easily. Unfortunately, we're usually not intending to be rude or pushy. Yet, with only the words we choose to put on a screen and send to an author, we can seem like a rude or pushy reviewer.

Don't use that tone with me!

One thing about tone of voice—it applies to authors too! When responding to feedback, authors also have a responsibility to follow the two Politeness Principles. Whether you're participating in the code review as an author or reviewer, there will likely be moments when you feel unsure about the feedback or comments you just wrote.

In such an event, try asking yourself these questions:

- Do you mention the person a bit more than the code? If so, try rephrasing what you are saying to discuss technical elements or code-focused topics.
- Is the overall feeling polite, friendly, and outcome-focused? Great, keep that going!
- On the other hand, are there combative, commanding, or passive-aggressive undertones? Take a moment or a break to interrupt the disruptive mindset you may be in. Grab a drink, take a walk, or take some deep breaths for 5 minutes. Afterward, go back to your comment and try to understand what led you to write your comments in such a way. Then, try to rewrite your comment in a more productive way. If it helps, use the Triple-R pattern to help organize your thoughts and keep you focused on the code rather than the person.
- Does the comment add value? Will it drive productive discussion?
- Can any parts of your comment be lost in translation, misconstrued, or not apply? For example, if you are working with a global team and make an analogy ("It's like a football field"), would it apply to everyone? If not, take it as a challenge to find a more universal analogy that everyone can understand.
- If you're in the middle of a discussion, does it feel like you're getting nowhere with the other person? Are things resulting in a deadlock? If so, you might consider bringing another developer into the mix and see whether their perspective can remove the deadlock or make some sort of progress.

Ideally, using the patterns, processes, and principles described in this chapter will make it rare for your team to misinterpret each other. For those edge cases that feel a bit off, try going through this list to see whether it helps you spot why!

However, we can mitigate this lack of context. If we keep just two practical principles in mind, we can vastly improve that comment.

PRINCIPLE 1: REPLACE NOTIONS OF "YOU" WITH "WE"

Referencing the author in comments goes against our responsibility as reviewers (focus on the code, not the developer). It also makes it more likely for the author to feel directly attacked or defensive (though they also have a responsibility not to). This problem can easily be solved by referring to the team—in this case, the *membership "we"* rather than the more direct "you." Let's change our example:

```
"We should move the Vehicle class to a separate file."
```

Quite the difference, right? Even though we know that the author will be doing this work, using the more polite "we" reinforces that the quality of the codebase is the whole team's responsibility.

PRINCIPLE 2: ASK, DON'T COMMAND

Comments that are framed as requests rather than commands are much more well-received. Imagine if I said, "Use a Boden mug for my latte" or "Alter this dress so that it's fitted in the waist"; no one (that's a decent and respectful human being) actually talks like that! Instead, "Could you use a Boden mug for my latte?" and "Is it possible to alter this dress so that it's fitted in the waist?" are much more approachable and inviting ways to communicate. In code reviews, we need to err on the side of being approachable, inviting, and polite:

```
"Can we move the Vehicle class to a separate file?"
```

One thing to note here: let's say we didn't follow principle 1 and just rephrased our original comment as a request:

```
"Can you move the Vehicle class to a separate file?"
```

It's subtle, but do you hear the difference? Focusing back to the author, despite reframing this as a request, still sounds a bit too frank. By changing one more word and asking the collective "we," it's a bit more courteous. We can't be too courteous in code reviews ☺.

Don't forget to add context!

We spent the bulk of this chapter learning how to write effective comments. The final thing we can do to improve this comment is to add context, especially since we're making a suggestion! As we've learned, these types of comments would benefit from a clear comment signal and a justification on why to make this change:

```
needs change: Can we move the Vehicle class to a separate file? This
follows our team guidelines (link) and will improve the readability of
this section.
```

With the addition of a comment signal, there's less ambiguity in whether or not this is a suggestion. Likewise, adding the justification for the request makes it less likely to be interpreted as a personal preference but rather as providing an objective rationale. If you want to make sure your tone of voice rarely leads to misinterpretation, either of your comments or your character, let those two principles—let's call them the Politeness Principles—guide you during code reviews.

This part of code reviews is so important that others in the industry have this principle in one form or another on their own development teams! Glenn Reyes (software engineer at Kadena) says it's important to "Keep it constructive and objective" in code reviews. Marilag Svennevig (CIO at Dewise) feels similarly about her teams: "We only have a simple principle when reviewing: just be pragmatic, be curious, and be kind."

And, luckily for Jonah, a senior Azure consultant at Solidify, an awful experience with a code review ended up being a positive lesson. Jonah's story finishes:

> ○ *After many years of development, coding, and learning by doing, I have learned that I do not want to be that "rude" code reviewer, I want to be able to suggest my fellow developer how to write better code by being neutral and I always try to keep my PR comments to be constructive, logical yet kind and respectful.*

6.3 Code compliments

When you see something you like in a code review, do you say something? Are there moments where you think, "Wow, that's actually a really clever way to do this!" but feel like adding these thoughts to the review is unnecessary? You're not alone. In fact, some developers don't even consider positive feedback during a code review. I think we should change that. Code reviews don't have to live on as the critical, demeaning, or demotivating process we may be used to. If you find an outstanding piece of code, say so!

"It's a waste of time" is a common response I hear when I advocate for code compliments. To that, I say, everything in moderation. Of course, if you start pointing out all the little things you may like in a code review, it will take longer, and your positive comments will lose their luster and impact. If everything is good, nothing is truly good. So, save your compliments and positive feedback for the code that truly deserves it—a clever (read: smart yet still human-readable) implementation of a performance optimization, a display of the author's deep understanding of a programming language, or even for teaching you something new.

Some great examples of a code compliment are as follows:

```
What an elegant solution. I would have never thought to approach it in that
way. Bravo!
Huh, I didn't know JavaScript could do that. Today I Learned :)
I wasn't aware of this library. That's super useful!
Daaaang. Your optimizations brought our load times down to 3ms! *Bows in
awe*
```

The only exception to adding compliments is if you are reviewing an intern's or junior's code. Give them all the praise. Your positive feedback will make them feel more confident in their abilities and reinforce what "good" code looks like, which is the kind to continue writing.

Summary

- We aim for codebase maintainability, so we write comments in a code review. If it won't contribute to this goal, it's likely not a comment you need to write.
- Effective comments depend on effective communication. They are also objective, as specific as possible, and have a focused outcome.

- Objective comments focus on the code and can be easily traced back to objective resources as supporting arguments. The 5P process (Pause and Ponder, and then choose Pass, Propose, or Postpone) can be used to determine objective suggestions, and the MMG Exchange can help you find middle ground on topics that aren't as clear cut.

- Specific comments denote if something needs to be done and explicitly call out the relevant code in question. Try comment signals, MoSCoW comments, or Conventional Comments to make it clear about whether something needs to be done. Write out variable/method/class names, list exact line numbers, and link to exact references—the more definitive you can be, the clearer you can be to the author.

- Outcome-focused comments tell the author exactly what to do. They typically include transformative verbs, which are actions that tend to change the state of the code. The outcome's results are also easily measured.

- The Triple-R pattern (Request, Rationale, Result) is a useful way to write comments that require a change or fix. Being specific about the request, giving your rationale behind it, and having a clear result to compare against make it easier for the author to understand and accept.

- If you see something you like that's really novel or is one of a kind, say so! Code compliments are always welcome in code reviews.

- Respect manifests in your tone of voice—meaning the way you write comments and the words you choose are important. Remember the two Politeness Principles: change notions of "you" to "we" and ask, don't command.

- Ultimately, be polite and be kind, always.

References

[1] Efstathiou, V., & Spinellis, D. (2018, May). Code review comments: Language matters. In *Proceedings of the 40th International Conference on Software Engineering: New Ideas and Emerging Results* (pp. 69–72). IEEE.

[2] Qiu, H. S., Vasilescu, B., Kästner, C., et al. (2022, May). Detecting interpersonal conflict in issues and code review: Cross pollinating open-and closed-source approaches. In *Proceedings of the 2022 ACM/IEEE 44th International Conference on Software Engineering: Software Engineering in Society* (pp. 41–55). ACM/IEEE.

Part 3

Dealing with dilemmas

Why does Anna always get her PRs approved?"

"This review will be at least a week; we only have one Senior Developer."

"What's the point of this process if Ralph doesn't have to go through it?"

"Review? We don't have time. This is an emergency!"

After a code review process has been established, these words have all been uttered in the years that followed. Teams change. Goals shift. Projects evolve. Through all the transformation, code reviews can become lackluster or morph into something you had never intended: an ineffective process your team no longer follows or enjoys. This part of the book talks about the very real dilemmas you might face once you've been using your code review process for some time.

Chapter 7 eases you into the types of code reviews you want to avoid. Chapter 8 talks specifically about lengthy code reviews; chapter 9 digs into process loopholes. Both chapters 8 and 9 guide you through the different conundrums your own team might face and what to do about them (or how to stop and prevent them entirely).

Finally, after discussing how things can go wrong in code reviews, we talk about the Emergency Playbook in chapter 10, a tool that helps your team stick to the right path. At this point, you've absorbed the most paramount information about code reviews; you should be able to maintain and adapt your team's process as you see fit. You'll also know what to keep an eye out for so that the process your team has worked so hard to build doesn't disintegrate or dissolve.

At this point, you might be interested in how your newly acquired knowledge fits in with other practices. If so, part 4, Pairing code reviews with other practices, may be of interest to you and your team. It can also be a great conversation starter, even if you don't implement the mentioned practices yourselves.

How code reviews can suck

This chapter covers

- Common pain points that can pop up in a code review
- Some real developer stories of code reviews gone wrong

Imagine being on a team of five. You're working on a relatively straightforward, monolithic application. Unfortunately, everyone is pushing their code to the main branch whenever they complete an assigned feature (or worse, whenever they want). You're stepping on each other's code, introducing varied naming conventions, overwriting and probably duplicating code, and much worse. It's the wild, wild West, and it's what having no code review process can feel like.

If you've worked on a team that did not have a code review process in place (or some quality checks as part of a CI/CD pipeline), you have probably experienced these pain points first-hand. A lot of time is wasted fixing things that shouldn't have been deployed into production in the first place. It becomes nearly impossible to revert to a good, working version of your application. And when those random bugs surface from the legacy code? You automatically multiply your story point estimate to resolve them since the code is quite cryptic—and, of course, the developer who wrote it is no longer here.

These effects compound when you have more complex applications, larger teams, distributed teams, or all three! Imagine working on an application that consists of 25 microservices. Your team of 10 engineers is responsible for five microservices, and the team is spread across the globe. Take the same symptoms from our earlier example, apply them here, and you'll end up with some very costly mistakes.

This pain point—the lack of any code review process at all—may even be the very reason you got this book! Luckily, you may already be applying what you've learned from parts 1 and 2 of this book to help you fix that problem. Unfortunately, there are other code review conundrums that can pop up once you do have a process in place. That's what I'll share with you in this chapter.

7.1 Code review pain points

Code reviews can be amazing if we can keep them consistent, maintainable, and effective. However, there are many ways code reviews can morph into a process we don't like or want. Usually, what gets in the way of (or starts chipping away at) a great code review process is a lack of communication and trust between members of a team or a lack of clear code review guidelines. Both manifest into the typical pain points that worsen code reviews to the point that people would rather have none at all. Here, we'll proactively explore the kinds of code reviews we don't want to have.

7.1.1 The lazy code review

One type of code review that is a major source of frustration for software developers is the lazy code review. There may be a process in place, but for one reason or another, the review itself is lackluster, done in haste, or done improperly. This kind of code review comes in many forms.

LOOKS GOOD TO ME SYNDROME

You've just received an email notification: a new PR was submitted by your colleague and is awaiting your review. You have some time, so you decide to take a look. Upon reaching the pull request (PR), you find 32 files changed, 1,078 lines deleted, and 1,345 lines added—and that's all you remember; the rest gets kind of fuzzy. You pride yourself on always giving proper, thorough reviews, but this is something else. You feel a bit icky, but you leave the infamous "LGTM 👍" ("Looks good to me 👍") comment and approve the PR. No one's really going to review that many files, right?

"Is it 5pm already?
Eh, LGTM 👍"

IT'S OK, IT'S AN EMERGENCY!

It's 3 am, and you've been paged as the on-call developer. There's a major problem in production: a random spike is occurring in one of your European regions, causing your cache to grow way past its threshold. You have automated processes in place that should prevent this from ever happening, but here we are. Despite having an established code review process, a big production fire like this seems to warrant a hotfix. After finding a solution (quite hastily), you quickly integrate your hotfix code straight into production, bypassing the established process. This works, and it was warranted for the situation at hand. However, an unhealthy precedent with your team has been established: if something is urgent enough, a process can be ignored. From this moment on, dangerous workarounds start to become the norm rather than the exception.

Code review?
We need that hotfix NOW!

THE (BIASED) BUDDY SYSTEM

After a rare focused afternoon, you've finally completed the feature you've been assigned this sprint. Proud and relieved, you open your PR, carefully adding helpful context for the reviewer. The following day, you check on the status of your PR. It's still open. However, your other colleagues' PRs are all approved. You're a bit annoyed. When you look closer, you can't believe it—two team members who are good friends have only been approving each other's PRs within minutes of being opened. And they've been doing this for a while. While not the result of code reviews, this behavior still affects the team's perception of the process. And when a process like the code review brings to light the flaws of poor team dynamics, it can quickly become the scapegoat.

LGTM! Let's get outta here :D

THE MISUSED CHAT SYSTEM

Your team has recently instituted a new code review policy: at least one reviewer needs to approve any PR that is submitted. You notice, however, that most PRs get approved within 5 minutes. For a moment, you consider whether your team is large enough to accommodate this pace and even conduct multiple reviews per day: you have 11 software developers in total. Unfortunately, you soon discover how the PRs are actually getting approved so fast: your team has found a workaround in the team chats. Instead of relying on proper reviews, an author posts a message in your team space and asks for a quick approval any time a new PR is created. Scouring through the long list of messages and requests, you find that whoever reads the latest message would jump into the PR and approve it without actually checking the code. You've even found that a QA (quality assurance) engineer, a "serial approver," would approve any open PR. Despite having a policy in place, things weren't working as they were supposed to.

Can I get one of those
nifty approvals?

Lazy code reviews are useless. In all of these scenarios, the pain points are clear: enforcing the process for some, but not all, and giving improper reviews (due to laziness or workarounds) can lead to resentment, tension, and major stress. This poor dynamic is amplified if the team's tech lead or manager ignores or condones the team's code review behavior.

7.1.2   *The mean code review*

An unnecessarily harmful code review type, the mean code review can wreak irreparable damage to your team. If you've ever been on the receiving end of an overly negative code review, comments, or comments that seem to focus more on you as a person than the code itself, you've unfortunately experienced this type of code review. It's this kind of process, and those kinds of comments, that developers dread the most. Let's see a couple of scenarios on how this could pan out.

I HAVE NO FILTER

On a public repository for an open source CSS Framework, the comment in figure 7.1 was found in one of the PRs. This was not photoshopped (other than redacting some identifying info and some light censorship), unfortunately. This is on a real repository out on the internet.

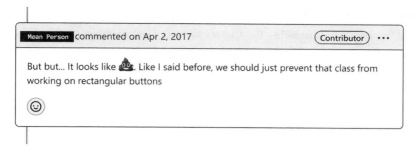

Figure 7.1   An actual comment on a PR (on an open source project)!

If the person who opened this PR was contributing to open source for the first time, I can guarantee you that they will likely not contribute again. Regardless of who submitted that PR, they may no longer feel welcome on this particular project, nor would they continue to support it. As for the commenter, this is a fairly clear example of comments that should never be written. There are better, more constructive ways to make your point.

YOU DON'T BELONG HERE

Say you're relatively new to the team. You're not new to software development, but you are new to this company. Nervous but excited, you are eager to contribute to the codebase and begin acclimating to your project and teammates. After much effort and careful inspection, you open your first PR. Unfortunately, a few hours later, you come back to a barrage of comments. They detail things to fix that are quite subjective, point out "stupid" mistakes using similar language, and really make you feel bad. This isn't a great start at all.

Now, imagine replacing yourself in the previous scenario with a junior developer or someone starting their first professional software development role. What would that experience do? How would this kind of introduction to code reviews affect this person's views of the process? Would you want to stay on a team like this? Work for a company that ignored exchanges like this? Stay in an industry where this is the norm? I think you can answer these questions quite passionately.

```
Maybe software development
       isn't for me.
```

Code reviews shouldn't be mean. In these code reviews, tact is nonexistent, and constructive criticism is an unknown concept to the reviewers. However, these mistakes can cause the most harm to the team.

7.1.3 *The shape-shifting code review*

Here, code reviews are impossible for the reviewers to manage, resulting in frustration and tension. These code reviews tend to drag on for so long because the code you started with is not the one you end up reviewing!

STACKING PRS

When one PR is based on another PR, which is based on another PR (and so on, though I hope not), this is known as stacking PRs. The original intent and context of the PR become unclear, making it quite difficult for the reviewer to give a proper review. Do I take into consideration the changes in the other PRs? Will my comments apply since there are so many pieces to consider that may or may not be part of this PR? What if the other dependent PRs are by different authors? Do I @mention them and pull them into this PR? The whole thing becomes unmanageable for the reviewer.

THE MOVING TARGET

You've been assigned a "quick" PR to review. Lovely. You take your time, almost reach the end of your review, and then BAM! New commits have been pushed, meaning you need to start over. Luckily, the new changes only include a few additions. You go through the changed files again, taking into account the new changes, and right when you click the Approve button, you find that the PR has automatically reverted to Needs Review status. Why? You guessed it, new changes were yet again pushed. How many times will this occur? Why did this person open a PR if they aren't finished? How do I not waste my time doing multiple reviews on the same PR?

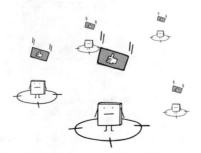

"Do you want a review or not?"

Code reviews need to be manageable. In these two shape-shifting scenarios, we see how frustrating code reviews can be for the reviewer when the PR is not ready or is not clear in its intent. Unless the review itself has established changes that need to be made, code reviews that keep changing their target will become unsustainable in the long run. Not to mention, you'll have some pretty annoyed colleagues.

7.1.4 The stringent code review

On the other end of the spectrum, there can be such a thing as "too much" code review, especially when no automation is in place. If the code review process involves too many steps or is too inflexible, unnecessarily complex, too reliant on manual tasks, or extremely strict, people will work around the process rather than follow it. The demanding nature of a code review like this can quickly turn into its biggest weakness.

DID YOU DO X, Y, AND Z—OH, AND D, E, AND G?

One of my past roles had a less-than-ideal code review process to deploy something to production. First, several manual scripts needed to be run to confirm some checks. This was to be self-acknowledged on the PR that they completed successfully. Next, as part of the PR, several links were required: a generated link to a staging environment where a preview could be viewed, a link to a report log from that staging environment, and a link to its corresponding work ticket (because the version control system was different from the task management system and could not be integrated). Once these were in place, a reviewer could finally start their review. If anything needed to be fixed, I had to complete all of those steps all over again. I'd manually update the newly generated staging links *each time* I responded to feedback that resulted in code changes. Sometimes, the service that generated these staging links would error out, time out, or be too busy to respond to my request. Did I mention there was a single agent that was responsible for creating these links for an organization of over 120? 😵 As you can imagine, our team despised this process.

"Our code review process is
outlined in those manuals."

EVERYTHING HERE GOES THROUGH ME

In another role in a smaller company, the code review process was mostly ideal. We had a testing, staging, and production environment and properly promoted code through each environment. We had quality checks that were mostly automated but required the appropriate approvals from our QA team and our colleagues. This was all great until a second mandatory approval from our project manager was introduced for all stages. This requirement meant that integrating a new feature into our testing environment required a code review from a fellow developer and the project manager. Once a QA engineer conducted their tests, their approval and the project manager's approval were required to promote the changes to a staging environment. To complete the series and for the changes to get deployed into production, the CTO and project manager needed to approve them.

"We're just waiting on one more
approval, then we can merge your PR!"

On the surface, this sounds extra secure. In reality, it meant our team was reliant on this project manager to be available and ready to approve, delaying an already cumbersome and long-running process.

Code reviews should be seamless with the rest of your workflow. As my first story illustrated, if your team gets bottlenecked by the processes surrounding the code review before you've even reached the review phase, there's something wrong. As my second story shows, if you have a situation where a quick fix needs to be deployed, but several approvals must be acquired, signatures collected, and other gate checks to jump across, people will undoubtedly grow tired of the process. In addition, the longer the delay in releasing new features or value to your customers, the costlier that can be for your organization's bottom line and reputation. At the worst end of this spectrum, people stop caring, which is detrimental to both your team and the codebase.

7.2 So, what do we do?

Phew, that was a wild ride, wasn't it? If you were reading some of those scenarios and regretfully nodding along in agreement, you've likely felt the pain of an ineffective or bad code review. The good news is that lots of those pain points can usually be attributed to some common problems, such as not having a collaborative understanding of team expectations, not knowing what is supposed to happen in a review and what each participant's responsibilities are, not using automation to the team's advantage, and not knowing how to communicate effectively during a review. We've covered how to do all of that in the earlier part of this book. This next part will deal with some of the trickier stuff. Let's see how to make our code reviews even better!

Summary

- Code reviews can present some challenging conundrums as time goes by.
- Proactively prevent code reviews from becoming lazy, mean, unmanageable, or too complicated. Heading in that direction can morph your code review process from good to real, real bad.

Decreasing code
review delays

8

This chapter covers

- Why code reviews take too long (and what to do about it)
- What to do about the "single senior developer reviewer" problem
- Knowing when to take discussions offline
- Uncovering gaps in other parts of your development lifecycle that result in gargantuan pull requests (and how to fix them)

Good code reviews take time—but not too much time, or everyone will hate them. It's a fine line between giving a review its due diligence and delaying the whole development workflow altogether. Take too long to get a PR opened (or ready, which are two different things!), and code reviews become bottlenecks. Take too long during the review, and it delays the value to your people. It's a lose–lose situation when you're experiencing both.

It should come as no surprise that code reviews that take too long are a common reason [1] developers don't like the process [2]. But why do they take so long?

176

Most causes are within our control, some are not (but we can try to mitigate that), and others are just plain excuses (shock!).

This chapter focuses on all of those pesky stealers of time and offers suggestions on what to do about them. After examining each one, you may find that there's actually a snag somewhere else in the process, with consequences only coming to light during the code review. In the end, we've been unfairly using the code review as the scapegoat for time delays.

> **NOTE**   I use *pull request* (PR) also to mean *merge request. Pull request* is a GitHub term, while *merge request* is a GitLab term. Both are mechanisms to propose changes to a main repository.

8.1   "We only have a single senior developer to review our PRs"

One common reason code reviews take too long is that teams require their most senior developer to be a reviewer on every PR. Whether that's because the senior developer has "always done it this way," is the best/ideal reviewer for the team's PRs, naturally gets assigned by the rest of the team on all PRs, or a myriad of other reasons, it has become a problem that many teams deal with.

This phenomenon is usually paired with the fact that there's only one senior developer on the team. And so, a bottleneck is formed. One I like to call the "single senior developer reviewer" problem. Of course, asking a single person to handle every PR is overwhelming. In most cases, teams need to readjust their perspective on who should review.

Code Reviews.

SUGGESTION 1: ANYONE ON THE DEVELOPMENT TEAM SHOULD BE ABLE TO APPROVE A PR

Senior developers get a lot of inherent respect and perceived authority on teams. This becomes a blessing and curse for those individuals, and the single senior developer reviewer problem is an example of why. However, just because someone is a senior developer doesn't mean they must be the reviewer. Anyone on the team should be able to approve a PR. Yes, anyone. New team members, junior developers, and others you might feel shouldn't have approval privileges. And their approval should carry the same weight as a senior developer's approval.

Anyone should be able to approve a PR.
(with a proper system of safeguards in place)

"But what if something breaks?" you nervously wonder. That's where a proper system of safeguards comes into play. That can come in the form of multiple environments or stages to deploy to; the ability to revert a deployed change easily; a CI pipeline that runs multiple, thorough, automated checks; a suite of proper unit and integration tests; a shared obligation toward accountability among the team; and a blameless culture. We mentioned plenty of these safeguards in the form of automations and self-checks in chapter 5. The more safeguards you employ, the easier it is for your team to contribute equally and be confident in each other's reviewing and approving abilities. If you're not there yet, that's OK. The goal would be to reach such a state and implement such a robust system that anyone on the development team can approve a PR, and no one will freak out.

At the end of the day, we place a lot of responsibility and assurance on the senior developer to make sure things don't break. If they approve a PR, it is good enough and can be recognized as safe to deploy. We should know that this is not always the case. Senior developers also make mistakes. Senior developers also miss things. As Glenn Reyes, a software engineer at Kadena, shares:

> 💬 *I've worked with very knowledgeable mentors that basically know about all best practices of doing code reviews and we still managed (due to laziness) to ship code that came with bugs and errors after.*

Instead of a single person taking on all that responsibility, it should be spread evenly across the team. Giving everyone the ability and responsibility to approve PRs can reduce the number of PRs the senior developer has to review.

SUGGESTION 2: NOT ALL PRS SHOULD BE ASSIGNED TO THE SENIOR DEVELOPER
Speaking of sharing responsibility, not all PRs should be the senior developer's obligation. If there are small changes—say, trivial configuration changes, the addition of some unit tests, or typos in some documentation—that don't require the senior developer's expertise or, more appropriately, the PR contains changes that should be shared across the team, assign those PRs to other teammates. Spread that knowledge around and build up the team's expertise on these other key parts of the code base. Ideally, this strategy leaves more room for the senior developer to focus on PRs that do require their expertise or background knowledge.

Share the PR Load.
(Not ALL PRs have to be assigned to the Senior Developer)

Another thing? I've seen many developers reassign a PR that's been assigned to them. Their reason? "I don't know too much about this part of the code base. It should go to [person's name, usually the senior developer]". But if not now, when? Also, if this practice ultimately leads to the single senior developer reviewer problem we previously discussed, this routine perpetuates the problem and will likely not change.

SUGGESTION 3: TAKE CODE YOU AREN'T FAMILIAR WITH BUT ARE ASKED TO REVIEW AS AN OPPORTUNITY TO LEARN
If you receive a PR and feel like you may not be the best person to review it or maybe even get the urge to reassign it, take a moment. Ask yourself some questions:

- Is there any point in the future that you may be asked to work with, refactor, or take over the code you've been asked to look at?

- Does the code belong to a code base that is well within the realm of your team's jurisdiction to work with?

If you nodded "yes," even in a hesitant way, you shouldn't ignore the PR. In fact, now's the time to get acquainted with it!

Intimidating PRs

Go through the code. Try to understand what is happening. Take notes and jot down the questions you may have. Then, have an offline discussion with the author. Seek to understand that part of the code base that may be new to you. You'd be surprised at how much more thorough a review from someone like you can be than from someone familiar with the code. In fact, that may be the very reason you were assigned the PR.

At some point, that part of the code base may be your responsibility, meaning you'd have to go through the same learning phase anyway. So why not now? If you stay within the comfort zone of code that's familiar to you, how will you ever expand your understanding of the application as a whole? And how will your team sustain the number of code reviews required if most members aren't well-versed in the entire application? The goal is to level up the entire team over time and eventually eliminate the single senior developer reviewer problem for good.

8.2 *"I don't understand the PR"*

Ever review someone's code changes, and upon reading them, you thought to yourself, "What the [insert expression of choice]?!" Regrettably, you're not alone. In fact, confusion while reviewing a PR is a common reason it's delayed [1]. This confusion comes down to something intuitive: the PR is missing key information or context, making it unclear.

SUGGESTION 1: MAKE SURE YOUR PRS CAPTURE THE NECESSARY CONTEXT AND INFORMATION NEEDED TO COMPLETE A REVIEW

The obvious mitigation strategy for this problem is to make sure PRs are primed. We discussed the elements of a good PR and what's within the author's responsibilities at length in chapter 2. PR templates and PR validations, discussed in chapter 5, are two tactics to avoid this problem. PR templates can help authors make sure they don't forget anything in the description. You can even use different templates for different kinds of PRs. PR validators can automate and enforce consistent PRs; use them to autolabel your PRs and enforce consistent PR title formats.

SUGGESTION 2: REMIND AND ENCOURAGE AUTHORS THAT THEIR EFFORTS IN PREPARING THEIR PRS INFLUENCE HOW LONG THE REVIEW LASTS

What's less obvious is that authors of code changes need to put in a bit of effort to prepare their PRs! It really comes down to that. From adding the context and justification for their changes to organizing their work into manageable chunks to telling a clear story with their commit history and documentation, it's up to the authors to make it happen.

Authors, before opening a PR:

"YOU can influence how long this review lasts.
YOU decide how well your PR is prepared."

That might seem overwhelming, but I don't think it needs to be. You see, this is another one of those long-standing beliefs in software development that we need to challenge—that putting in the effort to prepare a proper PR is a burden. Much like unit tests or writing documentation, some developers scoff at the inconvenience they believe these essential functions bring. This attitude, however, sounds like the mindset of someone who "just writes code."

Since you're reading this book, however, I don't think you are someone who thinks they "just" write code. You are a developer who knows that we do so much more and that "much more" is where we bring the most value. It's the compilation, organization, and communication of knowledge surrounding our code that comprises a larger and more useful part of our role. It's the caring part. The giving a damn part. It's what makes us better software developers.

If we can convince those developers, the ones who "just write code" to care just as much, we can improve a heck of a lot more than just the PRs. Especially as professional software developers, we can't view code reviews, among other tasks, as an afterthought, a "nice-to-have," or a one-off task. We lead by example and pride ourselves on doing things the right way, not the most convenient or quick way. If we want to call ourselves professional software developers, we need to embody the due diligence innate in professional software development.

> **NOTE** Due diligence is part of the job. Unit tests, documentation, and properly preparing code to be reviewed are not burdens but essential functions of professional software development. To be a professional software developer is to exhibit due diligence.

8.3   *"There are too many files to review"*

Next up is the review with 50+ files (or more). Code reviews with copious file counts tend to leave the reviewer confused, which is understandable but hardly intended. And from what we learned earlier, confusion in reviews leads to unnecessary delays. Too many files in a review can be indicative of a few things: the author has poorly organized their work, the code changes in question are likely not atomic (meaning granular and with a single purpose), there are unrelated code changes crammed in with the intended one to be reviewed, or the most rare, a small, but repetitive change actually warrants the number of files in the review (like renaming a variable or refactoring of some sort). Whatever the case may be, they all point to the same solution: breaking down the code changes into smaller portions (and doing that way earlier in the process). We talk more about how to do that in section 8.4.

SUGGESTION 1: IF IT'S TOO LATE (OR TOO DIFFICULT) TO BREAK APART INTO SEPARATE PRS, ASK THE AUTHOR TO EXPLAIN EXPLICITLY HOW TO NAVIGATE THE CHANGES

Whether that's a very detailed outline in the PR description or through a direct conversation with the author (actually, do both), the state of the PR requires the author to put in a bit of extra effort. Ask them to describe how the changes are organized, what parts are critical to focus on versus which ones may not, and what files or areas can be safely ignored/have a low risk of causing major problems. Communicating with the author is similar to having a travel guide with you in a foreign country: you'll be directed to the most interesting parts, know what spots to ignore, and have a direct person to answer your questions and explain peculiarities as you explore.

Too late to break down a large PR?

Authors need to help you navigate the changes. Better yet, have them explain their large PR to the team (and review the PR as a team).

SUGGESTION 2: CALL THE TEAM TOGETHER FOR AN IMPROMPTU MOB CODE REVIEW

If things are a bit more critical or the PR is too much for even a pair of people to go through, it may be worth it to call in the entire team to handle this review. As in our first suggestion, have the author outline the changes in a meaningful way. Then, with more people to help, try reviewing each critical part together. Ideally, more eyes and brains will be able to conduct the proper review of a PR this large. More importantly, everyone on the team needs to be aware of such large changes in case something regresses or introduces new bugs.

8.4   "Feature is too large to review"

Features that are too large to review are a specific kind of bottleneck that needs to be singled out. Even though it is a single feature, it still has too many files and way more lines of code than can properly be reviewed. We already recognize that this kind of PR is prone to the same consequences as the typical overloaded PR.

What's more concerning about large feature PRs is that they may indicate a gap in your planning/design phase. If the initial feature's scope is large, the resulting PR will also be large. If a feature is designed in a way that cannot be broken down into smaller, logical parts, the feature may be too big. These considerations need to be addressed during the planning and design phase, not in the code review. By that point, it's too late; completed work may be harder to break apart. In the worst-case scenario, a large feature is pressured to be approved and deployed, encouraging a hasty and incomplete review. Even if feedback is gathered on the large feature with a promise to be taken care of in a future PR, that PR may never come. Instead, it likely goes to a place many developers know and fear: the back of the backlog 😱. So what can we do instead?

SUGGESTION 1: AS A TEAM, FIND WAYS TO SHRINK OR BREAK DOWN FEATURES DURING THE PLANNING OR DESIGNING PHASES

Try to take PR review time into account when designing and planning your features. If something touches several areas of your codebase, consider splitting logical parts into their own tasks and, subsequently, their own PRs.

Sometimes, this process is quite clear, like splitting a feature based on user persona, user role in the application, target device, or some other delineation that makes it easy to group related functionality together. Sometimes, the way to break a feature apart is right in front of you, but you haven't thought about it in that way! A common example is to implement sorting and filtering in an application. Because we like to think of this functionality as something that goes together, we group them together in a single feature. If that happens to be too big, simply splitting sorting into its own task and filtering into another may be enough to break the feature into manageable parts. You can go even further and split each *style* of sorting or filtering as its own feature, truly making them atomic features and, by default, atomic PRs.

Other times, we group functionality together to optimize the work. At first, the tasks we are asked to work on seem small and harmless to work on together. However, the possibility of scope creep, unforeseen problems while development occurs, or other uncertainties and risks may arise, which can result in unexpectedly large PRs.

If you're having trouble breaking down a feature, try some of the strategies outlined in table 8.1. The more you can proactively split features or tasks into smaller ones, the less likely you'll run into large feature PRs.

Table 8.1 Feature breakdown strategies

Strategy	How to implement
Spell out your acceptance criteria	When a feature has ambiguous or no acceptance criteria, a feature tends to do too much. Related functionality is tacked on, best guesses while developing it are made, and an implicit understanding of the feature is what's built. Instead, push through and define the acceptance criteria for a new feature. You may find that a valuable but simplistic version is all you need for now, with nice-to-have functionality or updates still available to add later on. You may also find that amid your discussion, your list of acceptance criteria is getting too large, encouraging you to split up the related changes into smaller features.
Enable separating UI components from business logic	If features have a customer-facing component, you can try splitting the frontend work from the backend and into their own stories. This gives your team the opportunity to work on and deploy UI components and then follow with the backend logic. Placing UI components in a separate location, like an admin-only screen or sandbox area, lets you see the component in isolation, even while its backend work isn't finished. This is a great way to split up really large components.
Use feature flags	Feature flags allow you to enable or disable functionality in your application, usually through "toggles" (AKA checks in your code). You can use them to make features available for developers and QA engineers or on nonproduction environments while disabling them in production, which is very convenient. You can take advantage of feature flags when you split a large feature into smaller ones and work on them one by one, but you don't want to leave your production app in a broken state (because all parts of the feature need to be deployed). Here, you get to work on atomic features, review atomic features, and then enable them in production when the full feature is complete. Some great feature flag providers include LaunchDarkly, Split, and Harness. They integrate with almost all of the major platforms (like Jira, Datadog, and Azure DevOps).
Separate details from integration	If a feature can be split into isolated details and a final "integration" task that puts the details together, that is something to consider. For example, when adding a new endpoint to an API, certain parts of the endpoint, like the view or model layers, can each be an atomic piece of work, which leads to an atomic PR. The final integration of the new endpoint—say, the entire flow of this new endpoint, from the request to the view—can be the final PR that combines all of the isolated detail PRs together.
Separate refactoring from pure features	Sometimes, working on new features places us in a specific area of the codebase we *know* needs a bit of cleanup or refactoring. What tends to happen is that we combine our new feature work with our refactoring work. This makes it really difficult for a reviewer to go through. Instead, try making refactoring tasks and feature tasks separate and focused. This should also be submitted as separate PRs: a refactoring PR for the refactoring work and a new feature PR for only the code changes that contribute to the new feature.

SUGGESTION 2: AS AN AUTHOR, TAKE ADVANTAGE OF GIT

If you've already opened a large feature PR, consider reorganizing related changes into their own smaller PRs. You can do this using Git's `cherry-pick` command (https://git-scm.com/docs/git-cherry-pick). Assuming your commits were atomic and the changes you want to isolate and reorganize are self-contained in those commits, you can use Git's `cherry-pick` command to choose individual commits and copy them to a separate branch. These smaller clusters of related changes can then be reviewed in smaller PRs.

Alternatively, you can try to rebase your work and organize it into more meaningful atomic chunks. You can do this using the Git's `rebase` command (https://mng.bz/V2zP). This solution is a bit more advanced; if you are uncomfortable with how rebasing works in Git, I recommend asking for some one-on-one guidance from a colleague.

8.5   *"There's too much discussion back and forth"*

Once the hurdles have been cleared at the start of the review, the next few challenges may appear during the review itself. The most common reason for delay? Discussion between the reviewer and author. Lively conversation, meaningful clarifications, and an exchange of ideas are not bad things; it's the conversation that drags on with no understanding between the two parties that we want to avoid.

The best way to address long discussions is to take the conversation offline (or, at least, face to face and in real time). So, if you're sensing some blockers or are feeling stuck commenting back and forth, make the quick chat your first inclination to get unstuck. You'll likely find that direct, real-time conversations yield better results and understanding between people. Let's first take a look at some scenarios that may lead to an offline conversation.

SCENARIO 1: AS A REVIEWER, I HAVE A LOT OF OUTSTANDING QUESTIONS

If it takes you more time to write out your questions than to reach out to the author, you should reach out to the author. Note that this is not the same as reaching out because the PR is not primed. Rather, you are reaching out to the author because you see multiple matters of concern, key use cases not addressed, a misinterpretation of requirements, or some other reason where a conversation is warranted.

When the questions start piling up as you conduct your review, take a moment to note them and reread all the information at your disposal. Check out the description, review any linked documentation or supplemental info, have a quick gander at the labels used, etc. Just as we rely on authors to make an effort to prepare a proper PR, we, as reviewers, also need to make an effort to go through them thoroughly. If you are still left with questions, leave a comment on the PR that indicates the status and your next steps. Summarize your outstanding questions and note that you are contacting the PR author for an offline conversation to discuss. This comment lets anyone viewing the PR know that an offline conversation is happening and will likely result in another update (an important task we'll talk about momentarily). Contact the author directly, either through your messaging platform, a tap on the shoulder, or a video call. Ask them your questions, bring up your concerns, and then sit and listen.

SCENARIO 2: AS A REVIEWER, I SEE THAT MAJOR REWORK OR REVISIONS NEED TO TAKE PLACE

As before, leave a comment on the PR that summarizes your concerns and note that you are contacting the PR author for an offline conversation to discuss. Next, reach out directly to the author. Clarify your understanding of the code changes with them and make sure you are on the same page. Having set a baseline, bring up the areas of rework or revision you have encountered and explain your reasons behind them. Keep in mind that they may not be necessary after all. Sit and listen to the author.

SCENARIO 3: AS A REVIEWER WHO'S ALREADY LEFT COMMENTS, I SEE THE UPDATED CHANGES STILL DON'T ADDRESS THOSE COMMENTS

Since the initial set of comments were not understood, instead of continuing to communicate asynchronously, reach out to the author directly (and be sure to leave a comment on the PR that you are clarifying some things with the author). Explain that you've looked over the updates, but there are still some items to address. Assure the author that talking through the items is more direct, lowers the chance of misunderstandings, and gives the author a chance to ask questions and clarify what the reviewer is discussing. Continue this conversation until both parties are satisfied and confident they are on the same page.

PR Discussion going nowhere?

Take it offline!
(or directly communicate via video call)

I'm sure you see a theme here. Instead of dragging out the PR asynchronously, shorten it by spending some time synchronously! Direct conversation tends to clear up a lot of the confusion that is caused in PR discussions. Once you have those conversations, do not forget the important last step.

IF YOU HAVE AN OFFLINE CONVERSATION, UPDATE THE PR WITH THE OUTCOME
Getting to that understanding is wonderful, but don't forget to do something with it! This step is frequently forgotten. As a result, these one-off conversations can contribute to the siloed knowledge between team members and a fractured understanding of the decisions that affect a codebase. Instead, and at the very least, update the PR with the outcome of your conversation. This step provides closure to the PR's timeline; you've clearly indicated that a conversation related to this PR happened offline, and you've shared the results. Here's what that could look like:

- *If the conversation confirms major rework/revisions need to be done*—Both the author and reviewer add an update comment to the PR so that everyone knows what has been decided. The reviewer highlights the main considerations and justifications for the rework or revisions discussed in the offline conversation. The author adds an acknowledgment and notes that a new PR will be opened with the discussed changes. Then, close the PR. Since major rework needs to be done, a fresh PR with the appropriate implementation of the code changes will lend itself better to knowledge transfer with the team rather than continuously updating the flawed PR. By adding the summarization comments, any team members who view the PR know that another one is on the way and that they can focus their energy on that one once it is ready for review.

- *If conversation results in a decision that affects the codebase*—Sometimes, a conversation clarifies concerns between a reviewer and the author, and no changes need to be made to the current PR. However, an observation or future consideration might be discussed that the whole team should know about. When these insights happen, note them down and then add them to your update comment. As before, explain the outcome of your conversation, the resulting decision you've made, and the insights brought up that the whole team should be aware of.

Finished with your discussion?

Update the PR (and the rest of
your team) on the outcome.

To recap, when you need to leave a large number of comments or have lots of items to clarify as a reviewer, favor contacting the author directly and having a discussion. Doing so can save a lot of time that would otherwise be spent going back and forth between novel-length comments and asynchronous replies. Be sure to "bookend" this conversation with some update comments. First, leave a comment on the PR stating an offline conversation is being held, and then leave another comment summarizing the outcome of the offline conversation. This keeps everyone in the loop and encourages the communication of decisions and insights that come up in conversations.

8.6 "Code needs to be refactored (sometimes over and over)"

In this situation, a repetitive pattern occurs: a PR is opened and asked to be reviewed; a reviewer conducts a review, finds a lot that needs to be changed, and asks the author to do so; the author obliges and makes some updates; the reviewer finds the new changes still need work. And so, the cycle begins again.

Too much rework can be indicative of a feature's unclear or ambiguous design, unclear or ambiguous acceptance, an author who is fairly new to or unaware of the team's coding conventions or standards, an author who is new to programming in general, or an author who is not being diligent about their work. What do you do in this situation? In most cases, the best solution starts long before the code review. Let's go one by one.

THE DESIGN IS UNCLEAR/AMBIGUOUS

Similar to features that are too large, an unclear or ambiguous design can often be mitigated by properly discussing and defining the design of the proposed changes. This step should happen during the planning and design phase when tasks/user stories are written and before they are assigned. This is where the team should ask their questions, clarify assumptions and edge cases, discuss potential implementations, and gain an understanding of how it fits into the overall architecture of your codebase and applications. The more you can answer and explicitly define in this stage, the more successful your teammate will be in implementing it correctly the first time around.

ACCEPTANCE CRITERIA ARE UNCLEAR/AMBIGUOUS

Good design docs usually have clear acceptance criteria, so the same considerations apply here. If you discuss and define the acceptance criteria early, you'll have a better chance of implementing a feature correctly or with much less rework involved.

THE AUTHOR IS NEW TO/UNAWARE OF TEAM CODING STANDARDS

When a teammate is unfamiliar with how things are done, a little more guidance, a lot more empathy, and a good bit of coaching can be an effective solution. One approach is to use review milestones. Less involved than full-on pair programming but more involved than a single, final code review, review milestones are a happy middle path, with reviews happening at team-appointed intervals or "milestones." These milestones act as check-in points; a more experienced developer can go over the newer developer's code, give feedback on their current implementation, answer questions, and help the new developer get accustomed to their new team's codebase.

Common milestones include after an initial implementation or bug fix, throughout a developer's progress on a feature (say, after every commit for those that need a lot of guidance), or once at task assignment, once halfway through the deadline, and once right before opening a formal PR. These are just some examples I've encountered in my own career; you can adjust these intervals in ways that make sense for you.

Review Milestones

Less involved than full-on pair programming, but more involved than a single, final code review, **review milestones** are a happy middle path, with reviews happening at team-appointed intervals (milestones).

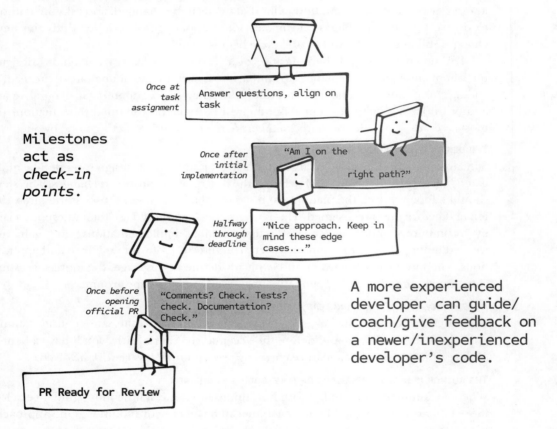

Once at task assignment — Answer questions, align on task

Milestones act as *check-in points.*

Once after initial implementation — "Am I on the right path?"

Halfway through deadline — "Nice approach. Keep in mind these edge cases..."

Once before opening official PR — "Comments? Check. Tests? check. Documentation? Check."

PR Ready for Review

A more experienced developer can guide/coach/give feedback on a newer/inexperienced developer's code.

By the time code is submitted in a PR, it has been iterated on and pre-reviewed, making it less likely to need major refactoring.

THE AUTHOR IS NEW TO PROGRAMMING IN GENERAL

Review milestones, as previously mentioned, are a very effective way to guide, reflect, give feedback, and keep newer developers on the right track. What may also help is extra attention to codebase reference samples, documentation, and extremely clear acceptance criteria. Essentially, this strategy looks similar to pair programming with them and supporting them through their first PR. Once they've reached that milestone, you can let the hand-holding and guidance soften a bit so that they can start building up their skills.

The more opportunities you can give new developers a way to answer their own questions or see concrete examples, the better prepared they are to accomplish building their first feature or resolving their first bug fix. Accompany that with intentional time to discuss their work, provide a judgment-free zone for them to ask questions, and clearly define how their work fits into the bigger picture, and you'll provide the best possible outcome for newer developers to acclimate to a professional software development team.

Summary

- Good code reviews take time, but not too much time. Eliminating unnecessary delays in the code review process can make them less dreaded.
- Almost all delays can be attributed to a lack of clarity or due diligence.
- Just because there's a single senior developer, it doesn't mean they should be assigned to every code review. Changes that don't require the senior developer's expertise should be reviewed evenly among the team, eventually leveling everyone's knowledge up on the team.
- If a PR is assigned to you that you may be unfamiliar with but is well within the realm of your team's responsibility (or could be in the future), take the opportunity to learn more about that code. Because if not now, then when?
- Authors are responsible for preparing their PRs in a way that sets the reviewer up for success. Make sure you review your own PR to see that all the context and information required to understand the code changes are available.
- Smaller code changes equal smaller PRs. Break up your code changes and files into smaller portions and do it *before* the PR. A bit of planning early on can be the difference between small and (overly) large PRs.
- Check your design/planning phase for gaps. Spell out your acceptance criteria, enable the separation of UI components from business logic, or use feature flags to help break down large features. The smaller the feature, the smaller the resulting PR.
- When discussions go back and forth more than once, take the conversation offline and come to an understanding. Then, add updates to the PR: one when an offline conversation occurs and another with the outcome of that offline conversation.
- Depending on the cause, breaking down features, implementing quicker and more frequent reviews before the formal code review (like using review milestones), or pairing with a more experienced developer can help keep the code

changes on track and up to standard. It can also prevent PRs from having to be reworked over and over.

- Due diligence is part of our job. The more we accept and shift into this mindset, the better this process, among others, will be for all developers.

References

[1] Ebert, F., Castor, F., Novielli, N., & Serebrenik, A. (2019, February). Confusion in code reviews: Reasons, impacts, and coping strategies. In *2019 IEEE 26th International Conference on Software Analysis, Evolution and Reengineering (SANER)* (pp. 49–60). IEEE.

[2] MacLeod, L., Greiler, M., Storey, M. A., Bird, C., & Czerwonka, J. (2017). Code reviewing in the trenches: Challenges and best practices. *IEEE Software, 35*(4), 34–42.

Eliminating
process loopholes

This chapter covers

- How loopholes happen
- The different loopholes that can emerge in a code review process
- How to fix those loopholes

It should go without saying: even the best code review processes can have loopholes! Whether they come about because of the wrong incentives or were never found from the start, code review loopholes are something that teams should give extra care and attention to. This chapter is especially relevant to the tech leads and engineering managers reading this book; keep an eye out for these loopholes on your own team and try to stop them before they become a bigger problem.

9.1 How do loopholes happen?

A loophole is defined as a means or opportunity to evade a rule, law, etc. [1]. In our case, the "rule" is the code review itself, and the loopholes are all the ways we skip it or conduct it in a superficial manner. It sounds so obvious and glaring that you'd think we'd recognize any loopholes creeping into our own review processes.

However, anything from the company culture to the tools we use can sneakily introduce the gaps where loopholes can begin to grow.

Sometimes, the tools we use with code reviews don't have proper safeguards, aren't configured correctly, or don't integrate easily with the rest of our toolset. Sometimes, the process changes, and it's not documented, communicated, or enforced. Other times, strict deadlines, overburdened workloads, or mandates from management obligate us to forget about code reviews "just this time." Most of the time, the way we do reviews on teams (if they are even used) is unclear, not well understood by the team itself, and not consistently enforced.

If you start to spot any of these cues on your own team, there might be a loophole in your process. Don't worry, though. This whole chapter's dedicated to the typical loopholes you may come across—and how to fix them!

9.2   *Loopholes (and how to fix them)*

During my own time working as a junior .NET developer, I was first introduced to the concept of code review loopholes. As naive as I was in my first real development job, I always assumed that I'd be the one making mistakes, that I'd have to keep up with the example of the senior developers on my team, that I'd need to learn the ropes of what a proper code review process was. Guess what? I think I was the only one who cared about code reviews!

I saw one senior developer committing straight to production. I saw a manager who had access to our repositories and would approve their own PRs (you know, because they're a manager). And I saw a different process each time code was committed. Sometimes, the code went through a strenuous review and needed the entire team's approval. Other times, people just committed whenever they felt like it. I learned a lot during that position.

The most important thing I learned (other than that juniors can be insightful, alert, and diligent, sometimes even more than the seniors) is that having no clear process, which means having an inconsistent process, can be really detrimental to a team and its codebase. I want to make sure that doesn't happen to you. We'll go through some loopholes that you should look out for, starting with the one I consider the most important. Then, I'll give some suggestions on how to close them.

9.2.1   *An undefined code review process*

As I've shared, one of my previous teams had no defined code review process at all. It got really bad. We had many production fires, our team didn't trust each other, and resentment grew. Our manager was no help either; they actually ignored the signs of our team breaking apart and even contributed to this loophole getting wider!

When your team is unsure of how code is reviewed (if it's reviewed at all), this confusion can become a glaring loophole (figure 9.1). Not knowing what steps are involved (or which are actually followed) makes it easier for developers to skip the process altogether. Not knowing who is responsible for reviewing code encourages developers to pick random people to review or even self-approve their own code. And no defined code review process means reviews are more likely to be ad hoc, ineffi-cient, and of varying levels of thoroughness.

Figure 9.1 No defined code review process results in inconsistencies.

As you can imagine, a lack of a defined process also invites a jumble of policies to be created. Sometimes, it's OK to merge straight into production, but sometimes, at least two approvals are needed (as was the case on my team). Sometimes, a pair pro-gramming session counts as the code review, but another time, a formal PR was requested.

The lack of consistency hurts your team, as trust in the code review process is unlikely ever to be built. Different developers will have different understandings of the process and will continue to perpetuate their knowledge to new team members, jumbling the process even further. I think you get the idea by now.

THE SOLUTION: DEFINE YOUR CODE REVIEW PROCESS

The very first thing you can do is to document your current code review process (if any). Whatever you think is happening is the first thing to jot down. This serves as your baseline. It is also the bare minimum that should be documented in your Team Working Agreement (chapter 4). Then, you'll work with your team to see what's really happening. Let's break down what can be done by role.

AS A TECH LEAD, SENIOR DEVELOPER, OR ENGINEERING MANAGER

You should be fully aware of the code review process your team uses. You are likely the one who helps enforce it and has played a role in defining it. As a more senior member of the team, other members may also look to you for guidance, ask questions about the process, or engage in conversation about changing parts of the process. Understanding your code review well enough to accommodate these scenarios would be beneficial to you and your team.

To start tackling the problem of an undefined code review process, it would be helpful to lay out the basic workflow as it currently exists (as you understand it), as shown in figure 9.2. I find the best way to do this is to draw it out on the whiteboard or use a Web-based whiteboard tool that can be edited or annotated. Miro (https://miro .com/), Figma (https://www.figma.com/), or Draw.io (https://www.drawio.com/) are optimal choices.

Baseline - Drafted by team lead or engineering manager

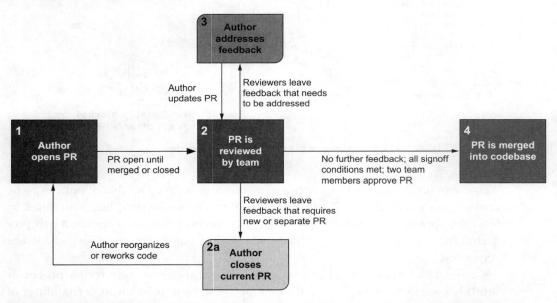

Figure 9.2   Starting point, or baseline workflow: Outline of what team lead/engineering manager assumes is the current code review process

Your workflow ideally answers these questions:

- What steps are involved in the code review process?
- Who is responsible for reviewing code?
- Who is responsible for approving code?

- What conditions need to be met for an approval?
- What conditions need to be met to proceed with merging changes?

Even if your initial draft can't answer all of these questions just yet, or you are simply unsure, don't worry. The full exercise you complete with your team should get you there, even if it takes a few iterations.

Once you have a working draft you can share, ask your team to confirm that the base steps you've laid out are correct. Let them modify the basic workflow at a high level. Get to a baseline workflow you all agree on. Assure your team that more detailed annotations will be possible and encouraged, but for now, you are just setting a baseline you can compare against later on.

When you've agreed to a baseline workflow, the next step is to decide how long you'd like to gather notes—say, a few sprints, a quarter, or a small project. Make it long enough that your team can make varied observations about the code review process but short enough that you can accurately compare it against the baseline you've created.

Meanwhile, when the duration has been set, ask your team to jot down any notes about the code review process they observe—pain points, skipped steps, delineations from the baseline, or other anecdotes related to the code review. You'll do the same.

Once your set time range is up, ask your team to modify, add, or correct parts of the baseline, this time using their notes. This part is extremely important: this exercise may reveal much more than you'd expect! From exposing erroneous steps that are completed, steps of which you were unaware, and steps that are skipped to revealing team-wide beliefs about the process that are outdated or incorrect, you'll likely develop the most accurate picture of what's really happening with your team.

As a developer

As a developer, you participate in the code review process first-hand. Your opinion is especially important when it comes to fixing the loophole of an unclear or undefined process.

After you've agreed on a high-level, baseline workflow with your team lead/engineering manager, you'll be asked to keep some notes about your code review process for a set duration. These should be little (or big) things you notice about your reviews as you go about your workday. These notes will make the edits phase (where you add your corrections and annotations to the baseline workflow) a more fruitful process. It will also help you remember smaller details, like PRs being open for too long or your code review tool allowing an author to approve their own PR. Some things you may want to keep a note of include the following:

- Are there confusing steps or steps that don't make sense?
- Do you find yourself stuck at certain phases of the review and require more guidance on what should happen next?

- Do you find you are doing more or less during the review process than your colleagues?
- Are there bottlenecks in the process that you feel don't provide value to the review process?
- Are there missing steps in the process that you feel would make the review process more valuable?

Collect these notes until you regroup to edit the baseline workflow. When that quarter or project is over, and your team lead/engineering manager requests your feedback, don't hold back! Your observations and suggestions are valid data points, and so are your colleagues'. Documented in this way, it can disclose to the team the real process versus the one everyone thinks is happening. Figure 9.3 provides an example workflow.

Baseline & Edits - Corrections and annotations added by team

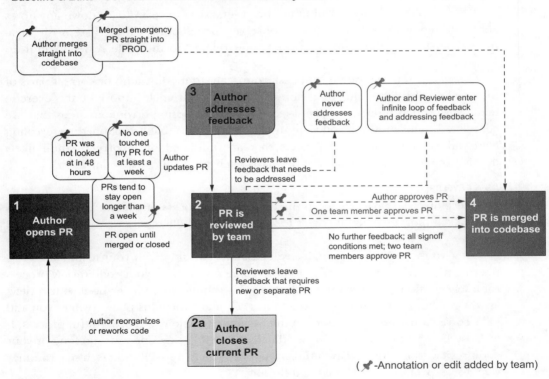

Figure 9.3   The real workflow: Edits and corrections added to the baseline by the team

Whoa. So that's what's actually going on around here. Only when your team members are all on the same page about your code review process can you start to see the cracks and weaknesses you need to fix. We'll get to that in a moment, but first, let's see what your team can do in their role.

AS A TEAM

So now you've got an overly detailed workflow to reference. You may or may not even have some red threads connecting different parts into a conspiracy-like web. What do you do now?

1. COMMENT CONSOLIDATION

The first thing to look for are duplicate edits or annotations. Are several developers pointing out that PRs stay open too long? Make that a single comment. Is there a consistent theme of authors merging straight into production? Make that a single comment. In each of these consolidations, feel free to keep the original comments as supplemental info within the consolidated comment. The goal is to condense the comments into distinct issues or weaknesses in your workflow, as shown in figure 9.4.

Consolidating recurrent/similar comments

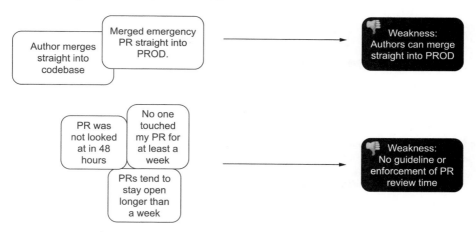

Figure 9.4   Consolidating duplicate comments into a single, identified weakness

Once all possible comments are condensed, replace that portion of the workflow with the consolidated weakness, as shown in figure 9.5. Leave any comments distinct enough to be their own weakness as-is, but add a label or change its color so you can still identify it as a weakness. Doing this will make the next step easier and clearly show you the glaring weaknesses in your process.

Baseline & Consolidated Weaknesses

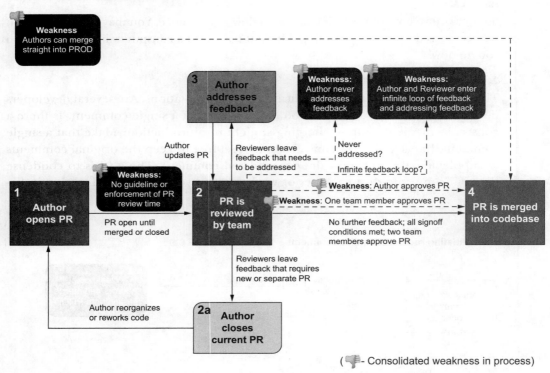

Figure 9.5   Consolidated comments and distinct weaknesses placed on baseline workflow

2. THE WEAKNESS WALKTHROUGH

Working together, walk through your reannotated workflow, stop at each weakness, and address it, as shown in figure 9.6. Yes, really. Discuss why it's a weakness and what the ideal state would be instead. Is it getting rid of it altogether? Is it shortening that step? Is it requiring enforcement? Whatever it is, figure out a way to get from where you are to where you want to be.

When you've addressed the weakness, replace that portion of the workflow with the agreed-upon solution. Only then should you continue your walkthrough, as shown

Weakness Walkthrough - Finding solutions one at a time

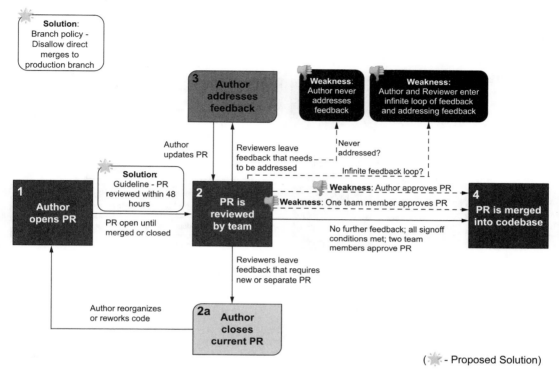

Figure 9.6   Finding team-approved solutions for two weaknesses

in figure 9.7. I'm serious. As you move along the steps, address the next weakness you arrive at, and don't move on until you do. Yes, it can be tedious. Yes, it may take several discussions. And yes, your team may not think this exercise is worth it while doing it. In the end, you'll create a workflow that aligns with what your team always assumed was happening but also addresses any problems that were actually happening. You'll be laughing about it later, I promise.

Remember, your ideal team workflow might take a few discussions, a few sprints, and a few creative solutions before reaching it. It might even change over time! The good news is that you'll end up with a referenceable, clear, and co-created code review process that everyone is aware of. If you feel like your process is slipping (or just want to regularly assess your code review process), you can use this collaborative exercise to pinpoint and fix any hidden loopholes.

Completed Weakness Walkthrough - Several iterations and a few weeks of discussions

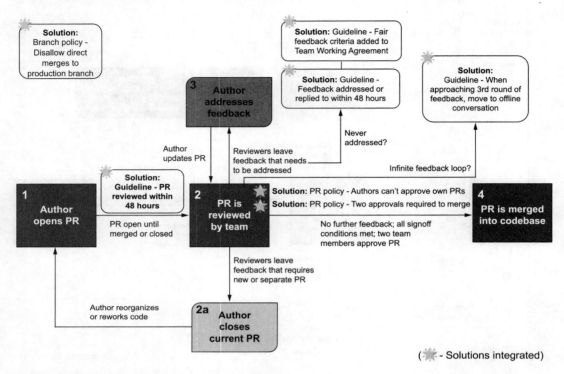

Figure 9.7   Final workflow, all weaknesses accounted for

9.2.2   *Lack of time for code reviews*

This loophole typically happens when the organization or engineering department as a whole looks down upon code reviews. When this is the case, development teams are either improperly incentivized to hit target metrics, such as higher Deployment Frequency or lower Mean Lead Time for Changes (DORA metrics), or have performance reviews or bonuses tied to the deployment of net new features. While developers may not necessarily agree with the lack of code reviews, some teams may feel like they don't have a choice when it comes to the culture of their organization or department.

Sometimes, this loophole also happens when there's only a single person who is doing all of the reviews, like a senior developer of a small team. When they start to feel like a bottleneck or lack support in reducing the code review load, it becomes tempting to bring up the lack of time the team has to do code reviews and skip them altogether. The "best" case scenario for this loophole? Reviewers skim the PRs they are assigned to so that they can get back to coding. As I hope you are aware, any scenario with a "lack of time" for code reviews means there is a fundamental misalignment between the development team and the larger department or organization, and the code base suffers for it.

I'm always reminded of the saying, "We always have the time to fix things, but never the time to do it correctly from the start." I think this statement is a painfully accurate description of teams who skip code reviews. Some engineering teams' philosophy is to "go fast" and deliver value—even if that means skipping safeguards like a code review—but then have no choice but to spend time fixing problems if they do occur.

"Luckily, we were able to allocate some extra time for production issue troubleshooting this quarter."

THE SOLUTION: MAKE PRS SMALLER

With smaller PRs, there can really be no excuse for skipping a review. Having no time for code reviews is usually attributed to pull requests that take too long to review. We discussed in chapter 8 why PRs can take too long, but the same lesson holds true here: the smaller the PR, the less likely the PR will take too long. Developers, reread that chapter to find all the ways you can make your PRs smaller.

Funnily enough, smaller PRs mean isolated, atomic changes, and smaller changes mean that code can be reviewed much more quickly. Smaller PRs mean there are fewer files changed, fewer lines of code to review, and less cognitive overhead to account for. The smaller you can plan, design, and develop your changes, the smaller your resulting PRs will be.

As a tech lead or engineering manager, you can influence how much time is dedicated to code reviews. If you plan for and consider code reviews as nonnegotiable, required tasks (which, at this point, we all agree they are), the team will be more likely to do them. Consider these ideas:

- Some teams add the estimated review time to the overall story during planning.
- Others separate and list the code review as its own task, treating it like a bug fix or technical debt task.
- Another option is to carve out a specific day for code reviews, though that doesn't always align with the flow of the development team. An alternative is to carve out specific hours of the day to be dedicated to code reviews.

- One more option is to have your team take on less work each sprint/quarter/[insert cadence of choice] so that you purposefully carve out time to do the reviews. And if you're working at a project level with clients, you should build reviews into your planning estimates.

This discussion reminds me of how we dealt with technical debt on one of my previous teams. I'm sure many teams can relate when they've just accepted technical debt as something that will never be addressed. It becomes an ever-expanding bucket of things that we really should work on or carve out some time to address but never do. When it got to a point where we couldn't fill the bucket anymore, we sat down and did some proper planning. This resulted in committing to 20% of each sprint as technical debt work. Even if it meant a single task was worked on that sprint, we progressed more than we ever had. Our manager was able to convince upper management because we still agreed to take on new feature work. And those who took on a technical debt task during the sprint were treated like someone on-call: they were allowed to focus on just the technical debt task and keep their other obligations to a minimum. With this setup, support upwards and within the team, and with consistent discipline, of course, we slowly chipped away at our technical debt, 20% of each sprint at a time. If we can address technical debt, you can certainly plan for dedicated time to review code. Even more so if you focus on creating small, manageable PRs!

9.2.3   *Tool (mis)configurations*

Did you know that the tools we use are prime candidates for loopholes? How many times do we have aspirational thoughts and good intentions about our process, only to find that our tools' configurations don't match? "Oh, we don't let anyone approve their own code. That's ridiculous!" Yet, the checkbox to enforce that is not checked. "We always require two people to approve a PR before it can be merged," but the settings show no minimum has been set. These are, at best, honest mistakes we have forgotten to configure and, at worst, deliberate choices made by a team.

Sometimes, the tools are difficult to use or hard to navigate, which can lead developers to find a way to go around them. Sometimes, we're using the wrong tools, ones that don't match our workflow or allow us to set up safeguards the way we need them. In the end, loopholes can come about because we use our tools improperly or not to their fullest extent.

THE SOLUTION: ALIGN YOUR HUMAN INTENTIONS WITH YOUR TOOL CONFIGURATIONS

This is where your defined code review process really comes into play. When you have a list of your intended guidelines and policies in a single place makes it easier to check whether they are implemented correctly.

As a tech lead, senior developer, or engineering manager (or those who have access to setting policies in tools, go through each policy and guideline you have and check that it is configured in your tools, similar to the previously discussed weakness walkthrough exercise. Are the right toggles checked? Are permissions granted to the right people? Do things generally align?

Of course, you can always ask your team to help you test the policies and ensure things act as your team expects. In fact, whenever your code review process changes (along with any policies or guidelines), a separate task to confirm your tools' configurations are also updated should be done. Then, ask your team to test the new process, which helps ensure your human intentions around your code review process match your tools' configurations.

9.2.4 Lack of feedback culture

For some teams, giving or receiving feedback is not typical, which can lead to a culture of "going with the flow." In this culture, individuals are reluctant to give feedback to or receive feedback from each other. Or worse, feedback is always positive, which is rarely the honest case. In a code review, this culture poses some challenges.

To start, it can be really difficult for the reviewer to raise concerns or draw attention to troubling matters without fear of offending the author or creating conflict. In the most extreme cases, reviewers can also fear retaliation from the authors for bringing up items during the code review. Consequently, reviewers may overlook flaws or purposely forget to mention them in a code review to save themselves from conflict. Reviewers may also give really superficial feedback to keep the team happy and avoid offending the author. As is obvious, this lack of honest feedback results in a less-than-ideal code review, one that might as well not happen at all.

"Yeah, everything looked great!
I already approved your PR."

As an author, not being open to feedback can make the code review process more difficult for everyone. Granted, authors can certainly receive ineffective or unnecessary pieces of feedback. For that, please direct your reviewers to chapter 6. However, when a reviewer brings forward constructive feedback or a relevant concern, the author may still choose to ignore or be offended by it, which contributes to a lack of feedback culture for your team. Without a viable way to communicate with each other due to always being cautious around one another, the code review process becomes pointless.

THE SOLUTION: INTEGRATE AND CELEBRATE FEEDBACK MECHANISMS

I've been on teams where we could give each other honest feedback, and I've been on teams where we could not. It was a night-and-day difference. On the teams with a feedback culture, I felt like my voice mattered, that I was an equal part of the team, and I felt confident that even after disagreeing with a colleague, we'd still like each other afterward and could progress with our work. On the feedback-averse teams, I constantly felt anxious and worried. I filtered my thoughts and opinions into vague, agreeable statements. Discussing something new or brainstorming how to do something was difficult because no one wanted to be judged.

If your team is one of those without a feedback culture or is struggling to get there, consider the following actions. *Tech leads and engineering managers*, one of your top priorities should be to create a safe environment for your team. This starts with you—you set the tone and serve as an example to the rest of your team. Some questions to consider:

- Are you open to feedback yourself?
- Do you incentivize positive feedback and disincentivize negative feedback? Do you do it intentionally or unintentionally?
- Are team members retaliated against, judged unfairly, or treated differently when feedback is brought to your attention?
- When hearing feedback, is there more focus on the person rather than the behavior?
- Are there options for your team to give feedback—anonymously or directly?
- Do you hold regular retrospectives with individuals and the team as a whole? Are they effective, or do they devolve into a "blame game"?
- When feedback is brought to your attention, does anything come of it? Whether it's a resolution to a request, an implementation of a change, or even an update on any progress, does your team know that it is taken seriously?

After some deep introspection and confirmation that you are modeling the behavior you'd like to see in your team, the next step is to ask those same questions of your team. Are most individuals capable and willing to give and receive constructive feedback? Can you provide guidelines on how to do that? Chapter 6 is a great resource for code review comments and constructive feedback.

Some other tactics to try with your team include the following:

- Encourage individuals to add their perspectives during retrospectives and team meetings.
- If team members successfully implement feedback they've received, celebrate those wins with them!
- Slowly make discussion and requests for feedback a normal part of your team dynamic. From planning meetings to retrospectives to deciding where to go for lunch, the more comfortable your team feels speaking up about something, the greater the chance for a feedback culture to take hold.

This change in culture may not happen right away; you'll have to stay consistent and disciplined, upholding a feedback culture with your team for a while. The work you do in building trust with and among your team will pay off in the long run, though!

Developers, you are the other critical component in this equation. Ask yourself if you're truly contributing to or hindering a culture of feedback. Some questions to consider:

- Are you quick to point out flaws in your colleagues' ideas when they're initially shared?
- Do you tend to agree with the team or your manager, even if you don't internally?
- Are you dismissive of constructive critique of your work?
- Have you ever asked for feedback on any of your work?
- Do you regularly ask a colleague to double-check or do a quick review of your work?
- Do your colleagues have a way to discuss something with you one on one?

You'll likely answer the questions quickly; you know yourself! If you answer honestly and find you are less open to feedback but more comfortable critiquing others' work, that's a starting point. Ask yourself why you aren't open to feedback. Are you worried about what your colleagues think of you? Do you take any feedback you receive personally? Does the thought of feedback stir up feelings of imposter syndrome within you? If you can pinpoint what's holding you back from being open to feedback, you'll have a better chance of overcoming it.

9.2.5 *Approval-driven metrics*

Approval-driven metrics, where DORA (and other) metrics may inappropriately drive teams to cut corners on their process or skip reviews altogether, can create a loophole due to a lack of time for code reviews. This loophole can also emerge when teams are measured on their code review approval rates or how quickly they can process code reviews. Instead of focusing on giving a proper review and allowing the code review to progress naturally, teams focus on the quickest path to approval.

Reviewers most likely skim or hardly look at the code at all. Those who do try to take their time and give a proper review may be pressured to give an approval before they are ready. Even if problems crop up in production due to superficial reviews, it doesn't seem to sway the team to make changes to their process. A hyperfocus on specific metrics like these tend to do more harm than good!

On the other side of this loophole, authors usually lack accountability as the goal is to get their changes approved and merged. What happens when something causes a problem? *Another pull request with a fix has been opened, and it had better be approved quickly!* Instead of targeting potential problems in the code or taking the time to do a proper review, teams are incorrectly incentivized, creating a harmful loophole.

THE SOLUTION: USE METRICS AS A SIGNAL, NOT A GOAL

Don't let any metrics drive you to cut corners on code reviews. It should go without saying that if there's a metric, there's almost certainly a way to abuse it. That's what happens when you tie individuals or teams too closely to a "magical" measurement that explains everything.

When people learn they will be judged on a number, they will do what they can to make sure that number is on the favorable end. Whether that's faster review times or less time between commit to production deployment, these metrics only tell part of a story. They should be used to indicate a team's progress and whether it is improving or declining.

As a team lead or engineering manager, this loophole may be the most important one you can directly influence. There are several facets to fixing this loophole, but they all focus on achieving the same thing: removing the notion that metrics are goals that must be met.

- *Refocus on quality and collaboration*—Shift emphasis away from meaningless numbers and back to things that matter. Things like code quality, knowledge sharing, and team mentorship should be prioritized over meeting arbitrary metrics like review speed or merged PRs per day. At the same time, encourage your team to have meaningful conversations about code readability, maintainability, and how to improve their processes overall. Spending their creativity and time on things that truly matter means less wasted creativity and time on boosting their numbers.

- *Use metrics as signals, not goals*—Use metrics to spot areas for improvement and track trends. For example, your team's review turnaround time or approval rates may be higher in one quarter and lower in another. Does that tell the whole story? Of course not, which is why metrics used in isolation and set as rigid targets incentivize shortcuts. Instead, take that data and contextualize it. Factor in the code complexity, project urgency, unplanned tasks, and other information to help you interpret the metrics before deciding what to do next. Finally, adjust your metrics as needed, regularly reviewing and tweaking your metrics to make sure they align with broader team goals.

- *Emphasize improvement, not competition*—Instead of using individual metrics to monitor your code reviews, set team-wide targets. Encourage collaboration and reward collective achievements and team successes. This doesn't mean individual performance will be forever neglected or considered; there's a time and place for that. Instead, leaving them out of the picture means there's less motivation for developers to engage in bad code review practices.

SO, WHAT SHOULD YOU MEASURE?

With a fundamental agreement and understanding that your team will not have any arbitrary measurements used against them, there are some useful things you can measure to determine the effectiveness of your code reviews. Incorporate these metrics with more detailed discussions and team check-ins to indicate trends and areas for improvement for the team as a whole. Check out table 9.1 for some to consider.

Table 9.1 Code review metrics

Metric	What does it measure?	How to measure it	Effect
Code churn	How often a given piece of code is changed/reworked after a review	Track lines of code added, deleted, and reverted after a review.	High churn can suggest overly stringent reviews or submitted code that is subpar/unclear. Low churn can indicate improved quality and legibility.
Review time	How long an average code review lasts	Track the time between opening a PR and merging it.	Faster review cycles can indicate timely feedback, greater alignment between author and reviewer, and manageable PR sizes. Slower review cycles can indicate communication bottlenecks, larger PR sizes, and a lack of clarity in requirements.
Review participation	How active team members are in code reviews	Track the number of reviews participated in, comments left, and average review time per developer.	High rates suggest a more collaborative culture and thorough individual reviews. Low rates can suggest uneven PR workload distribution, communication and feedback difficulties, or less engagement in reviews overall.
PR size	The average size of a pull request	Track the number of files/lines of code a PR has.	Larger sizes can indicate unclear work tickets or acceptance criteria. Smaller sizes can suggest better planning and alignment on work tickets.

9.2.6 Taking advantage of emergencies

Finally, we come to the last loophole: taking advantage of an emergency. Maybe there's a production fire, and there's no time to waste! Forget the established process; we need to push this hotfix now! That's one way to circumvent your code review.

If you account for emergencies and have some protocols in place, but they are quite simple, their misuse can become a loophole, too. The next time someone doesn't want to go through a code review, they can go around the process under the guise that it's an "emergency." If everything starts to become an emergency, and emergencies become the norm rather than the exception, you have a big problem.

THE SOLUTION: MAKE EMERGENCY PROCEDURES INTENTIONALLY TEDIOUS

When emergencies happen, there should be procedures to address them. What your team needs to do, however, is make the procedures intentionally tedious so that no one would consider taking advantage of them! In a true emergency, extra steps, lots of documentation, and requiring approvals are warranted; in a scenario where someone just wants to skip the code review because they don't feel like it, it'll be really unappealing even to consider.

We discuss the creation of these emergency procedures in great depth in the next chapter. Read on to see how you can make them thorough yet loophole-proof!

Summary

- Loopholes can exist in the best code review processes or emerge over time. Keep a vigilant eye out for them!
- A lack of a well-defined code review process leaves the door open for inconsistent reviews or individuals skipping the reviews altogether. Instead, have your process explicitly defined in your Team Working Agreement.
- If you need to define (or realign on) what your process is, try developing and agreeing to a baseline workflow, monitor any friction points or areas of improvement for a set amount of time, update your baseline workflow with the weaknesses, and then, over time, find solutions to address each of those weaknesses.
- A lack of time for code reviews can be attributed to unmanageably large PRs. Make your PRs smaller; there will be no excuse for failing to review small PRs.
- A team that lacks a culture of feedback makes a lot of things really difficult, with code reviews being a critically affected duty. First, as team leads or engineering managers, an honest look at how you set the tone is needed. If you aren't modeling the behavior you'd like your team to see, start by improving there.
- Encourage and reinforce feedback among your team. The more they get used to, see the value in, and perform different feedback mechanisms as part of their daily routine, the easier it will be to foster a feedback culture.
- Don't let metrics influence you to cut corners on code reviews. Instead, pair metrics with contextualized discussion as a signal of your team's code review efficacy. Some metrics to consider include code churn, review time, review participation, and PR size.
- Make emergency protocols intentionally tedious. Doing so can discourage individuals from taking advantage of them to circumvent the established code review process.

Reference

[1] Loophole. Dictionary.com. https://www.dictionary.com/browse/loophole

The Emergency Playbook

10

This chapter covers

- What an Emergency Playbook is and whether your team should use one
- How to properly create an Emergency Playbook and put it into practice

Despite your best intentions, emergency situations will occur that don't fit neatly into the established process. How do you deal with these taunting and troublesome incidents? More importantly, how do you determine whether a situation warrants bypassing your team's process? These questions can be answered with something like an Emergency Playbook.

10.1   *What is an Emergency Playbook?*

An *Emergency Playbook* is usually a collection of formal steps, actions, and decisions that can be taken during an emergency situation where there is no other choice but to bypass the process. Usually, hotfixes to patch a production problem quickly generate the need for an emergency response.

Sometimes, Emergency Playbooks are called runbooks, although they are not completely the same. You may also know them as Standard Operating Procedures (SOPs), a common tool businesses use to ensure consistency and quality in the completion of a task. They are also "break glass" procedures, analogous to the glass boxes you literally break in case of an emergency. Those who have ever been on call or know on-call engineers likely also recognize Emergency Playbooks; they may have used one during their shift.

Playbooks vs. runbooks

Used interchangeably but not quite the same, a runbook and a playbook differ in specificity. Runbooks are the more detailed and deliberately laid out steps or actions used to complete a task. Think, "How to Rollback a Deployment to the Last Working Version" or "How to Resolve a Merge Conflict." Runbooks walk you through carefully curated steps that have been proven to repeatedly and reliably complete the task and/or solve the problem. Effective and well-written runbooks are also more likely to be automated—a typical goal.

In contrast, playbooks are not as focused on a single task; rather, they focus on strategically handling a process. Playbooks can comprise a wider range of tasks, steps, and actions, including multiple runbooks. Playbooks also involve actions that require human intervention and decision. With this strategic focus and broader reach and because human decisions also play a part, the term *Emergency Playbook* is used to describe how we deal with those one-off approved bypass scenarios in a code review process.

An effective Emergency Playbook is detailed but concise, can be understood on its own, can walk the reader through an emergency scenario from start to finish, and, to the best of its ability, can account for all the typical scenarios it will guide the reader through. To do this, Emergency Playbooks need to have a few key sections.

Before we go into detail, let me explicitly state that you should treat the Emergency Playbook like insurance. It's better to have it and not need it than to need it and not have it. I should also repeat that this playbook should be used as rarely as possible, and this notion needs to be instilled in your team.

To ensure its limited use, keep the Emergency Playbooks you develop intentionally tedious. As you progress through the emergency processes' instructions, it should feel like you're stepping outside the established norm—you want to be paying extra attention as a result. The last thing you want is for your team to use this playbook as another workaround or as the norm rather than as an exception.

Lastly, these types of playbooks often need to be aligned with your organization's security and compliance policies. As you consider building your own, and especially as you build out the procedures to be followed, make sure to invite folks from both departments into your team's discussions. You'll all need to be aligned; otherwise, you may not be able to develop playbooks that are possible at your organization! With that discussion out of the way, let's see what goes into a typical Emergency Playbook.

10.2   What goes in an Emergency Playbook?

Emergency Playbooks can be quite broad and cover scenarios beyond what's relevant for the code review. Consequently, this section will focus on how to handle situations that justify circumventing your team's code review process.

10.2.1   Decision trees

One of the first things that should be part of your Emergency Playbook is a decision tree, as shown in figure 10.1. This decision tree should help you determine whether you should ignore your code review process. It answers the question, "What trigger conditions warrant an emergency scenario?"

Ideally, this decision tree will be strict: there should be fewer paths that lead to a "yes" decision. Try to stick to your code review as much as possible! If every situation justified skipping the process, what's the point of having a process at all? You can also produce a table/chart version of a decision tree, as shown in table 10.1.

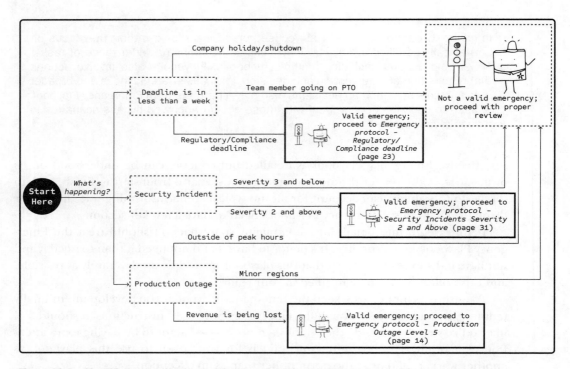

Figure 10.1   Simplified example of a decision tree: Deciding whether an incident is an emergency

Table 10.1   Is it an emergency?

Scenario	Valid Emergency?	Considerations
Need to meet boss's deadline	No	While deadlines are important, skipping the code review process in this scenario makes doing it again more likely. We don't want to make this a habit!
Need to deploy something before someone goes on PTO	No	PTO is usually planned; deadlines that overlap with someone going on PTO need to be considered during team planning so as not to cause a hasty deployment.
Need to meet a regulatory/compliance deadline	Yes	Failing to comply with regulations or compliance rules could mean severe fines, legal repercussions, or other negative penalties for the company, so this usually counts as an emergency! What should be discussed, however, is how this scenario came to be and what steps will be put into place so that it never happens again. While most likely a valid emergency, it should not become a regular backup plan to use the Emergency Playbook for such scenarios.
Security incident	Yes	Especially whether data is at risk or external users are affected. It could justify an emergency if the potential loss caused by the incident outweighs the risk of not doing a proper review.

Table 10.1   Is it an emergency? *(continued)*

Scenario	Valid Emergency?	Considerations
Revenue is being lost	Yes	One of the most serious emergencies, it should be treated similarly to a regulatory/compliance scenario.

10.2.2 Authorization process

If your situation is an emergency, the next section should detail who can initiate an Emergency Playbook process and how.

WHO IS AUTHORIZED TO INITIATE AN EMERGENCY PLAYBOOK PROCESS?

Typically, these are team leads, software development managers, or senior developers. This list can also include those on the current on-call shift (if your team participates in that) or a predetermined group of individuals that comprises a small emergency response team. This list is usually very small; the fewer people, the more secure and better it is. Whatever that list looks like for your team, be sure to double-check with your security, DevOps, infrastructure, and/or site reliability teams to make sure the list you propose aligns with any policies already in place.

One other thing—different processes might have different lists of authorized people. For example, if your process entails something riskier, it might involve a higher-level manager or someone from a different team to initiate the emergency process. Be sure to account for this factor and explicitly list out the proper individuals per process.

HOW DO YOU INITIATE AN EMERGENCY PLAYBOOK PROCESS?

Next, outline the exact steps to invoke the emergency procedure. This process definitely involves documentation, sometimes a series of approvals in tools, or a mix of both.

It's quite common to open a ticket or fill out a specific form that details the justification and rationale for invoking an emergency process. This form will be completed by someone on the authorized list. This ticket or document can also await an approval from senior leadership or someone else on the authorized list. With that, the emergency process is considered "invoked," and the authorized person may proceed.

10.2.3 Bypassing mechanisms

Once the emergency process is sanctioned, the next stage should describe the actual bypassing mechanism—the temporary operations or access permitted because it is an emergency. In our case, we're talking about bypassing the code review process you've established for your team.

It's rare for code changes to be deployed directly to production without any review at all, even in an emergency. Rather, some steps are expedited, and requirements for approval are loosened. Here are the common tactics used in emergency scenarios:

- *Requiring a single approver*—More than one approval on a PR should be the standard. In the emergency scenario, a single approver can be used to expedite the review process.
- *Requiring no approvers*—Not recommended; if choosing this as an option in your playbook, be sure to accompany it with lots of documentation and communication tasks.
- *Allowing a self-approval on own PR*—Justification steps should be put into place if choosing this option. For example, when a PR is detected to have been self-approved, an additional step should request the author to input a reason. Additionally, automated notifications should be reported to the team or tech lead/manager that a self-approval has occurred.
- *Allowing a manager or other stakeholder to approve a PR*—When there are no other choices, the pool of developers is small, or something really needs to get deployed, having a manager or other trusted stakeholder be an approver on a PR can be used as a bypassing mechanism. Justification steps should still be put into place, including the reason for requesting this particular approval.

Once a bypassing mechanism is chosen, describe the actions to be taken. Depending on what those actions are, they could involve

- Granting temporary elevated permissions
- Creating a temporary privileged account
- Temporary reconfiguring of settings or configuration

Make sure to list out the range of time this bypassing mechanism and its respective actions are valid. Also, detail who is to perform these actions.

10.2.4 *Next steps*

Once the chosen bypassing mechanism's actions have been taken, the next section needs to define the next steps. This should include documentation, communication, and postincident analysis.

DOCUMENTATION

Probably the most important part of any emergency procedure that's executed is its own documentation. This point cannot be stressed enough. We already have documentation to justify doing something. What should accompany that is documentation that records what was done.

While the person who initiates the emergency procedure can also carry it out, that's not always what happens. More likely, a different person or group performs the actual bypassing mechanism (and its respective tasks/actions) than the one who initiates the emergency procedure. For example, your team lead might initiate the emergency procedure, but you carry it out. In this event, it's even more imperative to document what has occurred.

Some key items you seriously need to document:

- Who was involved.
- Who actually carried out the bypassing mechanism.
- What was actually done. (Yes, the steps that should be taken need to be followed, but emergencies don't always go according to plan! That's why it's important to log everything that happens, even deviations from the official actions. In the best-case scenario, this log will look exactly like your bypassing mechanism steps. In the worst case, it will have a few more steps.)
- What temporary access/controls were granted.
- Which tools/accounts were affected.
- When (and if applicable, where) it took take place.
- The justification for the emergency procedure. (This should be a link to the justification document we discussed earlier. Without justification, your team should consider it a grave misuse of the Emergency Playbook). Consider this the official Emergency Procedure Execution Record (EPER).

COMMUNICATION

Once the emergency has been resolved (hopefully 🤞), it's easy to feel like the job is done. The hard part is, for sure, but an often forgotten next step is to communicate what actually happened. Depending on your organization, this communication can be a thorough and formal process or as simple as bringing it up at the next meeting. Be sure to check with your security and compliance teams to see whether any formal report is needed on their end. The Emergency Procedure Execution Record comes in really handy here! The information captured there would be critical to have on any kind of report.

With our Emergency Playbook focused on a process we mostly control (our own code review process), communication will involve the direct team. Again, this process could be a key topic to discuss at the next team meeting. Present to the greater team what happened, what made the situation a valid emergency, and what Emergency Playbook procedure was used. Summarize its success (or failure) and remind the team that this is a one-off; emphasize that it shouldn't happen unless absolutely necessary!

More questions may come up, or further discussion may be required to improve the procedure. For that, your team should enter the final step.

POSTINCIDENT ANALYSIS

I'm sure the first thing that comes to mind in an emergency is, "What's causing the problem?" Most teams have a postmortem analysis, a discussion, and a process to figure out the root cause of the emergency to prevent it from happening again. This step is important and should certainly be done.

For Emergency Playbooks, I think it's also important to do a postincident analysis. From determining how well the emergency procedure worked to identifying improvement areas or needed changes, your team would benefit from holding this discussion shortly after an Emergency Playbook procedure is executed.

10.3   *When do we use the Emergency Playbook?*

Emergency Playbooks should be used only on the rarest of occasions and only when absolutely necessary. Seriously! It can become tempting to misuse the powers the Emergency Playbook bestows. That's why it's equally as important to make the processes somewhat tedious. The additional steps and seemingly redundant checks and balances should make sense in the context of an emergency yet be too laborious for someone intending to abuse the process.

Template: Starter Emergency Playbook

To help your team get started with an Emergency Playbook, I've provided a Starter Emergency Playbook template, which is available in appendix B and the accompanying GitHub repo to this book. It is intended to get your team conversing with each other and to jumpstart the creation of your own Emergency Playbook.

This template takes the information discussed in Chapter 10 and condenses it into a template your team can choose to use and adapt. It contains the most important parts of the Emergency Playbook and asks your team to discuss the various sections that will go into it. Remember, this is just a template; yours doesn't have to adhere strictly to these sections nor be organized in the way you see here. Feel free to adapt it (which is strongly encouraged!) to fit your needs. Even more encouraged, file an issue on the GitHub repo with any mistakes, suggestions, improvements, or other ideas so we can continue to evolve the template for everyone to use and share!

Summary

- An Emergency Playbook is a collection of formal steps, actions, and decisions that can be taken during an emergency situation.
- An Emergency Playbook is an invaluable tool when used correctly and created collaboratively. Bring security and compliance teams into your discussions as you start to build out your own Emergency Playbook, especially when building out the actual procedures.
- Each emergency procedure included in an Emergency Playbook should comprise decision trees, an authorization process, the bypassing mechanism, the respective actions/tasks to take, and detailed next steps after completion, like documentation, communication, and postincident analysis.
- Emergency playbooks should only be used in true emergencies, like a hotfix for a production outage causing lost revenue.

Part 4

Pairing code reviews with other practices

You've made it this far, congratulations! 👏 🎉 🥳

In this last part, you can choose to learn more about code reviews within the context of other software development practices before I leave you with my thoughts on the future of code reviews.

If you pair program or are curious about it, chapter 11 focuses on the popular practice within the context of code reviews. A general introduction is provided, then some obvious questions are answered: Do we still need code reviews if we pair program? Why should we combine the two? How do we do both successfully? Chapter 12 does pretty much the same thing, but this time, with mob programming.

Finally, chapter 13 discusses code reviews and AI (at the time of this writing, you really couldn't ignore or run away from AI, so here we are). There were many ways I could have gone about writing this chapter; I chose to explore what's possible right now in terms of AI functionality in code reviews and to remind everyone what to be mindful of as we (inevitably) introduce AI into our code review processes.

Code reviews and pair programming

This chapter covers

- What pair programming is
- Code reviews or pair programming—which one?
- How pair programming complements code reviews
- Integrating pair programming
- Considerations for effective pair programming

Pair programming is an approach to software development where two programmers work together on a single workstation or a shared, online collaborative IDE [1]. There are several styles of pair programming (which we'll talk about briefly), but the driver–navigator style is the most commonly used one. Here, one developer is the driver and focuses on writing the actual code, while the other is the navigator and focuses on reviewing the code being written in real time. A pair typically sits at a shared workstation where both have an equal view of the screen, and often, each developer has their own mouse and keyboard. Both developers are encouraged to communicate constantly and to switch the roles of driver and navigator often so that neither role is confined to a single person.

In this setup, a navigator reviews a driver's code in real time. They point out glaring flaws as the driver writes the code and bring up alternative edge cases that may have been missed. They're likely to point out unclear logic or vague variable names much sooner and can discuss more difficult problems (and the possible solutions to those problems) with their pair programming partner. And since they work together closely, a lot of context and decision-making is shared between the driver and navigator. For these reasons, many developers think code reviews are no longer needed if they already engage in pair programming. Is that true?

11.1 Do we do code reviews or pair programming?

Do we do code reviews or pair programming? Both. Whether to conduct pair programming and code reviews shouldn't be an either/or question. In my opinion, when done well and engaging in both, you achieve two very different goals. Pair programming (or pairing) gets you to the most effective solution. Code reviews communicate what's happening to the codebase to the entire team. If we look at these two practices in this way, both need to be considered as they enhance rather than replace one another. Of the benefits each mechanism brings, some overlap, but others remain distinct (figure 11.1).

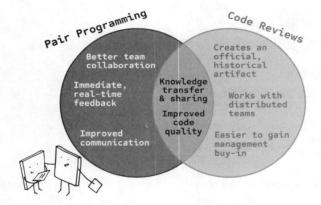

Figure 11.1   A comparison of pair programming to code reviews

Google has pair programming as a core practice within its engineering culture. Microsoft encourages its developers to pair program. ThoughtWorks advocates for "collaborative coding," which includes pair programming. GitHub encourages pair programming with its engineers, especially for those in remote environments [2]. All of these companies employ pairing but also engage in code reviews. Though each approach is different, each company's engineering teams combine the practices to achieve similar goals: to enhance code quality, improve team communication and collaboration, and increase the knowledge sharing that happens between teams.

11.1.1   Complementing code reviews with pair programming

Doing both pair programming and code reviews really comes down to this: more eyes on the code at different times during the development cycle results in better code. One or the other is better than none; using both is superior to some.

EARLIER DETECTION OF PROBLEMS

Real-time feedback in pairing stomps more bugs before they hatch. Since both developers constantly have someone to point out problems, edge cases, or even knowledge they may not have themselves, more potential problems can be caught long before the code review. Two perspectives and skill sets strengthen code. Single-minded code can sometimes miss the mark.

QUICKER CODE REVIEW PARTICIPATION BY NEW TEAM MEMBERS

Pair programming fast-tracks new team members' ability to participate in code reviews. Use the tour guide style and pair an experienced developer with a new colleague to help them skip the learning curve of your system. The new colleague can navigate your codebase in a guided way, have their questions answered, and have the quirks of the system explained by the experienced developer. The sooner they can get up to speed with your codebase and code review process, the sooner they can participate.

RESOLVE CODE REVIEW FEEDBACK FASTER

Drowning in PR comments? Stuck in an endless feedback–fix–resubmit loop? Surface the critical details and context of a reviewer's feedback through a pairing session instead. These items, often lost in a sea of PR comments, increase the number of updates needed and delay deployments. By using pairing during the code review (which is totally acceptable), you can address a reviewer's feedback and revise your changes much faster than replying to yet another comment on your PR. 😊

BETTER DESIGN DECISIONS FROM THE START

Often, reviewers find something needs to be completely rewritten during their code review, which is way too late. Worse, catching a bad implementation or poor design at the code review stage can be difficult to fix. What tends to happen, though some won't admit it, is that the change gets merged anyway to meet a deadline or arbitrarily mark a task as "done."

With pair programming, a pair may realize much sooner that their current implementation is insufficient, incorrect, or inadequate and scrap it. Through pairing's immediate feedback system, the two developers have a higher likelihood of catching bad design decisions earlier and start navigating down a better path.

11.1.2   Pair programming can't replace code reviews

Despite having similar outcomes, code reviews and pair programming produce different results. Pair programming shifts some of the reviewing process earlier but does so at the expense of some advantages only gained through a code review. These advantages are why pair programming can't replace code reviews. Let's talk about those.

NO HISTORICAL ARTIFACT IS CREATED

Pairing shines at real-time feedback, but PRs document. This is, in my opinion, the most important reason pair programming can't fully replace code reviews.

Yes, context, understanding of how code works, and rationale may be shared between the two paired developers; if all of that isn't documented anywhere (say, in a formal code review), that knowledge stays with those two individuals. No code review means no audit trail, no documented rationale behind the code changes, and no official records to look back on for the rest of the team. PR-based code reviews provide that critical record.

LIMITED KNOWLEDGE TRANSFER WITH A GREATER TEAM

Skipping the PR? Say goodbye to those pair programming insights. Without a PR or final code review, the knowledge gained through pairing remains limited to the initial two developers. There would be no mechanism to communicate changes to the rest of the team. While the two developers in the pairing may benefit from the collaboration, the rest of the team does not. Even if you place this information elsewhere, like a separate ticketing platform or bug-tracking software, it's less likely for the rest of the team to go there and read it out of their own volition. With a code review, you explicitly call for other team members to be aware of changes and to review them rather than hope they keep apprised of the changes on their own time.

LACK OF UNBIASED PERSPECTIVE

Paired developers reviewing each other's code tend to agree with each other. It's a less damaging version of the "buddy-reviewer system" but suffers from a similar disadvantage: a lack of fresh eyes on something. When the same people look at the same code, especially when they've developed it together in a paired session, they can still miss potential problems or develop blind spots. More eyes on the same code is always a better bet.

Having a neutral reviewer in a formal code review means code can be inspected and evaluated objectively. Having both in-the-moment reviews during the pairing session and a neutral, "final" review by someone who is not in the pair means a more robust review rather than only having one or the other.

LIMITED SCOPE

Two minds, one scope: though two developers focus and review the same code in a pairing session, the scope of their work mirrors that of a single developer—within the specific task at hand. Paired developers typically work on iterating, improving, and optimizing the code that's in front of them. All the decision–making and problem-solving tend to be within that zoomed-in scope. The same holds true for the reviews that happen between the pair.

Without an objective code review after the pairing and with eyes different from those of the original authors, a more holistic review of the code with an expanded scope may not occur. How the code fits into the overall codebase, alignment to existing architecture, and other broader conflicts could be missed if we only relied on reviews in pairing sessions.

11.2 Integrating pair programming

If you're convinced that pair programming may be something worthwhile for your team, congrats! The following sections are a compilation of info that I think will be the most relevant for you at this stage—everything from conversation starters about trying pair programming to pairing styles to how to make pairing more effective. This may be especially helpful for tech leads and managers if you're trying to introduce pairing on your teams.

Keep in mind that the following information isn't meant to be a full replacement for more involved learning on the practice of pair programming. For that, check out *Extreme Programming Explained* by Kent Beck (https://mng.bz/n0p4), the book that first introduced pair programming to a wider audience; this awesomely detailed and comprehensive blog post "On Pair Programming" by Birgitta Böckeler and Nina Siessegger (https://mng.bz/vJdr); the video "I've Pair Programmed for 30,000 Hours: Ask Me Anything!" from Joe Moore (https://mng.bz/4p5v); and another video "You Must Be Crazy to Do Pair Programming" from Dave Farley (https://mng.bz/QVdQ). They certainly have your back when it comes to more detailed information on pair programming!

> **NOTE**   The rest of this chapter discusses pair programming and how you may introduce and integrate it into your team. Feel free to skip if this chapter isn't applicable to your team. You can always refer to this chapter should you decide to use pair programming in the future!

11.2.1 *Convincing your team to try pair programming*

So, you're excited to try pair programming. Now, how do you convince your team? A good place to start is to open a discussion at your next team meeting. You'll want to get everyone's opinion on this.

The first way you can bring up the subject is by focusing on the advantages of pair programming. If there's an advantage you read in the previous section that fits especially well for your team's circumstances, use that! For example:

> *I've been reading up on pair programming and how, among other things, it can be a really effective way to spread knowledge on the team. Would anyone be interested in trying it out for this next sprint? We'll be working on some legacy code this sprint, so this might be a good way to get some knowledge out of Ben's (senior developer) brain while we see whether pairing is something we like!*

Here, a direct observation of something the team can improve (siloed legacy code knowledge) and an opportunity to test out pair programming ("We'll be working on some legacy code this sprint") make it a great way to bring it up to the team. Another example:

> *In the last few months, we've had to rework a bunch of features. I know no one is a fan of that, especially since we usually catch these things a bit too late. What do you think about pair programming for a bit to see if it can help us catch these problems sooner?*

Again, finding a direct link to something your team is experiencing that can potentially be improved or fixed by pair programming makes it a more compelling conversation starter!

The next thing that might happen is that someone voices some concerns about pair programming on your team. Please listen! They may have read opposing, unflattering information about pair programming, have tried it on other teams, and have had a negative experience, or, in all fairness, be averse to a new way of working. Encourage your team to share any experience they may have with pair programming so that you can 1) possibly address their concerns and 2) see what can be done to make it better on this team. For example:

I realize that pair programming is something new for most of us. Can we discuss some ground rules and expectations we can all agree on before we try it out?

If your team is still hesitant, try to put some boundaries on the pair programming itself. Maybe you only try it out for a week or a sprint:

What if we tested pair programming just for this sprint? Then, during our sprint retrospective, we can discuss how well it worked (or didn't work) and go from there.

Maybe you encourage supershort pairing sessions on smaller tasks to see how it feels for the team:

Don't worry. I'm not saying we're switching to pair programming from this point on! How about we try pairing when we get stuck on something? We'll limit the pairing session to 30 minutes.

Still, you might have some members of your team who may not be convinced. At this point, you can start experimenting with pair programming on a voluntary basis. Those who are more interested in it will likely be more successful than those who are forced into trying it! Once you've identified who's willing to test out pairing with you, you can consider how you'll pair.

11.2.2 *Pairing styles*

While the driver–navigator style of pair programming may be the first to come to mind, there are other styles of pair programming! These have come about to accommodate different combinations of developers. Different styles can also be used over the evolution of a team or the course of a project. Different styles also make more sense for certain tasks.

A note for the tech leads and managers: not all of these styles will make sense for your team; some might work for certain pairs while others won't. Some styles will be the go-to for specific tasks, while others will have no place in your development workflow. The following sections will go through each style in detail while table 11.1 neatly summarizes the pros and cons of each. If your team is testing out pair programming for the first time, it's ideal to start with the driver–navigator style and pair individuals on your team with comparable skill levels. It's also good to pair individuals with similar or nonclashing personalities (a topic so important, there's a whole section dedicated to it later in this chapter called Personality Matches!). Finally, do this in small doses. Try it for an hour at a time or for a small task per sprint or project, and assess how it works with your team. Do they like it? Does the team feel like it enhances their development process? Are they open to doing pair programming more often or on other tasks? As you answer these questions, you can start to tweak the styles of pair programming you use, how you use them, and how often you engage in pair programming overall.

DRIVING SCHOOL

Ever heard of a backseat driver? Where someone instructs you on how to drive and tells you exactly how to perform each action but isn't in the driver's seat themselves? This is similar to the driving school pairing style. The navigator gives much more tactical instructions to the driver and is more detailed and direct when telling the driver what to do. This approach is sometimes called the strong style or backseat navigator style. I wonder why?

This might work when a pair has discussed the solution they are about to implement and agree to work in this way. Sometimes, this style unintentionally happens when a stronger personality developer gets paired with a more timid developer (a concept we'll discuss in a bit).

POMODORO

Similar to the productivity technique with the same name, the pomodoro pairing style sets timed intervals for the pairing sessions. These intervals consist of 25 minutes of coding followed by a 5-minute break. Once this timed interval is up, the driver and navigator switch roles. After four of these 25-minute intervals, a longer 20-minute break is taken.

This is a popular pairing style as it gives both developers equal time to participate and to enforce the switching of roles. It also helps break apart the pairing sessions into manageable chunks.

TOUR GUIDE

In the tour guide style, the driver acts as a tour guide on a bus; they are responsible for both tactics (typing out their implementation) and strategy (by explaining their thought process) as a tour guide both drives the tour bus and points out interesting facts to those on board. Meanwhile, the other individual in the pairing session passively listens to the driver.

Your gut may be telling you that this is not an ideal long-term or permanent style of pair programming, and your gut would be right! This style is more suitable for pairings where an experienced developer walks through an implementation with newer developers or new team members. This style shouldn't be relied on, though; passive listeners can grow bored or lose focus as they don't get to participate in the actual writing of code.

PING-PONG

Usually combined with test-driven development, the ping-pong style is the most active and evenly-divided way to pair-program (in my opinion). One developer writes a test and then switches control to the other developer. The active developer now writes code to pass the test. After writing acceptable code to pass the test and before returning control to the other developer, the active developer writes the next test. With the next test prepared, the two developers switch control; now, the initial developer needs to write code to pass the newly written test. This cycle repeats as necessary, passing control back and forth as necessary (or sometimes throughout the entire development cycle), akin to a game of ping-pong.

This style can be incredibly useful for a range of skill levels; frequent switching gives the pairs room to work together and learn from each other while contributing at a near-even rate. When used with two developers of comparable skill levels, it can even become a fun activity where one tries to outwit the other and encourages the other to really stretch their problem-solving skills.

TAG-TEAM

In the tag-team style, the driver and navigator switch roles, but not according to any rules (like in ping-pong) or time intervals (like in pomodoro). It's a much more casual, free-form style of pairing, where the switching occurs when the individuals decide to—when the navigator has an idea they'd like to pursue, when the driver gets stuck or tired, or any other reason the pair decides to switch.

Table 11.1 Pair programming pairing styles

Pair style	How it works	Pros	Cons
Driver-navigator	One driver: focuses on writing the actual code One navigator: focuses on reviewing the code being written in real time	Most common; the pair has equal chances to contribute and review	Uneven personality matches might result in a single driver the entire session; the passive navigator might not review as effectively
Driving school	One navigator: focuses on giving tactical, direct, and detailed instructions to the driver One driver: follows the navigator's instructions	Can be useful if the pair has previously discussed a solution about to be implemented	Stronger personality might unintentionally perform this style when paired with a more timid developer
Pomodoro	One driver, one navigator (as in driver–navigator style) Pair program in 25-min intervals; 20 min coding, 5 min break. Then switch roles	Equal participation time between the pair; naturally breaks down pairing sessions into manageable chunks	Constant switching might be hard for some developers; can be difficult for pairs with different skill levels Timing might be an anxiety driver ("I only have 5 min left to finish this")
Tour guide	One driver: focuses on explaining and implementing code Multiple navigators: passively listen to driver	Useful for onboarding or when new implementation has to be shared with the greater team	Passive listeners can grow bored or "zone out" as they don't get to participate in actual code writing
Ping-pong	One writes a test; developers switch; currently active developer writes code to pass the test. Writes the next test and then switches; cycle continues	Great with Test-Driven Development; useful for range of skill levels	Constant switching might be hard for some developers; can be difficult for pairs with different skill levels
Tag-team	One driver, one navigator (as in driver–navigator style); switch driver role as the pair sees fit	Casual, free-form; developers decide when to switch	If one favors more control or is more passive, switching may not occur as frequently

In a past role, I was asked to fix a bug in the legacy part of our system. There were layers upon layers of dependency injection and abstraction. There were inconsistent naming conventions. There were barely any unit tests. It was a classic legacy nightmare. As you'd expect, this bug, estimated to take one sprint (which was two weeks for us) to debug and fix, was quite difficult to find. It took one sprint to debug and an additional two sprints to fix. I had to ask for another colleague's help constantly as they had a bit more historical context on this part of the application than I did. And since so much effort was devoted to fixing a lot of this technical debt, many of the shiny new features that we wanted to work on stayed put in our backlog.

There's some good to this story, though. After slowly tackling that technical debt through pair programming and making extensive use of code reviews to share the how and why of this refactor with the team, our application's health improved significantly. Bugs were not only less frequent but much easier to find. Instead of overflowing my head with several layers of abstraction and keeping track of inconsistent variable names, I could easily diagnose where a problem would be likely to occur and start my debugging there. With everyone much more acquainted with the newly refactored system, there was less reliance on the "tenured" colleagues to assist, meaning they could focus on their work. It took some initial investment in terms of time and pair programming effort, but it was so worth it to have healthy code that was maintainable in the end! You may have already engaged in this style without knowing it—when you get stuck on something and ask a colleague to take a look and see if you're missing anything!

11.2.3 *Considerations for effective pair programming*

Once you've figured out a pairing style to start with, the next thing to consider is how to actually do the thing. Some teams make a hard switch and begin developing in pairs for the whole workday or an entire project. That might work for a slim minority of teams that can adjust to major change; props to those teams! For the rest of us, especially if pair programming is something new to the team, a gentle introduction is best. First, let's explore how to set your in-person teams for pairing success. Then, we'll discuss remote team considerations. Tech leads and managers, this section's for you.

PAIRING WORKSTATIONS

Ideally, pair programming is done in a separate area that has dedicated, purpose-built workstations. Both developers should have a clear view of the code. Switching driver and navigator roles should be effortless. An environment that fosters focus for both developers (especially the navigator) while also respecting the rest of the team is crucial. Some things that can help make this happen:

- *Both developers should have their own keyboard and mouse*—Each developer's peripherals should have easy access to the monitor(s) they are using.
- *Make sure both developers clearly and comfortably see the code*—A single monitor works if both can easily read the code without requiring either developer to sit uncomfortably or adjust themselves into a weird position. Two monitors typically ensure this.

- *Find the right place for pairing*—Placing workstations in an area away from the main open floor or where the pair's constant conversation will not bother others keeps everyone on the team happy. Even if all team members will be engaged in a pairing session, having some distance between pairs will lessen the likelihood of getting distracted or being unable to focus due to others' conversations.

DURATION OF PAIRING SESSIONS

Don't force pairing on your team for the whole workday! From Birgitta and Nina (https://mng.bz/XV2p) to Nat Bennett (https://mng.bz/yoxy), many developers agree that pairing all day or even more than a few hours can be exhausting. Denis Kranjčec, a staff engineer at Infobip, says 3 to 4 hours a day is the limit for his team:

> 𝒪 *We paired for 3–4 hours a day, as we had other operations and support we needed to attend to. Not to mention that pair programming requires complete focus and can be exhausting, so 3–4 hours per day was the maximum anyway.*

Instead, build in some time for developers to work on their own and limit pair sessions so that they don't take up the bulk of the day. The Pomodoro pairing style is an obvious choice to start with, as time intervals are built-in. Tag-team and ping-pong styles are worth trying when setting explicit time limits for them, too. Start with 30 minutes to an hour of pairing sessions and see how that feels for your team.

PAIRING ON SPECIFIC TASKS

Not all tasks make sense for pair programming. Denis shared some more insights:

> 𝒪 *We gave up on pair programming on routine, repetitive, and simple tasks because we didn't get any added value. In that case, pair programming did prove too expensive.*

Find those tasks that will really benefit from having two minds and perspectives. Denis mentions, "When adding new features, we saw more and more benefits [from pair programming]." Other tasks include

- Work on critical systems
- Work on core libraries
- Complex problems with unclear solutions
- New architecture design
- Complex refactors
- Experimental solutions

On the other hand, less complex or "routine" code is probably better suited for single developers. Imagine someone looking over your shoulder as they watch you write basic getters and setters or set up boilerplate code from a template. It would be boring. It would be a poor use of your and your pair's time. And it's the type of code that doesn't require the combined power of both of your intelligent brains.

Wait, who gets credit on the commits?

One common worry about pair programming is that one developer may not receive credit for the code written in a pairing session. Especially when using the ping-pong, pomodoro, or even driver–navigator style with a fairly even split between switching roles, most developers think a single developer will have all the commits tied to their name. Don't worry! That's not the case.

In GitHub and GitLab, co-authored commits are possible using a `Co-authored-by` commit trailer [3]. So, as you write your commit message:

```
git commit -m "feature: add sorting filter to Table component"
```

You'll add two empty lines instead of finishing your commit with a closing quotation like you normally would:

```
git commit -m "feature: add sorting filter to Table component"
>
>
```

And it's here you'll add each developer's name and email address like so:

```
Co-authored-by: ADRIENNE BRAGANZA <ADRIENNE@EXAMPLE.COM>
Co-authored-by: MARIO TACKE <MARIO@EXAMPLE.COM>
```

Once you're finished adding all of the collaborators, you finish the commit message with the closing quotation mark. With that, each developer in a pairing session gets attribution in the pull request and in their contribution graph [4].

SKILL LEVEL MATCHES

One thing I hear over and over again is that pairing sessions require developers with equal or complementary skill levels. Otherwise, it becomes imbalanced, and the pairing session does not produce the benefits we hear about.

On the one hand, that can be true: pairing an experienced developer with a new developer would likely result in the experienced developer taking the reins and transferring lots of knowledge to the new developer. This isn't to say that a new developer can't teach an experienced developer something. Rather, it likely results in the experienced developer spending more of their time in the driver role and the new developer passively agreeing and watching. One user on Reddit, Tulikettuja, points out:

> 💬 *When I was a junior I was told pair programming was "the way" so I didn't question it. It meant I was usually stuck with someone who sat silently doing the work, occasionally narrating what they were doing and would sigh and roll their eyes if I asked if I could do the next bit. I realised very quickly I didn't like it at all. . . . But in the early days I think juniors can become passive and allow themselves to be steamrolled. It takes a rare senior to sit back and allow the junior space to explore.*

A pairing that seems to work better is two junior developers or two senior developers. Since both are somewhat equal in experience, they are more likely to learn from each other when pairing. Two juniors can help each other when they get stuck and can see different approaches and thinking styles. A final code review from a more senior developer can help refine that final code. Two seniors can help each other see more edge cases, iterate through several implementations, and optimize their code as much as possible. A final code review can then communicate the context and decision-making behind the optimized solution to the rest of the team. These scenarios, though, are ideal and highly dependent on the next topic.

PERSONALITY MATCHES

Extrovert versus introvert. Communicative versus contemplative. Collaborative versus independent. There are all kinds of people in the world, and that includes developers.

Depending on how one likes to work, pair programming can be the greatest thing ever or absolute hell. This is why personality matches are cited as a condition for success with pair programming. Garrett McCullough, a senior frontend engineer at Virta Health, agrees:

> *I think it's going to be personality dependent. If I'm learning a new code base, I need time to think by myself and build a mental model of the code. I don't learn anything by watching other people drive a pairing session. And if I'm driving while trying to learn, I don't think I'll have the time and space to build that mental model.*

The key element that unites those who don't like pair programming? Whether or not it was forced upon the team. I'm sure you can understand that the less likely the team was for it, the less likely it would be accepted or adopted.

Team members who naturally want to pair or have a complex problem worth discussing will typically arrange a pairing session on their own. If you find that most of your team prefers to work in this way, you can suggest (rather than mandate) pairing on tasks that make sense to the team. You can also rotate the developers that make up the pairs to see if someone works better with another.

I know you're probably thinking, "If someone is that stubborn or averse to collaboration, that's a bigger problem to deal with." The truth is that pair programming is quite difficult for anyone to get used to, even extroverted developers. The best outcomes usually lie in compromises that work for your team. Again, this could be deciding to pair only on appropriate tasks, limiting the time pairing sessions take, giving team members lots of room to adjust, taking a break from one another, and having plenty of time to work on a problem independently. In the end, if someone really doesn't want to pair, and reasonable steps have been taken to gently introduce and try it, there's no benefit to forcing anyone to pair program if they don't want to do it!

Once the initial weirdness of having someone over your shoulder is tackled, some might grow to like pair programming. In a study that researched integrating pair programming into software development processes, a key observation seems to support this: "Many programmers are initially skeptical, even resistant to programming with a partner. It takes the conditioned solitary programmer out of their 'comfort zone.' Shortly, however, most programmers grow to prefer pair programming" [5].

This happened to me in my first role. I typically like working alone. I like being tucked away in my cubicle, headphones on, and solving problems at my own pace. I didn't want my coworkers to know what I googled or how many times I rewrote something. Even if I got stuck on something, I knew I could figure a way out by myself. It was only when our tech lead noticed I was taking a bit too long on a task that pair programming was (at that time) made mandatory for that task.

I needed to switch out an API key and then update the corresponding endpoints with the newer versions. This was a big deal. I had access to something that, if I messed up, could bring down an entire university's email system. We didn't have some safeguards in place; a lot of things were manual copy/paste jobs (I know). So, my tech lead sat next to me that day and said, "Alright, walk me through what you understand about the task and then show me what you have so far." That was one of the scariest questions anyone had asked me in my career (so far)! I explained what I had accomplished, including my many concerns of potentially messing up, and stumbled over my excuses as to why I wasn't finished yet. In turn, my tech lead dispelled many of my fears, showed me what I could do if I did mess up, and told me that if I ever felt worried about something, I could always message her for a quick pairing session.

Over time, she helped me get out of my shell, taught me how to ask for help, and helped me move forward in my work. David Alexander, a software engineer at Optum, sums it up pretty well:

> 💬 *Pair programming adds a social element so you aren't as isolated, and it's easier to not just descend into a brain fog. I typically output significantly more work when pair programming, and it's better work too.*

Give it a try, don't do it all day, and don't force it upon the team. By then, you'll probably figure out whether pair programming will be a fit (and potentially learn more about your individual team members' personalities)!

PAIR PROGRAMMING AND REMOTE TEAMS

Pair programming, like most practices in software development, works well but is not the holy grail. For all the good pairing can bring, it tends to depend on teams that are in-office and have a good dynamic. What happens when your team is mostly distributed across time zones or fully remote (which is becoming more prevalent)?

It's been established that collaborative practices are more challenging when done online [6,7]. This is the same for pair programming. When done virtually, you lose the ease and convenience of being present with your partner and co-located at a single workstation. You succumb to the pitfalls of online communication, like misinterpretation of tone, lost verbal cues, and a weakened ability to interpret body language or facial expressions. And you're at the mercy of tools and a stable internet connection to facilitate a decent pairing session.

Despite these challenges, the reality of your team may require you to pair program virtually anyway. If that's the case, try these suggestions to further set your virtual pairings up for success:

- *Use video!*—If at all possible, turn on your video while pairing remotely. Remember all of those lost verbal cues and missed body language or facial expressions? Having video on can help bring those back and lessen its ability to affect your communication with your partner.
- *Find a quiet place*—As we've all learned (or maybe not), being in a quiet place when taking a virtual meeting benefits everyone involved. The more you can get away from excess noise, the better your pairing's audio will be, which facilitates better understanding between the two of you. Use noise-canceling headphones to further focus on your partner's voice. The more you can imitate being present with each other in a focused workstation, the better off your pairing session will be.
- *Choose tools that facilitate pair programming*—There's a whole slew of tools that have been built to try and solve the remote pair programming problem. There's Tuple (https://tuple.app/), which has been purpose-built to facilitate pair programming. CoScreen is another tool that's used for "video collaboration for technical teams." And yet another tool is Pop (https://pop.com/), which promises "seamless remote pair programming." I promise, I have no affiliation with

these tools or get any kickbacks 😊. These are just the tools I've heard developer teams use and like when having to pair program remotely! Dedicated tools aren't the only choice either: many developers use a hybrid approach of a collaborative IDE (online code editors or environments that allow multiple people to write, edit, and debug code at the same time) and a video conferencing tool (Zoom, Teams, WebEx, Slack). One popular choice is Live Share (https://mng .bz/1aWQ), an extension for VS Code to collaborate in real time. When I worked at MongoDB, I used this with a colleague on a live coding stream, and it worked pretty well! As long as you have a clear way to talk to each other, see each other, and see and control each other's screen, you'll make your pairing sessions with remote team members that much easier.

- *Consider additional tools to replace in-person methods*—In person, it's quite common to use a whiteboard or sketch things out while pairing. Virtually, those techniques don't have to disappear! Most remote pair programming tools or video conferencing software have collaborative tools built-in. If not, tools like Miro (https://miro.com/online-whiteboard/), Browserboard (https://browserboard .com/), Canva (https://mng.bz/aVyo), Figma (https://www.figma.com/), and Draw.io (https://www.drawio.com/), to name just a few, give you a collaborative whiteboard and diagramming tool to use with your partner. My favorite tool for this spontaneous task was Google Jamboard, but alas, it is going away at the end of 2024.

Summary

- Pair programming is an approach to software development where two programmers work together on a single workstation or a shared, online collaborative IDE.
- Both pair programming and code reviews should be considered; they enhance each other rather than replace one another.
- Pair programming and code reviews achieve distinct goals: pair programming (or pairing) gets you to the most effective solution. Code reviews communicate what's happening to the codebase to the entire team.
- Pair programming enhances code reviews in a few ways, including earlier detection of problems, quicker code review participation by new team members, faster resolution of code review feedback, and better design decisions from the start of development.
- Pair programming does not replace code reviews for several reasons. The most important? No historical artifact is created. Without an official record, the rationale behind changes stays with the paired developers. Other reasons include a limited transfer of knowledge with the rest of the team, a lack of an unbiased perspective, and limited scope with which the code is reviewed.
- Driver–navigator pair programming style is the most common, but others to consider are driving school, pomodoro, tour guide, ping-pong, and tag-team styles.

- Effective pairing depends on several things: dedicated workstations that allow effortless switching between developers, shorter pairing sessions (two hours or less), only pairing for specific tasks, and skill level and personality matches encourage the most effective pairing sessions.
- Pair programming presents some challenges for remote teams: you lose the ease and convenience of being present with your partner and co-located at a single workstation.
- To bolster more effective remote pair programming, emulate as much of the in-person stuff as possible: turn on and use your video, find a quiet place, use noise-canceling headphones, and choose tools that facilitate pair programming (screen-sharing, collaborative editing, virtual sketching/diagramming, etc.).

References

[1] Atwood, J. (2023, May 20). Pair programming vs. code reviews. *Coding Horror.* https://mng.bz/KD8Z

[2] Andaker, M. & Pieper, T., hosts. (2021, April 7). Jason Warner, CTO @ GitHub, on remote work culture, team productivity & engineering workflows (no. 9) [Audio podcast episode]. *The Deep Collaboration.* https://mng.bz/9o4o

[3] Creating a commit with multiple authors. (n.d.). GitHub Docs. https://mng.bz/j0zp

[4] Califa, J. (2019, January 16). Commit together with co-authors. *The GitHub Blog.* https://mng.bz/86vB

[5] Williams, L. (2001, February). Integrating pair programming into a software development process. In *Proceedings 14th Conference on Software Engineering Education and Training: "In search of a software engineering profession."* (Cat no. PR01059, pp. 27–36). IEEE.

[6] Alsharo, M., Gregg, D., & Ramirez, R. (2017). Virtual team effectiveness: The role of knowledge sharing and trust. *Information & Management, 54*(4), 479–490.

[7] Morrison-Smith, S., & Ruiz, J. (2020). Challenges and barriers in virtual teams: A literature review. *SN Applied Sciences, 2,* 1096. https://doi.org/10.1007/s42452-020-2801-5

Code reviews and
mob programming

This chapter covers

- What mob programming is
- Code reviews or mob programming—which one?
- How mobbing complements code reviews
- Integrating mob programming
- Mob programming challenges

Mob programming (also known as "mobbing") is where more than two team members work together to solve a problem. They typically huddle around a single workstation or a shared, online collaborative IDE. Similar to pair programming, there is a driver that focuses on coding and a navigator that gives out instructions, only this time, there are more navigators. Switching at timed intervals is more prevalent. And when one of the navigators gets stuck or needs guidance, they can ask the "mob" of people who are participating (the other navigators) for help.

With a whole team working together, communicating, sharing ideas, and bringing way more domain knowledge into the mix, surely code reviews are unnecessary now, right?

12.1   *Do we do code reviews or mob programming?*

Do we do code reviews or mob programming? Both. Hear me out! As with pair programming, mob programming and code reviews serve valuable purposes. Mobbing excels at knowledge sharing within the team. Code reviews fulfill the main (and sometimes only) record-keeping function of codebase changes and the decisions behind them. Both are needed and can achieve similar goals, but they are not interchangeable. Tech leads and engineering managers, it's worth noting that for mob programming to be effective (and to reap its unique benefits), your team needs to be comfortable talking with each other. Speaking up, feeling safe enough to do so, and respecting one another's ideas are absolutely key if you want to adopt mobbing. Already have a culture of feedback and are collaborative by nature? Mobbing is worth trying out! You may find that doing this will only contribute to and improve those things even more.

If we revise our diagram from the previous chapter, we can see how mob programming relates to pair programming and code reviews, as shown in figure 12.1. Visually, we can see the similarities mob programming has to code reviews: both

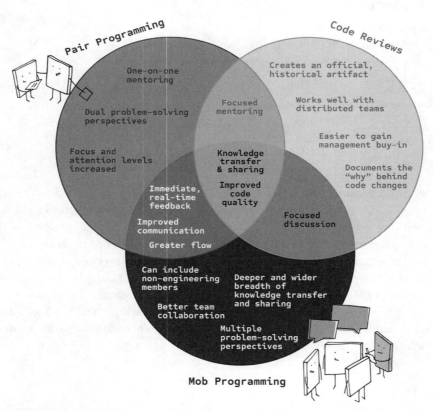

Figure 12.1   Comparing code reviews, pair programming, and mob programming

can be used to improve code quality and as a means of knowledge sharing and knowledge transfer. As a result, it's tempting to think that one can replace the other. But how these practices achieve those similar goals—the differences between mob programming and code reviews—is where we start to recognize the importance each brings.

12.1.1 Mob programming strengths

Before we get into how mob programming and code reviews complement each other, it's worth noting what unique strengths mob programming alone presents. They all occur because of the extra people mobbing throws into the mix.

REAL-TIME VS. ASYNCHRONOUS KNOWLEDGE SHARING

Two developers, a product owner, a tech lead, and a DevOps engineer walk into a conference room. . . . After a few hours, they walk back out with a caching solution that finally works!

That's the promise of mobbing, anyway. Bring a group of intelligent people with different perspectives together to solve a big, complex problem in the same room at the same time. They each talk through what's possible, what's not possible, what hasn't been tried yet (and why), what has been tried and hasn't worked (and why), and effectively spread this otherwise institutional knowledge in real time. As conversation flows and questions arise, the group can respond to each other right then and there. And as ideas come up, they can try them together, building upon each other's solution.

While all this interaction is happening, and as people take turns in the driver's seat, others can see how they work. They learn keyboard shortcuts they never knew about, see how individuals like to approach a problem, observe how and what they may Google, and study how different people get themselves unstuck when they come across an obstacle. This kind of knowledge sharing can only happen in this real-time, collaborative environment, similar to pairing.

Now, knowledge sharing can also happen during code reviews. However, it's at a much slower, asynchronous pace. When someone has a question, they'll likely get an answer, but only when the responder finally (or actually) responds. Compared to code review knowledge sharing, mob knowledge sharing is quicker and more comprehensive and typically involves more of the team. You can also gain institutional knowledge through code reviews, but nowhere near the speed (and sometimes depth) you do during mobbing. Rarely do you get to discover how your teammates work, either.

GROUP VS. PAIR PROBLEM-SOLVING

One interesting distinction mobbing has from pair programming is that those in the mob don't necessarily have to be developers. They can be a product owner, scrum master, QA tester, UX designer, software architect, or any other individual who can support the problem-solving process with their particular expertise. This widens the group of navigators you have access to. You can truly widen the breadth and depth of institutional knowledge sharing through mobbing because more people can be involved.

On the other hand, pair programming typically requires both people to be developers on the team. The frequent switching of the driver and navigator roles with each other relies on coding abilities to make pairing effective. While the two devs can discuss and work with each other, if both get stuck, then the problem-solving takes a pause. The pair can certainly ask others for help or other ideas, but this starts verging into a mob session rather than the initial pairing session that was started.

GROUP VS. INDIVIDUAL PROBLEM-SOLVING

In a study that compared participants' brain waves during solo, pair, and mob programming, researchers found that the perceived difficulty of problems increased when working alone and decreased as the group became larger [1]. Even though the problems had the same level of difficulty, a solo person showed a 36% increase in perceived difficulty, while the mob programming group only showed a 1% increase when compared to the neutral state [1].

I think this makes a lot of sense. Whenever we are on our own and get stuck, we usually ask for help. Sure, while working alone, "help" can mean researching the internet for a good blog post or, hopefully, an answered, recent, and still relevant StackOverflow question. If you think about it, though, other people created those resources that we seek assistance from. So we're really seeking help from others. Asking for help can also be more literal: tapping a colleague on the shoulder or sending a message to ask, "Do you have a couple of minutes to chat about this problem I'm having?" Working with others, especially on more complex challenges, will typically get you to a faster and sometimes better solution than working alone.

12.1.2 Complementing code reviews with mob programming

Mob programming complements code reviews in many of the same ways as pair programming: earlier detection of issues, better design decisions from the start, and quicker code review participation by new team members. We talked about those benefits in the last chapter. The major difference? With the addition of more people, mob programming changes the code review's role.

BETTER CONTEXT DURING CODE REVIEWS

In chapter 2, we discussed how important context is for code reviews and how it's the pull request (PR) author's responsibility to provide it. Now, imagine that all potential reviewers had the same base knowledge and context needed by the time changes need to be reviewed. That's exactly how mob programming enriches code reviews. If the entire team works together on a major feature or a significant code change, the context and decisions behind the final changes in the PR are preloaded into each team member's brain. It doesn't replace the need to document that information; that's why code reviews are still needed. However, reviewers can provide more effective feedback when they are familiar with the code and have discussed it with teammates beforehand.

TARGETED CODE REVIEWS

As your team mobs and figures things out, you may find that specific decisions made or paths chosen are a key part of the code changes. These changes can become targeted areas reviewers can focus on during the actual code review. Was everything discussed during the mob session? Does looking at the code with fresh eyes and without the group setting surface some concerns not previously discussed? Looking at the code individually, does it still make sense outside of the group setting? By focusing on the key parts of the code, reviews can become more effective and offer reviewers the chance to target what matters most.

COMPREHENSIVE CODE REVIEWS

Doing both mob programming and individual code reviews can give you the most comprehensive code reviews. Silly snags, like missing return statements or a forgotten null check, and major errors, like calling the wrong library or performing an incorrect calculation, can be caught early on while mobbing, preventing them from ever reaching the code review. Adding an individual code review on top of mobbing can serve as a final check. Things that might be glossed over, put aside, or potentially missed during mobbing are important here: adherence to team standards or conventions, ensuring consistency with other parts of the code base, yet another edge case, etc.

Mobbing certainly catches a lot of this stuff because you're working together; adding a final check via a code review adds another level of quality assurance. It provides another opportunity for fresh eyes, and eyes that are not in a group environment, to take one last look to make sure everything is OK.

SHORTER CODE REVIEWS

At the end of the day, mob programming streamlines coding and reduces the need for extensive code reviews through real-time feedback and collaborative problem-solving:

- *Immediate guidance*—The team acts as a collective pair of eyes, identifying potential issues and edge cases as they arise, leading to higher-quality code from the start. This reduces the need for rework later during a formal review.
- *Continuous feedback*—The in-session review loop eliminates the back-and-forth typical of traditional code reviews. Questions, clarifications, and suggestions are addressed immediately, preventing delays and misunderstandings.
- *Shared learning*—Mobbing naturally incorporates goals like code quality improvement, mentoring, and knowledge sharing. Through discussion and collaboration, team members learn from each other, often exceeding the benefits of individual code reviews in these areas.

Still, mob sessions lack the historical documentation that traditional code reviews provide. A condensed, focused review is necessary to capture the decisions and context behind the code changes. I'll talk about the specifics of this shorter review in a later section.

12.1.3   *Mob programming can't replace code reviews*

We've explored why mob programming is pretty great and how it complements code reviews. Still, mob programming alone can't replace code reviews. We've touched on it already, but it's worth saying again.

NO HISTORICAL ARTIFACT IS CREATED

Like pair programming, mobbing shines at gathering real-time feedback on code changes, but code reviews document why the change was made. This lack of documentation is still why I believe mobbing can't fully replace code reviews.

We've made the problem-solving and knowledge-sharing aspects way more effective with mobbing, no doubt. We've even sped up the feedback, design, and review loops because we have more people working together in the same place at the same time. What good does that do if we don't have an official record of it?

Even if the entire team has the context and rationale now, what happens when you gain a new team member? When one team member leaves? When your team has to go back into this code a year from now? The same weakness still applies whether you're working solo, in a pair, or in a mob: the context fresh in your head(s) now will likely deteriorate over time. That's why having any documented record of how changes came to be or why certain decisions were made will always be valuable to a team.

GROUPTHINK

If your team starts to mob more often or even switches to that default way of working, you might start offering the same perspectives or thinking about the same solutions. You might "go with the flow" because the current line of thinking makes sense. You may place your faith in the most senior developer's opinion, even if they may be wrong. Even though we try our best to avoid it, groupthink—the phenomenon in which a group collectively agrees without taking into account individual opinions and dissenting viewpoints [2]—can happen.

With code reviews, an opportunity to review code individually is provided. Items can always be missed in a mobbing session or given less importance if the group thinks it's warranted. By continuing to do both, code reviews can be a more structured way to analyze and reflect on the code. Sometimes, being able to do that on your own can surface opinions or thoughts that would otherwise not occur while working with a group.

TECHNICAL DEPTH MAY BE GLOSSED OVER

One of my reviewers also brought up a great point about mob programming. In their experience, "when non-devs are part of the mob, the technical checks tend to get overlooked more since devs are more inclined to avoid getting too deep technically" (thanks, reviewer #18!). Just as the mob can benefit from having more folks in the process, it can also present challenges.

This only strengthens the point that code reviews should be combined with mob programming. Instead of limiting who you invite to a mob session, you can rely on the technical validations with a code review, as those are typically done by your immediate team. Alternatively, you could also hold separate mob sessions, one with a more diverse set of people who may not all be developers and another session that is more technically focused and explicitly focuses on including folks who can participate on a deeper technical level. Paired with a final code review, you'd have several layers of checks you can be proud of.

12.2 Integrating mob programming with code reviews

Mob programming tends to work well with collaborative teams. Individuals who can give their opinions while considering others' opinions will find mobbing a delight. And having access to varied, relevant perspectives—especially those outside the engineering team—makes mobbing something worth trying. If you want to try mob programming but aren't sure how to integrate it into your team's workflow, the techniques in this section are a good start.

> **NOTE** The rest of this chapter discusses mob programming and how you may integrate it into your team. Feel free to skip this chapter if this topic is not applicable to your team. You can always refer back to this chapter should you decide to use mob programming in the future!

12.2.1 Complementary approaches

Adopting both mob programming and code reviews might seem like a tall order (and large time commitment), but it doesn't have to be. Depending on how you integrate mobbing into your workflow, you can adjust the purpose and length of your code reviews to match. Let's see what some complementary approaches to mobbing and code reviewing look like.

AGREE AND THEN SPLIT

The gentle introduction to mobbing is to use it in the most organic way: discussion and agreement of higher-level matters before splitting off into the nitty-gritty, individual work (figure 12.2). This method works well for agreeing to or "hacking" an initial implementation of a feature, discussing the goals and new design of a major refactor,

Agree, then Split approach

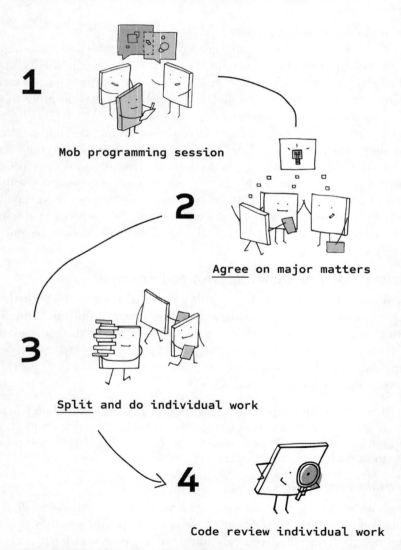

1 Mob programming session

2 Agree on major matters

3 Split and do individual work

4 Code review individual work

Figure 12.2   Agree and then split approach to doing both mob programming and code reviews

or laying the foundation of a new framework the team will start working within. These kinds of scenarios naturally produce questions, uncertainty, and a variety of possible approaches to pursue. Instead of having a single developer (or even a pair) figure all of that out on their own, having a wider conversation with the team sets up that type of work for greater success. Finally, since individual work is still performed, code reviews still take place on individual work but with much greater context for all involved.

In one of my past jobs, we were considering breaking apart a very monolithic application into separated but more manageable parts. The senior developer of our team initiated a few mob programming sessions with the rest of us to discuss this major rework. What was interesting to me was how different each individual's understanding of this proposed work was. Our senior developer started talking about a much greater level of separation and actual work: they wanted to completely redesign the architecture of our monolithic app to microservices. To me, breaking apart our monolithic app meant restructuring our code base so that if a change happened in one area, the entire codebase did not have to be built, sent to code review, and deployed as a whole. And yet, to another developer, "breaking apart the monolith" meant refactoring the monolith itself, just adding a few more patterns to make the existing code "more readable."

As you can see, if the senior developer hadn't initiated this mobbing session, we would have ended up with a brand-new application with architecture that only they understood! Luckily, the discussions and mini-hackathons prompted important questions: Why did we all agree that "breaking apart the monolith" was needed? To what extent did "break apart" mean? What frustrations with our existing application did we all experience that may have prompted this work in the first place?

In the end, we realized that it came down to how slowly we actually deployed features. Since our codebase needed to be deployed all at once, regardless of the size or location of the actual changes we made, it became a really big bottleneck for us. I could create a few changes to a CSS file, but I needed to redeploy the entire code base. My colleague could change a few unit tests, but again, the entire code base needed to be redeployed. We deployed once every few months. We wanted to deploy whenever we made a vetted, code-reviewed change!

After several discussions and hacking through our own code as a team, we figured out that we should start by restructuring our code base first and then see if that helped our deployment cadence. Our monolithic application was theoretically composed of five main domains. We decided to split the application along those logical domains and moved each into its own projects and code bases. We also created a few shared libraries that housed utilities and shared components used in all five projects. Agreeing to this major design, we still split our work individually and over two-week sprints. This meant we still held code reviews for our work. When we finished this major redesign, we were able to unblock each other during future deployments. Changes made in one project only triggered a build and release of that particular project. With the much faster deployment process, we went from monthly releases to almost daily releases. In the end, it was the right way to go; implementing a full-blown microservices architecture would have been too much. Only refactoring parts of the existing monolith may have made our code base less of a headache to work with, but we would have still encountered the deployment bottlenecks.

INTO THE VOID

While researching a bit more on how mob programming is used in real life, some research paper participants [3], some developer blogs [4,5], and a general sentiment of Reddit users [6] all point to a consistent declaration: mob programming works best when the group has to work on something they are unfamiliar with.

"We don't know what we're doing,
but we'll figure it out together."

This makes sense. Any time fleeting bugs, new features, or new domains are introduced to a team, there is an initial feeling of uncertainty about how to proceed. Instead of figuring it out on your own, having multiple perspectives tackling the unknown together seems to work very well.

If you're looking for scenarios that tend to do well with mob programming, here are a few:

- Implementing a new service
- Making an architectural decision
- Refactoring core logic
- Major production issue
- Migrating to the cloud
- Switching a frontend framework
- Figuring out contracts for different components
- Changing components that involve several feature teams

In the end, a research paper participant summed it up best: "When there's a big risk of the acceptance criteria getting a bit fuzzy or that they change during development then it's really good to have a Mob session where you can have different people" [3].

CAPTURE AND CHRONICLE

If you engage in mobbing for most of your development work, your code review can be condensed. Since many goals of the code review can be fulfilled in the mobbing phase instead, the code review can be reduced to its single, most important purpose: to create a historical artifact of why these changes came to be. You can create this artifact using what I like to call the capture-and-chronicle approach.

Mobbing produces code collaboratively, transfers and disperses in-depth knowledge to the team, and enables real-time review of the code changes. Decisions and context behind the changes—the "why"—can also be captured during mobbing. With much of that key info captured during the mob session, a lighter form of code review to chronicle it is typically all that's needed. If you create a checklist for what to chronicle, you can even fill out the PR as you mob, much like taking notes during a meeting. Table 12.1 is a good place to start your own checklist.

Table 12.1   Lightweight chronicle PR checklist

Checklist Item	Information to chronicle	Examples
Why/context	■ Why are we making this change? What's the context behind this change? ■ What decisions led to this solution? ■ How did we come to an agreement on this solution?	"This change addresses a really esoteric edge case we didn't catch but recently caused a major production issue (#323)." "We have to use this (rather than the FetchUser function available in version 9.3) because our internal packaging system is pinned to version 8.9.6. Until this has been updated company-wide, we have to continue using this workaround method."
Skipped solutions	■ What alternative solutions were discussed, and why were they skipped? ■ What "gut-feeling" solutions turned out to be wrong?	"We considered Next.js, but they don't seem to support relative paths for the exported content. They still have an open ticket on GitHub requesting this support, but they are ignoring it." "Lambda Functions incur an additional charge when writing to S3, so we skipped."
Considerations (brought up during mobbing)	■ Will these changes impact other teams? ■ Other parts of the code base? ■ Does this need to be deployed in a certain way?	"This needs to be feature-flagged until the corresponding 'Seller' component is ready." "With this refactor, we can remove the AccountUtilities library entirely. Let's place that work in a separate PR, though!"

Mobbing allows your team to work smarter, spread cognitive load, take advantage of multiple perspectives, and arrive at solutions faster. Capturing the key observations and decisions that mobbing helps to surface ensures you can chronicle the most important information for your PRs. This gives you the best of both worlds.

MOB CODE REVIEW

Finally, if mob programming is something your team needs to ease into, you can consider mob reviewing together! A mob review session is fairly easy to set up. As long as everyone involved can see a shared screen of the code to be reviewed clearly and has a way to communicate with the rest of the group, you're good to go.

Mob reviews offer a powerful way to achieve the knowledge sharing and collaboration traditionally associated with mob programming. By reviewing a colleague's work as a team, you tap into diverse expertise and perspectives. This real-time interaction streamlines the feedback loop, aligning the author with the team's technical goals more quickly. It also fosters shared responsibility and collective codebase ownership, ultimately leading to smoother development and less frustration for your team.

One developer I spoke to shared that they do "emergency mob reviews" when someone submits a really large PR that, due to their own constraints and management expectations, needs to be merged in ASAP. Instead of placing the pressure on the two reviewers assigned to that large PR, the entire team (a group of seven) pitches in to help. Making this assistance available has allowed them to more confidently break up PRs and help each other reference other parts of the codebase when making a suggestion to the PR.

This approach definitely takes up more time; however, they found that putting in the initial effort to improve those kinds of PRs, even if only by a little bit, benefits the team in the long run. In the best-case scenario, they are able to untangle the PR spaghetti and chop it into more manageable and meaningful chunks. Those PRs were much easier to review.

In the worst-case scenario, if they had to merge a large PR, they were all aware of it and would be familiar with the code when it came to inevitably debugging something in the future. It's not perfect, but it's a tool they use every now and then. Last I checked in with that developer, they are working on reducing their PR sizes from the start. I applauded their efforts!

Now, mob reviews don't have to be the only way you do code reviews from now on; individual code reviews are just as effective! However, choosing to employ mob reviews on complex or multistep changes or to review junior or new team member PRs can be a great way to use them.

12.2.2 *Mob programming challenges*

While mob programming has some unique strengths, it can also present challenges. Keep an eye out for these!

TOO MANY PEOPLE

Something to look out for is having too many people in the mob session. At a certain number of people, the mob session becomes less effective than deciding to work in pairs or even alone.

Overloading your mob session tends to happen when there are too many navigators or "just in case" people participating in the mob session. If you find that it's difficult for anyone to get a word in, it's taking a lot of time just to hear each person's opinion, or you have more passive, nonparticipating individuals in the group, it could be indicative of a group that's too large.

So, how many people should be in a mob session? There's no magic number that's been appointed as "correct"; it really depends on the team. To be considered a mob session, at least three people need to participate. To start, I think each developer on the team should take part. Set up a mob session in this way and only add other participants if the initial group gets stuck or needs additional context from someone not already in the group.

LOSS OF FOCUS

With more people being asked to participate, it can be tempting for individual members to wander off a little bit. While the rest of the mob is tackling whether an edge case should be considered, you might think, "Hmm, let me just check my messages real quick" or "Oh, I wonder what the lunch special is for today." Distractions happen; it's when the majority of navigators wander off for more than a bit that it truly starts to affect the mob session.

To counter this lack of focus, be sure to take several breaks while mobbing. Be sure that everyone has enough time to go to the bathroom, grab some snacks or drinks, stretch, intentionally rest their minds for a bit, and then regroup at an agreed-upon time. Giving the group plenty of breaks can help keep everyone focused when it matters.

MORE EFFECTIVE WHEN EVERYONE HAS GOOD COMMUNICATION SKILLS

I hinted at this earlier, but it goes without saying: mobbing doesn't mean your team will suddenly be blessed with great communication skills. You'll see this firsthand when you have your first mobbing session and have a team that isn't used to communicating in this way.

As we also know, teams are very different. Some are fast-paced and debate-heavy, and team members speak up for themselves. Others are more analytical and take their time. And many may not feel comfortable speaking up or contributing their opinion at all. For mobbing to work, everyone needs to participate!

REMOTE TEAMS

In the last chapter, we established that collaborative practices are more challenging when done online. This challenge is quite apparent when trying to engage in mob programming when parts or all of your team are remote. Yes, it is possible, and yes, there are tools that facilitate mob programming online. However, when done virtually, you lose the ease and convenience of being present with your teammates. Not to mention, there's a social factor and sense of unity [7] mobbing brings that can't be replicated online. It's unfortunate, but it must be acknowledged.

Despite these challenges, there are some things you can do to make online mobbing better:

- *Even if parts of your team can physically meet, have everyone join the mob session remotely*—Otherwise, the side conversations (and potential knowledge sharing) that happen on-site can't be transferred to the virtual participants.
- *Use video!*—Seeing everyone adds more facial expressions and body language cues, leading to a greater likelihood of being understood.
- *Use a Git "handover"*—Typically, you switch driver roles on-site by passing over the keyboard to the next person or switching seats. This is obviously not possible

online. Instead, a neat tactic can be to "hand over" a temporary Git branch with WIP commits [8]. After each person finishes their turn as the driver (or "typist" as they call it in the *Remote Mob Programming* book; https://www.remotemobpro gramming.org/), they push a WIP commit to their temporary branch. Then, the next person can pick up quickly where the last person left off and continue the mob session quickly. At the end of the mob session, the WIP commits are then squashed into more expressive commits before they merge. One incredibly useful tool to facilitate this is mob (https://mob.sh). Using three commands—`mob start`, `mob next`, and `mob done`—you and your team can do Git handovers more seamlessly when mobbing virtually.

- *Use time intervals to keep things moving*—Using time intervals allows you to make sure each team member has a chance to participate and to prevent one or two individuals from hogging the entire session. Effective mob sessions try to accomplish a single goal; having everyone participate at shorter intervals (10 minutes was the sweet spot for Simon Harrer, Jochen Christ, and Martin Huber, authors of the book *Remote Mob Programming*; https://mng.bz/PNp8) kept everyone more focused. Consider using MobTime (https://mobti.me/) or Mobster (http://mobster.cc/), two purpose-built timers for mob programming!

Mob programming online is definitely doable; it just takes a bit of effort and engagement from the entire team.

Code reviews aren't going away, even if you participate in pair or mob programming. What we are all really wondering now, though, is, "Do humans have to do any of this at all?" With AI truly the hottest thing since sliced bread at the moment, the next logical step to cover, and a great way to end the book (in my opinion), is if AI can take over code reviews for us and, better yet, if they should.

Summary

- Mob programming (also known as "mobbing") is where more than two members work together to solve a problem. They don't need to be developers and can include any individual who can support the problem-solving process with their particular expertise.
- Both mob programming and code reviews should be done. They fulfill different goals, so they aren't interchangeable.
- Mob programming excels at knowledge sharing. It can even provide a deeper and wider breadth of learning for those involved than traditional code reviews.
- Code reviews fulfill the only record-keeping function in a workflow. By only engaging in mob programming, you lose the context and decision behind the code changes produced during mobbing.
- Mob programming complements code reviews, so both are worth doing. Mob programming provides a real-time feedback and review loop that enables the greater team to share knowledge with each other at an incredible rate. In turn,

    code reviews can be shortened, more targeted, and more effective since reviewers are well-versed with the code they are reviewing.

- Some approaches to integrating mobbing into your workflow include
  - *Agree and then split*—Mobbing is used to agree on major design decisions or to agree on high-level matters before splitting off into doing individual work (and individual code reviews).
  - *Into the void*—Mobbing is used to tackle problems the entire team is unfamiliar with.
  - *Capture and chronicle*—Mobbing is the default way of working, and a lighter-weight version of a code review is used to chronicle the context behind the changes produced during the mob session.
  - *Mob code review*—The team works together to review code rather than produce code.
- Mob programming does present its own challenges. Keep an eye out for having too many people in a group, a loss of focus, groupthink, less effective mob sessions due to a lack of communication skills, and the obstacles that remote mob programming can bring.

References

[1] Shiraishi, M., Washizaki, H., Saito, D., & Fukazawa, Y. (2021). Comparing participants' brainwaves during solo, pair, and mob programming. In Gregory, P., Lassenius, C., Wang, X., Kruchten, P. (eds.), *Agile Processes in Software Engineering and Extreme Programming. XP 2021. Lecture Notes in Business Information Processing* (Vol. 419). Springer.

[2] Educative. (n.d.). What is groupthink and how to avoid it. DevPath. https://www.devpath.com/blog/what-is-groupthink

[3] Dragos, L. (2021). Mob vs pair: Comparing the two programming practices—A case study. https://mng.bz/JNXz

[4] Nycander, P. (2019, June 14). Why you should not (only) do mob programming. DEV Community. https://mng.bz/w57B

[5] Dungimon. (2022, September 29). A review of pair programming. I. M. Wright's "Hard Code." https://mng.bz/q07N

[6] xnadevelopment. (2021, June 23). Has anyone actually done mob programming? Reddit. https://mng.bz/75BV

[7] GOTO Conferences. (2020, April 20). Mob Programming and the Power of Flow, Woody Zuill, GOTO 2019 [Video]. YouTube. https://www.youtube.com/watch?v=28S4CVkYhWA

[8] Remote mob programming. (n.d.). [Homepage]. https://www.remotemobprogramming.org/

Code reviews and AI

13

This chapter covers

- Benefits of AI in code reviews
- Limitations of AI in code reviews
- AI-powered code review tools
- The future of code reviews: Human-AI collaboration

AI is having its moment right now. We have AI-powered coding tools like GitHub Copilot (https://github.com/features/copilot) and Amazon CodeWhisperer (https://aws.amazon.com/codewhisperer/), which promise faster code writing and better code quality. We have Codium AI (https://www.codium.ai/) that "analyzes everything in and about your code and then suggests tests as you code." We even have tools like DocuWriter.ai (https://www.docuwriter.ai/) to generate documentation for your code. AI is everywhere.

A 2023 GitHub survey asked 500 US-based developers at companies with more than 1,000 employees about how managers should consider developer productivity, collaboration, and artificial intelligence (AI) coding tools [1]. Some key findings are quite interesting: 92% of US-based developers are already using AI coding tools both in and outside of work [1]. Four out of five developers expect AI coding tools will make their team more collaborative. And 70% say AI coding tools will offer them an advantage at work. Naturally, the next thing developers wondered: What about AI code reviews?

At first, AI seems to solve many existing challenges with code reviews: it's always available, more consistent, and probably more thorough in its reviews, and it can shorten reviews altogether. But, diving a bit deeper, you'll find that AI-powered *anything* will have its limitations, code reviews included. In this final chapter (whoo, you made it!), I hope to give you a balanced exploration of what AI can mean for code reviews now and in the future.

13.1 Benefits of AI in code reviews

There are four main benefits that result from integrating AI into code reviews: expedited reviews, code quality improvement, review consistency, and review scalability for large teams and codebases.

13.1.1 Expedited reviews

Probably the most obvious advantage of AI in code reviews is that it makes them faster. This happens in several neat ways.

Developers commonly cite getting feedback in a timely manner [2] as a challenge in code reviews. To combat this, AI tools can be used to offer initial feedback and suggestions as soon as a PR is opened. For example, in a study [3] that proposed the use of the AI-powered code review tool AICodeReview, researchers found that developers using the tool took less time to complete reviews. AICodeReview uses the GPT-3.5 large language model (LLM) to analyze code snippets for potential problems, including syntax errors, anti-patterns, and bad design decisions. Then, the tool offers suggestions for improvement with explanations for the reasoning behind the suggestions.

If you remember the chapter on writing effective comments, this AI tool would be a perfect example of putting this into action. Explaining your reasoning and clearly articulating your feedback as a reviewer enables a faster review. Instead of going back and forth through comments trying to understand each other, using an AI tool to assist in communicating can get rid of that delay for good.

Another AI-powered tool, CodeRabbit (https://coderabbit.ai/), which we'll talk more about in a later section, enables quicker feedback in a slightly different way. Once you open a PR, CodeRabbit allows you to ask questions and get feedback on your changes. Conversing through comments, you can typically get real-time responses—something that isn't common when waiting on your human reviewers.

13.1.2 Code quality improvement

AI-powered tools can supercharge code reviews when it comes to code quality. When used as a first review, both on the author's and reviewer's side, developers can hone their critical thinking and judgment skills through validating the AI's review. This also leaves more time for reviewers to focus on solution design, architectural fit, and project alignment—the higher-stakes issues we'd ideally use code reviews for. AI can improve code quality in several ways:

- *Thorough feedback*—In the same study [3] that examined the use of the AICode-Review tool, researchers found that the tool detected more code smells than a manual review. Also, through the tool's suggestion feature, developers refactored a greater number of detected code smells than those performing a manual review. Using AI-powered tools in this way can ensure lower-stakes issues are found. Combined with a human review, developers can use the additional time to review higher-stakes issues, benefiting from the dual review.

- *Earlier feedback*—We've discussed the importance of automation in chapter 5 and how the earlier you're able to address things, the less likely they can delay your code review. A study [4] that proposes partially automating the code review process supports this. Researchers investigated the potential of applying machine learning to code reviews and developed a model that would specifically help authors. This model would analyze code changes suggested during past reviews and recommend them to authors before they submit a PR. This can be particularly useful for recurring problems that need to be corrected. Receiving this feedback earlier in the review process acts similarly to how we'd use a linter or formatter: fix any known issues *during* development so that they can be left out of the review, reducing the noise a reviewer would have to sift through.

- *Faster resolution*—Sometimes, discussing feedback, particularly changes or rework that needs to be done, and aligning on how to implement them can delay a code review. The second model developed in the code review automation study [4] proposes an AI-powered solution. As reviewers compose their comments and explain what is to be done, the model attempts to translate their natural language comments into the corresponding code modifications. With the explicitness and outcome-focused Triple-R pattern we discussed in chapter 6, this concept could really excel! In their results, the reviewer-assisting model achieved an accuracy of 31% in translating comments into code. We'll talk about AI's limitations in more depth in a moment. This is just a good reminder that AI is available to use, but it still has a way to go before we can rely on it fully without human review.

13.1.3 Review consistency

Let's be honest: we may try to give a consistent review each time we look at PRs, but the concentration and care we give each will differ. We're only human. Sometimes, we get tired. Other times, we might be pressured into doing a quicker review. And still, we might pay more attention to one colleague's code and less to another.

AI doesn't get tired or will be any more or less thorough in its review. It will equally review every PR. It will give all code changes the same scrupulous eye, regardless of who submitted them. It can be relied upon to check for the same issues and code smells (as configured or taught) every single time. That kind of consistency makes AI the ideal "first-pass review." Consolidating these checks in a repeatable manner makes it easy to scale (which we will discuss next) and offers any developer the opportunity to review them with insights to guide them.

13.1.4 Review scalability for large teams and codebases

By automating the tedious and time-consuming parts of a code review, humans are left to do the ideal parts. AI can serve as an effective, time-reducing starting point by initially performing its own review. AI can help us understand the code we're reviewing, ensure our PRs are context-filled without much effort, suggest code improvements or optimizations, and do a more thorough inspection to detect code smells than we ever could. With its assistance, AI can cut down on the delays that larger teams experience waiting for feedback and make time zones obsolete by always being available.

That said, AI won't replace developers just yet, especially during code reviews. Let's discuss why in the next section.

13.2   Limitations of AI in code reviews

Despite the potential AI brings to revolutionizing our code reviews, one fact still remains: human oversight is still required. Whether writing code or reviewing it—and with where our current technology stands—the limitations of AI mean it can assist us but not replace us. Here, we'll see why AI can't take over our code reviews just yet.

13.2.1 Difficulty understanding context and domain knowledge

There was a time when I thought the song "You'll Be in My Heart" was by the band Genesis. Same with "In the Air Tonight." Before I knew any better, I would get into silly debates with friends and my husband, insisting that Genesis was the original artist of those songs. It wasn't until a trivia night when "In the Air Tonight" played, and I incorrectly guessed Genesis as the artist that I found out I was so wrong. Phil Collins was the original artist. The thing is, hearing Phil Collins' unmistakable voice automatically meant it was a Genesis song for me. The context I was missing? Phil Collins was the lead singer for the band Genesis. And Phil Collins also had a solo career, completely separate from Genesis. I just didn't put those two facts together 🤦 🤖 💡. (I've since apologized to those friends and my husband for being so, so wrong.)

An AI can run into similar conundrums when it performs code reviews. It might not have—or have difficulty understanding—specific context or domain knowledge behind a code base. It will review based on the patterns it sees and knows. It will make decisions on those patterns. And, overall, the way it reviews will be highly dependent on the datasets that were used to train it. In a code review, an AI could make an ill-informed decision, much like I did without knowing the Phil Collins-Genesis connection. This leads to a few problems. For example, a developer might write a function to handle sensitive customer data that an AI immediately flags as a security vulnerability. What it doesn't recognize is that additional security measures have been implemented in the function, mitigating any security risk. If we fully rely on AI for a code review, this incorrectly flagged issue might hold up the rest of the process. Alternatively, if a human still reviews what the AI has flagged, the developer may chase a false issue and spend time on something that was not an issue at all.

Another example: PRs may be prepared and opened with the intent to merge the changes at a later date. This could be a change that scales infrastructure for a peak event, a migration event that depends on some prerequisite tasks, or another change that considers the context. If AI tools are used to automate the entire code review process, an AI might miss the understanding that these changes should not be autom-erged despite being "valid."

Alongside context and domain knowledge, an AI's inability to understand nuance can limit its effectiveness in code reviews. Sometimes, a developer makes deliberate coding choices that make sense to the team but not to an AI. For example, a senior developer might implement a slightly less efficient but more readable function because human comprehension is more important to the team. What is "readable" and "understandable" are difficult notions for an AI to determine. Instead, it will see the function's suboptimal efficiency and flag it as a problem rather than understand the benefit readability brings.

Until AI can replicate the human ability to understand context, nuance, and complex domain knowledge, it's unlikely to fully automate or take over the entire code review.

13.2.2 Capabilities are highly dependent on training data

Despite being trained on vast datasets of code, AI is, in a way, limited to that code. This presents several limitations. First, if the AI hasn't encountered specific examples of code that produce weird scenarios or rare edge cases or will trigger bugs only under the most uncommon of circumstances, it may not flag those items while reviewing your code, resulting in false negatives. Alternatively, it can go in the opposite direction and become too strict, flagging items that shouldn't be flagged at all. These are known as false positives. Both can greatly reduce the quality of support an AI can give during the code review.

Next, an AI's inability to adapt to new technologies can result in similar disadvantages. Let's say yet another JavaScript framework is released, and your team decides to use it. It's highly unlikely that the AI's training data would have any examples of the new JavaScript framework, and it would likely struggle to review that code effectively. This intuitively makes sense as we constantly refuse to review code we are unfamiliar with or make a "best-guess effort" when we are presented with new code to review.

This also leads to something called AI hallucinations, a phenomenon where LLMs tend to see patterns or objects that don't really exist, resulting in output that is completely inaccurate or downright ridiculous. You could say that the AI is "imagining" things!

For example, developers at Pretius experimented with an OpenAI Reviewer, an AI code reviewer, and encountered such AI hallucinations. Small changes to the code "caused the AI to make things up, repeat itself, make mistakes; it highlighted errors in the code, but showed the exact same code as a solution" [5]. I'm optimistic that our technology and learning models will improve over time. As of now, this is a major limitation to keep in mind when considering AI in code reviews. It also means human validation still plays a required part in AI-assisted reviews.

13.2.3   *Over-reliance on AI can hinder human reviewer expertise*

One thing I think we don't acknowledge is that there's a very high chance of becoming too reliant on AI. There's a difference between using AI to streamline and automate the tedious parts of our code review and using it as the code review. If we choose the latter and just let AI take care of code reviews, I see some long-term complications arising.

First, the more we rely on AI to find concerning manners in the code review, the more we neglect our own critical thinking skills. We can become complacent because we assume AI will catch all the problems in a review.

For example, say you add an AI-powered code review tool to your code review process. At first, you get used to it, diligently checking the problems it has flagged to see whether they are relevant. You still continue to do your own review of the code after the AI's review. This should be the proper way to do AI-assisted reviews, by the way. As time goes by, you start to trust in the AI's review more and more. You check its review, but not as thoroughly. Your own reviews start to get quicker as well. It can get to the point where you no longer do your own review and even skip your audit of the AI's review. The code review process has now become an AI-powered review, with nothing else afterward. What's brought up by the AI is trusted and not looked at again.

Without doing our own review and only relying on AI to flag potential issues, we don't exercise our own analytical and critical thinking skills as often. We become used to being told what problems may exist rather than finding them ourselves. If we don't keep an eye out for this, an overreliance on AI could reduce the overall team's code review skills.

Another snag? Focusing only on the AI-powered code review's findings can divert our attention away from the bigger picture. Architectural considerations, team maintainability, human readability, or larger, overarching project goals might be dismissed if we simply rely on AI to be *the* code review.

13.3   *What can an AI-powered code review do?*

Now that we know the benefits and limitations of AI in code reviews, it's time to explore what's actually out there. If you didn't already guess, code reviews now have a dash of AI in them as well. In this section, I'd like to give you a snapshot of what's possible right now with AI in code reviews. What can and should be "powered by AI"? I've chosen some examples of how I think AI fits perfectly into code reviews. I've also noted any caveats to keep in mind, as many of these features and tools are still quite new. Finally, I've given my overall opinion on whether it's worth considering at all!

> **NOTE**   I am not affiliated with or sponsored by the tools and services I reference in this section (I wish!). These are simply AI-powered tools that I've found in my research that are available right now and can potentially augment our code reviews for the better. Who knows what will be available in a year or two!

PR SUMMARIES

When we open pull requests, wouldn't it be nice to automatically generate a high-level summary of the changes? With AI, we can. Different tools implement this in different ways.

Copilot for Pull Requests (https://mng.bz/QVOR; only available with a Copilot Enterprise subscription) generates a summary of the changes made in a pull request, which files they affect, and what a reviewer should focus on when they conduct their review. Developers have to explicitly request a summary via the Summary tool, as seen in figure 13.1. These summaries can be added to the description of a new pull request, in the description of an existing pull request (by editing the opening comment), or in a comment on the main timeline of a pull request.

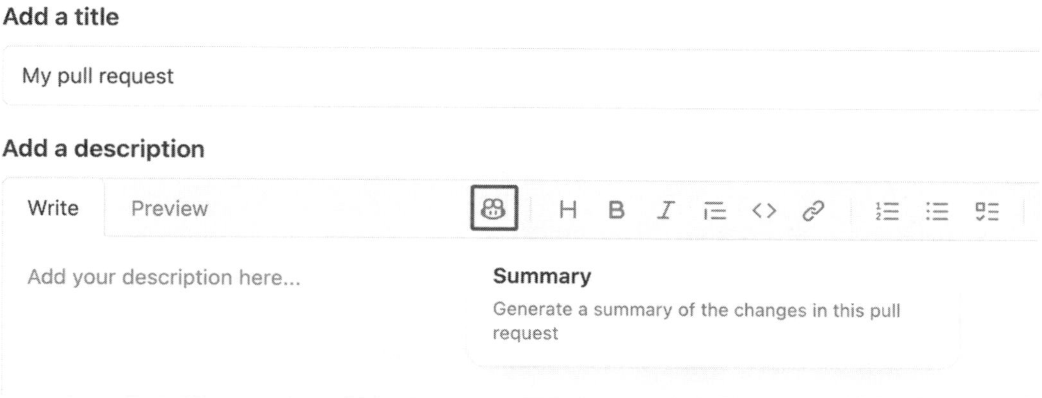

Add a title

My pull request

Add a description

| Write | Preview |

H B *I* ≔ <> 🔗   ⌗≡ ≔ ☑≡

Add your description here...

Summary
Generate a summary of the changes in this pull request

Figure 13.1   GitHub Copilot for pull request summaries button, seen in PR description editor toolbar

Qodo (https://www.qodo.ai/) gives developers an array of commands to run against their PR. An "AI PR Agent" powers these commands. Using the /describe command (https://mng.bz/pKQE), you can generate not only a description of your changes but clear PR titles, an "impact summary," which describes the potential effect of your code changes, a code walkthrough, and autolabel your PR, as seen in figure 13.2.

Type

Enhancement

Description

This PR introduces several enhancements to the PR description generation:

- The `changes_title` field has been added to the file label dictionary to provide a more informative title for the changes in the files.
- The table style and alignment in the `process_pr_files_prediction` method have been improved for better readability.
- The `insert_br_after_x_chars` function has been modified to handle new line characters and code tags, improving the formatting of the PR description.
- The `changes_title` field has been added to the `FileDescription` class in the `pr_agent/settings/pr_description_prompts.toml` file, allowing for a more detailed description of the changes in the PR.

Changes walkthrough

	Relevant files	
Enhancement	▼ **pr_description.py** Improved PR file description and table formatting pr_agent/tools/pr_description.py • Added `changes_title` to the file label dictionary. • Adjusted table style and alignment in `process_pr_files_prediction` method. • Modified `insert_br_after_x_chars` function to handle new line characters and code tags.	+49/-22
Configuration changes	▶ **pr_description_prompts.toml** Added `changes_title` field to FileDescription class	+4/-1

Figure 13.2   Output of Qodo `/describe` command, showing type of change, PR description, and change walkthrough

You can customize what to generate with this command, too, so if you only need the description, you can configure it that way. And if you'd like to automatically run the `/describe` command every time a new PR is opened, an existing PR is reopened, a PR is moved from Draft to Open, or when a review is manually requested, that can be done via a GitHub Action.

There are many other tools, like CodeRabbit or What The Diff, that also offer automated PR summarizations that can be configured to run when PRs are opened!

Any caveats? Of course, there are a few. Most of these tools convert the code diff into an LLM prompt, typically using GPT-4. These are used to generate the summaries you see. As with any tool that uses generalized LLMs, the potential for hallucinations or difficulty understanding the input exists, resulting in an unusable output. Another caveat? The larger your PR, the longer the processing times will be for generating a summary. For example, Copilot for Pull Requests has documented requests taking more than a few minutes to return some output. A few minutes might seem like nothing, but as a developer who wants to get things done faster and more efficiently, that minor wait alone may encourage them not to use the tool at all. If they do wait, well, it might cause the team to question whether AI is really helping if the process takes just as long. Another thing to watch out for with larger PRs is the omission of files over a certain threshold. With Copilot for Pull Requests, they've witnessed only "the first 30 files being accounted for and then any additional files being omitted from the summarization" [6].

Is this something to consider? Absolutely. I've stressed how important it is to make sure PRs are detailed and full of context. If AI can help us be more consistent with that or reduce the time it takes to make sure our PRs are that detailed, it is very much worth considering. PR summaries can serve as a great starting point for authors to describe the "why" of their changes. It provides a quick overview for reviewers, allowing them to focus on what matters in the PR. Having humans validate the summaries and striving to keep PRs small, we can mitigate most of the caveats. Overall, I think it's worth augmenting your team's code review with AI in this way.

CODE SUGGESTIONS/INSTANT CODE REFACTORING

Whether it's issue detection or a suggested improvement, inline code refactoring is another neat way AI can assist in the code review. Not only can AI point these items out, but it also makes it simple to integrate the related code change right in the PR. Again, different tools achieve this in different ways.

What The Diff allows you to comment on the lines of code that you want refactored with the `/wtd` command followed by a description of the changes you want. After a few moments, What The Diff suggests changes in the pull request, which can be accepted with one click, as seen in figure 13.3. This is a great way for authors to quickly address—or at least get a head start on—feedback from their reviewers.

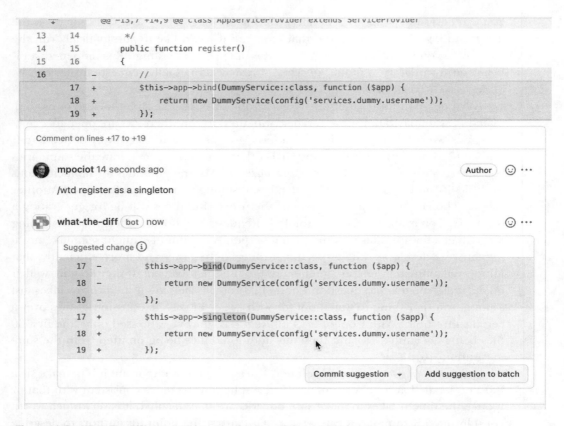

Figure 13.3   What The Diff generated suggestion to register selected code as a singleton

Qodo has an `/improve` command (https://mng.bz/OBV2) that can suggest how your PR code changes can be, well, improved. For larger PRs, a more comprehensive review can be done through the `--extended` flag of the `/improve` command. This segments larger PRs and generates proportionate suggestions, like maintainability improvements or best practices that were not considered, as seen in figure 13.4.

Both reviewers and authors alike can use this command: authors, to help them be their own first reviewer and propose the best version of their changes, and reviewers, to help them articulate a change they can't quite put their finger on but know needs to be modified.

Google has internally implemented instant code refactoring via ML-suggested edits. Using the Dynamic Integrated Developer ACTivity (or DIDACT; https://mng .bz/M1aD) methodology, Google applied machine learning to develop a model to help developers automatically resolve code review comments. With the millions of reviewer comments they see per year, the ability to train their model based on their

Figure 13.4   Output of Qodo /improve command with the --extended flag

developers' code reviewing habits, and refinement of the model through captured ratings of helpfulness (or not), they were able to create a model that addresses 52% of comments with a target precision of 50% [7]. Now, as a part of their internal code review tool, ML-suggested edits are generated for every review, with 40% to 50% of all previewed suggested edits applied by code authors [7].

Metabob (https://metabob.com/) takes a slightly different approach to generating code suggestions. Using special neural networks (called *graph neural networks*), Metabob examines and learns the relationships between different parts of your code.

With this understanding, Metabob can pinpoint and categorize code issues while taking the surrounding code (context) into account. Once a problem is identified, Metabob explains it and feeds this explanation, along with the problematic code, into generative AI models. Metabob then generates context-sensitive code recommendations that specifically address the identified issue.

Any caveats? Not too many, just the typical ones to keep in mind. These tools are powered by similar LLMs, so there's always the possibility of false positives, false negatives, and hallucinations to watch out for. Using them to assist rather than replace the review process, paired with the ever-constant need for human validation, should mitigate these risks.

Is this something to consider? Absolutely. Authors can take advantage of these tools to be their own first reviewer. They can help us understand why one implementation is better (or not). And they can significantly reduce the feedback–response cycle as authors can get a head start on addressing those comments. This is a great example of where AI and humans can work in harmony.

AUTOMATED REVIEW

This deserved its own section! Though inline code refactoring and code suggestions play a part in automated reviews, intentional "review" features tend to focus on an overall assessment of the submitted PR.

Qodo is the most comprehensive automated review I have found so far. Triggered using the `/review` command (https://mng.bz/YD8e), Qodo's PR-agent provides a wealth of information about the PR it inspects: what type of change it is, a summary of the changes, whether relevant tests were added, an estimate of how much effort is required to review the PR, security concerns—you get the idea. This information is configurable and is generated as a PR Analysis, as seen in figure 13.5.

PR Review

⏱ **Estimated effort to review [1-5]**	2, because the changes are straightforward and mainly involve removing code and updating documentation. The logic simplification in `pr_reviewer.py` is the primary area needing a closer look to ensure nothing critical was removed or broken.
✏ **Relevant tests**	No
🔍 **Possible issues**	**Possible Bug:** The removal of `remove_previous_review_comment` functionality without ensuring that duplicate comments are handled might lead to clutter in PR comments if the system was previously relying on this to clean up old comments.
🔒 **Security concerns**	No

Figure 13.5   Qodo's PR Analysis output after running the `/review` command

As you can see in the figure, more in-depth PR feedback is also generated, from general suggestions to feedback on specific files. This is, in my opinion, a reviewer's best friend. Again, it doesn't replace what we have to do, but having a curated synopsis at our disposal can make the review process much less painful than it has to be. By automating away the tedious checks, like making sure necessary tests are included or that no obvious security vulnerabilities are found, we can turn our reviewing attention straight to the code. These types of overviews are also really helpful for onboarding new members or getting colleagues who are unfamiliar with that part of the code base, well, more familiar with it once and for all.

CodeRabbit does its own automated review on submitted pull requests, where the main output is review feedback that is posted through comments. It also makes use of code suggestions to help address the very comments it added. While it doesn't have the same thorough overview of the PR as Qodo, one unique feature it provides is a Code Walkthrough. This summarizes what the changes do overall, followed by an individual summary of each file changed in the PR. It attempts to relate the changes to each other to make it easier for the reviewer to understand the PR, as seen in figure 13.6.

Any caveats? AI-powered reviews can be incredibly helpful, but it's crucial not to let them become a crutch. While the level of detail and accuracy can vary, some reviewers might be tempted to simply run an automated review and consider their job done. This shortcut mentality can backfire. Instead, reviewers need to use AI as a starting point. Take advantage of its initial review and the time it saves you. However, remember your responsibility to validate the findings and use that saved time to focus on the bigger picture. This means prioritizing higher-level issues and using your human expertise to ensure a truly thorough review.

Is this something to consider? Absolutely. Tools like this can make the reviewer's job especially productive: we can use them to make sure we don't miss anything, provide a consistent review, give us a focused starting point, and reduce the time we spend reviewing overall. What's important to remember is that our human judgment and final decision-making are even more important now; just because an AI flagged an issue or suggested a code improvement doesn't mean it is valid. We need to make sure these suggestions are sound and make sense to pass on to the author.

PR FEEDBACK CHAT

Another troublesome area in code reviews? Waiting on feedback from our reviewer. Sometimes it's a legitimate reason, like waiting for colleagues in a different time zone to reply. Other times, you just have to wait until your reviewer can respond. Using AI, a tool has been built to counter this problem.

CodeRabbit is an AI-driven platform that offers, among other cool things, the ability for you to have a conversation with your PR. Once it performs a review (another feature we'll discuss shortly), an author can ask questions in the context of the

coderabbitai `bot` commented 2 weeks ago · edited ⌄   ···

Walkthrough

The changes introduce a new feature to remove internal comments from the OpenAPI output. This is achieved by adding new command-line options, modifying the `Registry` struct, and creating a new function to handle comment removal. The changes also include generated code for handling HTTP requests and forwarding them to gRPC endpoints.

Changes

File	Summary
`Makefile` , `.../BUILD.bazel`	Addition of a new `buf generate` command and inclusion of a new proto file in the proto_library.
`.../remove_internal_comment.pb.gw.go`	Generated code for handling HTTP requests and forwarding them to gRPC endpoints.
`.../remove_internal_comment.proto`	New protocol buffer file defining a gRPC service with specific comments to be excluded from the OpenAPI output.
`internal/descriptor/registry.go`	Introduction of two new fields and their getter and setter methods to the `Registry` struct.
`protoc-gen-openapiv2/defs.bzl`	New command-line options added to control the handling of comments in the generated OpenAPI output.
`.../genopenapi/template.go`	New function introduced to remove internal comments from a given string.
`.../genopenapi/template_fuzz_test.go`	New test function added to fuzz the `removeInternalComments` function.
`protoc-gen-openapiv2/main.go`	New command-line flag introduced to remove all substrings in comments that start with `(--` and end with `--)`.

🐰 "In the land of code so bright,

A rabbit hopped through day and night.

With each hop, a change was made,

In the world of software, a new layer laid.

Comments hidden, secrets kept,

Through lines of code, the rabbit leapt. 🐰"

Figure 13.6   CodeRabbit Code Walkthrough output

changes. For example, if CodeRabbit comments on a line of code to make a suggestion, you can reply to that comment and ask for an explanation or more details, as seen in figure 13.7. As you use this over time, CodeRabbit learns from your (and your team's) interactions, refining its model to match how your team works. Qodo offers something similar with its `/ask` command (https://mng.bz/Ge8V), where you can converse on the main timeline of your PR.

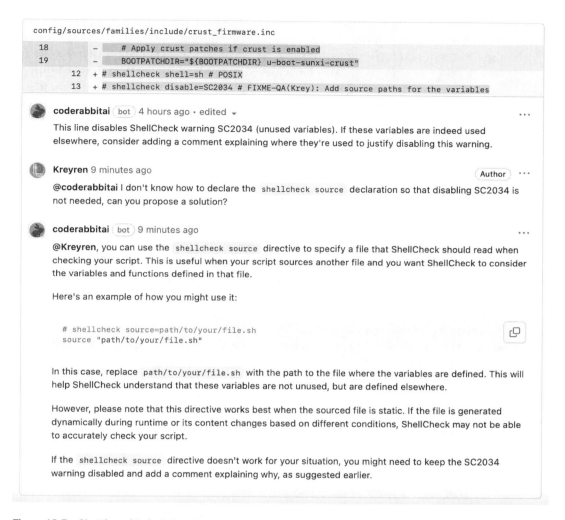

Figure 13.7   Chatting with CodeRabbit AI on a piece of PR feedback

Any caveats? Both CodeRabbit and Qodo hinted at it: these tools get better over time. Naturally, if you want to start using these tools right away, it may not work as accurately or as you hoped. Also, the more you use these tools, the more data it has at its disposal make better decisions in the future. If your team is hesitant to use it and would rather speak to someone with context and organizational knowledge now or just uses it occasionally, the resulting model might be incomplete, obsolete, or inaccurate. As long as your team is aware of this and has the time to dedicate to building and training that model with its participation, I think you can build a model that aligns with your expectations.

Is this something to consider? Maybe. I think if your team is really bogged down by waiting for reviewer feedback or must work with colleagues who are in really disparate time zones, it is something to consider. As a team, clear expectations need to be set: what level of assistance can truly be achieved in the beginning? What level of support will be given to the team in terms of learning how to use it, how to configure it, and how to refine it? What kind of participation is required? Will it be used on every PR or only on more complex changes? The more you can level-set with the entire team on how long it might take to get to a working model and the expected participation it requires from everyone, the better it will be for all.

ISSUE VALIDATION

One unique feature I've seen is the attempt to validate PR changes against a linked GitHub or Gitlab issue. Unfortunately, not much information is available on it on CodeRabbit's website or docs, but the thought is enticing. Based on what's written in the linked issue, CodeRabbit interprets "aspects" of the issue to fulfill. It then reviews the code in the linked PR to see whether it properly fulfills each aspect of the ticket. In other words, it's a pretty convenient way to say, "Yup, you've correctly and comprehensively addressed the issue!"

Any caveats? Many. First, this feature only supports GitHub or Gitlab issues at the moment. This can be problematic if (a) you aren't using GitHub or Gitlab or (b) your team primarily uses a different method to track work items, like a Jira board. If you use a different tool to track your work items, you'd have to duplicate them as issues for this to work. Next, this assumes issues are filled out in explicit detail and in a way that is interpretable by CodeRabbit. If issues are written in a lackluster way or without clear, verifiable "aspects," the issue validation may not work as intended.

Is this something to consider? At the moment, I don't think so. The restrictions (only available through GitHub or Gitlab issues) and the required level of additional effort (writing accurate, detailed, and thorough issues) defeat the purpose of using it.

13.4 *Integrating AI into your code reviews*

I think AI can truly change our code reviews for the better. While they can't do the entire review for us, they can handle some hefty parts and reduce the overall time a review takes.

If you've decided to integrate one of the AI-powered tools or an AI-assisted service into your code review process, I've outlined a path to safely and effectively do so. This path relies on the notion of levels. Levels, of which we have Low, Medium, and High, will represent the team's confidence in the AI's accuracy. As you continue to use the AI, you'll observe and track how it fares with your process, determine whether it has learned your code base and team decisions adequately and, ultimately, decide whether it provides review capabilities that your team can be confident in.

LOW

Start out with ignoring and being very lenient with AI suggestions. As implied by the level, your team's confidence in the AI will be quite low at this point. Use the AI-assisted tools to provide you with initial analysis, but don't block a PR because of what an AI brings up. See what it flags. Determine what it doesn't flag. Is it right? Is it really wrong? Since you're just starting out with the tool, it needs to get used to your team, its coding style and conventions, and learn how your team reviews its code. If your tool has the notion of rating the AI's output, make sure to use it.

As a team, it would be good to set expectations as well. What do you expect to use the AI tool for? What threshold of incorrect vs correct issues or suggestions would your team feel comfortable with before graduating to a Medium level? What's the official expectation on addressing AI-generated reviewer feedback? The more you can adapt your Team Working Agreement to handle the AI adjustments being made to your process, the more your team can align on its integration. As time evolves, and you find that the AI's suggestions are more refined and correct, graduate to Medium.

MEDIUM

At this level, your team's confidence in the AI is medium. AI's suggestions are taken more seriously but can still be overridden by human decisions if they are incorrect. Your AI tool has had time to get to know your code and your team's coding style. It has likely reduced the number of totally inaccurate suggestions and false positives and negatives. Depending on the variety of changes it has witnessed through your team, it might be missing some context and domain knowledge, but it's working as expected for your routine changes. Once the AI's record of correct and helpful suggestions starts to pass a 90% threshold, you can elevate your team's confidence level to High.

HIGH

The ideal, final level, High, is where the AI has become so attuned to your team and your code base that the suggestions and issues it flags are correct more often than not. It has become so accurate and sparks human discussion due to its findings that you actually withhold approval on a PR until the AI's issues are fixed. It may take some time to get to a high level of confidence, but it will be well worth it.

Please don't use my data

Watch out for requests (or requirements) to use your code base as part of an LLM's training model. Often, AI-assisted tools will add your code to the vast datasets that are used to power it and make it better. However, security issues, leaked, proprietary internal code, or just simple privacy concerns are all valid concerns when considering an AI tool to use.

If you have the option to opt out, that's a good sign that the AI-powered tool or service is being transparent with you and its offerings.

If you have the option to self-host an instance of your AI tool, that's even better. This gives you more control over your data and ensures you aren't unintentionally and indirectly providing your source code to the public.

13.5   *The future of code reviews: Human-AI collaboration*

Imagine a future where code reviews are effortless, efficient, and bias-free. AI is pushing us towards that reality, and you have the power to be a part of it. Some of you may even be using AI tools in your code reviews already! (Living in the future, I see.) If you're considering adding AI-powered tools to your own code review, embrace them! Let AI be your tireless first reviewer, crafting clear PR descriptions and titles and catching basic code smells. Let AI enable you to understand your code faster, resolve feedback quicker, and gain peace of mind with consistent, unbiased reviews.

But here's the X-factor: AI is a powerful assistant, not a replacement. It can't replicate your human intuition. It won't understand that `"mdspc"` is a terribly abbreviated variable name and that `"monthlyDessertSpecial"` is much better. It won't grasp the context behind your comments, nor can it use your team's collective knowledge. That's why human validation is crucial. Don't become reliant on AI; it's young and ever-changing. It's an amazing copilot (😊), but it can't fly the code review plane—yet.

So, the future? Human-AI collaboration. Pairing human expertise and judgment with AI's tireless assistance will be the key to unlocking the full potential of code reviews.

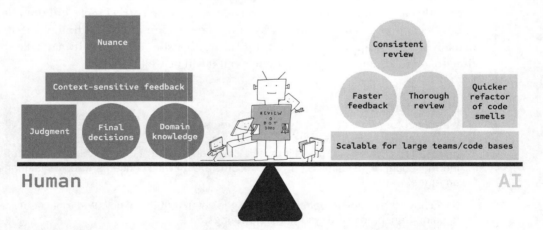

Human-AI Collaboration in Code Reviews

AI can't **replace** our human judgment and final decision-making in code reviews, but it can **assist** us in making the review faster, easier, and more effective than a human-only review. The right balance between both results in the ideal AI-assisted code review.

Figure 13.8   The future of code reviews relies on a balance between human and AI responsibility.

My advice on AI will be fleeting, but one thing remains constant: code reviews are here to stay. They'll always be a cornerstone of our responsibility as developers. And with the knowledge in this book and the magic of AI, you can transform them into the most fulfilling and effective process your team has ever experienced. Go forth and write (and review) amazing code!

Summary

- AI is here, and it's not a bad thing, but we have to be mindful of how we integrate it into code reviews.
- AI can be a wonderful assistant; it can speed up reviews, be a consistent reviewer, help larger teams be more effective with reviews, and further improve the quality of code that passes our review.
- Despite these benefits, we still have a part to play in code reviews. AI's limitations, like difficulty understanding context and nuance and dependence on training data, mean it's not quite ready to fully take over the code review process. Humans are still required to make final decisions and validate the AI's job.
- An important thing to keep in mind is to avoid an overreliance on AI in code reviews (and in general). Not doing so could hinder our skills in critical thinking and code comprehension.
- What can AI do? Many time-saving things: PR summaries, code suggestions, inline code refactoring, PR feedback chats, and PR analysis. It can do all of that, but it can't take over the entire code review. Your human judgment and validation are still required to make sure AI is doing exactly what we intended.
- Integrating AI into your code reviews is encouraged if it makes sense for your team, and it is introduced cautiously with a plan in mind. Use the Low-Medium-High path to slowly build confidence in the AI you plan to use with your code reviews.
- The future of code reviews? AI won't replace them (sorry!), but it will certainly augment them in a way that makes developers' time more effective. Code reviews will be about human–AI collaboration, where AI can provide helpful insights, automate tedious tasks, and be an extra check for humans, and humans can focus their time on more meaningful tasks, take advantage of their ability to make sense of nuance and context, and ultimately make the final decision in a review.

References

[1] Shani, I. (2024, February 8). Survey reveals AI's impact on the developer experience. *The GitHub Blog*. https://mng.bz/eVZG

[2] MacLeod, L., Greiler, M., Storey, M. A., Bird, C., & Czerwonka, J. (2017). Code reviewing in the trenches: Challenges and best practices. *IEEE Software, 35*(4), 34–42.

[3] Almeida, Y., Albuquerque, D., Dantas Filho, E., et al. (2024). AICodeReview: Advancing code quality with AI-enhanced reviews. *SoftwareX, 26,* 101677.

[4] Tufano, R., Pascarella, L., Tufano, M., et al. (2021, May). Towards automating code review activities. In *2021 IEEE/ACM 43rd International Conference on Software Engineering (ICSE)* (pp. 163-174). IEEE.

[5] Kurek, T., Świś, L. (2023, November 30). AI code review: We've tried OpenAI at our company, and here's what we've learned. *Pretius*. https://pretius.com/blog/open-ai-code-review/

[6] About Copilot pull request summaries. (n.d.). GitHub Docs. https://mng.bz/px7R

[7] Resolving code review comments with ML. (2023, May 23). Google Research. https://mng.bz/Omej

appendix A
Team Working Agreement starter template

Welcome to the Team Working Agreement starter template. This is a modifiable Markdown file that you and your team can use to kickstart the creation of your TWA. It will also be available on the accompanying GitHub repo for this book. Feel free to modify and adapt it as suits your team!

Team Working Agreement Starter (Markdown)

```
# Team Working Agreement [Code Review]
_Starter Template made available through "Looks Good To Me: Constructive
Code Reviews" by Adrienne Braganza_.

_This template serves as a starting point for your team to discuss and fill
out collaboratively. Some items have been added as a starting point; add,
remove, or modify these items with your team as necessary. Other portions
have been left empty or as prompts: discuss and decide how to answer these
as a team._

_Remember: this can be changed as a team as many times as necessary!_

## Code Review Goals
Our prioritized goal(s) for our code review process is {finding
bugs|codebase stability & maintainability|knowledge transfer &
sharing|mentoring|recordkeeping/chronicling}.

What we want our code review process to do:

? As always, we encourage a collaborative, respectful, and constructive
environment during our code reviews. Focus on the code, never the
developer! Above all, be kind.
```

Our Tools/Platform and our Workflow
We will use {tool/platform of choice} to facilitate our code reviews. We chose this as a team because...

Our Workflow
Our general code review workflow: {insert workflow diagram here}.

Detailed Steps of our Workflow
1. The starting point
2. The review-requesting action
3. The review mechanism
4. The feedback-cycle mechanism
5. The signoff conditions
6. The ending point

Author Responsibilities
- **Be your own first reviewer**: Anticipate what question your reviewers may ask and proactively answer them. Ensure that your code changes are well-tested, formatted consistently, and follow the team's coding standards.
- **Make your PR manageable**: Submit well-defined pull requests (PRs) with a succinct title, clear descriptions of changes, and use links, labels, and anything else that adds context to the PR. Keep the PR itself short, atomic, and relevant. Ideally, your PR is less than 20 files or 500 lines of code changed.
- **Make your PR understandable**; Check off all required items in the PR template (if used).
- **You are not your code**: Leave your ego at the door.
- **Focus on the feedback, not on yourself or the reviewer**: Be open and responsive to reviewer feedback and try to address any blocking issues within 24 hours.

Reviewer Responsibilities
- **Leave your ego at the door**.
- **Focus on the code, not the developer**.
- **Constructive feedback**: Use comments to leave small or self-explanatory pieces of feedback. Make sure they are objective, specific, and outcome-focused. For larger pieces of or more complex feedback, communicate directly with the author, rather than through comments.
- **Don't abuse the leverage you are given in this role**: Try to complete reviews within 24 hours or as timely as possible. Suggest alternative approaches or improvements, but back them with facts.
- **Thorough reviews are expected**: What passes through your review, thorough or not, is your responsibility.

Our Guidelines
These guidelines establish what to do in our code review process and how to do it. They are here to keep our team and process on track and to align our team on the expectations we've collectively agreed to for reviews.

Our Review Focus
These are the main items to focus on during a code review (_template note: feel free to remove/add/modify items in this list_):

- **Complexity**: Can you understand the code? Is it easy to follow? Will it still be clear to a different developer (or even the original author) when

they revisit it in the future? Are there any opportunities to make the code more "human-friendly" and straightforward? Will you be able to make changes to this code in the future? Are there "workaround" or "temporary" bits of code that need to be addressed in a more permanent way?
- **Consistency**: Do the proposed changes follow any working, reliable, and established design patterns and practices already within the project? Is there an opportunity to reuse existing code or libraries?
- **Conventions**: Are industry-wide conventions being followed? Does the code follow any library, framework, language, or other established conventions?
- **Cross-platform compatibility**: Does your codebase need to consider cross-platform compatibility? Are there dependencies included that are not platform agnostic? Will other developers have a hard time running this code "out of the box"?
- **Documentation**: Will missing documentation be a blocker for approval (I think it should!)? Will updates to relevant documentation be a PR checklist item? Do explanatory comments in the code count as documentation? Do you differentiate between technical, user, architectural, and other forms of documentation? If so, which types are valid to address during the code review?
- **Error handling**: Are there clear guidelines on how to handle errors and exceptions? Are they implemented consistently across the codebase? Are there edge cases not handled?
- **Naming**: If your team has naming conventions, are they followed? Are variables, methods, functions, classes, and other key parts clear and understandable? How about a multilingual team? How strict will you be on naming and what rules regarding its enforcement will be important enough to add to your team working agreement?
- **Resource management**: Are the management of resources (like memory, network connections, I/Operations, etc.) properly considered?
- **Scalability**: Does the code lend itself to refactoring or rewriting without much impact? Can it handle future scenarios that are slightly different?
- **Security**: Are there glaring security vulnerabilities not caught by automated means? Are there security standards imposed by the industry you are in that are not followed?
- **Tests**: Are missing tests a blocker for approval? Will tests that purely increase code coverage be accepted? Are there acceptable scenarios where no accompanying tests will be allowed?

As reviewers, our time should be prioritized on keeping an eye out for the above issues.

Our Blocking vs Non-blocking Issues
These lists comprise the issues that **should block** a PR from being approved (blocking issue) and those that **should not block** a PR from being approved (non-blocking issue). If you encounter an issue that is not listed here, let's discuss as a team.

Blocking Issues
Issues that impact functionality, security, or maintainability; issues that need to be addressed by the author before it can be approved; issues that can block a PR from approval.

- **Core functionality**: Code doesn't meet the intended functionality, as outlined in the PR description or acceptance criteria.
- **Security issues**: Code introduces vulnerabilities which can expose personal or sensitive data or compromise the system.
- **Code standards violations**: Code deviates from established team, project, or style conventions and guides in a major way.
- **Code smells**: Code has poor structure, readability, or anti-patterns.
- **Regression**: Code introduces unintended side effects or breaks existing functionality.
- **Performance issues**: Code negatively impacts performance or resource usage.
- **Failing tests**: Code changes cause existing tests to fail.

Non-blocking Issues
Issues that do not impact functionality, security, or maintainability. Issues that should not block a PR from approval; issues that can be addressed through a separate pull request, minor update, or constructive feedback.

- **Style preferences**: Code style preferences that differ from your own. Small formatting issues: Minor things like inconsistent spacing or indentation.
- **Documentation nitpicks**: Minor inconsistencies, typos, or non-impacting issues in documentation.
- **Missing, but optional features**: If a PR fulfills core functionality, but doesn't have an optional feature that was mentioned in passing.
- **Minor refactor opportunities**: Code improvements that don't impact functionality but can be addressed in a separate pull request.
- **Unrelated improvements**: Suggestions that are unrelated to original PR, but can be addressed in a separate pull request.

Our approval policy
Here we outline **who gets to approve PRs** and **how many approvals are needed to merge a PR**.

Approver list
Those that directly contribute to the main repositories and have at least the "Write" role on those repositories are eligible to be an approver.

If you are added as a **Required** reviewer, you are expected to give a timely review on the assigned PR.

If you are added as an **Optional** reviewer, you are highly encouraged to treat the PR as a learning opportunity and to add an acknowledgement comment on the PR of your time spent learning about the code in the assigned PR.

Number of approvals
2 approvals (or more) are required before a PR can be merged. An author can't approve their own PR.\

Here's a preview of what this Markdown template will produce:

Team Working Agreement [Code Review]

Starter Template made available through "Looks Good To Me: Constructive Code Reviews" by Adrienne Braganza.

This template serves as a starting point for your team to discuss and fill out collaboratively. Some items have been added as a starting point; add, remove, or modify these items with your team as necessary. Other portions have been left empty or as prompts: discuss and decide how to answer these as a team.

Remember: this can be changed as a team as many times as necessary!

Code Review Goals

Our prioritized goal(s) for our code review process is (finding bugs|codebase stability & maintainability|knowledge transfer & sharing|mentoring|recordkeeping/chronicling).

What we want our code review process to do:

💡 As always, we encourage a collaborative, respectful, and constructive environment during our code reviews. Focus on the code, never the developer! Above all, be kind.

Our Tools/Platform and our Workflow

We will use (tool/platform of choice) to facilitate our code reviews. We chose this as a team because...

Our Workflow

Our general code review workflow: [insert workflow diagram here].

Detailed Steps of our Workflow

1. The starting point
2. The review-requesting action
3. The review mechanism
4. The feedback-cycle mechanism
5. The signoff conditions
6. The ending point

Author Responsibilities

- **Be your own first reviewer**: Anticipate what question your reviewers may ask and proactively answer them. Ensure that your code changes are well-tested, formatted consistently, and follow the team's coding standards.
- **Make your PR manageable**: Submit well-defined pull requests (PRs) with a succinct title, clear descriptions of changes, and use links, labels, and anything else that adds context to the PR. Keep the PR itself short, atomic, and relevant. Ideally, your PR is less than 20 files or 500 lines of code changed.
- **Make your PR understandable**: Check off all required items in the PR template (if used).
- **You are not your code**: Leave your ego at the door.
- **Focus on the feedback, not on yourself or the reviewer**: Be open and responsive to reviewer feedback and try address any blocking issues within 24 hours.

Reviewer Responsibilities

- **Leave your ego at the door**.
- **Focus on the code, not the developer**.
- **Constructive feedback**: Use comments to leave small or self-explanatory pieces of feedback. Make sure they are objective, specific, and outcome-focused. For larger pieces of or more complex feedback, communicate directly with the author, rather than through comments.
- **Don't abuse the leverage you are given in this role**: Try to complete reviews within 24 hours or as timely as possible. Suggest alternative approaches or improvements, but back them with facts.
- **Thorough reviews are expected**: What passes through your review, thorough or not, is your responsibility.

Our Guidelines

These guidelines establish what to do in our code review process and how to do it. They are here to keep our team and process on track and to align our team on the expectations we've collectively agreed to for reviews.

Our Review Focus

These are the main items to focus on during a code review (*template note: feel free to remove/add/modify items in this list*):

- **Complexity**: Can you understand the code? Is it easy to follow? Will it still be clear to a different developer (or even the original author) when they revisit it in the future? Are there any opportunities to make the code more "human-friendly" and straightforward? Will you be able to make changes to this code in the future? Are there "workaround" or "temporary" bits of code that need to be addressed in a more permanent way?
- **Consistency**: Do the proposed changes follow any working, reliable, and established design patterns and practices already within the project? Is there an opportunity to reuse existing code or libraries?
- **Conventions**: Are industry-wide conventions being followed? Does the code follow any library, framework, language, or other established conventions?
- **Cross-platform compatibility**: Does your codebase need to consider cross-platform compatibility? Are there dependencies included that are not platform agnostic? Will other developers have a hard time running this code "out of the box"?
- **Documentation**: Will missing documentation be a blocker for approval (I think it should!)? Will updates to relevant documentation be a PR checklist item? Do explanatory comments in the code count as documentation? Do you differentiate between technical, user, architectural, and other forms of documentation? If so, which types are valid to address during the code review?
- **Error handling**: Are there clear guidelines on how to handle errors and exceptions? Are they implemented consistently across the codebase? Are there edge cases not handled?
- **Naming**: If your team has naming conventions, are they followed? Are variables, methods, functions, classes, and other key parts clear and understandable? How about a multilingual team? How strict will you be on naming and what rules regarding its enforcement will be important enough to add to your team working agreement?
- **Resource management**: Are the management of resources (like memory, network connections, I/Operations, etc.) properly considered?
- **Scalability**: Does the code lend itself to refactoring or rewriting without much impact? Can it handle future scenarios that are slightly different?
- **Security**: Are there glaring security vulnerabilities not caught by automated means? Are there security standards imposed by the industry you are in that are not followed?
- **Tests**: Are missing tests a blocker for approval? Will tests that purely increase code coverage be accepted? Are there acceptable scenarios where no accompanying tests will be allowed?

As reviewers, our time should be prioritized on keeping an eye out for the above issues.

Our Blocking vs Non-blocking Issues

These lists comprise the issues that **should block** a PR from being approved (blocking issue) and those that **should not block** a PR from being approved (non-blocking issue). If you encounter an issue that is not listed here, let's discuss as a team.

Blocking Issues

Issues that impact functionality, security, or maintainability; issues that need to be addressed by the author before it can be approved; issues that can block a PR from approval.

- **Core functionality**: Code doesn't meet the intended functionality, as outlined in the PR description or acceptance criteria.
- **Security issues**: Code introduces vulnerabilities which can expose personal or sensitive data or compromise the system.
- **Code standards violations**: Code deviates from established team, project, or style conventions and guides in a major way.
- **Code smells**: Code has poor structure, readability, or anti-patterns.
- **Regression**: Code introduces unintended side effects or breaks existing functionality.
- **Performance issues**: Code negatively impacts performance or resource usage.
- **Failing tests**: Code changes cause existing tests to fail.

Non-blocking Issues

Issues that do not impact funtionality, security, or maintainability. Issues that should not block a PR from approval; issues that can be addressed through a separate pull request, minor update, or constructive feedback.

- **Style preferences**: Code style preferences that differ from your own. Small formatting issues: Minor things like inconsistent spacing or indentation.
- **Documentation nitpicks**: Minor inconsistencies, typos, or non-impacting issues in documentation.
- **Missing, but optional features**: If a PR fulfills core functionality, but doesn't have an optional feature that was mentioned in passing.
- **Minor refactor opportunities**: Code improvements that don't impact functionality but can be addressed in a separate pull request.
- **Unrelated improvements**: Suggestions that are unrelated to original PR, but can be addressed in a separate pull request.

Our approval policy

Here we outline **who gets to approve PRs** and **how many approvals are needed to merge a PR**.

Approver list

Those that directly contribute to the main repositories and have at least the "Write" role on those repository are eligible to be an approver.

If you are added as a **Required** reviewer, you are expected give a timely review on the assigned PR.

If you are added as an **Optional** reviewer, you are highly encouraged to treat the PR as a learning opportunity and to add an acknowledgement comment on the PR of your time spent learning about the code in the assigned PR.

Number of approvals

2 approvals (or more) are required before a PR can be merged. An author can't approve their own PR.

appendix B
Emergency Playbook
starter template

To help your team get started with an Emergency Playbook, I've provided this template. This is intended to get your team conversing with each other, agree to certain questions, and jumpstart the creation of your own Emergency Playbook.

Remember, this is just a template; yours doesn't have to adhere strictly to these sections nor be organized the way you see here. Feel free to adapt it (which is strongly encouraged!) to fit your needs. You can also grab a digital copy in this GitHub Repo I've prepared.

B.1 Name your emergency procedure:

What is this emergency procedure called?

B.2 Decision trees

This section should determine whether or not to ignore your code review process. It answers the following question:

What trigger conditions warrant an emergency scenario? Feel free to add your own decision tree workflows here.

B.3   *Authorization process*

If you have confirmed a valid emergency, this next section details who is allowed to initiate an Emergency Playbook procedure and how to start one.

Who is authorized to initiate an Emergency Playbook process? (List out specific individuals.)

How do you initiate an Emergency Playbook Process? (Outline the exact steps to be used to invoke the emergency procedure. This definitely involves documentation, sometimes a series of approvals in tools, or a mix of both.)

B.4   *Bypassing mechanism (and associated tasks)*

Here, you should describe the actual bypassing mechanism—the temporary operations or access permitted because it is an emergency. In our case, we're talking about bypassing the code review process you've established for your team.

Some examples include

- *Requiring a single approver*—More than one approval on a PR should be the standard. In the emergency scenario, a single approver can be used to expedite the review process.
- *Requiring no approvers*—Not recommended; if choosing this as an option in your playbook, be sure to accompany it with lots of documentation and communication tasks.
- *Allowing a self-approval on own PR*—Justification steps should be put into place if choosing this option. For example, when a PR is detected to have been self-approved, an additional step should request the author to input a reason. Additionally, automated notifications should be reported to the team or tech lead/manager that a self-approval has occurred.
- *Allowing a manager or other stakeholder to approve a PR*—When there are no other choices, the pool of developers is small, or something really needs to get deployed, having a manager or other trusted stakeholder be an approver on a PR can be used as a bypassing mechanism as well. Justification steps should still be put into place, including the reason for requesting this particular approval.
- *Other*—If any of the other options don't work, describe what *your* team's bypassing mechanism will be.

What's our bypassing mechanism?

What associated actions need to be taken? (Outline exact steps. Consider granting temporarily elevated permissions, creating a temporary privileged account, or temporary reconfiguring or settings/tool configurations, among other possibilities.) Be sure to also list the range of time these actions are valid for and who is to perform these actions.

B.5 Next Steps

Once the bypassing mechanism (and its respective actions have been taken), describe what happens next. These include three specific sections: Documentation, Communication, and Post-Incident Analysis.

B.5.1 Documentation

While the person who initiates the emergency procedure can also carry it out, that's not always what happens. What might be more likely is that a different person or group of people perform the actual bypassing mechanism (and its respective tasks/actions) than the one that initiates the emergency procedure.

Some key items you seriously need to document are

- Who was involved?
- Who actually carried out the bypassing mechanism?
- What was actually done? (Yes, the steps that should be taken need to be followed, but emergencies don't always go according to plan! That's why it's important to log everything that happens, even deviations from the official actions. In the best case scenario, this log will look exactly like your bypassing mechanism steps. In the worst case, it will have a few more steps.)
- What temporary access/controls were granted?
- Which tools/accounts were affected?
- When (and if applicable, where) did this take place?
- What justified this emergency procedure? (This should be a link to the justification document we discussed earlier. Without this, your team should consider it a grave misuse of the emergency playbook)

Consider this the official Emergency Procedure Execution Record or EPER.

COMMUNICATION

Next, *communicate* what actually happened. Depending on your organization, this can be a thorough and formal process or as simple as bringing it up at the next meeting.

Be sure to check with your security and compliance teams to see if any formal report is needed from their end. This is where the Emergency Procedure Execution Record we discussed previously comes in real handy! The information captured there would be critical to have on any kind of report.

Some examples include

- Make a Production Outage Record and Emergency Bypass Acknowledgement Record (if applicable) available in the emergency channel/space.
- Send an Incident Summary email to all affected teams.
- Send a Resolution Summary email to affected customers.

Outline what those communication tasks are for your team here.

POST-INCIDENT ANALYSIS

It's important to do a post-incident analysis. From determining how well the emergency procedure worked to identifying improvement areas or needed changes, your team would benefit from holding this discussion shortly after an emergency playbook procedure is executed.

Outline when your team should do this and what questions you should try to answer when holding a post-incident analysis.

appendix C
PR templates

I've created a few PR templates your team can use as starting points. They are all Markdown files; one for a new feature, one for a bug fix, and one for a documentation update. They each ask the author to provide useful pieces of information based on the type of PR. Again, these are a combination of what worked well on my teams and what would err on the side of over-communicating (which is usually helpful in these situations). As always, feel free to start out with these and then adapt or modify to your team's needs!

New feature PR template (Markdown)

```
# New Feature PR Template
---

## What is this?
Provide a sentence or two to describe the new feature.

## Why are we building it?
Provide justification/rationale on why this is needed now. Links to work
item/user story is ok, but copying it over to this description is even
better!

## How does it work?
Outline the high-level flow of how this feature works.

1.
2.
3.

## Documentation
Link accompanying documentation for this new feature
```

Acceptance criteria
What was the acceptance criteria for this feature? Links to work item/user story is ok, but copying it over to this description is even better!

Regression Risk
Are you confident these changes do not introduce any regressions?

Have you addressed any known regressions as a result of these changes?

New Feature Checklist

- [ ] Work Item/User Story # is linked
- [ ] Design document linked
- [ ] New unit tests have been added to accommodate new code

Notes
Is there any other context or information to share that would be helpful to know about this feature (especially if it helps the reviewer)?

Thanks for working on this awesome new thing!

Bug fix PR template (Markdown)

Bug Fix PR Template

What's happening?
Provide a sentence or two to describe the bug.

Reproduction Steps
Outline the steps you took to reproduce the bug. Be sure not to forget any steps and that they are in the right order!

1.
2.
3.

Root Cause
What was the root cause of the bug? How did you identify it?

Fix
Explain the fix in a sentence or two. Then, go into detail about **why** this fix solves the problem.

Testing Strategy
How was the fix tested to make sure the bug is truly resolved?

Impact
Are there any implications this fix may have on other parts of the application?

Regression Risk
Are you confident this fix does not introduce new issues? If you think this
fix may have some regression risk, what steps have been taken to mitigate it?

Bug Fix Checklist

- [ ] Issue # is linked
- [ ] Fix has been tested locally and works
- [ ] New unit tests have been added to prevent future regressions
- [ ] (If applicable) Relevant documentation has been updated

Notes
Is there any other context or information to share in order to understand the
fix or its impact?
Thanks for (hopefully) squashing this bug!

Documentation update PR template (Markdown)

Documentation Update PR Template

What are we changing in the docs?
Provide a sentence or two about the documentation update.

Why are we changing this?
Explain **why** these documentation changes are necessary. Feel free to
provide more details about the changes here.

Items Impacted
Briefly list the components, pages, versions, etc. affected by this change.

Screenshots (if applicable)
If there are significant visual changes, please attach some before and after
screenshots.

Review Checklist

- [ ] Spelling and grammar check has been performed and is correct
- [ ] All links are working and correct
- [ ] Documentation accurately reflects the current state of the project
- [ ] Changes are clearly highlighted and easy to understand

Notes
Any other context or information to share that may be helpful for reviewers?

Thanks for keeping our documentation current and correct!

appendix D
List of resources

This appendix provides a list of resources organized by chapter, a list of linters by language, and a list of static analysis tools by language.

D.1 List of resources by chapter

Chapter 1

Git—https://docs.github.com/en/get-started/using-git/about-git

Chapter 2

git-email workflow—https://blog.djhaskin.com/blog/git-email-workflow-made-easy/
Conventional Commits—https://www.conventionalcommits.org/
Oh My Zsh—https://github.com/ohmyzsh/ohmyzsh
zsh—https://linuxhandbook.com/why-zsh/
ohmyzsh labels—https://api.github.com/repos/ohmyzsh/ohmyzsh/labels
Azure DevOps Draft PRs—https://mng.bz/BX0g
Github Draft PRs—https://mng.bz/dX7X
GitLab Draft MRs—https://mng.bz/rKGZ
Ready for Review PR state (GitHub)—https://mng.bz/VVwO

Chapter 3

GitHub—https://github.com/
GitLab—https://about.gitlab.com/
Gerrit—https://www.gerritcodereview.com/
Crucible—https://www.atlassian.com/software/crucible
Rhodecode—https://rhodecode.com/
Collaborator—https://smartbear.com/product/collaborator/

Review Board—https://www.reviewboard.org/

RBCommons—https://rbcommons.com/

Chapter 4

Google's Engineering Practices: Code Review—https://google.github.io/eng-practices/review/

How to Do a Code Review (Google Engineering Guidelines)—https://google.github.io/eng-practices/review/reviewer/

Writing Good CL Descriptions (Google Engineering Guidelines)—https://google.github.io/eng-practices/review/developer/cl-descriptions.html

Handling Pushback in Code Reviews (Google Engineering Guidelines)—https://google.github.io/eng-practices/review/reviewer/pushback.html

GitLab Code Review Guidelines—https://docs.gitlab.com/ee/development/code_review.html

Defining What a Domain Expert Is (GitLab Guidelines)—https://docs.gitlab.com/ee/development/code_review.html#domain-experts

Responsibilities of the Merge Author (GitLab Guidelines)—https://mng.bz/xKBY

U.S. GSA Technology Transformation Services Guide: Code Review—https://engineering.18f.gov/code-review/

Yelp Engineering Code Review Guidelines—https://mng.bz/AQD7

Preparing Your Code for Review (Yelp Engineering Guidelines)—https://mng.bz/Zlwa

What to Do When Reviewing Code (Yelp Engineering Guidelines)—https://engineeringblog.yelp.com/2017/11/code-review-guidelines.html#when-reviewing-code

Chapter 5

ESLint—https://eslint.org/

ESLint Extension for VS Code—https://marketplace.visualstudio.com/items?itemName=dbaeumer.vscode-eslint

no-var—https://eslint.org/docs/latest/rules/no-var

no-duplicate-imports—https://eslint.org/docs/latest/rules/no-duplicate-imports

no-await-in-loop—https://eslint.org/docs/latest/rules/no-await-in-loop

eqeqeq—https://eslint.org/docs/latest/rules/eqeqeq

no-alert—https://eslint.org/docs/latest/rules/no-alert

no-console—https://eslint.org/docs/latest/rules/no-console

no-unneeded-ternary—https://eslint.org/docs/latest/rules/no-unneeded-ternary

Roslyn—https://github.com/dotnet/roslyn

SonarQube—https://www.sonarsource.com/products/sonarqube/

Veracode—https://www.veracode.com/

Codacy—https://github.com/marketplace/codacy

Selenium—https://www.selenium.dev/

Puppeteer—https://pptr.dev/

Protractor—https://www.protractortest.org/

Postman—https://www.postman.com/automated-testing/

Newman—https://mng.bz/RVeO

semantic-pull-request—https://github.com/marketplace/actions/semantic-pull-request

Conventional Commit spec—https://www.conventionalcommits.org/en/v1.0.0/

installing as a GitHub action—https://github.com/marketplace/actions/semantic-pull
-request#installation

PR Label Manager—https://github.com/marketplace/actions/label-manager-for-prs
-and-issues-based-on-configurable-conditions

PR Size Labeler—https://github.com/marketplace/actions/pull-request-size-labelling

Pull Request Statistics—https://github.com/marketplace/actions/pull-request-stats

GitHub CODEOWNERS file—https://docs.github.com/en/repositories/managing
-your-repositorys-settings-and-features/customizing-your-repository/about-code
-owners

SonarQube GitHub Action—https://github.com/marketplace/actions/official
-sonarqube-scan

Microsoft's Inclusiveness Analyzer—https://github.com/marketplace/actions/inclu
siveness-analyzer

ZAP Baseline Scan—https://github.com/marketplace/actions/zap-baseline-scan

Jfrog's Frogbot—https://github.com/marketplace/actions/frogbot-by-jfrog

Zimperium's Zimperium zScan—https://github.com/marketplace/actions/zimperium
-zscan

SecureStack's SecureStack Web Vulnerability Analysis—https://github.com/market
place/actions/securestack-web-vulnerability-analysis

Nightfall AI's Nightfall DLP Action—https://github.com/marketplace/actions/night
fall-dlp-action

SecureStack's All-In-One GitHub Action—https://github.com/marketplace/actions/
securestack-all-in-one-github-action

Code Climate—https://github.com/marketplace/code-climate

GitHub "Code Review" Actions—https://github.com/marketplace?type=actions&cat
egory=code-review

Chapter 6

MoSCoW comments—https://dev.to/allthecode/moscow-the-best-code-review-technique
-you-re-not-using-2b0e

Conventional Comments—https://conventionalcomments.org/

Membership "we"—https://en.wikipedia.org/wiki/We#Membership_we

Chapter 7

No resources are mentioned in the chapter.

Chapter 8

cherry-pick—https://git-scm.com/docs/git-cherry-pick
rebase—https://git-scm.com/book/en/v2/Git-Branching-Rebasing

Chapter 9

Miro—https://miro.com/
Figma—https://www.figma.com/
Draw.io—https://www.drawio.com/

Chapter 10

No resources are mentioned in the chapter.

Chapter 11

Extreme Programming Explained—https://www.oreilly.com/library/view/extreme
-programming-explained/0201616416/
On Pair Programming—https://martinfowler.com/articles/on-pair-programming.html
I've Pair Programmed for 30,000 Hours: Ask Me Anything!—https://www.youtube
.com/watch?v=RCDfBioUgts
You Must Be Crazy To Do Pair Programming—https://www.youtube.com/watch?v
=t92iupKHo8M
The Mortifying Ordeal of Pairing All Day—https://www.simplermachines.com/the
-mortifying-ordeal-of-pairing-all-day/
Tuple—https://tuple.app/
Pop—https://pop.com/
Live Share—https://code.visualstudio.com/learn/collaboration/live-share
Browserboard—https://browserboard.com/
Canva—https://www.canva.com/online-whiteboard/templates/

Chapter 12

Remote Mob Programming book—https://www.remotemobprogramming.org/
mob—https://mob.sh/
MobTime—https://mobti.me/
Mobster—http://mobster.cc/

Chapter 13

GitHub Copilot—https://github.com/features/copilot
Amazon CodeWhisperer—https://aws.amazon.com/codewhisperer/
Qodo—https://www.qodo.ai/
DocuWriter.ai—https://www.docuwriter.ai/
CodeRabbit—https://coderabbit.ai/
Copilot for Pull Requests—https://docs.github.com/en/enterprise-cloud@latest/
copilot/github-copilot-enterprise/copilot-pull-request-summaries

Qodo `/describe` command—https://www.qodo.ai/products/ide-plugin/workspace -mode/describe/

What The Diff—https://whatthediff.ai/

Qodo `/improve` command—https://www.qodo.ai/products/ide-plugin/file-mode/ improve

DIDACT—https://ai.googleblog.com/2023/05/large-sequence-models-for-software.html

Metabob—https://metabob.com/

Qodo `/review` command—https://www.qodo.ai/products/ide-plugin/workspace -mode/ review

Qodo `/ask` command—https://www.qodo.ai/products/ide-plugin/workspace-mode/ ask

D.2   *List of linters by language*

I've put together this list with the help of the Awesome Linters repository (https:// github.com/caramelomartins/awesome-linters). Please check them out, as they'll likely have the most up-to-date information on linting tools! For now, the ones listed in the table should be worth checking out (by the time you read this book).

Table D.1   Linters by language

Language	Linter	URL
ABAP	abaplint	https://abaplint.org/
Ansible	ansible-lint	https://github.com/ansible/ansible-lint
AWS CloudForma-tion templates	cfn-lint	https://github.com/aws-cloudformation/cfn-python-lint/
Azure Resource Manager (ARM)	arm-ttk	https://github.com/azure/arm-ttk
C	clang-format	https://clang.llvm.org/docs/ClangFormatStyleOptions.html
C++	clang-tidy	https://clang.llvm.org/extra/clang-tidy
	cpp-lint	https://github.com/cpplint/cpplint
	clang-format	https://clang.llvm.org/docs/ClangFormatStyleOptions.html
	flint++	https://github.com/JossWhittle/FlintPlusPlus
C#	dotnet format	https://github.com/dotnet/format
CSS	stylelint	https://stylelint.io/
Clojure	clj-kondo	https://github.com/borkdude/clj-kondo
CoffeeScript	coffeelint	https://coffeelint.github.io/
Copy/paste detection	jscpd	https://github.com/kucherenko/jscpd

Table D.1   Linters by language *(continued)*

Language	Linter	URL
Crystal	crystal	https://crystal-lang.org/
Dart	Dartanalyzer	https://dart.dev/guides/language/analysis-options
	effective_dart	https://pub.dev/packages/effective_dart
	lint	https://github.com/passsy/dart-lint
Dockerfile	hadolint	https://github.com/hadolint/hadolint
EditorConfig	editorconfig-checker	https://github.com/editorconfig-checker/editorconfig-checker
Erlang	elvis	https://github.com/inaka/elvis
ENV	dotenv-linter	https://github.com/dotenv-linter/dotenv-linter
F#	FSharpLint	https://fsprojects.github.io/FSharpLint
Fortran	fprettify	https://pypi.python.org/pypi/fprettify
Gherkin	gherkin-lint	https://github.com/vsiakka/gherkin-lint
GitHub Actions	actionlint	https://github.com/rhysd/actionlint
Go/Golang	Golangci-lint	https://github.com/golangci/golangci-lint
	go-critic	https://github.com/go-critic/go-critic
	revive	https://revive.run/
GoReleaser	GoReleaser	https://github.com/goreleaser/goreleaser
Groovy	npm-groovy-lint	https://github.com/nvuillam/npm-groovy-lint
Haskell	HLint	https://github.com/ndmitchell/hlint
HTML	HTMLHint	https://github.com/htmlhint/HTMLHint
Java	checkstyle	https://checkstyle.org/
	google-java-format	https://github.com/google/google-java-format
JavaScript	ESLint	https://eslint.org/
	standard js	https://standardjs.com/
	xo	https://github.com/xojs/xo
JSON	eslint-plugin-json	https://www.npmjs.com/package/eslint-plugin-json
JSONC	eslint-plugin-jsonc	https://www.npmjs.com/package/eslint-plugin-jsonc
Infrastructure as code	Checkov	https://www.checkov.io/
Kubernetes	kubeconform	https://github.com/yannh/kubeconform
Kotlin	ktlint	https://github.com/pinterest/ktlint

Table D.1 Linters by language *(continued)*

Language	Linter	URL
Kotlin	diktat	https://diktat.saveourtool.com/
	ktfmt	https://facebook.github.io/ktfmt/
LaTeX	ChkTex	https://www.nongnu.org/chktex/
Lua	luacheck	https://github.com/luarocks/luacheck
Markdown	markdownlint	https://github.com/igorshubovych/markdownlint-cli#readme
Natural language	textlint	https://textlint.github.io/
Nim	nimfmt	https://github.com/FedericoCeratto/nimfmt
OpenAPI	spectral	https://github.com/stoplightio/spectral
Perl	Perlcritic	https://metacpan.org/pod/Perl::Critic
	perltidy	https://perltidy.sourceforge.net/
PHP	parallel-lint	https://github.com/php-parallel-lint/PHP-Parallel-Lint
	PHP built-in linter	https://www.php.net/manual/en/features.commandline.options.php
	PHP CodeSniffer	https://github.com/PHPCSStandards/PHP_CodeSniffer
	PHPStan	https://phpstan.org/
	Psalm	https://psalm.dev/
	twig-lint	https://github.com/asm89/twig-lint
PowerShell	PSScriptAnalyzer	https://github.com/PowerShell/Psscriptanalyzer
Protocol Buffers	protolint	https://github.com/yoheimuta/protolint
Python3	bellybutton	https://github.com/hchasestevens/bellybutton
	pylint	https://pylint.pycqa.org/
	fixit	https://pypi.org/project/fixit/
	flake8	https://flake8.pycqa.org/en/latest/
	black	https://github.com/psf/black
	isort	https://pypi.org/project/isort/
	ruff	https://github.com/astral-sh/ruff
	unimport	https://unimport.hakancelik.dev/
	wemake-python-styleguide	https://wemake-python-styleguide.rtfd.io/
	yapf	https://github.com/google/yapf
R	lintr	https://github.com/jimhester/lintr

Table D.1   Linters by language (continued)

Language	Linter	URL
R	styler	https://styler.r-lib.org/
Raku	Raku	https://raku.org/
Rego	Regal	https://github.com/styrainc/regal
Renovate	renovate-config-validator	https://docs.renovatebot.com/config-validation/
Ruby	ERB Lint	https://github.com/Shopify/erb-lint
	htmlbeautifier	https://github.com/threedaymonk/htmlbeautifier
	rufo	https://github.com/ruby-formatter/rufo
	RuboCop	https://github.com/rubocop-hq/rubocop
	Standard Ruby	https://github.com/testdouble/standard
Rust	Clippy	https://github.com/rust-lang/rust-clippy
	dylint	https://www.trailofbits.com/post/write-rust-lints-without-forking-clippy
	rustfix	https://github.com/rust-lang/rustfix
	rustfmt	https://github.com/rust-lang/rustfmt
Scala	Scalafmt	https://github.com/scalameta/scalafmt
	WartRemover	https://www.wartremover.org/
Secrets	GitLeaks	https://github.com/zricethezav/gitleaks
Shell	bashate	https://github.com/openstack/bashate
	ShellCheck	https://github.com/koalaman/shellcheck
	shellharden	https://github.com/anordal/shellharden
	shfmt	https://github.com/mvdan/sh
	sh	https://pkg.go.dev/mvdan.cc/sh/v3
Snakemake	snakefmt	https://github.com/snakemake/snakefmt/
	snakemake–lint	https://snakemake.readthedocs.io/en/stable/snakefiles/writing_snakefiles.html#best-practices
SQL	sleek	https://github.com/nrempel/sleek
	squawk	https://squawkhq.com/
	sql-lint	https://github.com/joereynolds/sql-lint
	sqlfluff	https://github.com/sqlfluff/sqlfluff
	tsqllint	https://github.com/tsqllint/tsqllint

Table D.1   Linters by language (continued)

Language	Linter	URL
Swift	SwiftFormat	https://github.com/nicklockwood/SwiftFormat
	SwiftLint	https://realm.github.io/SwiftLint
Tekton	tekton-lint	https://github.com/IBM/tekton-lint
Terraform	fmt	https://developer.hashicorp.com/terraform/cli/commands/fmt
	tflint	https://github.com/terraform-linters/tflint
	terrascan	https://github.com/accurics/terrascan
Terragrunt	terragrunt	https://github.com/gruntwork-io/terragrunt
TypeScript	Angular ESLint	https://github.com/angular-eslint/angular-eslint#readme
	ESLint	https://eslint.org/
	standard js	https://standardjs.com/
	tslint-clean-code	https://www.npmjs.com/package/tslint-clean-code
Verilog/System-Verilog	verible-linter-action	https://github.com/chipsalliance/verible-linter-action
Vim Script	vint	https://github.com/Kuniwak/vint
XML	LibXML	http://xmlsoft.org/
YAML	YamlLint	https://github.com/adrienverge/yamllint
Multiple Languages	biome	https://biomejs.dev/
	Goodcheck	https://sider.github.io/goodcheck
	Mega-Linter	https://nvuillam.github.io/mega-linter/
	Prettier	https://prettier.io/
	relint	https://github.com/codingjoe/relint
	SonarLint	https://sonarlint.org/
	Super-Linter	https://github.com/github/super-linter
	todocheck	https://github.com/preslavmihaylov/todocheck
	trunk	https://trunk.io/

D.3   *List of static analysis tools by language*

This set of resources was kindly borrowed from Analysis Tools (https://analysis-tools .dev/) and more specifically, their repository (https://mng.bz/o0Ov) on which the website is based. Analysis Tools uses user rankings and comments to help determine which tools should be suggested. I highly recommend going to their website to search for your specific tech stack and for the most up-to-date information available!

Table D.2   Static analysis tools by language

Language	Static analysis tool	URL
ABAP	*abapOpenChecks*—Enhances the SAP Code Inspector with new and customizable checks	https://docs.abapopenchecks.org/
Ada	*Codepeer®*—Detects run-time and logic errors	https://www.adacore.com/static-analysis/codepeer
	Polyspace for Ada ®—Provide code verification that proves the absence of overflow, divide-by-zero, out-of-bounds array access, and certain other run-time errors in source code	https://www.mathworks.com/products/polyspace-ada.html
	SPARK ®—Static analysis and formal verification toolset for Ada	https://www.adacore.com/about-spark
Awk	*gawk –lint*—Warns about constructs that are dubious or non portable to other awk implementations	https://www.gnu.org/software/gawk/manual/html_node/Options.html
C	*Astrée ®* —Astrée automatically proves the absence of runtime errors and invalid concurrent behavior in C/C++ applications	https://www.absint.com/astree/index.htm
	CBMC—Bounded model-checker for C programs, user-defined assertions, standard assertions, several coverage metric analyses	http://www.cprover.org/cbmc
	clazy—Qt-oriented static code analyzer based on the Clang framework	https://github.com/KDE/clazy
	CMetrics—Measures size and complexity for C files	https://github.com/MetricsGrimoire/CMetrics
	CPAchecker—A tool for configurable software verification of C programs	https://cpachecker.sosy-lab.org/
	cppcheck—Static analysis of C/C++ code	https://cppcheck.sourceforge.io/
	CppDepend ®—Measure, query, and visualize your code and avoid unexpected issues, technical debt, and complexity	https://www.cppdepend.com/
	cpplint—Automated C++ checker that follows Google's style guide	https://github.com/google/styleguide/tree/gh-pages/cpplint
	cqmetrics—Quality metrics for C code	https://github.com/dspinellis/cqmetrics
	CScout—Complexity and quality metrics for C and C preprocessor code	https://www.spinellis.gr/cscout

Table D.2   Static analysis tools by language *(continued)*

Language	Static analysis tool	URL
C	*ESBMC*—ESBMC is an open source, permissively licensed, context-bounded model checker based on satisfiability modulo theories for the verification of single- and multi-threaded C/C++ programs.	http://esbmc.org/
	flawfinder—Finds possible security weaknesses	http://dwheeler.com/flawfinder/
	flint++—Cross-platform, zero-dependency port of flint, a lint program for C++ developed and used at Facebook	https://github.com/JossWhittle/FlintPlusPlus
	Frama-C—A sound and extensible static analyzer for C code	https://www.frama-c.com/
	GCC—The GCC compiler has static analysis capabilities since version 10	https://gcc.gnu.org/onlinedocs/gcc/Static-Analyzer-Options.html
	Goblint—A static analyzer for the analysis of multi-threaded C programs	https://goblint.in.tum.de/
	Helix QAC ®—Enterprise-grade static analysis for embedded software. Supports MISRA, CERT, and AUTOSAR coding standards.	https://www.perforce.com/products/helix-qac
	IKOS—A sound static analyzer for C/C++ code based on LLVM	https://github.com/nasa-sw-vnv/ikos
	Joern—Open-source code analysis platform for C/C++ based on code property graphs	https://joern.io/
	KLEE—A dynamic symbolic execution engine built on top of the LLVM compiler infrastructure	http://klee.github.io/
	LDRA®—A tool suite including static analysis (TBVISION) to various standards, including MISRA C & C++, JSF++ AV, CWE, CERT C, CERT C++, and Custom Rules	https://ldra.com/
	PC-lint®—Static analysis for C/C++	https://pclintplus.com/
	Phasar—A LLVM-based static analysis framework, which comes with a taint and type state analysis	https://phasar.org/
	Polyspace Bug Finder®—Identifies run-time errors, concurrency issues, security vulnerabilities, and other defects in C and C++ embedded software	https://www.mathworks.com/products/polyspace-bug-finder.html
	Polyspace Code Prover®—Provide code verification that proves the absence of overflow, divide-by-zero, out-of-bounds array access, and certain other run-time errors in C and C++ source code	https://www.mathworks.com/products/polyspace-code-prover.html
	scan-build—Frontend to drive the Clang Static Analyzer built into Clang via a regular build	https://clang-analyzer.llvm.org/scan-build.html

Table D.2 Static analysis tools by language *(continued)*

Language	Static analysis tool	URL
C	*splint*—Annotation-assisted static program checker	http://splint.org/
	SVF—A static tool that enables scalable and precise interprocedural dependence analysis for C and C++ programs	https://svf-tools.github.io/SVF
	TrustInSoft Analyzer®—Exhaustive detection of coding errors and their associated security vulnerabilities	https://trust-in-soft.com/
	vera++—Vera++ is a programmable tool for verification, analysis, and transformation of C++ source code	https://bitbucket.org/verateam/vera/wiki/Introduction
C#	*.NET Analyzers*—An organization for the development of analyzers (diagnostics and code fixes) using the .NET Compiler Platform	https://github.com/DotNet Analyzers
	ArchUnitNET—A C# architecture test library to specify and assert architecture rules in C# for automated testing	https://github.com/TNG/Arch UnitNET
	code-cracker—An analyzer library for C# and VB that uses Roslyn to produce refactorings, code analysis, and other niceties	https://code-cracker.github.io/
	Designite®—Designite supports the detection of various architecture, design, and implementation smells, computation of various code quality metrics, and trend analysis.	http://www.designite-tools.com/
	Gendarme—Gendarme inspects programs and libraries that contain code in ECMA CIL format (Mono and .NET).	https://www.mono-project.com/docs/tools+libraries/tools/gendarme
	Infer#—InferSharp (also referred to as Infer#) is an interprocedural and scalable static code analyzer for C#.	https://github.com/microsoft/infersharp
	Meziantou.Analyzer—A Roslyn analyzer to enforce some good practices in C# in terms of design, usage, security, performance, and style	https://github.com/meziantou/Meziantou.Analyzer
	NDepend®—Measure, query, and visualize your code and avoid unexpected issues, technical debt, and complexity	http://www.ndepend.com/
	Puma Scan—Puma Scan provides real-time secure code analysis for common vulnerabilities (XSS, SQLi, CSRF, LDAPi, crypto, deserialization, etc.) as development teams write code in Visual Studio.	https://pumasecurity.io/
	Roslynator—A collection of 190+ analyzers and 190+ refactorings for C#, powered by Roslyn	https://github.com/JosefPihrt/Roslynator

Table D.2 Static analysis tools by language (*continued*)

Language	Static analysis tool	URL
C#	*SonarAnalyzer.CSharp*—These Roslyn analyzers allow you to produce Clean Code that is safe, reliable, and maintainable by helping you find and correct bugs, vulnerabilities, and code smells in your codebase.	https://github.com/SonarSource/sonar-dotnet
	Wintellect.Analyzers—.NET Compiler Platform ("Roslyn") diagnostic analyzers and code fixes	https://github.com/Wintellect/Wintellect.Analyzers
C++	*Astrée* ®—Astrée automatically proves the absence of runtime errors and invalid concurrent behavior in C/C++ applications.	https://www.absint.com/astree/index.htm
	CBMC—Bounded model-checker for C programs, user-defined assertions, standard assertions, several coverage metric analyses	http://www.cprover.org/cbmc
	clang-tidy—Clang-based C++ linter tool with the (limited) ability to fix issues, too	https://clang.llvm.org/extra/clang-tidy
	clazy—Qt-oriented static code analyzer based on the Clang framework	https://github.com/KDE/clazy
	CMetrics—Measures size and complexity for C files	https://github.com/MetricsGrimoire/CMetrics
	cppcheck—Static analysis of C/C++ code	https://cppcheck.sourceforge.io/
	CppDepend ®—Measure, query, and visualize your code and avoid unexpected issues, technical debt, and complexity.	https://www.cppdepend.com/
	cpplint—Automated C++ checker that follows Google's style guide	https://github.com/google/styleguide/tree/gh-pages/cpplint
	cqmetrics—Quality metrics for C code	https://github.com/dspinellis/cqmetrics
	CScout—Complexity and quality metrics for C and C preprocessor code	https://www.spinellis.gr/cscout
	ESBMC—ESBMC is an open source, permissively licensed, context-bounded model checker based on satisfiability modulo theories for the verification of single- and multi-threaded C/C++ programs.	http://esbmc.org/
	flawfinder—Finds possible security weaknesses	http://dwheeler.com/flawfinder/
	Frama-C—A sound and extensible static analyzer for C code	https://www.frama-c.com/
	Helix QAC ®—Enterprise-grade static analysis for embedded software. Supports MISRA, CERT, and AUTOSAR coding standards	https://www.perforce.com/products/helix-qac

Table D.2   Static analysis tools by language *(continued)*

Language	Static analysis tool	URL
C++	*IKOS*—A sound static analyzer for C/C++ code based on LLVM	https://github.com/nasa-sw-vnv/ikos
	Joern—Open-source code analysis platform for C/C++ based on code property graphs	https://joern.io/
	KLEE—A dynamic symbolic execution engine built on top of the LLVM compiler infrastructure. It can auto-generate test cases for programs such that the test cases exercise as much of the program as possible.	http://klee.github.io/
	LDRA ⍟—A tool suite including static analysis (TBVISION) to various standards including MISRA C & C++, JSF++ AV, CWE, CERT C, CERT C++, and Custom Rules	https://ldra.com/
	PC-lint ⍟—Static analysis for C/C++. Runs natively under Windows/Linux/MacOS. Analyzes code for virtually any platform, supporting C11/C18 and C++17.	https://pclintplus.com/
	Phasar—A LLVM-based static analysis framework that comes with a taint and type state analysis	https://phasar.org/
	Polyspace Bug Finder ⍟—Identifies run-time errors, concurrency issues, security vulnerabilities, and other defects in C and C++ embedded software	https://www.mathworks.com/products/polyspace-bug-finder.html
	Polyspace Code Prover ⍟—Provide code verification that proves the absence of overflow, divide-by-zero, out-of-bounds array access, and certain other run-time errors in C and C++ source code	https://www.mathworks.com/products/polyspace-code-prover.html
	scan-build—Frontend to drive the Clang Static Analyzer built into Clang via a regular build	https://clang-analyzer.llvm.org/scan-build.html
	splint—Annotation-assisted static program checker	http://splint.org/
	SVF—A static tool that enables scalable and precise interprocedural dependence analysis for C and C++ programs	https://svf-tools.github.io/SVF
	TrustInSoft Analyzer ⍟—Exhaustive detection of coding errors and their associated security vulnerabilities	https://trust-in-soft.com/
	vera++—Vera++ is a programmable tool for verification, analysis, and transformation of C++ source code.	https://bitbucket.org/verateam/vera/wiki/Introduction
ColdFusion	*Fixinator* ⍟—Static security code analysis for ColdFusion or CFML code. Designed to work within a CI pipeline or from the developer's terminal	https://fixinator.app/

Table D.2   Static analysis tools by language *(continued)*

Language	Static analysis tool	URL
Crystal	*ameba*—A static code analysis tool for Crystal	https://crystal-ameba.github.io/
Dart	*Dart Code Metrics*—Reports code metrics, checks for anti-patterns, and provides additional rules for Dart analyzer	https://pub.dev/packages/dart_code_metrics
Delphi	*Fix Insight ©*—A free IDE Plugin for static code analysis	https://www.tmssoftware.com/site/fixinsight.asp
	Pascal Analyzer ©—A static code analysis tool with numerous reports	https://peganza.com/products_pal.html
	Pascal Expert ©—IDE plugin for code analysis	https://peganza.com/products_pex.html
	SonarDelphi—Delphi static analyzer for the SonarQube code quality platform	https://github.com/integrated-application-development/sonar-delphi
Dlang	*D-scanner*—D-Scanner is a tool for analyzing D source code.	https://github.com/dlang-community/D-Scanner
Elixir	*credo*—A static code analysis tool with a focus on code consistency and teaching	https://github.com/rrrene/credo
	dialyxir—Mix tasks to simplify use of Dialyzer in Elixir projects	https://github.com/jeremyjh/dialyxir
	sobelow—Security-focused static analysis for the Phoenix Framework	https://github.com/nccgroup/sobelow
Elm	*elm-review*—Analyzes whole Elm projects, with a focus on shareable and custom rules written in Elm that add guarantees the Elm compiler doesn't give you	https://package.elm-lang.org/packages/jfmengels/elm-review/latest
Erlang	*dialyzer*—The DIALYZER, a DIscrepancy AnaLYZer for ERlang programs. Dialyzer is a static analysis tool that identifies software discrepancies, such as definite type errors, code that has become dead or unreachable because of programming error and unnecessary tests in single Erlang modules or entire (sets of) applications.	https://www.erlang.org/doc/man/dialyzer.html
	Primitive Erlang Security Tool (PEST)—A tool to do a basic scan of Erlang source code and report any function calls that may cause Erlang source code to be insecure	https://github.com/okeuday/pest
Fortran	*i-Code CNES for Fortran*—An open source static code analysis tool for Fortran 77, Fortran 90, and Shell	https://github.com/lequal/i-CodeCNES
Go	*aligncheck*—Find inefficiently packed structs	https://gitlab.com/opennota/check

Table D.2   Static analysis tools by language *(continued)*

Language	Static analysis tool	URL
Go	*bodyclose*—Checks whether HTTP response body is closed	https://github.com/timakin/bodyclose
	deadcode—Finds unused code	https://github.com/tsenart/deadcode
	dogsled—Finds assignments/declarations with too many blank identifiers	https://github.com/alexkohler/dogsled
	errcheck—Check that error return values are used	https://github.com/kisielk/errcheck
	errwrap—Wrap and fix Go errors with the new %w verb directive	https://github.com/fatih/errwrap
	flen—Get info on length of functions in a Go package	https://github.com/lafolle/flen
	go tool vet –shadow—Reports variables that may have been unintentionally shadowed	https://golang.org/cmd/vet#hdr-Shadowed_variables
	go vet—Examines Go source code and reports suspicious	https://golang.org/cmd/vet
	go-consistent—Analyzer that helps you to make your Go programs more consistent	https://github.com/Quasilyte/go-consistent
	go/ast—Package ast declares the types used to represent syntax trees for Go packages.	https://golang.org/pkg/go/ast
	goconst—Finds repeated strings that could be replaced by a constant	https://github.com/jgautheron/goconst
	gofmt -s—Checks if the code is properly formatted and could not be further simplified	https://golang.org/cmd/gofmt
	gofumpt—Enforce a stricter format than gofmt, while being backwards-compatible	https://github.com/mvdan/gofumpt
	goimports—Checks missing or unreferenced package imports	https://pkg.go.dev/golang.org/x/tools/cmd/goimports
	gokart—Golang security analysis with a focus on minimizing false positives	https://github.com/praetorian-inc/gokart
	goroutine-inspect—An interactive tool to analyze Golang goroutine dump	https://github.com/linuxerwang/goroutine-inspect
	gosec (gas)—Inspects source code for security problems by scanning the Go AST	https://securego.io/
	gotype—Syntactic and semantic analysis similar to the Go compiler	https://pkg.go.dev/golang.org/x/tools/cmd/gotype
	govulncheck—Govulncheck reports known vulnerabilities that affect Go code.	https://go.dev/blog/vuln

Table D.2   Static analysis tools by language *(continued)*

Language	Static analysis tool	URL
Go	*ineffassign*—Detect ineffectual assignments in Go code	https://github.com/gordonklaus/ineffassign
	misspell—Finds commonly misspelled English words	https://github.com/client9/misspell
	nakedret—Finds naked returns	https://github.com/alexkohler/nakedret
	nargs—Finds unused arguments in function declarations	https://github.com/alexkohler/nargs
	prealloc—Finds slice declarations that could potentially be preallocated	https://github.com/alexkohler/prealloc
	staticcheck—Go static analysis that specializes in finding bugs, simplifying code and improving performance	https://staticcheck.io/
	structcheck—Finds unused struct fields	https://gitlab.com/opennota/check
	structslop—Static analyzer for Go that recommends struct field rearrangements to provide for maximum space/allocation efficiency	https://github.com/orijtech/structslop
	test—Shows location of test failures from the stdlib testing module	https://pkg.go.dev/testing
	unconvert—Detects redundant type conversions	https://github.com/mdempsky/unconvert
	unparam—Finds unused function parameters	https://github.com/mvdan/unparam
	varcheck—Finds unused global variables and constants	https://gitlab.com/opennota/check
Groovy	*CodeNarc*—A static analysis tool for Groovy source code, enabling monitoring and enforcement of many coding standards and best practices	https://codenarc.github.io/CodeNarc
Haskell	*Liquid Haskell*—Liquid Haskell is a refinement type checker for Haskell programs.	https://ucsd-progsys.github.io/liquidhaskell-blog/
	Stan—A command-line tool for analyzing Haskell projects and outputting discovered vulnerabilities in a helpful way with possible solutions for detected problems	https://kowainik.github.io/projects/stan
	Weeder—A tool for detecting dead exports or package imports in Haskell code	https://github.com/ocharles/weeder

Table D.2   Static analysis tools by language *(continued)*

Language	Static analysis tool	URL
Haxe	*Haxe Checkstyle*—A static analysis tool to help developers write Haxe code that adheres to a coding standard	https://haxecheckstyle.github.io/docs/haxe-checkstyle/home.html
Java	*Checker Framework*—Pluggable type-checking for Java. This is not just a bug-finder, but a verification tool that gives a guarantee of correctness	https://checkerframework.org/
	checkstyle—Checking Java source code for adherence to a Code Standard or set of validation rules (best practices)	https://checkstyle.org/
	ck—Calculates Chidamber and Kemerer object-oriented metrics by processing the source Java files	https://github.com/mauricioaniche/ck
	ckjm—Calculates Chidamber and Kemerer object-oriented metrics by processing the bytecode of compiled Java files	http://www.spinellis.gr/sw/ckjm
	CogniCrypt—Checks Java source and byte code for incorrect uses of cryptographic APIs	https://www.eclipse.org/cognicrypt
	Dataflow Framework—An industrial-strength dataflow framework for Java	https://github.com/typetools/checker-framework
	DesigniteJava ®—Supports the detection of various architecture, design, and implementation smells along with the computation of various code quality metrics	http://www.designite-tools.com/designitejava
	Diffblue ®—A software company that provides AI-powered code analysis and testing solutions for software development teams	https://www.diffblue.com/
	Doop—A declarative framework for static analysis of Java/Android programs centered on pointer analysis algorithms	https://bitbucket.org/yanniss/doop
	Error Prone—Catch common Java mistakes as compile-time errors	https://errorprone.info/
	fb-contrib—A plugin for FindBugs with additional bug detectors	http://fb-contrib.sourceforge.net/
	forbidden-apis—Detects and forbids invocations of specific method/class/field (like reading from a text stream without a charset)	https://github.com/policeman-tools/forbidden-apis
	IntelliJ IDEA ®—Comes bundled with a lot of inspections for Java and Kotlin and includes tools for refactoring, formatting, and more	https://www.jetbrains.com/idea
	JArchitect ®—Measure, query, and visualize your code and avoid unexpected issues, technical debt, and complexity	https://www.jarchitect.com/

Table D.2   Static analysis tools by language *(continued)*

Language	Static analysis tool	URL
Java	*JBMC*—Bounded model-checker for Java (bytecode), verifies user-defined assertions, standard assertions, several coverage metric analyses	https://www.cprover.org/jbmc
	Mariana Trench—Our security-focused static analysis tool for Android and Java applications	https://mariana-tren.ch/
	NullAway—Type-based null-pointer checker with low build-time overhead; an Error Prone plugin (http://errorprone.info/)	https://github.com/uber/NullAway
	OWASP Dependency Check—Checks dependencies for known, publicly disclosed vulnerabilities	https://owasp.org/www-project-dependency-check
	qulice—Combines a few (pre-configured) static analysis tools (checkstyle, PMD, Findbugs, etc.)	https://www.qulice.com/
	RefactorFirst—Identifies and prioritizes God Classes and Highly Coupled classes in Java codebases you should refactor first	https://github.com/jimbethancourt/RefactorFirst
	Soot—A framework for analyzing and transforming Java and Android applications	https://soot-oss.github.io/soot
	Spoon—A metaprogramming library to analyze and transform Java source code (including Java 9, 10, 11, 12, 13, and 14)	https://spoon.gforge.inria.fr/
	SpotBugs—SpotBugs is FindBugs' successor. A tool for static analysis to look for bugs in Java code.	https://spotbugs.github.io/
	steady—Analyses your Java applications for open-source dependencies with known vulnerabilities, using both static analysis and testing to determine code context and usage for greater accuracy	https://eclipse.github.io/steady/
	Violations Lib—Java library for parsing report files from static code analysis	https://github.com/tomasbjerre/violations-lib
JavaScript	*DeepScan* ®—An analyzer for JavaScript that targets runtime errors and quality issues rather than coding conventions	https://deepscan.io/
	low—A static type checker for JavaScript	https://flow.org/
	hegel—A static type checker for JavaScript with a bias on type inference and strong type systems	https://hegel.js.org/
	NodeJSScan—A static security code scanner for Node.js applications powered by libsast and semgrep that builds on the njsscan CLI tool	https://opensecurity.in/
	Polymer-analyzer—A static analysis framework for Web Components	https://github.com/Polymer/tools/tree/master/packages/analyzer

Table D.2   Static analysis tools by language (continued)

Language	Static analysis tool	URL
JavaScript	*retire.js*—Scanner detecting the use of JavaScript libraries with known vulnerabilities	https://retirejs.github.io/retire.js
	standard—An npm module that checks for Javascript Styleguide issues	http://standardjs.com/
	tern—A JavaScript code analyzer for deep, cross-editor language support	https://ternjs.net/
Julia	*JET*—Static type inference system to detect bugs and type instabilities	https://github.com/aviatesk/JET.jl
	StaticLint—Static Code Analysis for Julia	https://github.com/julia-vscode/StaticLint.jl
Kotlin	*detekt*—Static code analysis for Kotlin code	https://detekt.github.io/detekt
Lua	*luacheck*—A tool for linting and static analysis of Lua code	https://github.com/lunarmodules/luacheck
	lualint—Performs luac-based static analysis of global variable usage in Lua source code	https://github.com/philips/lualint
	Luanalysis—An IDE for statically typed Lua development	https://plugins.jetbrains.com/plugin/14698-luanalysis
MATLAB	*mlint* ®—Check MATLAB code files for possible problems	https://mathworks.com/help/matlab/ref/mlint.html
Nim	*DrNim*—DrNim combines the Nim frontend with the Z3 proof engine in order to verify/validate software written in Nim.	https://nim-lang.org/docs/drnim.html
Ocaml	*Sys*—A static/symbolic Tool for finding bugs in (browser) code	https://github.com/PLSysSec/sys
	VeriFast—A tool for modular formal verification of correctness properties of single-threaded and multi-threaded C and Java programs annotated with pre-conditions and postconditions written in separation logic	https://github.com/verifast/verifast
PHP	*CakeFuzzer*—Web application security testing tool for CakePHP-based web applications	https://zigrin.com/tools/cake-fuzzer/
	churn-php—Helps discover good candidates for refactoring	https://github.com/bmitch/churn-php
	composer-dependency-analyser—Fast detection of composer dependency issues	https://github.com/shipmonk-rnd/composer-dependency-analyser
	dephpend—Dependency analysis tool	https://github.com/mihaeu/dephpend
	deprecation-detector—Finds usages of deprecated (Symfony) code	https://github.com/sensiolabs-de/deprecation-detector

Table D.2   Static analysis tools by language *(continued)*

Language	Static analysis tool	URL
PHP	*deptrac*—Enforces rules for dependencies between software layers	https://github.com/sensiolabs-de/deptrac
	DesignPatternDetector—Detection of design patterns in PHP code	https://github.com/Halleck45/DesignPatternDetector
	EasyCodingStandard—Combine PHP_CodeSniffer (https://github.com/squizlabs/PHP_CodeSniffer) and PHP-CS-Fixer (https://github.com/FriendsOf PHP/PHP-CS-Fixer)	https://www.tomasvotruba.com/blog/2017/05/03/combine-power-of-php-code-sniffer-and-php-cs-fixer-in-3-lines
	Enlightn—A static and dynamic analysis tool for Laravel applications that provides recommendations to improve the performance, security, and code reliability of Laravel apps	https://www.laravel-enlightn.com/
	exakat—An automated code reviewing engine for PHP	https://www.exakat.io/
	GrumPHP—Checks code on every commit	https://github.com/phpro/grumphp
	larastan—Adds static analysis to Laravel improving developer productivity and code quality	https://github.com/larastan/larastan
	Nitpick CI ®—Automated PHP code review	https://nitpick-ci.com/
	Parse—A Static Security Scanner	https://github.com/psecio/parse
	pdepend—Calculates software metrics like cyclomatic complexity for PHP code	https://pdepend.org/
	phan—A modern static analyzer from Etsy	https://github.com/phan/phan/wiki
	PHP Architecture Tester—Easy-to-use architecture testing tool for PHP	https://github.com/carlosas/phpat
	PHP Assumptions—Checks for weak assumptions	https://github.com/rskuipers/php-assumptions
	PHP Coding Standards Fixer—Fixes your code according to standards like PSR-1, PSR-2, and the Symfony standard	https://cs.symfony.com/
	PHP Insights—Instant PHP quality checks from your console	https://phpinsights.com/
	PHP Refactoring Browser—Refactoring helper	https://qafoolabs.github.io/php-refactoring-browser
	PHP-Parser—A PHP parser written in PHP	https://github.com/nikic/PHP-Parser
	php-speller—PHP spell check library	https://github.com/mekras/php-speller

Table D.2   Static analysis tools by language *(continued)*

Language	Static analysis tool	URL
PHP	*PHPArkitect*—Helps you to keep your PHP codebase coherent and solid by permitting the addition of some architectural constraint check to your work-flow.	https://github.com/phparkitect/arkitect
	PhpDeprecationDetector—Analyzer of PHP code to search issues with deprecated functionality in newer interpreter versions	https://github.com/wapmorgan/PhpDeprecationDetector
	phpDocumentor—Analyzes PHP source code to generate documentation	https://www.phpdoc.org/
	phploc—A tool for quickly measuring the size and analyzing the structure of a PHP project	https://github.com/sebastian bergmann/phploc
	PHPMD—Finds possible bugs in your code	https://phpmd.org/
	PhpMetrics—Calculates and visualizes various code quality metrics	http://www.phpmetrics.org/
	phpmnd—Helps to detect magic numbers	https://github.com/povils/phpmnd
	phpqa - jakzal—Many tools for PHP static analysis in one container	https://github.com/jakzal/phpqa
	phpqa - jmolivas—PHPQA all-in-one Analyzer CLI tool	https://github.com/jmolivas/phpqa
	PHPStan—PHP Static Analysis Tool—discover bugs in your code without running it	https://phpstan.org/
	Progpilot—A static analysis tool for security purposes	https://github.com/design security/progpilot
	Psalm—Static analysis tool for finding type errors in PHP applications	https://psalm.dev/
	rector—Instant Upgrades and Automated Refactoring of any PHP 5.3+ code	https://getrector.org/
	Reflection—Reflection library to do Static Analysis for PHP Projects	https://github.com/phpDocumen tor/Reflection
	Symfony Insight ℗—Detect security risks, find bugs and provide actionable metrics for PHP projects	https://insight.symfony.com/
	Tuli—A static analysis engine	https://github.com/ircmaxell/Tuli
	WAP—Tool to detect and correct input validation vulnerabilities in PHP (4.0 or higher) web applications and predicts false positives by combining static analysis and data mining	https://securityonline.info/owasp -wap-web-application-protection -project
PL/SQL	*ZPA*—An extensible code analyzer for PL/SQL and Oracle SQL. It can be integrated with SonarQube	https://felipezorzo.com.br/zpa/

Table D.2   Static analysis tools by language *(continued)*

Language	Static analysis tool	URL
Perl	*Perl::Analyzer*—A set of programs and modules that allow users to analyze and visualize Perl codebases by providing information about namespaces and their relations, dependencies, inheritance, and methods implemented, inherited, and redefined in packages, as well as calls to methods from parent packages via SUPER	https://technix.github.io/Perl-Analyzer/
	Perl::Critic—Critique Perl source code for best-practices	https://metacpan.org/pod/Perl::Critic
	zarn—A lightweight static security analysis tool for modern Perl Apps	https://github.com/htrgouvea/zarn
Python	*autoflake*—Autoflake removes unused imports and unused variables from Python code.	https://github.com/PyCQA/autoflake
	bandit—A tool to find common security issues in Python code	https://bandit.readthedocs.io/en/latest
	Bowler—Safe code refactoring for modern Python	https://pybowler.io/
	deal—Design by contract for Python	https://deal.readthedocs.io/
	Dlint—A tool for ensuring Python code is secure	https://github.com/dlint-py/dlint
	Dodgy—Dodgy is a very basic tool to run against your codebase to search for "dodgy" looking values	https://github.com/landscapeio/dodgy
	jedi—Autocompletion/static analysis library for Python	https://jedi.readthedocs.io/en/latest
	mccabe—Check McCabe complexity	https://pypi.org/project/mccabe
	mypy—A static type checker that aims to combine the benefits of duck typing and static typing, frequently used with MonkeyType (https://github.com/Instagram/MonkeyType)	http://www.mypy-lang.org/
	pyanalyze—A tool for programmatically detecting common mistakes in Python code, such as references to undefined variables and type errors	https://pyanalyze.readthedocs.io/en/latest/
	PyCodeQual ®—PyCodeQual gives you insights into complexity and bug risks.	https://pycodequ.al/
	pydocstyle—Check compliance with Python docstring conventions	http://www.pydocstyle.org/
	pyflakes—Check Python source files for errors	https://pypi.org/project/pyflakes
	pylint—Looks for programming errors, helps enforce a coding standard, and sniffs for some code smells	http://pylint.pycqa.org/en/latest

Table D.2   Static analysis tools by language *(continued)*

Language	Static analysis tool	URL
Python	*pylyzers*—A static code analyzer/language server for Python, written in Rust, focused on type checking and readable output	https://mtshiba.github.io/pylyzer/
	pyre-check—A fast, scalable type checker for large Python codebases	https://pyre-check.org/
	pyright—Static type checker for Python, created to address gaps in existing tools like mypy	https://github.com/Microsoft/pyright
	pyroma—Rate how well a Python project complies with the best practices of the Python packaging ecosystem and list issues that could be improved.	https://github.com/regebro/pyroma
	Pysa—A tool based on Facebook's pyre-check to identify potential security issues in Python code identified with taint analysis	https://pyre-check.org/docs/pysa-basics.html
	pytype—A static type analyzer for Python code	https://google.github.io/pytype
	pyupgrade—A tool (and pre-commit hook) to automatically upgrade syntax for newer versions of the language	https://pypi.org/project/pyupgrade-docs/
	refurb—A tool for refurbishing and modernizing Python codebases	https://github.com/dosisod/refurb
	vulture—Find unused classes, functions, and variables in Python code.	https://github.com/jendrikseipp/vulture
	wily—A command-line tool for archiving, exploring, and graphing the complexity of Python source code	https://github.com/tonybaloney/wily
	xenon—Monitor code complexity using radon (https://github.com/rubik/radon)	https://xenon.readthedocs.io/
R	*cyclocomp*—Quantifies the cyclomatic complexity of R functions/expressions	https://github.com/MangoTheCat/cyclocomp
	lintr—Static Code Analysis for R	https://github.com/jimhester/lintr
Ruby	*brakeman*—A static analysis security vulnerability scanner for Ruby on Rails applications	https://brakemanscanner.org/
	bundler-audit—Audit Gemfile.lock for gems with security vulnerabilities reported in Ruby Advisory Database (https://github.com/rubysec/ruby-advisory-db)	https://github.com/rubysec/bundler-audit
	Churn—A Project to give the churn file, class, and method for a project for a given check-in	https://github.com/danmayer/churn
	dawnscanner—A static analysis security scanner for Ruby-written web applications	https://github.com/thesp0nge/dawnscanner

Table D.2   Static analysis tools by language (*continued*)

Language	Static analysis tool	URL
Ruby	*Fasterer*—Common Ruby idioms checker	https://github.com/DamirSvrtan/fasterer
	flay—Flay analyzes code for structural similarities.	https://ruby.sadi.st/Flay.html
	flog—Flog reports the most tortured code in an easy to read pain report. The higher the score, the more pain the code is in.	https://ruby.sadi.st/Flog.html
	Fukuzatsu—A tool for measuring code complexity in Ruby class files	https://github.com/CoralineAda/fukuzatsu
	pelusa—Static analysis Lint-type tool to improve your OO Ruby code	https://github.com/codegram/pelusa
	reek—Code smell detector for Ruby	https://github.com/troessner/reek
	RuboCop—A Ruby static code analyzer, based on the community Ruby style guide	https://docs.rubocop.org/rubocop
	Rubrowser—Ruby classes interactive dependency graph generator	https://github.com/blazeeboy/rubrowser
	rubycritic—A Ruby code quality reporter	https://github.com/whitesmith/rubycritic
	Sorbet—A fast, powerful type checker designed for Ruby	https://sorbet.org/
	Steep—Gradual typing for Ruby	https://github.com/soutaro/steep
Rust	*C2Rust*—C2Rust helps you migrate C99-compliant code to Rust.	https://c2rust.com/
	cargo udeps—Find unused dependencies in Cargo.toml	https://github.com/est31/cargo-udeps
	cargo-audit—Audit Cargo.lock for crates with security vulnerabilities reported to the RustSec Advisory Database (https://github.com/RustSec/advisory-db/)	https://rustsec.org/
	cargo-bloat—Find out what takes most of the space in your executable	https://github.com/RazrFalcon/cargo-bloat
	cargo-breaking—cargo-breaking compares a crate's public API between two different branches, shows what changed, and suggests the next version according to semver.	https://github.com/iomentum/cargo-breaking
	cargo-call-stack—Whole program static stack analysis	https://github.com/japaric/cargo-call-stack
	cargo-deny—A cargo plugin for your dependencies. It checks for valid license information, duplicate crates, security vulnerabilities, and more.	https://embarkstudios.github.io/cargo-deny

Table D.2   Static analysis tools by language *(continued)*

Language	Static analysis tool	URL
Rust	*cargo-expand*—Cargo subcommand to show the result of macro expansion and #[derive] expansion applied to the current crate	https://github.com/dtolnay/cargo-expand
	cargo-geiger—A cargo plugin for analyzing the usage of unsafe Rust code	https://github.com/geiger-rs/cargo-geiger
	cargo-semver-checks—Scan your Rust crate releases for semver violations	https://crates.io/crates/cargo-semver-checks
	cargo-show-asm—cargo subcommand showing the assembly, LLVM-IR ,and MIR generated for Rust code	https://github.com/pacak/cargo-show-asm
	cargo-spellcheck—Checks all your documentation for spelling and grammar mistakes with hunspell (ready) and language tool (preview)	https://github.com/drahnr/cargo-spellcheck
	cargo-unused-features—Find potential unused enabled feature flags and prune them.	https://github.com/TimonPost/cargo-unused-features
	diff.rs—Web application (WASM) to render a diff between Rust crate versions	https://diff.rs/
	kani—The Kani Rust Verifier is a bit-precise model checker for Rust.	https://github.com/model-checking/kani
	lockbud—Statically detects Rust deadlock bugs	https://github.com/BurtonQin/lockbud
	MIRAI—An abstract interpreter operating on Rust's mid-level intermediate language and providing warnings based on taint analysis	https://github.com/facebookexperimental/MIRAI
	Prusti—A static verifier for Rust based on the Viper verification infrastructure	https://www.pm.inf.ethz.ch/research/prusti.html
	Rudra—Rust Memory Safety and Undefined Behavior Detection	https://github.com/sslab-gatech/Rudra
	rust-analyzer—Supports functionality such as `goto definition`, type inference, symbol search, reformatting, and code completion and enables renaming and refactorings	https://rust-analyzer.github.io/
	rust-audit—Audit Rust binaries for known bugs or security vulnerabilities	https://github.com/Shnatsel/rust-audit
	RustViz—RustViz is a tool that generates visualizations from simple Rust programs to assist users in better understanding the Rust Lifetime and Borrowing mechanism.	https://github.com/rustviz/rustviz
	warnalyzer—Show unused code from multi-crate Rust projects.	https://github.com/est31/warnalyzer

Table D.2   Static analysis tools by language *(continued)*

Language	Static analysis tool	URL
SQL	*dbcritic*—Finds problems in a database schema, such as a missing primary key constraint in a table	https://github.com/channable/dbcritic
	holistic—More than 1,300 rules to analyze SQL queries	https://holistic.dev/
	pgspot—Spot vulnerabilities in postgres extension scripts	https://github.com/timescale/pgspot
	sqlcheck—Automatically identify anti-patterns in SQL queries.	https://github.com/jarulraj/sqlcheck
	Visual Expert ®—Code analysis for PowerBuilder, Oracle, and SQL Server Explores, analyzes, and documents Code	https://www.visual-expert.com/
Scala	*Scalastyle*—Scalastyle examines your Scala code and indicates potential problems with it.	http://www.scalastyle.org/
	scapegoat—Scala compiler plugin for static code analysis	https://github.com/sksamuel/scapegoat
Shell	*i-Code CNES for Shell*—An open source static code analysis tool for Shell and Fortran (77 and 90)	https://github.com/lequal/i-CodeCNES
	kmdr—CLI tool for learning commands from your terminal	https://github.com/ediardo/kmdr-cli
	shellcheck—A static analysis tool that gives warnings and suggestions for bash/sh shell scripts	https://www.shellcheck.net/
Tcl	*Frink*—A Tcl formatting and static check program (can prettify the program, minimize, obfuscate, or just sanity check it)	http://catless.ncl.ac.uk/Programs/Frink
	Nagelfar—A static syntax checker for Tcl	https://sourceforge.net/projects/nagelfar
	tclchecker—A static syntax analysis module (as part of TDK [https://github.com/ActiveState/tdk])	https://github.com/ActiveState/tdk/blob/master/docs/3.0/TDK_3.0_Checker.txt
TypeScript	*fta*—Rust-based static analysis for TypeScript projects	https://ftaproject.dev/
	zod—TypeScript-first schema validation with static type inference	https://zod.dev/
Verilog/Sys-temVerilog	*Icarus Verilog*—A Verilog simulation and synthesis tool that operates by compiling source code written in IEEE-1364 Verilog into some target format	https://github.com/steveicarus/iverilog
	svls—A Language Server Protocol implementation for Verilog and SystemVerilog, including lint capabilities	https://github.com/dalance/svls

Table D.2   Static analysis tools by language *(continued)*

Language	Static analysis tool	URL
Verilog/SystemVerilog	*Verilator*—A tool that converts Verilog to a cycle-accurate behavioral model in C++ or SystemC. Performs lint code-quality checks	https://www.veripool.org/verilator
	vscode-verilog-hdl-support—Verilog HDL/SystemVerilog/Bluespec SystemVerilog support for VS Code	https://github.com/mshr-h/vscode-verilog-hdl-support
Multiple Languages	*ale*—Asynchronous Lint Engine for Vim and NeoVim with support for many languages	https://github.com/w0rp/ale
	Android Studio—Based on IntelliJ IDEA, and comes bundled with tools for Android, including Android Lint	https://developer.android.com/studio
	AppChecker ℗—Static analysis for C/C++/C#, PHP, and Java	https://npo-echelon.ru/en/solutions/appchecker.php
	Application Inspector ℗—Commercial Static Code Analysis, which generates exploits to verify vulnerabilities	https://www.ptsecurity.com/ww-en/products/ai
	ApplicationInspector—Creates reports of over 400 rule patterns for feature detection (e.g. the use of cryptography or version control in apps)	https://github.com/microsoft/ApplicationInspector
	ArchUnit—Unit test your Java or Kotlin architecture.	https://www.archunit.org/
	autocorrect—A linter and formatter to help you improve copywriting, correct spaces, words, and punctuation between CJK (Chinese, Japanese, Korean)	https://huacnlee.github.io/autocorrect
	Axivion Bauhaus Suite ℗—Tracks down error-prone code locations, style violations, cloned or dead code, cyclic dependencies and more for C/C++, C#/.NET, Java. and Ada 83/Ada 95	https://www.axivion.com/en/products-services-9#products_bauhaussuite
	Bearer—Open source static code analysis tool to discover, filter, and prioritize security risks and vulnerabilities leading to sensitive data exposures (PII, PHI, PD)	https://github.com/bearer/bearer
	Betterscan CE—Checks your code and infra (various Git repositories supported, cloud stacks, CLI, Web Interface platform, integrations available) for security and quality issues	https://github.com/tcosolutions/betterscan-ce
	BugProve ℗—BugProve is a firmware analysis platform featuring both static and dynamic analysis techniques to discover memory corruptions, command injections and other classes or common weaknesses in binary code.	https://www.bugprove.com/

Table D.2   Static analysis tools by language *(continued)*

Language	Static analysis tool	URL
Multiple Languages	*callGraph*—Statically generates a call graph image and displays it on screen	https://github.com/koknat/callGraph
	CAST Highlight ℗—Commercial Static Code Analysis which runs locally but uploads the results to its cloud for presentation	https://www.castsoftware.com/products/highlight
	Checkmarx CxSAST ℗—Commercial Static Code Analysis, which doesn't require precompilation	https://www.checkmarx.com/products/static-application -security-testing
	ClassGraph—A classpath and module path scanner for querying or visualizing class metadata or class relatedness	https://github.com/classgraph/classgraph
	Cobra ℗—Structural source code analyzer by NASA's Jet Propulsion Laboratory	https://spinroot.com/cobra
	Codacy ℗—Code Analysis to ship Better Code, Faster	https://www.codacy.com/
	Code Intelligence ℗—CI/CD-agnostic DevSecOps platform that combines industry-leading fuzzing engines for finding bugs and visualizing code coverage	https://www.code-intelligence .com/
	codeburner—Provides a unified interface to sort and act on the issues it finds	https://groupon.github.io/codeburner
	codechecker—A defect database and viewer extension for the Clang Static Analyzer with web GUI	https://codechecker.readthedocs .io/en/latest
	CodeFactor ℗—Automated Code Analysis for repos on GitHub or BitBucket	https://codefactor.io/
	CodeFlow ℗—Automated code analysis tool to deal with technical depth	https://www.getcodeflow.com/
	CodePatrol ℗—Automated SAST code reviews driven by security, supports 15+ languages and includes security training	https://cyber-security.claranet.fr/en/codepatrol
	codeql—Deep code analysis; semantic queries and dataflow for several languages with VSCode plugin support	https://github.com/github/codeql
	CodeQue—Ecosystem for structural matching JavaScript and TypeScript code	https://codeque.co/
	CodeRush ℗—Code creation, debugging, navigation, refactoring, analysis, and visualization tools that use the Roslyn engine in Visual Studio 2015 and up	https://www.devexpress.com/products/coderush

Table D.2   Static analysis tools by language *(continued)*

Language	Static analysis tool	URL
Multiple Languages	*CodeScan* ☮—Code Quality and Security for Salesforce Developers	https://www.codescan.io/
	CodeScene ☮—CodeScene is a quality visualization tool for software.	https://codescene.com/
	CodeSee ☮—CodeSee is mapping and automating your app's services, directories, file dependencies, and code changes.	https://www.codesee.io/
	CodeSonar from GrammaTech ☮—Advanced, whole program, deep path, static analysis of C, C++, Java and C# with easy-to-understand explanations and code and path visualization	https://codesecure.com/our-products/codesonar/
	DeepSource ☮—In-depth static analysis to find issues in verticals of bug risks, security, anti-patterns, performance, documentation and style	https://deepsource.com/
	Depends—Analyzes the comprehensive dependencies of code elements for Java, C/C++, Ruby	https://github.com/multilang-depends/depends
	DevSkim—Regex-based static analysis tool for Visual Studio, VS Code, and Sublime Text - C/C++, C#, PHP, ASP, Python, Ruby, Java, and others	https://github.com/microsoft/devskim
	Embold ☮—Intelligent software analytics platform that identifies design issues, code issues, duplication and metrics. Supports Java, C, C++, C#, JavaScript, TypeScript, Python, Go, Kotlin and more	https://embold.io/
	emerge—Emerge is a source code and dependency visualizer that can be used to gather insights about source code structure, metrics, dependencies, and complexity of software projects.	https://github.com/glato/emerge
	ezno—A JavaScript compiler and TypeScript checker written in Rust with a focus on static analysis and runtime performance	https://kaleidawave.github.io/posts/introducing-ezno/
	Find Security Bugs—The SpotBugs plugin for security audits of Java web applications and Android applications (also work with Kotlin, Groovy, and Scala projects).	https://find-sec-bugs.github.io/
	Fortify ☮—A commercial static analysis platform that supports the scanning of C/C++, C#, VB.NET, VB6, ABAP/BSP, ActionScript, Apex, ASP.NET, Classic ASP, VB Script, Cobol, ColdFusion, HTML, Java, JS, JSP, MXML/Flex, Objective-C, PHP, PL/SQL, T-SQL, Python (2.6, 2.7), Ruby (1.9.3), Swift, Scala, VB, and XML	https://www.microfocus.com/en-us/cyberres/application-security/static-code-analyzer

Table D.2   Static analysis tools by language *(continued)*

Language	Static analysis tool	URL
Multiple Languages	*Freeplane Code Explorer*—The Code Explorer mode in Freeplane is designed for analyzing the structure and dependencies of code compiled to JVM class files	https://docs.freeplane.org/ user-documentation/Code_ Explorer.html
	graudit—Grep rough audit - source code auditing tool	http://www.justanotherhacker .com/
	HCL AppScan Source ©—Commercial Static Code Analysis	https://www.hcltechsw.com/ products/appscan
	Infer—A static analyzer for Java, C and Objective-C	https://fbinfer.com/
	Kiuwan ©—Identify and remediate cyber threats in a blazingly fast, collaborative environment with seamless integration in your SDLC. Python, C\C++, Java, C#, PHP and more	https://www.kiuwan.com/ code-security-sast
	Klocwork ©—Quality and Security Static analysis for C/C++, Java and C#	https://www.perforce.com/ products/klocwork
	LGTM ©—Find security vulnerabilities, variants, and critical code quality issues using CodeQL queries over source code.	https://lgtm.com/
	lizard—Lizard is an extensible Cyclomatic Complexity Analyzer for many programming languages, including C/C++ (doesn't require all the header files or Java imports).	https://github.com/terryyin/lizard
	Mobb ©—Mobb is a trusted, automatic vulnerability fixer that secures applications, reduces security backlogs, and frees developers to focus on innovation.	https://mobb.ai/
	MOPSA—A static analyzer designed to easily reuse abstract domains across widely different languages (such as C and Python)	https://mopsa.lip6.fr/
	Offensive 360 ©—Commercial Static Code Analysis system doesn't require building the source code or pre-compilation	https://offensive360.com/
	OpenRewrite—OpenRewrite fixes common static analysis issues (https://mng.bz/zZJr) reported through Sonar and other tools using a Maven and Gradle plugin or the Moderne CLI	https://docs.openrewrite.org/
	OpenStaticAnalyzer—A source code analyzer tool that can perform deep static analysis of the source code of complex systems	https://github.com/sed-inf-u -szeged/OpenStaticAnalyzer

Table D.2   Static analysis tools by language *(continued)*

Language	Static analysis tool	URL
Multiple Languages	*oxc*—The Oxidation Compiler is creating a suite of high-performance tools for the JavaScript / Type-Script language rewritten in Rust.	https://github.com/web-infra-dev/oxc
	parasoft ℗—Automated Software Testing Solutions for unit-, API-, and web UI testing. Complies with MISRA, OWASP, and others	https://www.parasoft.com/
	Pixee ℗—Pixeebot finds security and code quality issues in your code and creates merge-ready pull requests with recommended fixes	https://pixee.ai/
	PMD—A source code analyzer for Java, Salesforce Apex, Javascript, PLSQL, XML, XSL, and others	https://pmd.github.io/
	pre-commit—A framework for managing and maintaining multilanguage pre-commit hooks	https://pre-commit.com/
	PVS-Studio ℗—A conditionally free for FOSS and individual developers (https://mng.bz/0QYm) static analysis of C, C++, C#, and Java code	https://pvs-studio.com/
	pylama—Code audit tool for Python and JavaScript	https://klen.github.io/pylama/
	Qwiet AI ℗—Identify vulnerabilities that are unique to your code base before they reach production.	https://qwiet.ai/
	ReSharper ℗—Extends Visual Studio with on-the-fly code inspections for C#, VB.NET, ASP.NET, JavaScript, TypeScript, and other technologies	https://www.jetbrains.com/resharper
	RIPS ℗—A static source code analyzer for vulnerabilities in PHP scripts	https://www.ripstech.com/
	Roslyn Analyzers—Roslyn-based implementation of FxCop analyzers	https://github.com/dotnet/roslyn-analyzers
	Roslyn Security Guard—Project that focuses on the identification of potential vulnerabilities such as SQL injection, cross-site scripting (XSS), CSRF, cryptography weaknesses, hardcoded passwords, and many more	https://security-code-scan.github.io/
	SafeQL—Validate and auto-generate TypeScript types from raw SQL queries in PostgreSQL.	https://safeql.dev/
	SAST Online℗—Check the Android Source code thoroughly to uncover and address potential security concerns and vulnerabilities.	https://sast.online/
	Scrutinizer℗—A proprietary code quality checker that can be integrated with GitHub	https://scrutinizer-ci.com/

Table D.2   Static analysis tools by language *(continued)*

Language	Static analysis tool	URL
Multiple Languages	*Security Code Scan*—Security code analyzer for C# and VB.NET	https://security-code-scan.github.io/
	Semgrep—A fast, open source, static analysis tool for finding bugs and enforcing code standards at editor, commit, and CI time	https://semgrep.dev/
	Semgrep Supply Chain ⓔ—Quickly find and remediate high-priority security issues	https://semgrep.dev/products/semgrep-supply-chain
	ShiftLeft Scan—Scan is a free, open source DevSecOps platform for detecting security issues in source code and dependencies.	https://github.com/ShiftLeftSecurity/sast-scan
	Sigrid—Helps you to improve your software by measuring your system's code quality, and then compares the results against a benchmark of thousands of industry systems to give you concrete advice on areas where you can improve	https://www.softwareimprovementgroup.com/solutions/sigrid-software-assurance-platform/
	Similarity Tester—A tool that finds similarities between or within files to support you in encountering DRY principle violations	https://dickgrune.com/Programs/similarity_tester/
	Snyk Code ⓔ—Snyk Code finds security vulnerabilities based on AI	https://snyk.io/
	SonarCloud ⓔ—Enables your team to deliver clean code consistently and efficiently with a code review tool that easily integrates into the cloud DevOps platforms and extends your CI/CD workflow	https://sonarcloud.io/
	SonarQube—Empowers development teams with a code quality and security solution that deeply integrates into your enterprise environment, enabling you to deploy clean code consistently and reliably.	https://sonarqube.org/
	Sonatype ⓔ—Reports known vulnerabilities in common dependencies and recommends updated packages to minimize breaking changes	https://www.sonatype.com/
	Soto Platform ⓔ—Suite of static analysis tools consisting of the three components Sotoarc (Architecture Analysis), Sotograph (Quality Analysis), and Sotoreport (Quality report)	https://www.hello2morrow.com/products/sotograph
	SourceMeter ⓔ—Static Code Analysis for C/C++, Java, C#, Python, and RPG III and RPG IV versions (including free-form)	https://www.sourcemeter.com/
	sqlvet—Performs static analysis on raw SQL queries in your Go code base to surface potential runtime errors	https://github.com/houqp/sqlvet

Table D.2   Static analysis tools by language *(continued)*

Language	Static analysis tool	URL
Multiple Languages	*StaticReviewer®*—Executes code checks according to the most relevant Secure Coding Standards, OWASP, CWE, CVE, CVSS, MISRA, and CERT, for 40+ programming languages, using 1,000+ built-in validation rules for Security, Deadcode, and Best Practices Available; a module for Software Composition Analysis (SCA) to find vulnerabilities in open source and third-party libraries	https://securityreviewer.atlassian.net/wiki/spaces/KC/pages/196633/Static+Reviewer
	Svace ®—Static code analysis tool for Java, C, C++, C#, and Go	https://www.ispras.ru/en/technologies/svace/
	Teamscale®—Static and dynamic analysis tool supporting more than 25 languages and direct IDE integration	https://www.cqse.eu/en/teamscale/overview/
	ThreatMapper—Vulnerability Scanner and Risk Evaluation for containers, serverless, and hosts at run time	https://github.com/deepfence/ThreatMapper
	trivy—A simple and comprehensive vulnerability scanner for containers and other artifacts, suitable for CI	https://github.com/aquasecurity/trivy
	TscanCode—A fast and accurate static analysis solution for C/C++, C#, and Lua codes provided by Tencent	https://github.com/Tencent/TscanCode
	Undebt—Language-independent tool for massive, automatic, programmable refactoring based on simple pattern definitions	https://github.com/Yelp/undebt
	Understand ®—Code visualization tool that provides code analysis, standards testing, metrics, graphing, dependency analysis, and more for Ada, VHDL, and others	https://www.scitools.com/
	Upsource ®—Code review tool with static code analysis and code-aware navigation for Java, PHP, JavaScript, and Kotlin	https://www.jetbrains.com/upsource
	Veracode ®—Find flaws in binaries and bytecode without requiring source.	https://www.veracode.com/security/static-code-analysis
	WALA—Static analysis capabilities for Java bytecode and related languages and JavaScript	https://github.com/wala/WALA
	weggli—A fast and robust semantic search tool for C and C++ codebases	https://github.com/googleprojectzero/weggli
	WhiteHat Application Security Platform ®—WhiteHat Scout (for Developers) combined with WhiteHat Sentinel Source (for Operations) supporting White-Hat Top 40 and OWASP Top 10	https://www.whitehatsec.com/platform/static-application-security-testing

324   APPENDIX D   *List of resources*

Table D.2   Static analysis tools by language *(continued)*

Language	Static analysis tool	URL
Multiple Languages	*XCode* ®—XCode provides a pretty decent UI for Clang's (https://clang-analyzer.llvm.org/xcode.html) static code analyzer (C/C++, Obj-C).	https://developer.apple.com/xcode

index

Numerics

5P process 145

A

abandoned TODOs 103
acceptance criteria 185
addressing feedback 20–22
affected projects 32
AI (artificial intelligence)
  benefits of 256–258
  code reviews and 261–270,
    273
  future of code reviews 272
  integrating into code
    reviews 270–271
  limitations of 258–260
AICodeReview tool 256–257
Alsharo, M. 238
Amazon CodeWhisperer 255
API testing, defined 125
Approved PRs 38
/ask command 268
authorization process 215
authors
  being own first reviewer 45
  contract for 49
  ego and 49
  making PR manageable 46
  making PR
    understandable 48
  overview of 45–49
  responsibility of 56

automated reviews 266
automated testing 124–125
automation 112
  as asset 113–114
  before review 118–125
  during review 126–140
  prerequisites for 114–118

B

before/after comparison 32
better applications 13
blocking issues 78
bottlenecks, code reviews
  as 100
breaking changes 32
  affected projects 32
  mitigation/next steps 32
Bug fix PR template
  (Markdown) 288–289
bugs, finding 60–61
Bus Factor 63
bypassing mechanisms 215,
  284

C

catch statements 115
categorizations 25
CD (continuous delivery) 5
CDN (content delivery
  network) 137
cherry-pick command 186
CI (continuous integration) 5

clarity, of PR (pull request)
  titles 23
Clausen, Christian 9
codebase stability and
  maintainability 61
Code Complete (McConnell) 8
code compliments 163
CODEOWNERS file 132, 134
CodeRabbit 256, 263,
  267–268
code refactoring 263
code review 15
  defined 13
  delays 182–186
  dissecting 15
  human-led 56
  hybrid 56
  labels 34
  participants and
    expectations 40–56
  systems 16–17
  tool-facilitated 56
code review comments
  effective 143–158
  references 164
code review delays 176
  single senior developer
    reviewer problem
    177–180
code review process
  approval-driven metrics
    207–208
  building, references 88
  choosing tools 67–72

code review process *(continued)*
  establishing goals 59–67
  guidelines, setting 73–81
  lack of time for 202–204
  refining 82–87
  tool (mis)configurations
    204
  undefined 194–201
code reviews 3
  AI and 255, 273
  AI-powered 261–270
  benefits of 10–12
  book structure 9–10
  building first process 58
  convincing team 12
  dilemmas 165
  elements of PRs 22
  essentials 89
  history of 19
  improving 12, 174
  integrating mob program-
    ming with 245–253
  labels 34
  lazy 168–170
  mean 170
  mobbing vs. 240–245
  overview 1
  pain points 168–174
  pairing with other
    practices 219
  pair programming and
    222–225
  references 13, 57, 238
  review states 36–38
  shape-shifting 172
  stringent 173
  who this book is for 7–9
  workflow of 19–22
code suggestions 263
Codium AI 255
Collaborator, code review
  tool 71
comments 142
  code compliments 163
  code review comments, tone
    of voice 158–163
  concerns 103
  effective 143–158
  mean code reviews 170
const declarations 113–114
context/justification 27

continuous deployment 6
Conventional Comments
  152–154
Creating a commit with multiple
  authors (GitHub Docs)
  238
Crucible, code review tool 70

D

decision, refining code review
  process 85
decision trees 213, 282
delays, code review
  confusion about PRs 181
  discussion back and
    forth 186–189
  large feature PRs 183–186
  refactoring code 189, 191
  too many files to review
    182–183
/describe command 261, 263
DIDACT (Dynamic Integrated
  Developer ACTivity) 265
documentation 30
Documentation update PR
  template (Markdown)
  289
DORA (DevOps Research and
  Assessment) 61–62
DORA metrics 57
draft PRs 36
driving school style 228

E

else statements 115
Emergency Playbook 211
  contents of 213–217
  decision trees 282
  defined 212
  emergency procedure
    name 282
  runbooks vs. 212
  starter template 282–286
  when to use 218
EPER (Emergency Procedure
  Execution Record) 217,
  285
eqeqeq rule 122
ESLint 113, 115

F

feature flags, defined 185
feedback culture 205–207
  integrating and celebrating
    feedback
    mechanisms 206
feeling unwelcome 171
Figma, whiteboard tool 196
finally statements 115
finding bugs 60–61
Five Lines of Code (Clausen)
  8–9
forgotten code 103
for loop 156
formatting 118–120

G

Gerrit 70
Git, cherry-pick command 186
GitHub 70
GitHub Copilot 255
GitLab 70
graph neural networks 266
group and individual reviewer
  assignment 118
guidelines, setting 73–81

H

human-led code review
  systems 16
hybrid code review systems 17

I

IDE (integrated development
  environment) 20
if-else construct 115
/improve command 264
Informational Reviewers 64
in-house coding standards 103
In Review PRs 37
integration task 185
issues
  expected 103
  numbers 30
  obvious 103
  tough 105
  validation 270

J

Johnson, Stephen C. 121

K

knowledge transfer and knowledge sharing 62–65

L

labels 34
language conventions 103
lazy code reviews 168–170
buddy system 169
emergencies 169
Looks good to me (LGTM)
syndrome 168
misused chat system 170
linking, defined 117
linting 103, 121–122
LLM (large language
model) 256
loopholes 194–210
approval-driven metrics
207–208
causes of 194
lack of feedback culture
205–207
lack of time for code
reviews 202–204
taking advantage of
emergencies 209–210
tool (mis)configurations
204
undefined code review
process 194–201

M

McConnell, Steve 9
mean code reviews 170
comments 170
feeling unwelcome 171
mentoring 65
Metabob 266
Miro, whiteboard tool 196
mitigation/next steps (breaking
changes) 32
MMG Exchange (Maintainable
Middle Ground
Exchange) 146–149

mob commands 253
mobbing
code reviews vs. 240–245
complementing code reviews
with 243–244
strengths of 241–242
MoSCoW comments 150–152
MRs (merge requests) 20, 22,
177

N

Needs Fixes PRs 38
new/changed code 20–22
New Feature PR template
(Markdown) 287
nitpicks, defined 107
nonblocking issues 78

O

objectivity 143–146
reviewers being
objective 145–146
Optional Reviewers 64
organizations
code reviews and 52, 57
overview of 52–56
persuading code review-resis-
tant organizations 52–56
outcomes, focused 155–157
asking author to make
change 155
Triple-R pattern 155

P

pair programming 221
code reviews and 222–225
integrating 225–237
ping-pong style 228
pomodoro style 228
PR gate checks 136–139
development secrets 138
formatting 137
inclusive language 137
linting 137
security 137
sensitive information 138
static analysis 137
test coverage 139
process loopholes 193

Production Outage Record 286
PR prechecks 117
PR (pull request) 5, 13, 17, 20,
22, 177
removing required line item
from PR template 85
requiring minimum of two
approvers for all PRs
86
workflow 20–22
PR (pull request) description
affected projects (breaking
changes) 32
before/after comparison 32
context/justification 27
documentation 30
linked tickets/issue
numbers 30
mitigation/next steps (breaking changes) 32
testing 29
use cases 29
PR (pull request) feedback
chat 267
PR (pull request)
summaries 261
PR (pull request)
templates 287–289
Bug fix PR template
(Markdown) 288
Documentation update PR
template
(Markdown) 289
New Feature PR template
(Markdown) 287
PR (pull request) titles
categorization prefixes 25
clarity of 23
PR templates 117, 126
PR validators 129–131
label manager 129
PR size labeler 130
PR title format 129
pull request stats 130
PRs (pull requests) 20
delays, large feature PRs
182–186
delays in code reviews 181
elements of 22
great PRs 56
reasonable sizes 102
stacking 172

Q

QA (quality assurance) 43
Qodo 261, 264, 266
quality gates 136

R

Ready for Review PRs 37
rebase command 186
recordkeeping/chronicling 65
refactoring code 189
  author new to programming
    in general 191
  author new to/unaware of
    team coding
    standards 189
  unclear/ambiguous accep-
    tance criteria 189
  unclear/ambiguous
    design 189
refining code review
    process 58–87
  decision 85
  discussion 82
  dissemination 85
  refinement scenario
    walkthroughs 85–87
refinement scenario walk-
    throughs
  removing required line item
    from PR template 85
  requiring minimum of two
    approvers for all PRs 86
regulatory/compliance
    deadline 214
reminders and escalations 139
remote teams, pair program-
    ming and 236
response times, determining for
    team 99
Review Board, code review
    tool 71
/review command 266
reviewers
  assignments 131–135
  contract for 44
  influence of 40–42, 56
  overview of 40–44
  responsibility for what passes
    through review 42–44

review requested 20–22
Rhodecode, code review tool 71
runbooks, vs. playbooks 212

S

self-approving PRs 106
senior developers, single senior
    developer reviewer
    problem 177–180
  anyone on development team
    should be able to approve
    PRs 178
  not all PRs should be
    assigned to senior
    developer 179
  take code you aren't familiar
    with as opportunity to
    learn 179
shape-shifting code reviews
    172
signoff 20–22
SOPs (Standard Operating
    Procedures) 212
specificity 149–155
  clarity of comments 149
  comment signals 149
  Conventional
    Comments 152–154
  highlighting code 154
  MoSCoW comments 150–152
static analyzers 123
stringent code reviews 173
  manual scripts 173
  reliance on project
    manager 174
Stroustrup brace style 115
style consistency 103
style guides 115–117
subjective comments 143

T

tag-team style 229–230
teams
  code review process and 50
  contract for 51
  deciding the tempo of the
    code review process 56
  overview of 49–51
  setting tempo 50

tech leads 51
  contract for 51
  enablement 51
  encouragement 51
testing 29
threaded discussions/
    conversations 117
tickets 30
time-based notifications 118
tone of voice 158–163
  asking, not commanding 162
  power of 'you' 159
  replacing 'you' with 'we' 160
tool-facilitated code review
    systems 16
tour guide style 228
Triple-R pattern 155
TWA (Team Working
    Agreement) 91
  defined 92
  establishing 95–98
  living document 109
  making changes to 110
  setting expectations with
    92–95
  starter template 275–278
  what to include in 98–109

U

UI components 185
UI testing, defined 124
unit testing, defined 124
use cases 29

V

Vacation Factor 63
var declarations 114

W

What The Diff 263
workflow, code review 73
  four parts of 56
workstations, pairing 230
/wtd command 263

Y

Yacc (Yet Another Compiler
    Compiler) 121